The LaSalle Quartet

Conversations with Walter Levin

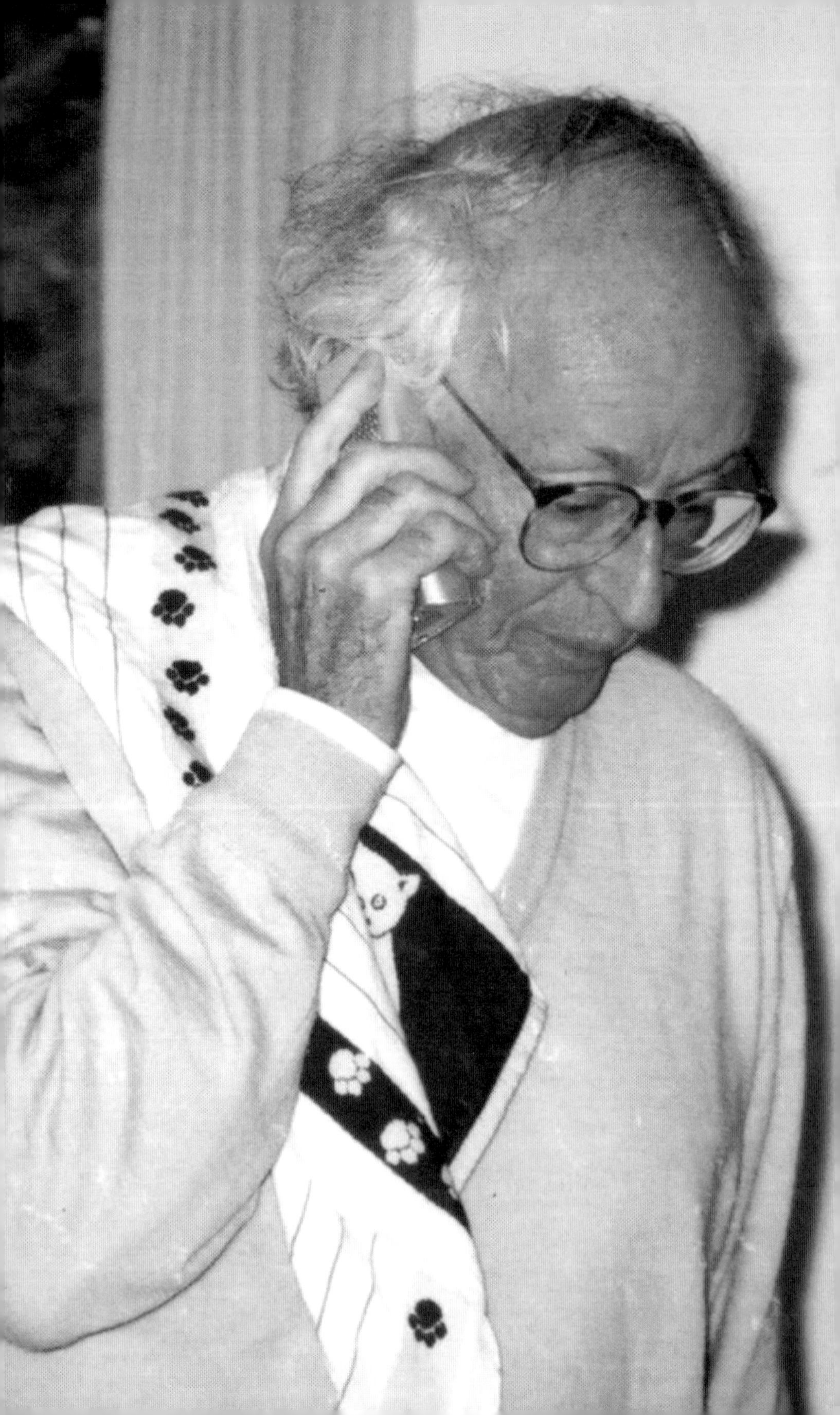

The LaSalle Quartet

Conversations with Walter Levin

Robert Spruytenburg

translated from the German
by Richard Howe

THE BOYDELL PRESS

Published 2014
The Boydell Press, Woodbridge

ISBN 978 1 84383 835 7

The translation of this work was funded by Geisteswissenschaften International – Translation Funding for Work in the Humanities and Social Sciences from Germany, a joint initiative of the Fritz Thyssen Foundation, the German Federal Foreign Office, the collecting society VG WORT and the Börsenverein des Deutschen Buchhandels (German Publishers & Bookseller Association).

The Boydell Press is an imprint of Boydell & Brewer Ltd
PO Box 9, Woodbridge, Suffolk IP12 3DF, UK
and of Boydell & Brewer Inc.
668 Mount Hope Ave, Rochester, NY 14620-2731, USA
website: www.boydellandbrewer.com

A catalogue record for this book is available
from the British Library

Printed on acid-free paper

Designed and typeset in Janson by
Richard Howe, New York, New York

In memory of my parents

Contents

List of Illustrations

Frontispiece

Walter Levin 2004 (photo courtesy of Günter Pichler)

The author and publishers are grateful to all the institutions and individuals listed for permission to reproduce the materials in which they hold copyright. Every effort has been made to trace the copyright holders; apologies are offered for any omission, and the publishers will be pleased to add any necessary acknowledgement in subsequent editions

The Members of the LaSalle Quartet 1946–1988

1st Violin

Walter Levin	1946–1988

2nd Violin

Henry Nigrine	1946–1948
Isidore Cohen	Summer 1948
Henry Meyer	1948–1988

Viola

Max Felde	1946–1949
Peter Kamnitzer	1949–1988

Cello

Jackson Wiley	1946–1951
Paul Anderson	1951–1952
Richard Kapuscinski	1952–1955
Jack Kirstein	1955–1975
Lee Fiser	1975–1988

Foreword to the German Edition

The LaSalle Quartet was founded by music students at the Juilliard School in New York in 1946 and concertized until 1987. After four years at Colorado Springs it was resident at Cincinnati from 1953 through the end of its career. Since its founding it made a name for itself above all through its efforts on behalf of the music of the 20th century: above all, the Second Viennese School – Arnold Schoenberg, Anton Webern, Alban Berg. With this repertory the LaSalle Quartet became famous. But its efforts were equally directed at the music of the immediate present. With never-flagging curiosity and energy, however, it also dedicated itself to unknown and neglected repertory, such as many rarely performed Haydn quartets, and through its performance and recording of the four string quartets of Alexander Zemlinsky contributed substantially to the renaissance of this composer who was scorned by the Nazis. Path-breaking for the development of the literature of the string quartet nevertheless were the commissions for compositions by the young composers of the post-war period. When in the middle of the decade of the 1950s the LaSalle Quartet first took part in the Darmstadt Summer Courses for New Music, it learned to its astonishment that no new string quartets were being written, supposedly because there was no ensemble that would play them. As a result of the commissions that the LaSalle Quartet thereupon awarded in the following years, there arose a whole series of works that the LaSalle Quartet premiered and presented to the world of music on tours as well as in part recorded. The string quartet by Lutosławski (1964), the second quartet by György Ligeti (1968), and *Fragmente – Stille, an Diotima* by Luigi Nono (1980) have in the meantime been accepted into the string quartet literature as classics. Characteristic of the unconventional way of the LaSalle Quartet is that only after twenty years of concertizing did it conclude a contract with a recording company, Deutsche Grammophon, from whence arose an extremely fruitful collaboration. Uncompromising, as in all its activities, it released as its first recording the string quartets by Krzysztof Penderecki and Witold Lutosławski together with the great and wholly neglected d minor quartet by Hugo Wolf: certainly an unpopular and commercially risky repertory. Thereupon followed, in 1971, against the initial resistance of Deutsche Grammophon, the path-breaking complete recording of the works of the Second Viennese School for string quartet: it became an unexpected commercial success and is surely the only quartet recording in history that after forty years is still on the market. The conception of the task of a string quartet ensemble that is implied by the preceding description was the exception in the late 1940s, the 1950s, and the 1960s. The forerunner in this respect was the Kolisch Quartet, cofounded with Arnold Schoenberg in Vienna in 1921, which in multiple respects was otherwise also exemplary for the LaSalle Quartet. Likewise the Juilliard Quartet, with whom the LaSalle Quartet studied at the Juilliard School, was distinguished by a related orientation.

Was the LaSalle Quartet an American quartet? Its entire career, everything that it was and became, was possible only in America: financially secured as Quartet in Residence at the College-Conservatory of Music at the University of Cincinnati and supported by a culturally interested, financially powerful circle of friends: the 'Sunday Group,' which made possible many interesting projects as well as commissions for works. In its essential core, however, the LaSalle Quartet had a deeply European stamp, since three of its four long-term members were German immigrants who had found their in part hazardous way to America. The family of Peter Kamnitzer (1922–), the violist, came from Berlin. They emigrated to London in 1938 and to America in 1941, after the war had already begun. Henry Meyer (1923–2006), the second violinist, grew up in Dresden and only by an unimaginable chain of real miracles in extreme circumstances survived the concentration camps of Auschwitz and Buchenwald. His whole family, however, perished. When Henry Meyer wanted to emigrate to America after the war, General Eisenhower intervened personally on behalf of the required financial guarantee, the affidavit. Until that was arranged, Henry Meyer spent three years in Paris and studied with René Benedetti and George Enescu. Walter Levin (1924–), the first violinist, only left Germany with his family in December, 1938, that is, after the '*Reichskristallnacht*' of the ninth of November, with Palestine as their destination. There Walter Levin spent seven extremely fruitful and formative years under the tutelage of first-class teachers, who were all also refugees from German-speaking Europe: Rudolf Bergmann as violin teacher, Frank Pelleg (formerly Pollak) as piano teacher, and Paul Ben Haim (formerly Frankenburger) his teacher for the music-theoretical subjects. In December of 1945 Levin travelled to New York in order to study at the Juilliard School of Music and to fulfill his life's ambition, namely to found a string quartet.

My wife and I first met Walter Levin in 1988, on the occasion of the last of the master classes given by the four members of the LaSalle Quartet at the Basel Academy of Music. Although I myself am not a musician, but rather a chemical engineer, I immediately felt an elective affinity with Walter Levin's analytical, unsentimental, approach to music, with his interpretive rigor, as well as with his drive for knowledge, his dry humor, and his abundant linguistic wit. That this was one of the central leading figures in the world of the string quartet was not clear to us from the beginning, but was something we only really became aware of when we discovered the reviews of the LaSalle Quartet's recordings in *The Gramophone* magazine, which in those years were being re-released on CDs.

In the years that followed we often followed Walter Levin and his wife Evi to the Steans Institute at Ravinia near Chicago to attend Walter Levin's courses in interpretation there as well as those he gave in Paris under the auspices of the organization ProQuartet. Naturally it was simpler to do so directly in Basel, where to our good fortune Walter and Evi Levin had their second, European, residence. As a result we could learn first hand in the quartet workshop at the Basel Academy of Music what many-sided decisions are constantly to be made in the realization of a score and, above all, how they are to be made. '"Because I like it" is not a criterion,' is one of Walter Levin's leading maxims. Instead one draws upon the original literature on performance practice of a given epoch, on authentic statements by the composers about their works, one uses urtext editions and reads the critical reports that accompany them, one plays from scores instead of parts. For practically every issue he had ready a rational approach based on his encyclopedic knowledge of music. And if occasionally he did not, he would stop and for minutes on end concentratedly consult a copy of the manuscript, of which he possessed a unique collection. Nothing was left to chance in rehearsing a piece: bowings had to match the phrasing and not vice-versa. Fingerings were refined with respect to security in their technical execution, since 'the main thing is to practice as little as possible,' he would add impishly, with a straight face. Rhythmic and other kinds of sloppiness, thoughtlessness, and imprecise ensemble playing weren't tolerated, and nothing escapes Walter Levin's relentless ear: 'F, not F sharp, in the second violin!' he can shout out in the midst of the densest uproar of a development. The legendary transparency of the interpretations of the LaSalle Quartet does not rest on any mystery but is rather the result of precise considerations and the conscious application of tone color as well as every other means of string technique. The fanatical precision in the implementation of the score, the great dynamic contrasts, as well as the rhetorical expressivity of the LaSalle Quartet are a legacy of the Kolisch Quartet and go back to Arnold Schoenberg's principles of performance, which were aimed at defending the works against the arbitrariness of interpreters.

During one of the legendary parties at Walter and Evi Levin's apartment, after the final concert of the 1989 chamber music course at the Basel Academy of Music, Rainer Schmidt, the second violinist of the Hagen Quartet, wanted to hear a live recording by the LaSalle Quartet of Beethoven's quartet Opus 59, Nr. 2. This recording became an elemental musical event for me: what the twelve year old Walter Levin experienced in Berlin when he heard a recording with the conductor Arturo Toscanini for the first time now happened to me also: I was 'thunderstruck.' Thus and not otherwise was how one must play; such forward propulsive intensity, rhythmic precision, and momentum I had never heard before. Of Beethoven's metronome marks, which of course the LaSalle Quartet observed, I still knew nothing at that time. From then on it was my primary goal to acquire a comprehensive knowledge of the interpretations of the LaSalle Quartet. Soon, however, I had to learn that the available discography covered only a limited part of its repertory: the classics, for instance, that is, the quartets by Haydn and Mozart as well as the early and middle Beethoven quartets were missing. At my request, Walter Levin then made tape cassette copies for us from his personal archive of the Beethoven performances missing in the discography. They began with the revelation unleashed by Opus 59, Nr. 2, and led to a fundamental rethinking of my previous conception of musical interpretation. These live recordings also, however, held in store a surprise for me: those of Opus 18, Nr. 2, and Opus 95 were from the year 1956; the recording of Opus 18, Nr. 1, from 1958; and that of Opus 18, Nr. 5, from 1962. Why then were there no more recent recordings of these quartets? Had the LaSalle Quartet later not played these pieces any more? This question stayed with me, unanswered, until in 2003 the happy event occurred that the LaSalle Quartet decided to entrust its entire archive to the Paul Sacher Foundation in Basel: so to speak right on my doorstep. Suddenly the entire repertory of the LaSalle Quartet was available on 236 CDs of live performance recordings from Cincinnati. In addition, there were eighteen albums with the complete concert and tour programs as well as newspaper reports and reviews: the so-called 'scrapbooks,' a kind of diary that Evi Levin maintained with iron discipline throughout the entire career of the LaSalle Quartet. Into this universe, which is what the collection revealed itself to be, I immersed myself in the years that followed. A web of connections and relationships was revealed in outline, about which I felt an ever increasing need to ask Walter Levin for clarifications and elucidations. That was how our conversations originated, at first still somewhat unstructured and spontaneous, then ever more targeted, in which the answers mostly led to new questions, so that in time layer upon layer of an uncommonly intense musical life as well as an exceptional quartet career were exposed.

The conversations transcribed in the present book took place between April, 2003, and May, 2008. This long span of time was a consequence of Walter Levin's extremely tight appointment calendar. They took place in the kitchen in Walter and Evi Levin's small attic apartment in Basel, overflowing with books, CDs, and scores. After supper the dishes were cleared away and the microphone set up. Tirelessly and drawing on a quasi-infallible memory Levin answered my questions readily and extensively, assisted by his wife.

It is the special gift of Walter and Evi Levin to make contacts and then to maintain them for decades. In this way an immense network of personal relationships, nearly incomprehensible to the outsider, arose that cannot possibly be surveyed in a few conversations. Those readers who have known Walter and Evi Levin for many years already will undeniably discover many gaps. The conversations documented here, however, are not memoirs and make no claim to completeness, as they have arisen from a very particular perspective. It was my intention to document the various influences that were decisive for the individual members of the LaSalle Quartet and for Walter Levin in particular, and which form the basis for the unique capabilities and career of this ensemble. Of equal importance were the countless and often incredible coincidences and turning points that decisively influenced the development of Walter Levin and the LaSalle Quartet and for the most part were connected with people who crossed their path at crucial moments. And – which was my original question – I was interested in how their repertory developed chronologically and in content.

The first seven chapters of this book [chapters 1–13 in the English edition] are of a biographical-historical nature and address the individual members of the quartet, portray Walter Levin's development, how the LaSalle Quartet worked together, its collaboration with recording companies, and the teaching activities of its members, which were of decisive importance for them. Chapters eight through twelve [chapters 14–18 in the English edition] address the composers in the repertory of the LaSalle Quartet and demonstrate how and why this repertory was built up step by step so as to be as we know it. Chapter 13 [English edition chapter 19] finally addresses certain specific problems of interpretation that arose for me in the course of listening to the many recordings, and the discussion of which is also revelatory of the way of thought of Walter Levin and the LaSalle Quartet as well as in more general respects. To illustrate the written text some examples are to be heard on the accompanying mp3-CD [not included in the English edition].

One aspect that to my regret cannot be conveyed by the transcription of the conversations is the extremely expressive speech ductus of Walter Levin, which is not so astonishing for such a strongly expressive musician. One would have to supply the text with signs indicating how it is to be read, such as Arnold Schoenberg supplied for his own lectures. So that the reader can, however, get some impression of Walter Levin's original tone, some few, particularly typical, passages from the conversations have been repeated on the accompanying mp3-CD.

Acknowledgements

Above all, I am profoundly grateful to Walter and Evi Levin for their generous hospitality and the warm-heartedness with which they welcomed my wife and me during all the years, and for their patience and willingness to answer my questions for hours on end. We owe to them an undreamt-of broadening of our cultural horizons and a lesson in inextinguishable joy in life.

My very special thanks go to Dr. Felix Meyer, the director of the Paul Sacher Foundation in Basel, who followed and supported this project from the outset with the greatest good will. The creation of this book would not have been possible without the Paul Sacher Foundation in Basel, which allowed me unlimited access to the LaSalle Quartet collection during countless working sessions. I would like to thank Frau Henrike Hoffmann in particular for her friendly and competent assistance. I am obliged in particular to thank the Paul Sacher Foundation for their generous financial support of the present publication.

Professor Volker Scherliess of the Lübeck Academy of Music kindly gave me his permission to use his December 2004 public colloquy at the Basel Academy of Music as the basis for the section on the years of Walter Levin's youth in Berlin. For this I owe him a particular thanks.

I am very grateful to Dr. Werner Grünzweig, director of the Music Archive of the Akademie der Künste in Berlin, for his spontaneous willingness to write the Afterword to this book. As a long-time connoisseur of the LaSalle Quartet and Walter Levin's conversation partner in the series of 26 programs, 'Walter Levin and the LaSalle Quartet,' broadcast by Deutschlandradio Kultur in 2009, Dr. Grünzweig was so to speak predestined to be the author of the Afterword to this book.

At this point Bálint András Varga is also to be thanked for his information regarding the composer László Kalmár.

My further thanks are addressed to Malgorzata Albinska-Frank, who prepared the material for the accompanying CD [not included in the English edition] with her own particular passion.

Günter Pichler, primarius of the Alban Berg Quartet, I thank for his wonderful photo of Walter Levin with kitchen towel and telephone during one of the legendary working vacations in Flims.

Finally I thank the publisher, who spontaneously responded to the manuscript with enthusiasm as well as Verlag edition text + kritik for their care with the manuscript and for their attention to some of my special requests.

With my whole heart I thank my wife Christiane, who was with me in all of the conversations with Walter and Evi Levin: together we undertook the journey of discovery in the world of music and its interpretation that was inspired by Walter Levin. Without her unerring support through all the years the realization of the present book would not have been possible.

— Robert Spruytenburg
Basel, January 2011

Foreword to the English Edition

Exactly like the German edition of my book, *Das LaSalle-Quartett – Gespräche mit Walter Levin*, the English edition of this book is a happy accident. Whereas for the German edition it was the publisher of edition text + kritik who became enthusiastic about my manuscript and spontaneously decided to publish it, in the present case it was Richard Howe who, after reading the German original, offered with comparable enthusiasm to translate it. Richard Howe, who studied with two of Walter Levin's closest friends, Herbert Brün and Wolf Rosenberg, and who knows and understands Walter Levin's intellectual universe, is an ideal translator of the present book. I owe him a special thanks for the linguistic elegance of his translation, which marvelously captures the tone and the spirit of the original.

My special thanks to the Börsenverein des Deutschen Buchhandels. Without the very generous contribution granted by the jury of the Geisteswissenschaften International the translation of this book would not have been possible.

I thank the publisher Boydell & Brewer for their interest in my book and for their willingness to publish the English translation.

Thanked also is the Paul Sacher Foundation in Basel, which had already generously supported the German edition, for their financial support of the English edition.

For Paolo Rosenberg's photograph of his father, which was missing in the German edition, I am obliged to heartfelt thanks to Pamela Rosenberg.

— Robert Spruytenburg
Basel, October 2013

Translator's Note

Of the many German Jewish immigrants to America whom I have known over the years, many of them musicians, no one of Walter Levin's generation speaks a more idiomatic informal American English than he, in particular as regards vocabulary and syntax. Even his accent, though scarcely Middle Western even after decades in Cincinnati, Ohio, is only a faint echo of his native German, though the cadences of his speech still betray their pre-war Berlin origins and perhaps even exaggerate them. Little is more characteristic of Walter's speaking voice than the sudden leap into a falsetto for one kind of emphasis, the drop into the cellar of his range for another, his *accelerandi*, *ritardandi*, *rubati*, his *Luftpausen*, his constantly modulating dynamic range from *pp* to *ff* and back, his movement from *dolce* to *marcato*, from the lyrical to the declamatory – to listen to Walter in conversation is to hear the same enormous range of expression as is to be heard in his violin playing and in the legendary performances and recordings by his LaSalle Quartet. And never more so than when he is telling any one of his favorite and oft repeated stories, so many of which have been captured for us in this book.

Translation is already a treacherous enough business even without attempting to carry Walter's expressivity across from spoken German to written English, something that might only be possible for a poet to achieve. But I have attempted to preserve as much as possible the rhythmical vitality of his speech and his shifts in register between formal and informal without becoming either pretentious – one could never call Walter that – or falling into carelessness. Even in the most casual conversation, Walter remains alert to the nuances of language and the value of *le mot juste*.

I would like to express my deep appreciation to Marianne 'Manni' Brün for her patient willingness to answer my innumerable questions of nuance and sometimes even plain sense in my search for English 'equivalence.' Manni died on January 6, 2014, at the age of 84, and so did not live to see the fruit of her efforts in print. She is sorely missed by me, and by many others as well. Thanks also to Evi Levin for answering many questions of biographical detail, to Professor Allen Otte of the Cincinnati College-Conservatory of Music for his numerous contributions regarding the school where the LaSalle Quartet was in residence for so many years; to Peter Kamnitzer for supplying me with additional information about his life, to Carol Perlstein for her recollections of the 'Sunday Group' in Cincinnati, to Michael Middeke of Boydell & Brewer for his constant editorial support, and to Rohais Haughton, also of Boydell & Brewer, for her support in seeing the book through the production process.

— Richard Howe
New York City
January, 2014

Notes on the Text and on Recordings

The conversations that are the basis of this book were recorded at irregular intervals between 2003 and 2008. Owing to their informality, the conversations were often wide ranging, not to say rambling, in character. They have been edited to put like together with like as much as possible; nevertheless, the text represents a series of large 'takes' and not a splicing together of minute bits and pieces that would sacrifice their spontaneous quality.

Levin frequently returned to a handful of his most important themes, but with different emphases, in different contexts. Footnotes supply cross-references to other places in the text where Levin has more to say on a given topic. The conversations have also been supplemented here and there by material drawn from Levin's master classes, lectures, and radio interviews, in order to more thoroughly present his views on a given topic.

Any number of minor slips of memory and other small errors of fact have been silently corrected.

The conversations make frequent reference to recordings by the LaSalle Quartet and others as well. WGUC, the radio station of the University of Cincinnati, recorded almost all of the LaSalle's 'at home' concerts; copies of these are now in the LaSalle Quartet archive of the Paul Sacher Foundation in Basel.

Owing to the extraordinary state of flux in the recording industry at this time, and the imminent disappearance of the CD in favor of on-line distribution, it has been felt advisable not to provide conventional discographic citations that will all too soon be out of date but simply to provide enough information, either in the text or in the footnotes, to enable the reader to locate a recording (if it is available) on the internet, or even through a record store, for those fortunate enough to live near one of this endangered species.

Part I

Walter Levin

from Berlin to New York

1 Berlin

VOLKER SCHERLIESS:[1] To begin with, Herr Levin, could you tell us a little bit about your family background?

WALTER LEVIN: My family comes from two very different parts of Germany. My father came from Schleswig-Holstein – he and his family could still speak the Mecklenburg dialect, which I, unfortunately, cannot. My father, Alfred Levin,[2] was born in Lübeck, less than a quarter of a mile from where the Academy of Music now stands, and where I taught from 1988 to 2008. As a child I never went with my father to visit the city where he was born, I only got to know Lübeck in the years when I was teaching there. I always had a rather odd feeling when I was on my way to the Academy of Music, I couldn't help being aware of the fact that I was passing the places where my father had played as a child, since in spite of the war the city hasn't changed all that much, or at least its street plan hasn't. So for me Lübeck is closely associated with my family. My grandparents moved to Berlin in 1907, when my father was fourteen.

My mother, Erna Levin[3] – her maiden name was Zivi – came from the Rhineland; she was born in Düsseldorf and studied at the Academy of Music in Cologne. My mother's father had studied singing and composition – he became the senior cantor at the synagogue in Elberfeld. I spent many vacations with my grandparents there, and so I got to know the atmosphere of a Jewish community in a small town in Germany at a time when living and working there was not yet life-threatening.

My father had set about to marry a woman who was a musician. Although he had been trained in business, he was a man with an immense love of music, and he was determined to have a wife who played professionally or who would at least play music at home – at any rate that was his main concern. And he actually did find her, while she was still a music student in Cologne. My mother was a superb musician, an organist and a pianist who could sight read anything, improvise fluently, and accompany arias and Lieder by ear. So I was born into a Berlin household that was always full of music.

I had no idea how unusual it was to have chamber music all the time at home: piano quartets and piano quintets, trios, and also string

[1] We are grateful to Volker Scherliess for his kind permission to use excerpts from a public colloquy led by him at the Basel Academy of Music on December 8, 2004, in honor of Walter Levin's 80th birthday. Volker Scherliess was a professor of musicology at the Lübeck Academy of Music, now retired.

[2] Alfred Levin (b. Lübeck, September 3, 1893; d. Tel Aviv, April 16, 1963).

[3] Erna Levin, née Zivi (b. Düsseldorf, June 21, 1894; d. Chur, August 6, 1973).

quartets – we were very fond of string quartets in particular. My parents' friends were very good amateurs, they played this literature very well. As a little boy I listened to my mother practicing the piano every day for hours on end, since the easiest way to get me to settle down was to have me sit on a little stool right under the piano – then I would keep still and just listen quietly. So without thinking anything about it I got to know a lot of the classical and romantic literature for piano – and the chamber music literature too, since I was allowed to stay up on the evenings when they played chamber music at home.

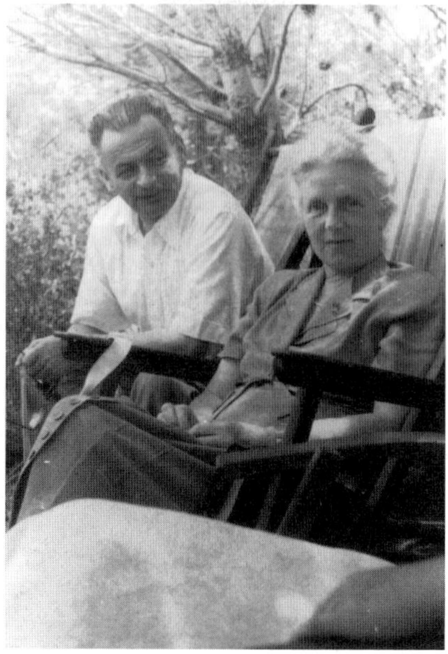

1 Alfred and Erna Levin, Ramat Gan (Tel Aviv), c. 1943

I actually cannot remember a time when I didn't know the major works of the classical and romantic chamber music literature, and I also had a very good memory for music: if someone couldn't remember the theme of a movement, my sisters would ask me and I would sing it right away. And so it wasn't long at all before the youngest member of the Levin family was allowed to take piano lessons just like his sisters did. I played everything by ear and my teacher, Marie Zweig, didn't notice at first that I couldn't read music. And since I could play by heart all the pieces my sisters played, I could just pretend to be reading the music. Of course when I finally had to play a piece I hadn't heard, I was completely lost, and then I had to begin the tedious effort of learning to read musical notation. Later on my teachers at school were also taken in by this kind of bluffing and often believed I knew something that I really didn't know at all.

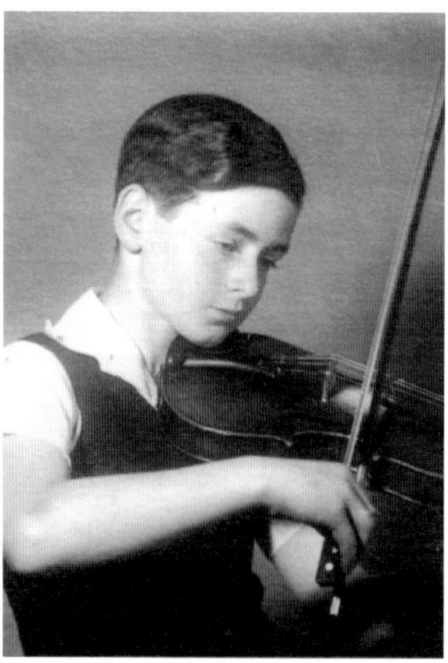

2 Walter Levin, Berlin, circa 1936

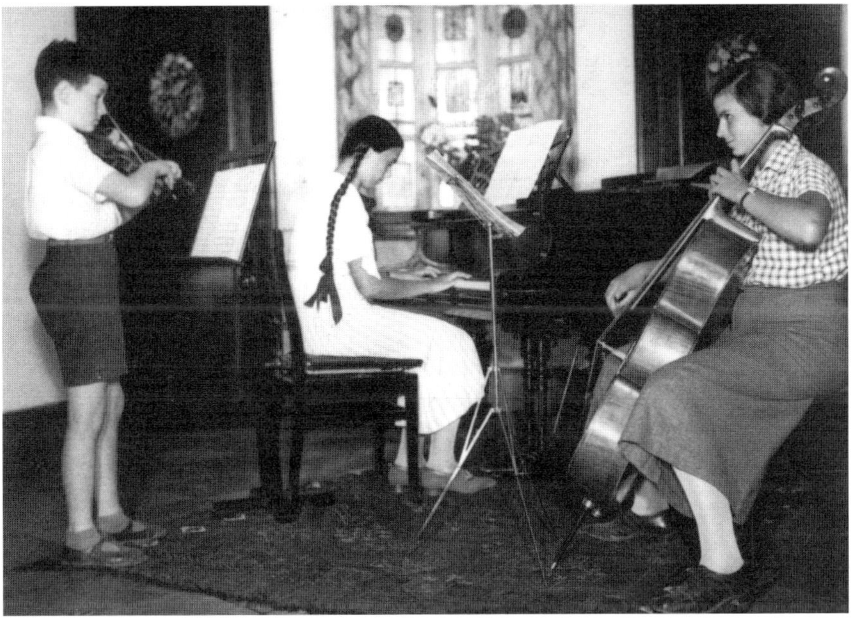

3 Walter Levin with his sisters Eva and Friedelore, Dahlem, Cäcilienallee 47 (today's Pacelliallee 47), c. 1936

VS If your first instrument was the piano, how did you become a violinist?

WL I got children's instruments all the time from people who had heard that I was musical: I had an accordion, a harmonica, a drum, a trumpet, and a children's saxophone, and I taught myself how to play all of them. The violin was my favorite instrument, though it was rather odd how I got my first one. When my grandfather – my father's father – celebrated his 70th birthday in Berlin, he invited his entire family, including all the grandchildren, to celebrate with him.[4] And on this occasion, he gave each of his grandchildren – that is, each of the boys – a violin, a real one. I have no idea why. I suppose he thought a violin would make a good children's toy. My cousin Peter Hamburger, who was a very close friend of mine, took his violin apart immediately to see what was inside. But I did what I did with every instrument I was given: I simply taught myself how to play it.

So I began to play the violin, as best I could. By watching the violinists on our chamber music evenings at home I could see how it was done. It went rather well playing simple pieces by ear, and my sisters encouraged me to play trios with them. I had only missed seeing one thing, which was that you can use all the fingers of the left hand when you play the violin. I played everything with just one finger, and so I developed

[4] On October 11, 1929, when Levin, who was born on December 6, 1924, was not yet five years old.

a really sensational technique for shifting the left hand position without making too much of a *glissando*, since *portamenti* were already taboo, even then. So that was how I got started playing the violin. And then on my mother's birthday the following June my sister and I played a little rondo by Beethoven for her. She was really quite taken with that, but she was also really upset that everything I'd taught myself about playing the violin was wrong, and so she decided that I had to start having lessons right away since otherwise the damage would be irreparable.

I got a wonderful violin teacher, Jürgen Ronis, a student of the great violinist Carl Flesch,[5] and I made progress very quickly. I took violin lessons from him until we emigrated to Palestine in 1938, and I loved it. I always found the violin quite easy to play, actually easier than the piano. Now that I could play two instruments it wasn't long before I could take part in our household's chamber music evenings, which of course had a big influence on me: the violinists and violists who played with us at home had very good taste and played, for instance, not only the well-known named quartets by Haydn like the 'Lark' or the 'Emperor' but also a few of his quartets that nobody ever plays. Sometimes they let me play second violin, which made me realize just how rich the quartet literature is.

My interest in string quartets quickly developed to such an extent that for my bar mitzvah when I was thirteen I got just one single present from my parents, but one that was really something: the whole of the quartet literature: classical, romantic, impressionist, and modern in a multi-volume set with parts – a whole library of chamber music in itself![6] It was a tremendous gift: I still have it and it's still the foundation of my music collection. It includes string quartets from the early classical period on through Haydn, Mozart, Beethoven, Schubert, Brahms, Schumann, Reger, and even the Bruckner quintet, but also – which still amazes me – the first and second quartets of Arnold Schoenberg. I have no idea how my mother happened to have that particular idea, since she was no great admirer of Schoenberg's music. But she did know some of Alban Berg's music, and my parents had been at the premiere of *Wozzeck*. To this day I still rather resent the fact that they didn't take me with them, but then I was just a year old and they probably thought I was really just a bit too young for that sort of thing.

This anthology of scores and parts was an incredibly farsighted and

5 Carl Flesch (1873–1944). His many well-known students included Szymon Goldberg, Ida Haendel, Ginette Neveu, and Henryk Szeryng. His *Kunst des Violinspiels* (Berlin, 1928–1929); *The Art of Violin Playing* (New York, 2000/2008) is one of the classics of violin pedagogy.

6 The set, published by Peters with the individual volumes bound in red linen, was called the *Kammermusik Notenbibliothek* (Library of Chamber Music), also included piano trios, piano quartets, and quintets.

important gift, possibly the most wonderful present I've ever gotten in my whole life. Even now I find it tremendously impressive that anyone can foresee what will turn out to be the life interest of a thirteen year old. And these scores got me extraordinarily motivated to learn all of this literature as quickly as possible, simply by playing it all by myself. On top of which, my grandfather – this time it was my mother's father – gave me a very nice violin for my bar mitzvah, a Pfretzschner violin, which was the first relatively decent violin I ever owned.[7] I even brought it to America with me.

VS Could you tell us something about your school years and your musical education in Berlin?

WL To begin with I went to an elementary school in Lankwitz, the suburb of Berlin where I was born, starting in early 1931. The school still exists, the building is still standing: I went to visit it a few years ago. As a child the way to school seemed to me to be unbelievably long and perilous. I had to cross some big streets, it was like a trip around the world. Three or four years ago I took a walk along this same route and discovered that the school is so to speak just around the corner from where we lived. It's astonishing, the sorts of impressions you form as a child. I actually had a good time at this school: I had a very nice classroom teacher, Frau Hermsen, and I also found the lessons very stimulating. But I didn't have much to do with my classmates.

Then came 1933 – meanwhile I had reached the third grade – and all at once something started happening that I wasn't at all prepared for. Some classmates of mine suddenly began pushing and shoving me in the school yard and calling me all sorts of names. I hadn't a clue how to respond, especially since I'd always thought of these classmates as friends of one sort or another – in any event we had always been civil to one another. Now all of a sudden they were hostile to me, and for what seemed to me to be no reason at all. It's not so nice when one of your classmates suddenly calls you a dirty rotten Jew. Obviously, as is always the case, he'd gotten this expression from his parents or their milieu. At that time such insults were in every Nazi newspaper, and the two worst hate rags, *Der Angriff* and *Der Stürmer*, were prominently displayed on the news stands for all the world to see. Children of course adopted this vocabulary uncritically.

I reacted violently: I punched the boy in the mouth and knocked one of his teeth out. That did it! I was promptly taken to task for this by the teacher in charge: whatever was I thinking of, hitting somebody like

[7] It was probably a violin made by Hermann Richard Pfretzschner (1857–1921) of the famous old family of German violin makers. He was best known as a bow maker.

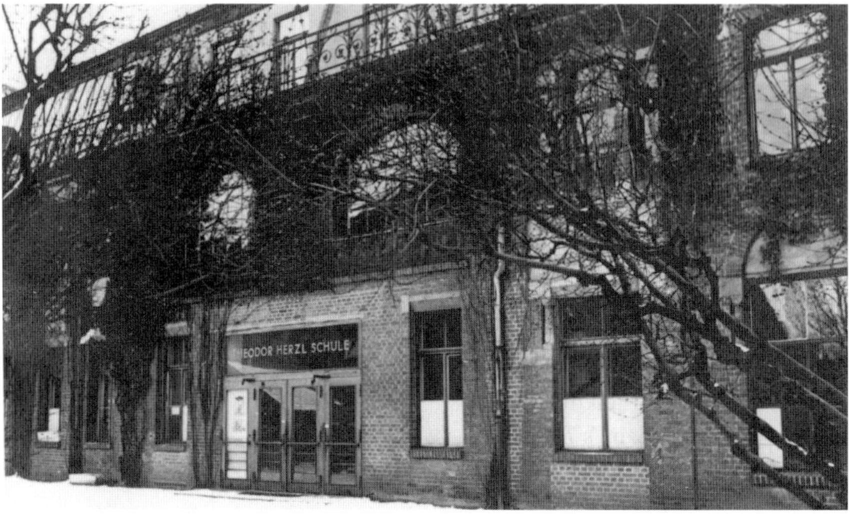

4 Theodor Herzl School, Kaiserdamm 78, Berlin

that? I replied that I wasn't going to let anybody call me a dirty rotten Jew. The teacher asked my classmate whether he'd really said that, and he shot back that yes indeed he had, and that I was one too! That was the first such experience I can remember. There were a number of later, less immediately personal experiences, but all the same one gets to be sensitive about such things. My parents very quickly came to the conclusion that you could no longer let a nine year old go to such a school, and they enrolled me in a private school run by the Jewish School Association, the Theodor Herzl[8] School on the Kaiserdamm, a Zionist school that stood right behind the building that housed the radio broadcasting studios on the Masurenallee. I went to school there from 1934 to 1938. We had Hebrew lessons every day so that we would learn our future country's native language.

At the Theodor Herzl School I got a really astonishingly interesting and even captivating education that also had a life-long influence on me. Thanks to the Nazis there were marvelous teachers there, and I began to appreciate subjects that I'd previously hadn't had a clue about or had simply found boring. They were taught in a way that would be taken for granted today, in a modern school system, but which was new to me then. As I later found out, the teachers were for the most part university professors who had been dismissed by the Nazis and were now waiting for a visa so that they could emigrate. This often took quite a long time, so in the meanwhile they took jobs as school teachers. I have very spe-

[8] Named for the founder of Zionism, the Theodor Herzl School was established in 1920 with a progressive curriculum that included vocational training as well as Hebrew in order to prepare students for emigration to Palestine.

cial memories of our music teacher. When he came into our classroom for the first time, he introduced himself as our new music teacher and made us the following proposition: for those of us who were interested, he would play operas and we would talk about them. But for those who weren't interested, he suggested that they go out into the school yard, divide themselves into two teams, and spend the hour playing soccer. But they had to keep their voices down, because of course it was forbidden. If anyone found out about it, we would all be kicked out of school.

Some 80 percent of the students went off to play soccer. But those of us who stayed got an incredible education. This man sat at the piano and with a rasping voice sang operas for us,[9] accompanying himself on the piano, and talking about them. There's a figure very much like him in Thomas Mann's *Doktor Faustus*, namely Wendell Kretzschmar: that's just what he did, and Adrian Leverkühn, the young composer in Mann's novel, learned a huge amount from him. And we too learned a huge amount – those were fascinating lessons. I thought I already knew something about music, but actually I knew nothing at all about it, as I now realized. This teacher was Willi Apel,[10] as I only learned much later on. That was the sort of people we had as teachers while they were waiting to emigrate. And it was just the same in physics, mathematics, painting, and wood and metal working: it was a terrific school. For instance, we had a year-long project to learn the *Urfaust*, to study it and perform it, even to build a puppet theater for it and to make the puppets ourselves. Fabulous teaching! That was the Jewish School in Berlin, so my experience in elementary school was exceptionally positive.

VS So that was already in the Nazi time; how did you experience it as a child in Berlin?

WL The actual experience of the time in which you are living is something completely different from the retrospective view you have later on, after you've come to know what really happened then or what was about to happen. Sometimes you project your retrospective view rather too strongly onto your earlier experiences. After all, life is experienced more by living it than by being especially conscious of it – at least that's how it is for me. I've always been preoccupied with whatever I was interested in. In those years I had to go to school in the morning and when I got back home I did my homework as quickly as possible so I could get to the

[9] Levin is alluding to some lines in Chapter 8 of Thomas Mann's novel *Doktor Faustus*.

[10] Willi Apel (1893–1988), pianist and musicologist. He emigrated to America 1936, and taught at Harvard, 1938–1942, and Indiana University, 1950–1970. Principally known as a medievalist, he also edited the classic *Harvard Dictionary of Music*. Levin and Apel met again when they both were teaching at Colorado College. See also p. 100.

violin or the piano or, sometimes, in the evening, go with my mother or with both my parents to a concert, or to the opera, which was even more important to me. But looking back on it now I have to ask myself, how was it possible to grow up relatively normally in the time in which the Nazis had come to power?

I'd gone to school in Berlin for a few years during the Weimar Republic too. And of course that was an incredible golden age for culture in Berlin: at the beginning of the 1930s there were three opera houses: the Staatsoper, the Deutsches Opernhaus, and the famous Kroll Opera. There were several symphony orchestras, of which the Berlin Philharmonic was by no means the worst, and many chamber music and solo concerts. I remember a sonata cycle by Georg Kulenkampff[11] with Edwin Fischer,[12] the Swiss pianist, and string quartets came to Berlin from all over the world. And whenever a quartet was playing, my mother took me with her to the concert. So even then I got to hear some very good string quartets. In 1935 I was allowed to go with my parents to the Staatsoper for the first time, which was a tremendous experience for me: from then on I became an avid opera fan. The last performance I went to in Berlin was in October, 1938, which was already a dangerous thing to do, since by then Jews were no longer allowed to go to the theater in Germany.

After 1933 something changed that I'm aware of today but wasn't so conscious of at the time: the roster of artists performing in public changed. All of a sudden some of the greatest and most important artists in Europe and America were no longer on the scene: all of a sudden Jews were no longer allowed to perform at public concerts or even to go to them. They were also no longer allowed to sing in the opera houses, and some of the greatest and most popular singers, for instance the bass Alexander Kipnis,[13] were no longer allowed to appear at the Staatsoper. They vanished. Some conductors were also forbidden to

[11] Georg Kulenkampff (1898–1948), German violinist, studied with Leopold Auer, and later formed a well-known trio with Edwin Fischer and Enrico Mainardi. Known for his interpretations of the romantic repertory, he succeeded Carl Flesch as violin professor at the Lucerne Conservatory.

[12] Edwin Fischer (1886–1960), Swiss pianist, conductor, and teacher, was one of the foremost interpreters of the German repertory, known especially for his Bach and Schubert, but also for his performances of Mozart piano concerti. His master-class students included Alfred Brendel, Paul Badura-Skoda, and Daniel Barenboim.

[13] Alexander Kipnis (1891–1978), one of the leading basses of his generation, appeared in all the world's major opera houses but was most closely associated with the Berlin Staatsoper, the Vienna Staatsoper, Covent Garden, and the Metropolitan Opera in New York; he also sang at Bayreuth and Salzburg, and was a favorite of Bruno Walter and Toscanini. In addition to his repertory of over 100 roles in German, Italian, French, and Russian opera, Kipnis was widely recognized as an outstanding exponent of Lieder, in particular of the songs of Brahms and Wolf.

continue practicing their profession in Germany. Now some of these people I didn't know anyway, and there were still famous artists playing in Germany who weren't Jewish, so as a child I didn't take much notice of this rather abrupt and radical shift, though later on I was to become acutely conscious of it.

ROBERT SPRUYTENBURG: You've often mentioned the Kulturbund, an organization that was at least ostensibly established to support Jewish artists in Germany. Could you tell us something about that?

WL When the Nazis came to power in 1933 they set about right away to exclude Jewish artists and academics as quickly as possible from every German organization, whether universities or orchestras, in order to make their lives ever more impossible. Later they even forbade Jews to work as private teachers. This all culminated in the *Lexicon of Jews in Music*[14] by Herbert Gerigk and Theophil Stengel: to have your name in this catalogue was reason enough to be deported to a concentration camp and murdered. It was so to speak the telephone book for Jews in German culture, in music. I have a copy, incidentally. It was reprinted in 1999 with a very interesting historical essay. My grandfather, the cantor, is also in it. So it became increasingly difficult, if not altogether impossible, for Jews to continue to work in Germany. Soon enough they were all out of work, and at the same time they were unable to emigrate, since in order to emigrate you needed a visa from another country, and the other countries weren't particularly interested in taking in a large number of unemployed Jewish refugees. Not one of these countries opened up its borders as you might have expected or as they should have done.

You can scarcely imagine now what it's like to be persecuted in your own country and to be forced to emigrate because you can no longer earn a living, and not one of the other countries will let you in. To get a visa you had to have financial guarantees. And where were you going to get them? In America, for instance, you had to have the so-called affidavit, which guaranteed that someone would be financially responsible for you if you came to America, so that you wouldn't end up as a burden on society. This may have been understandable, as the Great Depression was just ending, but for a would-be emigrant desperately trying to get out of Germany it was an enormous hurdle to get over. How many people this policy prevented from leaving Germany in time – there aren't many statistics about that. Far too many, in any event.

14 The 1940 *Lexikon der Juden in der Musik* has been reprinted in Eva Weissweiller's *Ausgemerzt! Das Lexikon der Juden in der Musik und seine mörderschen Folgen* (Cologne, 1999) See also the anthology *Geschlossene Vorstellung, Der Jüdische Kulturbund in Deutschland 1933–1941* (Berlin, 1992).

So people were stuck. They couldn't leave Germany but they had become unemployed, practically overnight, and could no longer support their families, since in 1933 Hitler had issued a decree called the 'Ordinance for the Reconstitution of the Professions,'[15] which was nothing more than a law requiring every organization and institution in Germany to immediately dismiss their Jews, without any compensation, without any reason at all other than the fact that they were Jews. And that's what happened. All at once thousands upon thousands of first rate people were unemployed with no prospect of any other employment. It was in response to this situation that the leadership of the Jewish communities in Germany established an organization that they called the Jewish Kulturbund, the Jewish Cultural Alliance.[16]

RS So the Kulturbund wasn't only for musicians?

WL No, it was also for actors, set designers, directors.

RS Painters too?

WL No, actually to begin with the Kulturbund was only for performing artists. Painters didn't work in groups that needed a public venue to perform in. The Kulturbund was for people who ordinarily sang or played in theaters. So this organization, the Kulturbund, was established, and indeed in collaboration with the Nazi regime. Reich Secretary for Culture Hans Hinkel was the man who was appointed by the Nazis to oversee the Kulturbund and to effect a segregation of Jewish from non-Jewish artists, which really meant isolating the Jewish artists. What the Germans had in mind from the outset was to round up the Jews and ultimately to murder them. It wasn't all that easy to do. First of all you had to identify them before you could round them up. You had to know where they were. And so they set up an organization that ideally would even appear to be helping the Jews. Like Theresienstadt, which was the same idea. From the outside it should look as if concentration camps were nothing more than a separation of the two peoples, who would go on working just as they had before, only they would be kept apart from one another. What this really meant was something else entirely.

When the Kulturbund was founded in 1933, it was a huge organiza-

15 The law was officially promulgated on April 7, 1933.

16 The Kulturbund der Deutschen Juden was founded in Berlin on July 15, 1933; in 1935 it was renamed Der Jüdische Kulturbund in order to emphasize that its members were not Germans. Its initial membership numbered on the order of 2,000 actors and musicians; it grew to include perhaps as many as 180,000. The Kulturbund was officially dissolved on September 11, 1941.

tion that set up orchestras, theaters, opera houses, and chamber music ensembles in every big German city for the Jews who had been let go. It was responsible for everything, including the whole administrative apparatus you need to organize all that – very interesting. Now there were opera performances and symphony concerts in special theaters. But you could go to them only if you were a member of the Kulturbund: non-Jews were forbidden to attend. You can imagine the caliber of these performances: the best people were in these orchestras and the best singers from the Staatsoper, were suddenly only to be heard by the Jews. The Kulturbund Orchestra in Berlin was first rate, Hans Wilhelm Steinberg was the conductor[17] – later on he rehearsed the Palestine Orchestra for Arturo Toscanini, and then in America he conducted the Pittsburgh Symphony – one of the really great conductors.

My first symphony orchestra concerts were at the Jewish Kulturbund. I remember exactly the first live *Eroica* I ever heard, it was with this orchestra under Steinberg. It was certainly a very good performance, one that made an enormous impression on me. Among my first impressions of opera was *Samson and Delilah*, which they allowed despite its Jewish subject: the permissible repertory was very restricted in that regard. And the Kulturbund persuaded many great artists to come back to Germany again. Alexander Kipnis, the great bass of the Berlin Staatsoper, came from abroad to give a special concert at the Kulturbund, and a great many opera lovers tried in vain to get tickets to this concert, but it was just as much forbidden for them to go to it as it was for a Jew to go to a non-Jewish theater or concert. Carl Flesch also came and gave a concert that made a huge impression on me, as I'd had very few chances to hear the great violinists, since almost all of them had been driven out of Germany. I have all the Kulturbund programs here with me! It was unbelievable! And it was for Jews only, the others would have given their right arms to get in.

RS Did the Kulturbund make it possible for musicians to earn a living again?

WL You could earn a living in the Kulturbund. So it seemed as if it really was possible to keep going in Germany in spite of everything. This was dangerous because it led people to the mistaken assumption that perhaps they really ought to remain in Germany. They deluded themselves that they were safe. But what else were they to do then? And the leader of the

[17] William Steinberg (1899–1978) conducted the world premiere of Arnold Schoenberg's comic one act opera *Von Heute auf Morgen* (From Today until Tomorrow) in 1930. After 1933 he led the Kulturbund Orchestra in Berlin, emigrating to Palestine in 1936, where he co-founded the Palestine Orchestra, which he conducted until 1938, when Toscanini invited him to the NBC Symphony. He led the Pittsburgh Symphony 1952–1976 and the Boston Symphony 1969–1972.

Kulturbund, the musical and administrative leader, Kurt Singer, a neurologist and a very intelligent man, colossally gifted, also as a conductor, fell for it, negotiating all the time with Hinkel, never understanding what the whole affair was about. His letters to people in the Kulturbund orchestra who had the opportunity to emigrate to Palestine and could get a position in the Palestine Orchestra prove this. Kurt Sommerfeld, for instance, the percussionist, got an angry letter from Singer, who took his departure as treason, accusing him of leaving the Kulturbund Orchestra in the lurch with no possibility of finding a replacement.

The Kulturbund had taken on a life of its own. And that good man, Kurt Singer, made a trip to America in 1938 and even though everyone told him to stay there he went back to Holland, where the Kulturbund had relocated to in the meantime. But what does that mean, 'relocated'? In Germany most of the Kulturbund's institutions were forced to close after the November, 1938, pogroms, and so people were compelled to go to Holland, where they were still able to work. Singer was arrested there by the Nazis in 1943 and died the following year in Theresienstadt. This total incomprehension! This inability to recognize the real emergency, this not wanting to leave people in the lurch, this misplaced sense of responsibility! Paula Fürst, the principal of my school in Berlin, the Zionist Theodor Herzl School, a wonderful woman, she also didn't emigrate. She had to know that all the children in her school were safe before she would go. And then it was too late, she was deported to Theresienstadt and died there. Sadly, there were many like her. But the Kulturbund was an important safety net for people who otherwise had no chance of earning so much as a penny.

I often wonder how it is possible to live in a time in which your own life, in the most literal sense of the word, is increasingly threatened, without really being able to see the consequences. Why, for instance, did my parents stay in Germany until the end of 1938, after the *Kristallnacht* of the 9th and 10th of November, that is, just a few months before the outbreak of the Second World War? The handwriting on the wall was obvious, but despite that some people couldn't bring themselves to leave. And that cost many, many people their lives. We know that today. But obviously at the time my father also wasn't so aware of the situation, although in 1933 his whole family had emigrated to Palestine immediately and had urged him to do the same thing. But he too just couldn't bring himself to leave.

When we did, finally, at the last moment, get an emigration visa from the English consulate – Palestine was still a British protectorate then – the German police authorities denied us our passports, without giving us any reasons at all. Eventually someone got the address of an attorney who seemed to know what to do. At his office my parents were told that they had to pay a rather large sum, the so-called Reich's Flight Tax,[18] into a special account, and then there would be nothing more standing in the way of our emigration. It later turned out that this money was for the private account of the chief of the Berlin police, at that time Heinrich Graf von Helldorf. Once the money had been paid, all of a sudden our emigration proceeded very quickly. We got a call from the police department telling us that our passports were being issued and that our departure was now being arranged so to speak under the supervision of the Berlin police. My last memory of Germany before the war is of our leaving Cäcilienallee Nr. 47 in Dahlhem to go to the Zoo train station, in December, 1938.

[18] The Reich's Flight Tax (*Reichsfluchtsteuer*) was used to seize the financial assets of Jews who were emigrating or who were suspected of planning to emigrate. Levin is making quite an understatement when he says 'a rather large sum': his family forfeited virtually their entire fortune.

2 *Decisive Musical Influences*

Menuhin, Heifetz, Flesch

ROBERT SPRUYTENBURG: You mentioned before that the decade prior to the Nazi takeover was a cultural golden age in Berlin. Can you still remember the first concert your parents took you to?

WALTER LEVIN: Absolutely, it made a profound impression on me. My first concert was an open rehearsal of the Berlin Philharmonic under Bruno Walter[1] in 1932 with Yehudi Menuhin[2] as the soloist. Menuhin played two works in this concert: the Mendelssohn violin concerto and a Mozart concerto. Of the two I was especially taken with the Mozart. It was the D major concerto Nr. 7, K. 271a, which hardly anyone knows, since officially there are only five Mozart violin concerti, besides a fraudulent sixth concerto. The authenticity of Nr. 7 is also still being contested, even today, since we have no autograph score. It's more virtuosic than the other five concerti – the violin part may indeed have been revised by someone else – but for me it's always been unmistakably Mozart: a fascinating and ravishing concerto, which I myself played later on.

This performance by Menuhin was and remained one of my greatest musical experiences for many years. At that time the rhythmical élan of Menuhin's playing in a work of the classical period was simply incomparable. Rhythmically he played the piece with tremendous verve and at the same time with a beautiful, intense, and singing tone that was never sentimental. Okay, he made certain *portamenti* that nobody would dare to do today, but he made them very tastefully. It was violin playing of the best kind, singing, also rhetorically expressive, and good humored too. It had all the qualities of the rhetorical style of playing Mozart, which are not often heard. Such a performance is extremely rare.

After I'd told my piano teacher, Marie Zweig, about my great enthusiasm for the young Yehudi Menuhin and told her I'd bought some recordings by him, she asked me whether I'd ever heard Jascha Heifetz.[3] And I

[1] Bruno Walter (1876–1962), German conductor and associate of Gustav Mahler, fled Germany in 1933 and settled in the United States in 1939. Known particularly for his advocacy of Mahler's music, he was regarded as one of the greatest of 20th century conductors.

[2] Yehudi Menuhin (1916–1999), American-born violinist and child prodigy, later based in the UK, was one of the greatest 20th century violinists, performing and recording extensively as a soloist, chamber musician, and conductor over a span of nearly seven decades.

[3] Jascha Heifetz (1901–1987), Lithuanian born American violinist and child prodigy, emigrated with his parents to America in 1917. Perhaps the most influential violinist of the 20th century, his recorded legacy is one of the monuments of the history of musical performance.

must in all honesty confess that at that point in time, around 1933, I hadn't even heard the name Jascha Heifetz, to say nothing of having heard any performances by him: it was already the Nazi time and there weren't any really internationally acclaimed violinists still playing in Germany. So I went to the record store and asked about recordings with Heifetz. They had the fifth Mozart violin concerto in a recording with the London Symphony Orchestra under Sir Malcolm Sargent,[4] which I listened to straight away and which was an absolute revelation to me. I'd never heard violin playing anything like it. The lyricism and the tone quality of Menuhin's violin playing were of a different kind, and also quite incredible for such a young violinist. But Heifetz' playing had an element of rhythmical vitality, momentum, and clarity of tone production that left every note, even the shortest, still sounding beautiful, and he played all of it strictly in tempo: he didn't make any unnecessary *ritardandi*, he played this music in a really classically pure way. For me that was just as impressive and influential as hearing Menuhin had been and as, somewhat later, hearing Toscanini would also be.

RS Did you have a chance later on to get to know Heifetz personally?

WL No, I didn't, but I heard him play quite often, and I had an astonishing experience of him once when I was studying with Ivan Galamian[5] in upstate New York. He was playing the Brahms concerto with the New York Philharmonic, and I went to hear it along with several friends from Galamian's summer school at Meadowmount. Before the concert we went backstage to the Green Room and peeked through the little window in the door. Heifetz was practicing, and he was practicing scales just like a student: one note at a time to begin with, then in thirds, then arpeggios, so to speak the Flesch scale system.[6] The greatest virtuoso of his time was practicing fundamental technique just like a young student – and this just before playing the Brahms concerto! That made a tremendous impression on us, we'd thought that the greatest soloists didn't need to practice at all any more. But Heifetz always practiced every day, and in the most thorough-going way, so to speak from the

[4] Malcolm Sargent (1895–1967), English conductor, was best known as the chief conductor of London's famous summer Proms concerts at the Royal Albert Hall.

[5] Ivan Galamian (1903–1981) studied with Konstantin Mostras in Moscow and with Lucien Capet in Paris. He emigrated to the United States in 1937 and taught at the Curtis Institute of Music in Philadelphia; from 1946 on he taught at Juilliard. In 1944 he founded his own summer academy at Meadowmount near Lake Champlain in upstate New York. Among his best known students are Itzhak Perlman, Pinchas Zukerman, Kyung-Wha Chung, Michael Rabin, and Miriam Fried. See also pp. 52–57.

[6] As outlined in Flesch's *Skalensystem* (Berlin, 1926); *Scale System* (New York, 1926).

ground up, starting with fundamental technique, then pieces, in a slow tempo to begin with, for intonation – just exactly how everyone should practice. You could take that as a real example for yourself. We didn't go into the Green Room, we wouldn't have dared to disturb him.

RS Could you still go to public concerts in Berlin after 1933?

WL Yes, I did – I didn't pay much attention to the Nazi proscriptions. And there were also the concerts that the Kulturbund sponsored. My parents joined the Kulturbund as soon as it was founded in 1933, and took me along to some of their earliest concerts, among them my first *Eroica* under Steinberg that I mentioned earlier. I heard many concerts at the Kulturbund, including solo recitals the likes of which are scarcely remembered any more. An important experience for me was a solo recital by Carl Flesch, the famous violinist and teacher at the Academy of Music in Berlin. Carl Flesch had emigrated to England in 1934 and then came back to Berlin to give a recital exclusively for members of the Kulturbund. Unfortunately there are only a few recordings by Carl Flesch, but they are unique documents and should be heard more often. They document a singing style of violin playing in its purest form, without any kind of sentimentality, a style that has, unfortunately, been lost. Flesch used both *portamento* – smoothly gliding between two notes like a singer – which is so despised today by violin teachers and young violinists, and *rubato*, a rhythmic freedom akin to speech. I got to be familiar with this kind of violin playing very early on, because my first violin teacher, Jürgen Ronis, was a student of Carl Flesch.

For me it's still a mystery, how the style of violin playing could change so radically in the course of just a few decades. Nowadays if I suggest a fingering to young students that would require them to glide between two notes like a singer would, they look perplexed and ask me if I really mean that they should play *portamento* and make a *glissando* between the two notes. Of course they should! That's what singers do, and the violin is a singing instrument! But they're all quick to tell me that one just doesn't do that sort of thing anymore. I discover over and over again that so many young instrumentalists are completely unfamiliar with the vocal literature. Nowadays, unfortunately, instrumentalists are usually concerned only with learning their own instrument, not with the literature of music in general. Violinists don't go to vocal recitals, often they don't know any of the operatic literature, and cellists don't know any Lieder. The Lieder of Schubert, Schumann, and Brahms are by and large unknown to the younger generation of instrumentalists, and they don't know any singers, so they don't ever get to hear what real singing is. The result is that the singing style is foreign to them, and they don't understand that it's essential to violin playing. As string players there's no question but that they should listen to singers and get to know the vocal literature, because that's where stringed instruments come from: they are singing instruments.

Opera and Song

RS For as long as I've known you, you've always spoken enthusiastically about opera. When did your passion for opera begin?

WL I got interested in vocal music very early on and was crazy about opera even as a child. My parents had a big collection of records with opera excerpts and I listened to them again and again for hours on end. The first opera I ever heard live, in 1935, was *Samson and Delilah* by Camille Saint-Saëns, in a production by the Kulturbund. A little later, in 1936, I went to a production of *Carmen* at the Staatsoper, conducted by Leo Blech,[7] a great musician. Dusolina Giannini[8] sang the role of Carmen. I saw many operas at the Staatsoper; it was my favorite opera house. I particularly remember a performance of Mozart's *Zauberflöte* in 1937 under Robert Heger,[9] because the Queen of the Night was sung by a singer who was to become one of my favorites: Erna Berger,[10] an extraordinarily distinguished coloratura soprano. For me that was an earth shattering experience: I'd never heard a coloratura soprano like that before, someone who could sing Mozart with such brilliant technique and at the same time so musically, with tremendous rhythmical verve and an incomparably beautiful voice.

In Berlin we often went to vocal concerts also, to Lieder recitals. Evenings of Lieder have become rather less commonplace today. At that time I heard many concerts by Heinrich Schlusnus,[11] since his accompanist,

[7] Leo Blech (1871–1958) conducted the Staatsoper in Berlin 1906–1937 and the Berlin City Opera 1949–1953. He was particularly noted for his *Carmen*, which he conducted over 600 times.

[8] Dusolina Giannini (1902–1986), soprano, sang leading roles under Bruno Walter and Toscanini at the Salzburg Festival; she later sang at the Metropolitan Opera in New York, and in Chicago and San Francisco. Her brother, the composer Vittorio Giannini, was Walter Levin's composition teacher at Juilliard.

[9] Robert Heger (1886–1978), conductor and composer, conducted at the Vienna Volksoper, the Munich Opera, the Vienna Staatsoper, and the Staatsoper in Berlin. After the war he conducted at the Berlin City Opera before returning to the Munich Staatsoper.

[10] Erna Berger (1900–1990), one of the most important German sopranos of the 20th century, was best known as the Queen of the Night in *Die Zauberflöte*, Violetta in *La Traviata*, Mimi in *La Bohème*, Gilda in *Rigoletto*, and Konstanze in *Die Entführung aus dem Serail.*

[11] Heinrich Schlusnus (1888–1952), baritone, sang at the Berlin Staatsoper 1917–1944. His best known roles were Wolfram in *Tannhäuser*, the title role in *Rigoletto*, and Giorgio Germont in *La Traviata*. He was internationally renowned as an interpreter of Lieder.

Sebastian Peschko,[12] was a friend of my eldest sister Friedelore and often came to our house in Dahlem. In this way, we got free tickets for Schlusnus concerts in the *Philharmonie* or in one of the halls where there were Lieder evenings. So he was one of the singers whose voice and style of singing I got to know quite early on. He was a very good Lieder singer. Another recital that made a big impression on me was by Alexander Kipnis, who was an internationally famous bass at the Berlin Staatsoper and the Vienna Staatsoper. He also came to Berlin, sometime around 1936, and gave a Lieder recital sponsored by the Kulturbund. That was the first truly great Lieder recital I ever heard. It opened with an aria from the Verdi *Requiem*, accompanied on the piano, followed by Lieder. It made an enormous impression on me. When you listen to recordings by Kipnis you can hear that his approach to singing is not at all unlike Carl Flesch's approach to violin playing. Kipnis also makes use of *rubato* – rhetorical, rhythmic freedom – as well as *portamento* – deliberately, expressively.

My whole conception of violin sound has always had a lot to do with singing, and it still does even today: it's modelled on the great singers of Lieder and opera, which is why opera was such a central component of my musical development. I always try to encourage my students to go to the opera, because opera has to do with the rhetoric of music, with its inflections, with concepts like *legato*, *portato*, *portamento*, and *messa di voce*, that is, all the criteria and specialities of the *bel canto*[13] technique of the Italian school. You can't conceive of them for the violin if you've never heard them. Long tones, for instance, cannot simply be held evenly the way they usually are today, they require an intensification in which one makes a crescendo into the middle of the note and then a diminuendo, the so-called *messa di voce*, or that you somehow otherwise enliven the note by varying its tonal quality. As a string player you have to know all these things that come from the art of singing.

Toscanini

RS A celebrated musician who was also a major influence on you at an early age was Arturo Toscanini.[14] How did you discover him?

[12] Sebastian Peschko (1909–1987) was a student of Edwin Fischer. He was a highly regarded accompanist of many eminent singers, including Schlusnus, Erna Berger, Walter Berry, Lisa Della Casa, Grace Bumbry, Christa Ludwig, and Hermann Prey.

[13] *Bel canto*, literally 'beautiful singing,' generally refers to the 19th century Italian school of singing that favored a light tone production to enable the singer to fluently execute the florid passages and complex ornaments of Rossini, Donizetti, and Bellini, while maintaining a perfect legato; beyond mere technical facility, *bel canto* at its best is characterized by a nuanced and supple expressivity of phrasing.

[14] Arturo Toscanini (1867–1957), Italian conductor, was perhaps the most famous as well

WL Toscanini was already familiar to me as a child in Berlin as the result of a trip to the record store I always stopped at on my way home from my violin lessons. For some strange reason we had only the second movement of Beethoven's seventh symphony at home, the recording with Weingartner[15] and the London Symphony on Columbia. One of the records had the end of the first movement and another had the beginning of the third movement, which seemed very unsatisfactory to me, and after a lot of nagging on my part my parents gave me the necessary 30 marks – at that time 78 rpm records were very expensive – and sent me off to buy the complete recording. When I got to the store I said that this time I didn't just want to listen to new releases as I usually did, I actually wanted to buy the five record set of the Beethoven seventh with Weingartner. But the girl who always played the new releases for me suggested that before I bought the Weingartner I should listen to a new recording that they'd just gotten in by the New York Philharmonic under a conductor by the name of Arturo Toscanini.

I knew nothing about Toscanini, but I listened to this recording and it was as if I'd literally been struck by lightning. That was the kind of experience you have only very rarely, where you instantly realize that this is just how music simply must be played. Such brilliant, rhythmical, exact, and fantastic orchestral playing was something I'd never even remotely heard anything like before. It wasn't like anything I was used to and I was simply overwhelmed by it. The way Toscanini conducted this Beethoven symphony, the way the orchestra played it, how it had been conceived and performed – I immediately felt that this was just exactly how it had to be. I don't know why I felt this way, I'd never seen the score and was actually in no way qualified to make such a judgment. But I was absolutely certain that this recording was incomparable, and I decided all by myself to buy the Toscanini recording instead of the Weingartner. Naturally that led to some consternation when I got back home. But over the course of many years the tremendous force of Toscanini's performances and his quest for truth in music have become more and more convincing to me, and the more I learned about music, the more I felt I was right to buy this recording, although Weingartner was not at all a bad conductor.

RS In what way was Toscanini influential for you?

as one of the most influential 20th century conductors. His weekly radio broadcasts with the NBC Symphony made him a household name in America, and his uncompromising opposition to the Fascist and Nazi governments of Italy and Germany in the 1930s gave him an unexampled moral stature as well.

15 Felix Weingartner (1863–1942), Austrian conductor, was the first to record a complete cycle of the Beethoven symphonies.

WL My colleagues in the LaSalle Quartet and I were great admirers of this kind of performance, this self-effacement, that hasn't confused self-expression with interpretation, but rather understands interpretation as a realization of the composer's intentions – that was always our ideal. You can always recognize a Toscanini recording by its rhythmical élan, its inner tension, and also by its transparency. And I do believe you can hear his influence in the rhythmical character and transparency of our own performances. Toscanini's way of rehearsing, his relentless pursuit of precision, his unwillingness to compromise, and his unsentimental conception of musical performance – all of these characteristics of his music making were exemplary for me from the very beginning.

RS You also got plenty of opportunities to hear Toscanini conducting the NBC Symphony in rehearsals and concerts.

WL Yes, but that was later on, in New York, when I was at Juilliard.

3 *Palestine*

ROBERT SPRUYTENBURG: When you arrived in Palestine at the end of 1938, you could already play the violin quite well, so you needed a good violin teacher. How did you come to find Rudolf Bergmann?[1]

WALTER LEVIN: Bergmann was recommended to us by Bronislaw Huberman.[2] My parents wanted to get an independent assessment of whether my gifts were sufficient to enable me later on to have a career in the somewhat precarious profession of music. My family knew Huberman because my uncle Erich was his doctor. And when they were looking for an advisor, my uncle arranged for us to visit Huberman at his hotel in Tel Aviv. My mother and I went there and I played for him. That was a memorable afternoon. He was very friendly and we had quite an intense conversation in which he wanted to know just exactly what my interests in music were and what I wanted to do with them. Afterwards he had a private conversation with my mother and told her that it would certainly be possible for me to have a career in music. His advice was that I should get a thorough training in all the fundamentals, and he recommended teachers with whom I should study. And they were the best recommendations imaginable: Huberman was obviously a teacher of genius along with everything else, he knew exactly what kind of teacher I would need.

So he recommended Rudolf Bergmann, one of his concertmasters in the Palestine Orchestra, whom he regarded highly, as my violin teacher. He thought Bergmann would be the right teacher for me since he also came from Germany. And since at that time I could scarcely speak Hebrew at all, in spite of having spent four years in Hebrew classes at the Theodor Herzl School, he thought it would be good for me to have a teacher who came from the same cultural milieu as I did. There were three other concertmasters as well: Andreas Weissgerber[3] did come from Vienna, but Jozéf Kaminski[4] was from Poland and

1 Rudolf Bergmann (1892–1961), German violinist, emigrated to Palestine early in 1936 to be one of the concertmasters of the newly founded Palestine Orchestra.

2 Bronislaw Huberman (1892–1947), Polish violin prodigy and virtuoso, whose performance at age fourteen of the Brahms violin concerto was acclaimed by Brahms himself, founded the Palestine Orchestra in 1936. See pp. 24–26.

3 Andreas Weissgerber (1900–1941) was a child prodigy who later studied at the music academies in Budapest, Vienna, and Berlin before resuming his successful career as a virtuoso violinist. He emigrated to Palestine in 1936.

4 Jozéf Kaminski (1903–1972) studied in Vienna with Arnold Rosé; he also studied composition with Hans Gál. He was concertmaster of the Warsaw Radio Orchestra and the founder of the Warsaw String Quartet. He emigrated to Palestine in 1937.

Lorand Fenyves[5] was from Hungary. Bergmann had studied the violin in Budapest with Jenö Hubay, one of the great violin teachers at that time,[6] along with Joseph Joachim[7] and Carl Flesch. In fact many string players in the Palestine Orchestra were students of Hubay, including Ödön Partos,[8] a fabulous violist and a wonderful musician with whom I had a lot to do later on.

There were a lot of Germans and Hungarians in the orchestra, since it had been Huberman's idea to establish an orchestra in Palestine to rescue Jewish musicians from the Nazis. He travelled all over Europe recruiting, which was salvation for many musicians. Huberman had read the signs of the times. There are two letters from musicians who saw where things were headed. One of them is from Schoenberg to Kandinsky[9] and the other is from Huberman to Furtwängler,[10] in which he explains why he wouldn't be playing with Furtwängler in the Brahms Festival. Those were people who had the courage to speak out about their moral convictions rather than evade them. There were also people who were not Jewish but who left Germany out of moral considerations: the Busch brothers Adolf, Fritz, and Hermann,[11] for instance, and also Casals,[12] who was not prepared to collaborate with the Franco regime in Spain. For such people it was simply out of the question to collaborate with the Nazis and with Franco: they were dictators, murderers.

[5] Lorand Fenyves (1918–2004) studied with Jenö Hubay. He made his debut at the age of fourteen and performed extensively in Hungary and elsewhere in Europe. He emigrated to Palestine in 1936.

[6] Jenö Hubay (1858–1937). His students included André Gertler, Stefi Geyer, Eugene Ormandy, Zoltán Székely, and Joseph Szigeti.

[7] Joseph Joachim (1831–1907), Hungarian virtuoso violinist for whom Brahms wrote both his violin concerto and his double concerto for violin and cello. The Joachim String Quartet, founded in 1869, was renowned as Europe's finest.

[8] Ödön Partos (1907–1977) studied violin with Jenö Hubay and composition with Zoltán Kodály. In 1933 he became the concertmaster of the Kulturbund Orchestra, and in 1938, Bronislaw Huberman invited him to be principal violist of the Palestine Orchestra, a position he held until 1956; he was also the violist of the Israel Quartet.

[9] Wassily Kandinsky (1866–1944), Russian artist, art theorist, and pioneer of abstract art, knew many of the European avant-garde in all the arts, including Schoenberg.

[10] Wilhelm Furtwängler (1886–1954), German conductor and composer, who elected to remain in Germany as conductor of the Berlin Philharmonic during the Nazi regime. His relationship to the Nazis and his recorded performances have remained controversial ever since.

[11] Adolf Busch (1891–1952), violin virtuoso and founder of the Busch Quartet and co-founder of the Marlboro Festival; Fritz Busch (1890–1951), conductor, best known for his performances of Mozart at Glyndebourne; Hermann Busch (1897–1975), cellist and member of the Busch Quartet and the Busch-Serkin Trio.

[12] Pablo Casals (1876-1973), renowned Spanish cellist, conductor, and teacher, refused to play in Spain after Franco's victory in 1938. He did not live to see the end of Franco's regime in 1975.

Huberman founded the Palestine Orchestra in 1936, which was a wonderful cultural contribution to the development of the country and which also saved the lives of as many as a hundred musicians and their families.[13] For if you could prove that you had a job as a musician in Palestine, the British Mandate administration would give you a visa and you could emigrate. The most extraordinary musicians came to Palestine as members of this orchestra. Huberman also convinced one of the greatest conductors of our time to conduct the orchestra's inaugural concerts at the end of December, 1936, and the beginning of January, 1937: Arturo Toscanini, who came to Palestine again in April, 1938.[14] Unfortunately I missed out on the inaugural concerts of the Palestine Orchestra with Toscanini, since we only arrived in Palestine at the end of 1938. But thanks to Huberman the basis of a musical life was established in Palestine on a level that one could never have imagined otherwise. Huberman was an incredible personality, both as a musician and as a human being.

RS Had you already known Huberman as a violinist at that time?

WL No, I only first met him when we talked at his hotel, and of course I immediately went to one of the concerts in which he was performing as a soloist with the Palestine Orchestra, playing the Brahms violin concerto. I should point out that at the age of twelve Huberman had already played this concerto for Brahms, and at a time when it was held to be practically unplayable. Brahms was so impressed that he inscribed a marvelous dedication in Huberman's score. When one heard Huberman live, as I did, he radiated an immense energy, and he played with an unparalleled recklessness, without regard for a certain hardness of tone that went along with that. Huberman's tone wasn't at all what a violinist today conceives of as the much lauded 'beautiful tone.' But what for Huberman was most important was the character of the music, and he produced it by setting aside every bit of caution. But by then the next generation of violinists had already won the day. Even violinists who had studied with Hubay in Budapest, like Szigeti, for instance, and later on my teacher Bergmann, didn't play like Huberman. Ever since then violinists have played with a tonal refinement that is the complete opposite of the kind of violin playing that aims at rendering the music's character. The great teacher Carl Flesch also wrote very negatively about Huberman's playing.

Even at the beginning of the 20th century, Huberman represented a lost world, since beginning with Kreisler everything is played with

[13] For more about Huberman's efforts to recruit Jewish musicians for the Palestine Orchestra, see Jehoash Hirshberg, *Music in the Jewish Community of Palestine 1880–1948* (Oxford, 1995), and Barbara von der Lühe, *Musik war unsere Rettung* (Tübingen, 1998).

[14] During his two visits to Palestine Toscanini conducted a total of 21 concerts, taking an honorarium for none of them.

vibrato, whereas Huberman played for long stretches without much vibrato, reserving it for the expressive places. Nowadays, in our era of authentic performance practice, that's become popular again, but for a long time, especially during the second half of the 20th century, it was considered totally unacceptable. Which is why Huberman was already a violinist from a by-gone era, even in the 1930s. What was also striking about Huberman is his rhythm: he made scarcely any *rubati* and played extremely precisely rhythmically. That too is unusual today, since for a very long time everything has been highly romanticized and played with a lot of rhythmic freedom and *rubato*. In any case, at a time when I was still learning to play the violin it was an incredible and formative experience for me to hear how a truly great musician and soloist interpreted a work like the Brahms concerto. On top of which this man apparently had an inexhaustible fund of energy: on that evening he played three of the very greatest violin concerti: Bach, Brahms, and Mendelssohn, one right after the other, and in between them a few encores from the Bach solo sonatas as well. All these things made a very strong impression on me, and on the members of the Palestine Orchestra too. My teacher Bergmann always spoke of Huberman with the greatest respect.

RS Let's get back to your teacher Rudolf Bergmann again. What was Bergmann doing in Germany before he emigrated to Palestine?

WL He was the concertmaster and widely known soloist of the Wiesbaden Municipal Spa Orchestra under its permanent conductor, Carl Schuricht. In February 1933 he was dismissed on account of his being Jewish, but got a new position in Frankfurt in 1934 as concertmaster of the Kulturbund Orchestra there. He emigrated to the Netherlands already in 1935 and from there to Palestine in 1936, where Huberman engaged him as one of the concertmasters of the Palestine Orchestra.

RS You said once that there was a direct line of descent from your violin teacher Bergmann all the way back to Beethoven.

WL Yes, that's right. As a young violinist Bergmann studied briefly with Joseph Joachim, and Joachim was a student of Joseph Böhm, who had worked with Beethoven to prepare the second performance of his string quartet Opus 127.

RS What method book did Bergmann use in teaching the violin?

WL Just like Jürgen Ronis in Berlin, Bergmann used Carl Flesch's *Art of*

Violin Playing,[15] and he recommended that I get a copy: a fabulous book! In it everything is analyzed so precisely that if you were clever enough you could learn from the book all by itself: how to practice, how to tune, how to stand, how to make vibrato, the correct position of the thumb, the Franco-Belgian method of holding the bow, and everything in it about interpretation – incredible! I was already familiar with all that from my studies with Jürgen Ronis. But Bergmann was concerned not only with violin technique but also with music itself, with interpretation: how to perform grace notes in Mozart and how to deal with questions of interpretation generally, that is, to rely on urtext editions and original sources and to realize the composer's intentions as precisely as possible – everything that was important to me later on. Pedagogically Bergmann was excellent. It was from him that I learned how to teach the violin, and I began very early on, while I was still in Palestine, to give violin lessons myself.

RS What kind of violin literature did you study with Bergmann?

WL I worked on the Mozart violin concerti with him, but also on concerti by Giovanni Battista Viotti and Pierre Rode. Astonishingly, Viotti's 22nd concerto was one of Brahms' favorite concerti, and for that reason Bergmann convinced me to take this concerto seriously too, since one could learn an enormous amount from it. I then learned the concerto Nr. 8 'In the Form of a Vocal Scene' by Louis Spohr, a piece that I later tormented my own students with, because it's such an excellent preparatory study for the Beethoven concerto. Nowadays, unfortunately, Spohr is almost totally neglected. I also studied the Kreutzer etudes – etudes are scarcely used any more by violin teachers. Herbert Brün and I rehearsed some Mozart sonatas with Bergmann, as well as two big Beethoven sonatas, and the great C major Fantasy by Schubert, since we wanted to give a sonata recital together. Later on of course came the Beethoven concerto, at around age sixteen the Brahms concerto, and then the great virtuoso violin literature like the concerti of Vieuxtemps and Wienawski.

RS For you then, Rudolf Bergmann was not only a violin teacher but also a highly educated man.

WL Indeed. He mentored me intellectually and strongly encouraged my intellectual interests. I spent whole afternoons and evenings with Bergmann, and he showed me books that I'd previously never heard of. For instance, it was he who first showed me the ten volume *Handbook of*

[15] Berlin, 1928/1929; New York, 2000/2008.

Musicology[16] which had been published relatively recently, and he lent me the volume on performance practice. I had never even heard of performance practice! Whenever a question came up in our conversations, he showed me the relevant literature and gave me a book about it, urging me to read it. This was how I got to know a great many of the classics of German literature. For me it was like discovering a whole new world. He always treated me like an adult. I'm still grateful to Bergmann for having put me on a path that set the course for my whole future, and I'm forever grateful to Huberman for having sent me to Bergmann as a student.

Bergmann was very pleased that I was always interested in everything he did. He also composed, albeit with great difficulty, and he always played for me what he'd written and was very interested in hearing my critique. I really wasn't qualified to do that, as I still was pretty clueless about music, though I did have a good sense of what worked and what didn't, and, moreover, I had two friends, Herbert Brün[17] and Wolf Rosenberg,[18] both of them very advanced students of composition with Stefan Wolpe. And Wolpe was a student of Webern and an avant-garde composer.[19] So I heard a lot about what really was new music and I passed that along to Bergmann. But composition was frustrating for him. I believe he never finished a single piece.

RS So you had a lot of music lessons and had to practice a great deal. But besides that you also had to go to school.

WL In my first year in Palestine, when I was fourteen years old, I went to the Shalva High School.[20] After that I had only private instruction. My father wanted me to get my *Abitur*,[21] the equivalent of which in Palestine was called a 'Matriculation Certificate,' a 'Matric' for short, which was the qualification for admission to the English universities, since one of course

16 Ernst Bücken, ed. *Handbuch der Musikwissenschaft* (Wildpark-Potsdam, 1928–1934).

17 Herbert Brün (1918–2000), composer and graphic artist; see pp. 41–42 and 287–289.

18 Wolf Rosenberg (1915–1996), composer and critic; see pp. 289–292.

19 Stefan Wolpe (1902–1972), composer and polymath of the arts, studied with Johannes Itten, Paul Klee, and others at the Weimar Bauhaus 1920–1924; he later got to know the Dadaist Kurt Schwitters and the Marxist Hanns Eisler and absorbed elements of both into his music. Forced to leave Germany in 1933, Wolpe studied briefly with Anton Webern in Austria before emigrating to Palestine in 1934, teaching at the Conservatory of Music and Dramatic Arts in Jerusalem, where Brün and Rosenberg were, later, students. He left for New York in December, 1938. Better known as a teacher than as a composer, his students in America included Morton Feldman, Ralph Shapey, and David Tudor.

20 *Gymnasium:* in the classical German educational system, a school with a curriculum oriented to preparing students for university admission.

21 The *Abitur* is the German equivalent of English 'A-levels'; the American equivalent might be the combination of a high school diploma together with suitably high college admissions test scores.

wanted to study at a European university. In England you had to have the matriculation certificate in order to do that, and since it was offered in the whole of the British empire, you didn't have to go to London to get it. Since Palestine was administratively a British Mandate and therefore under British law, the Matriculation Certificate was also offered there: you could take the exam once a year. But you had to prepare for it in evening classes, since many young people who wanted to study for it were already older, in their early twenties, and had to work for a living during the day. So there were all sorts of schools in Tel Aviv that specialized in evening instruction: they offered four or five of the subjects you had to study for the Matriculation. There were many first rate teachers in these schools who had lost their positions in Europe, just as there were in music. For three years I went to evening school three or four times a week, from 8 pm to 11 pm, and passed my Matriculation exam in 1943.

RS Were the subjects required for the Matric what you would expect?

WL Yes, mathematics, English,[22] music, history, and a foreign language, for which I picked German. There were special books from England that were written specifically for the Matriculation exam and that had all the questions you would have to answer. I didn't worry about the course in music since the questions you got on the music exam for the Matriculation Certificate testified to a scarcely believable degree of simple narrow-mindedness. On Rudolf Bergmann's recommendation I had wonderful private lessons in music: for piano he had recommended Frank Pollak, who later adopted the Hebrew name Pelleg,[23] since I played the piano as well as the violin, and Paul Ben-Haim,[24] who had changed his name from Frankenburger,[25] for composition, theory, harmony, and analysis.

[22] Levin began learning English as a child in Berlin after his parents hired an English nanny; the Levins also vacationed in the UK, at Swansea in Wales. Like music and German, English was for him a 'slam dunk' subject for the Matric.

[23] Frank Pelleg (1910–1968), pianist and harpsichordist, emigrated to Palestine from Prague in 1936 at Bronislaw Huberman's invitation. After the war he made many international tours, playing with Otto Klemperer, Sergiu Celibidache, and Georg Solti, among many others. He was a founding member of the Research Institute for Jewish Music in Jerusalem in 1939 and of the Haifa Symphony Orchestra in 1951, where he was managing director until the end of his life. On his initiative the 1954 ISCM (International Society for Contemporary Music) festival took place in Haifa. The LaSalle Quartet played there on its first international tour. See pp. 124–126. Herbert Brün was also a student of Pelleg's.

[24] Paul Ben-Haim (1897–1984) had launched a career in Germany as an opera conductor before emigrating to Palestine in 1933. He conducted the Palestine Orchestra on several occasions, but concentrated on teaching and composition, becoming Israel's most famous composer.

[25] It was not unusual for immigrants from German-speaking Europe to adopt Hebrew names in Palestine, and not only out of Zionist convictions or out of gratitude to their

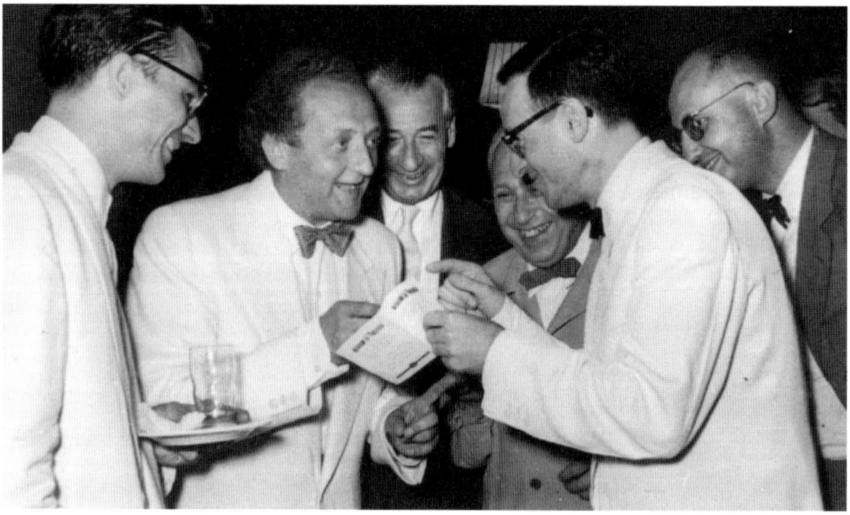

5 Richard Kapuscinski, Frank Pelleg, Erich Levin (Walter Levin's uncle), Rudolf Bergmann, Walter Levin, Ernst Schreuer (husband of Eva, née Levin), Tel Aviv, 1954

Ben-Haim was a wonderful man, the very image of a Protestant minister: tall, serious, quiet, blond. He was a composer as well as a theoretician and conductor. Later on I came to have a high regard for him as a Mahler conductor, and also as an accompanist and a chamber music player. I had music theory lessons with him once a week. I revered Ben-Haim. His wife wasn't Jewish. Remarkably, none of the wives of my three teachers were Jewish, but they had all gone with their husbands to Palestine.

I had piano lessons with Frank Pelleg twice a week. Pelleg came from Prague and was an exceptional soloist, on the piano as well as on the harpsichord. He was a Bach specialist and very early on had specialized in the harpsichord, following the example of Wanda Landowska,[26] but he also played the classical piano repertory. In the Mozart concerti he even played his own cadenzas, as I was later to hear Artur Schnabel[27] do, but up until then I had never heard such a thing. So I got a very comprehensive and insightful education from all three of my teachers. They taught me to see the connections between things and to see them in context.

adopted country: German emigrants were often derided by the prior generations of immigrants as *yekkes* (from German *Jacke*: 'jacket') for their difficulties in assimilating. Levin was pestered to change his name to Zvi, which he refused to do.

26 Wanda Landowska (1879–1959), Polish harpsichordist, is largely credited with the revival of interest in the instrument in the early 20th century.

27 Artur Schnabel (1882–1951), pianist and composer, was the first to record all 32 Beethoven piano sonatas; he is recognized as among the most intellectually profound of the great 20th century pianists. For Schnabel's music, see pp. 318–332.

I was also immersed in the culture of Prague and Vienna, which at that time I knew nothing about. Karl Kraus,[28] for instance, wasn't of any interest to my parents. I first saw the red covers of Karl Kraus' journal *Die Fackel* at Frank Pelleg's. But I didn't understand what it was really all about: I still had a lot to learn. So in Tel Aviv I was in a completely German cultural milieu. My friends Herbert Brün, Wolf Rosenberg, and Wolfgang Hildesheimer[29] all spoke German, and I also spoke only German with my teachers.

RS It's actually astonishing that you learned Hebrew at all!

WL It was only because of school, Shalva High School, where the instruction was all in Hebrew. My father understood the importance of that right away, he told me that I was going to go to school until I'd learned enough Hebrew to be able to understand the teachers. The passion for Thomas Mann that one of my fellow students at Shalva High School had kindled in me was very helpful in that regard, a German boy who sat next to me in class and who had been in Palestine longer than I had. He spoke very good Hebrew and was always very calmly reading a book hidden under his school desk. I asked him what it was he was reading all the time. He told me it was *Buddenbrooks* by Thomas Mann. I wanted to know if it was really all that interesting. His only response was to say I should read it myself sometime! Of course I found it right away on my parents' bookshelves, and so I read *Buddenbrooks*. I was utterly enchanted. I read one book after another by Thomas Mann – they were all in my parents' bookcase.

Since I had to learn to actually speak as well as understand Hebrew, I was also in an after-school Hebrew study group, led by an amateur trumpet player, Galibow. Galibow came from Bulgaria, had a German wife, and was an excellent Hebrew teacher. Everyone in the group had to give a talk on some subject of interest to them. He asked me what I wanted to give a talk on, and I told him *Tonio Kröger* by Thomas Mann. I wrote my talk in German and with Galibow's help translated it into Hebrew, which taught me a lot about the language.

[28] Karl Kraus (1874–1936) is held by many to be the greatest 20th century satirist in the German language; some would go further and rank him with Jonathan Swift among the greatest satirists ever. Kraus published all of his work in the journal *Die Fackel (The Torch)* which he founded in 1899. His solo performances of Shakespeare, Nestroy, Raimund, and Offenbach drew a large following among the Viennese intelligentsia and avant-garde. His greatest work, the play *Die letzten Tage der Menschheit (The Last Days of Mankind)*, is an epic satire on the corruption of everyday life in Vienna during the First World War.

[29] Wolfgang Hildesheimer (1916–1991), German writer, was a founding member of the Gruppe 47, the famous post-war association of concerned writers formed in Germany in 1947. In 1977 he published an important, if controversial, biography of Mozart. He was a particularly close friend of Rosenberg's. See pp. 43–44.

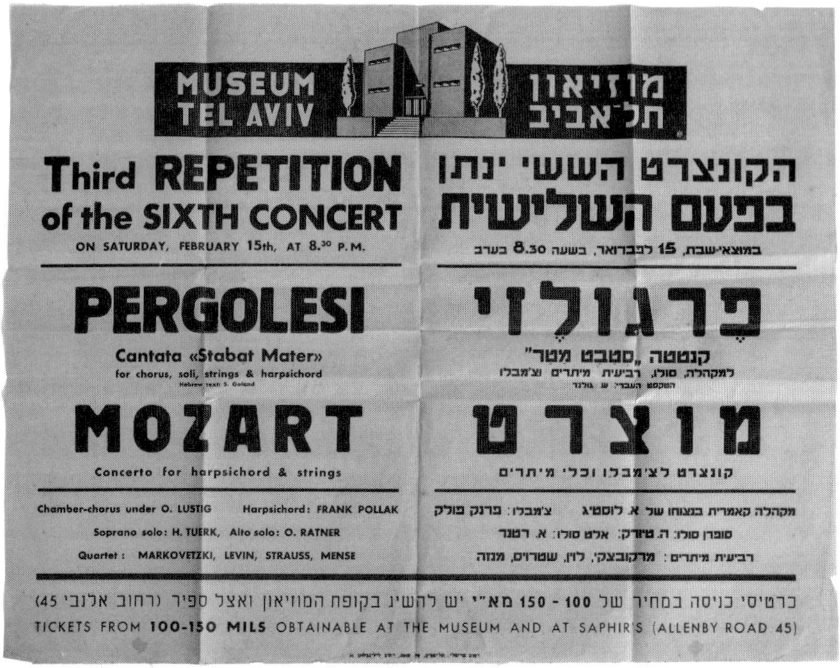

6 Poster for a concert with Frank Pelleg [Pollak], and Walter Levin, Tel Aviv, February 15, 1941

It was already hard enough to learn subjects like mathematics, geometry, or history taught in a language I scarcely knew at all. But what was even worse was that I also had to take Arabic as a foreign language, and it too was taught in Hebrew. That was dicey, as I was only just beginning to learn Hebrew. But I absolutely had to get a passing grade, because of a stringent requirement my father had imposed on me: not until I could keep up with my classes would he consider whether or not to let me study music. So I had to get a relatively decent grade in Arabic. I transcribed some stories into the Latin alphabet, learned them by heart in bed in the mornings, and recited them in school. The accent wasn't hard for me, I always had a good ear for that, but I didn't understand a single word of what I was saying. But the teacher thought it was quite good, and I actually passed. This was the same sort of bluffing I had used as a child in Berlin, pretending to be able to read music.

RS You made up your mind very early on to become a quartet player, and you started a quartet of your own not long after you arrived in Palestine. How old were you then?

WL When I arrived in Palestine I had just turned fourteen. In Tel Aviv I soon

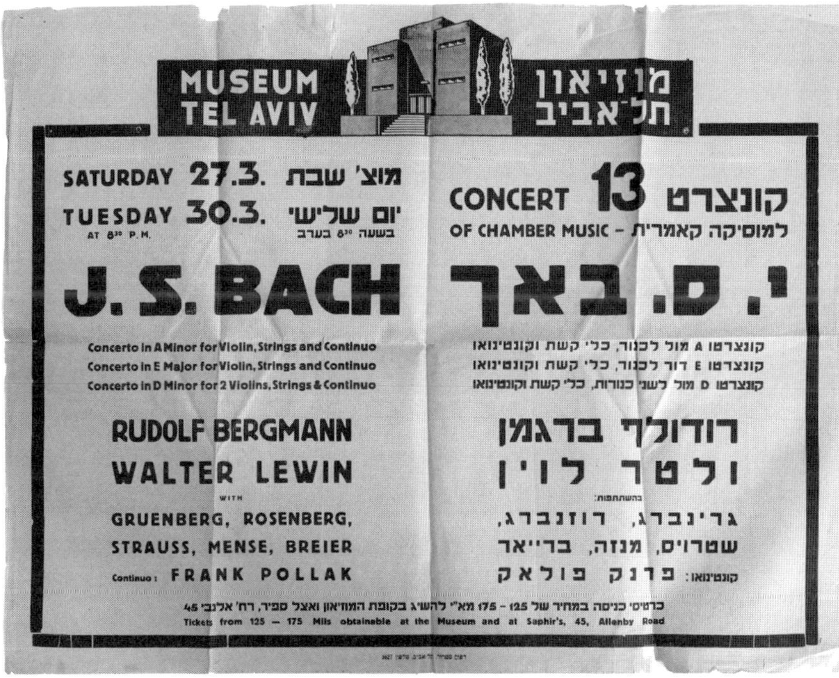

7 Poster for a concert with Rudolf Bergmann, Frank Pelleg [Pollak], and Walter Levin, Tel Aviv, March 27, 1943

got to know Gideon Strauss, a violist who was some ten years older than me. He had also emigrated to Palestine and worked at the Bank Leumi, the national bank. He was an enthusiastic violist who hadn't become a professional musician since he couldn't earn a living that way. But in his free time he played the viola superbly, and he was one of those amateurs who are as good as professional musicians and who have an immense knowledge of the musical literature: an intelligent, well-read intellectual who knew a lot. He'd been intensely involved with playing chamber music his whole life long, starting in Berlin. He was an incredible inspiration for me. He actually became my mentor for chamber music. Of course Bergmann was a fabulous violin teacher, who also played in a quartet, but his job was to teach me the violin. My quartet playing was actually put on the right track by Gideon Strauss. For example, he insisted on our studying the score to whatever quartet we were rehearsing, instead of just playing from the parts. And I rather quickly got to know a whole bunch of young musicians, which wasn't hard to do in Tel Aviv. Something like a third of my classmates at school played the violin and the other two-thirds played the piano, and very well too. There were also one or two cellists and violists, and in the lunch breaks we had a chamber orchestra and played Bach, the third Brandenburg Concerto, and *concerti grossi* by Handel and Vivaldi.

So I had musicians for friends right away, including some very good violinists. My classmate Chaim Taub became the first violinist in the Tel Aviv String Quartet and was later concertmaster in the Israel Philharmonic. Many of my classmates were really very good instrumentalists who were in the Palestine Orchestra later on. When I was fifteen I started a quartet with them and some other friends: it was my idea, I had always wanted to play quartets. I changed the roster a little from time to time when I realized it wasn't right yet. So to begin with I had two colleagues who also studied with Bergmann, an insanely gifted violinist, Itzhak Markowetzki, who was a sort of 'gypsy' or 'coffee house' violinist, an incredible virtuoso who could play anything and everything effortlessly, but who didn't have much of a clue about music. Bergmann was very upset that he wasn't able to teach the boy how to play correctly, he simply played everything by instinct.

Markowetzki was with me in the quartet in the beginning. At first I played second violin and he played first. Erich Grünberg[30] also played in the quartet with me, and we constantly traded places as first and second and went on tour to the kibbutzim together. My friend Werner Torkanowsky[31] was also a violinist in the quartet. As my cellist I had Jaakov Mense,[32] who was still going to school at the Herzlia High School in Tel Aviv. Along with my sister Friedelore, he was a student of Theo Salzmann,[33] one of the principal cellists in the Palestine Orchestra. Among other things we played Beethoven's Opus 18, Nr. 4, in the Ohel Theater, one of the biggest theaters in Tel Aviv. In concerts at the Tel Aviv Museum[34] we also played chamber music arrangements of Bach's fifth Brandenburg concerto, his d minor concerto, and his triple concerto, all three with Frank Pelleg as harpsichordist. That was in February 1941, when I was just sixteen, which is rather young to have the experience of playing with such an extraordinary soloist. From Pelleg you learned to listen incredibly closely, and also learned a way of making music based on its sheer sonority that I've scarcely ever encountered again from a keyboard player.

The quartet went to Kibbutz Givat Brenner once and gave a con-

30 Erich Grünberg (1924–) was concertmaster of the Palestine Broadcasting Orchestra 1938–1945; he subsequently held that position in the Stockholm Philharmonic, the London Symphony Orchestra, and the Royal Philharmonic.

31 Werner Torkanowsky (1926–1992), violinist and conductor, led the New Orleans Symphony 1963–1977.

32 Jaakov Mense later became the cellist in the New Israeli String Quartet.

33 Theo Salzmann (1907–1982) studied with Julius Klengel in Leipzig and was appointed principal cellist of the Vienna Symphony at age nineteen. He emigrated to Palestine in 1938 and was principal cellist of the Palestine Orchestra until 1947, when he moved to Australia. He was engaged by William Steinberg as principal cellist of the Pittsburgh Symphony in 1951.

34 Now Independence House, the building was originally the home of Tel Aviv's first mayor, Meir Dizengoff. It housed the Tel Aviv Museum 1930–1971.

cert in the *chadar ochel*, the dining hall, since that was the only big hall they had. One of the nicest things about Palestine was that if you played music you were welcome everywhere: the kibbutz residents were extraordinary music lovers. You got free accommodations, sat together with everyone at dinner, and ate the wonderful food they grew there. Afterwards the chairs were rearranged and we played a concert program. The people were enthusiastic, and we played a lot of different encores, but the encores weren't the end of it, since the most important part of the evening was yet to come: the requests. You did very well to be prepared for this, since they requested the most difficult pieces for quartet. As a result, we very quickly got to know our way around the great quartet literature. The members of the kibbutzim also knew their way around it, even the late Beethoven quartets, and a majority of the listeners followed our performances with pocket scores. This went on for hours, on into the early morning.

One time, on one of these kibbutz tours, someone came up to us and asked us if we wouldn't like to play the Schubert Quintet. It was Chaim Rothschild, a cellist. He worked the whole day long on the kibbutz and played the cello in the evening, and how! He had studied in Leipzig with Julius Klengel[35] and he too knew the whole of the quartet literature, just like Gideon Strauss – there were exceptionally cultivated, knowledgeable people on the kibbutzim. Subsequently we went on tour with him as our cellist. We went on foot from one kibbutz to the next, and we were welcomed everywhere with open arms and treated as if we were the closest of relatives. We would play a concert and spend the night in each kibbutz, often outside under mosquito nets when it was very hot. I'd never seen anything like it, people who knew this music inside out, and who shared everything they knew with you: that in itself was a very valuable lesson and a terrific experience. Those were concerts the likes of which I never experienced again. I learned a lot in Palestine. It was a completely different atmosphere from what I had known in Berlin. Life on a kibbutz at that time radiated a wonderful atmosphere of harmony, that was the biggest impression I got from these tours with my quartet, and there were incredible people living on the kibbutzim. As you know, my sister Eva also went to live on a kibbutz.

RS Did you rehearse regularly with your quartet?

WL As often as possible, whenever we had time. In that sense it wasn't a regular quartet, we all had other things to do too. But whenever we had the opportunity, we rehearsed pieces we could take on tour. For instance, we

[35] Julius Klengel (1859–1933), principal cellist of the Leipzig Gewandhaus Orchestra 1881–1924. Among his best known students were Emanuel Feuermann and Gregor Piatigorsky.

selected and rehearsed a Haydn quartet, and then we played Tchaikovsky's Opus 11 and Schubert's quartet in a minor.

During this time I also learned a great deal about how you work as a quartet, that you have to work together with your colleagues, that you can't just stubbornly insist on getting your own way, you have to give other opinions their due. In this regard Gideon Strauss was always a calming influence on me, also later. I remember that he heard the LaSalle Quartet in San Francisco and came up to me afterwards and told me that my intonation could be better, that I'd played a bit sharp, and asked me if I knew why. It was because I used the kind of vibrato that goes to the high side of the notes. If you do that, they sound sharp, because the ear orients itself toward the higher frequencies. I knew this, but I did it anyway. I had to learn not to do that. Gideon was always a very good listener who helped me a lot. He also knew how to get through to me. He also came to visit us in Colorado, and for years afterwards we saw him regularly, since he came to America with his family and lived in New York for a long time.

RS Did most of the proposals for the quartet's repertory come from Gideon Strauss?

WL Yes, they did. I didn't have much of a clue about it. All I knew was that I very much wanted to play Beethoven's Opus 59, Nr. 2 and his Opus 127, because I'd heard the Calvet Quartet play them in Berlin. But Gideon advised against it – he said there would be time for that later on.

RS Actually you had scarcely any models for quartet playing, since there weren't that many quartets in Palestine then.

WL There were several, though. In Palestine each of the four concertmasters of the Palestine Orchestra had his own quartet: Rudolf Bergmann, Jozéf Kaminski, Lorand Fenyves, and Andreas Weissgerber together with his brother, the cellist Joseph Weissgerber. Bergmann's was a very good quartet which gave regularly concerts in the Tel Aviv Museum on the Boulevard Rothschild. Its other members were a second violinist from the Palestine Orchestra, the violist Renée Galimir, and the cellist Theo Salzmann. This quartet was exemplary for me in every respect because it gave thoroughly rehearsed performances of the great works of the literature like the late Beethoven quartets, the quartets of Brahms, and the Mozart quartets dedicated to Haydn, as a result of which I got to know this literature professionally for the first time. Renée Galimir was a phenomenal violist. But I didn't know until much later what a splendid musician it was who was playing in Bergmann's quartet. She was one of Felix Galimir's three sisters, with whom he had founded the Galimir Quartet in Vienna in the 1920s: Adrienne Galimir played second violin and Marguerite Galimir played cello.[36] Felix Galimir and his sister Renée joined the Palestine Orchestra in 1936, at Huberman's invitation, but he was enticed by Toscanini to go to New York to play in the NBC Symphony in 1938,[37] while Renée Galimir spent the rest of her life in Palestine.

Even in their younger days, the Galimir Quartet played an enormous role in the musical life of Vienna, but Renée Galimir was very modest and never mentioned the fact that as a young girl she had gotten to know and had played an entire repertory that wasn't played in Palestine at this time. For example, in the late 1920s, shortly after the world premiere by the Kolisch Quartet,[38] the Galimir Quartet rehearsed Alban Berg's *Lyric Suite* – not a piece normally played by teenagers. In April, 1931, they invited Berg to their first performance of the work, and he was so impressed that he inscribed a wonderful dedication in Felix Galimir's score. In 1936 the Galimir quartet even recorded the *Lyric Suite* in Paris, for which they won the *Grand Prix du Disque*.[39] When you hear their recording today, it testifies to what an outstanding ensemble the Galimir Quartet had been. But I only got to know Felix Galimir in New York. One of the first concerts by the LaSalle Quartet was played in Stefan Wolpe's New York apartment in 1949, and Felix Galimir was one of the listeners who were present.

Of the good professional quartets at that time, in Berlin I had heard only the Calvet Quartet,[40] since the Busch Quartet no longer played in Nazi Germany. None of the really good quartets played in Germany any longer. To this day I still don't understand why the Calvet Quartet played in Nazi Germany, since at least one member, Daniel Guilet, was Jewish.[41]

36 Felix Galimir (1910–1999) founded the Galimir Quartet together with his three sisters Renée (1908–1975), Adrienne (1912–1997), and Marguerite (1905–1985) on the occasion of the 1927 centennial of Beethoven's death. Under the special tutelage of their chamber music teacher Simon Pullman, the quartet developed into an outstanding ensemble, specializing in contemporary music.

37 Felix Galimir was concertmaster of the NBC Symphony 1939–1954. Adrienne Galimir married the violinist Louis Krasner in 1936 and emigrated with him to America.

38 The Kolisch Quartet was founded in 1921 in conjunction with Schoenberg's Society for Private Performances and premiered many important 20th century contributions to the quartet literature, among them Bartók's fifth and sixth quartets, Schoenberg's third and fourth quartets, Alban Berg's *Lyric Suite*, and Webern's Opus 28.

39 The Galimir Quartet had hoped that Berg himself could supervise these recording sessions; fortunately, they were able to get his advice about certain details of the score prior to his untimely death in 1935.

40 The Calvet Quartet was active 1919–1940.

41 Daniel Guilet (1899–1990) was the second violinist in the Calvet Quartet 1929–1940. He joined Toscanini's NBC Symphony in 1944, becoming its concertmaster in 1951. In 1942 he founded the Guilet Quartet, and in 1954, together with pianist Menahem Pressler and cellist Bernard Greenhouse he founded the Beaux Arts Trio.

RS Up until then you had mostly heard the quartet literature that was played in your parents' house concerts.

WL That's right. But that was just a sophisticated dilettantism, and they played only the classical-romantic literature. In Palestine too I didn't really get beyond the romantic literature and the occasional impressionistic piece. At that time Palestine was very reactionary as regards musical taste. I first heard modern music in Tel Aviv with my friends Herbert Brün and Wolf Rosenberg. Through them I got to know something about twelve-tone music for the first time, which I had never heard at all before then. They tried to teach me about it, but I wasn't particularly interested. But then on Saturdays, on *Shabbat*, there was an opportunity to go to concerts of recordings on the rooftop of musicologist Peter Gradenwitz's house in Tel Aviv.[42] Gradenwitz was a tremendously stimulating personality. He got interesting recordings and played not only the usual repertory but also an extraordinary series of recordings made for Schoenberg's 70th birthday. Alfred Newman, a well-known film composer and a student of Schoenberg's, had arranged for the Kolisch Quartet – who at that time were completely unknown to me – to record Schoenberg's four quartets in a film studio in Hollywood.[43] These recordings were issued privately and sent to friends and former students. That's how I heard the third and fourth Schoenberg quartets for the very first time. It was an unbelievable shock and, for me, a book with seven seals: I understood absolutely nothing and had absolutely no idea how you would play such music at all or how you would get your bearings in it.

If you look at the dates of these recordings, it turns out that the recording of the fourth quartet was made on the afternoon of the day of the world premiere, which was that evening. That the Kolisch Quartet could have taken such a risk is a riddle for me still, even today. Even more unbelievable is the fact that the Kolisch played the first three Schoenberg quartets from memory. So here for the first time was a music that had scarcely anything to do with the music I was familiar with: I absolutely had to get to know it. That's how I first came upon the Schoenberg quartets. I only got to know Webern and Berg later on in New York. But the memory of those rooftop recordings concerts at Peter Gradenwitz's has stayed with me my whole life. It was the same experience all over again that I'd had hearing the Calvet Quartet play Beethoven. Like the two

42 Peter Gradenwitz (1910–2001), German musicologist and composer, married Rosi Wolfsohn, the daughter of Schoenberg's doctor in Berlin. He and his wife emigrated to Palestine in 1936, where he was a co-founder of the national chapter of the ISCM; in 1949 he founded the first Israeli music publishing house to achieve international stature: Israeli Music Publications.

43 These recordings were made privately at the end of December, 1936, and the beginning of January, 1937, at the United Artists studios in Hollywood.

Beethoven quartets I'd heard in Berlin, the third and fourth Schoenberg quartets were among the first pieces I later rehearsed with the LaSalle Quartet: I couldn't shake them off – I felt that I simply had to learn these pieces in order to understand how one learns such a piece.

RS On top of all that, you also started an orchestra in Tel Aviv?

WL Indeed. That happened after my playing had progressed far enough for my teacher Bergmann to recommend me as a substitute player for the Palestine Orchestra. When part of the orchestra went on tour to Egypt, the part that was left at home gave concerts in the kibbutzim. But sometimes they needed a bigger roster and now and then I could play with the orchestra. That was how I first played the Mahler fourth symphony, which was quite an effort for me, I had no idea how difficult the Mahler symphonies are. We went to the kibbutzim with a Mozart horn concerto, with early Beethoven symphonies and Mozart symphonies – that was how I got to know all of that literature. As a result of this experience, I said to myself that if later on I had to play in an orchestra professionally, then I'd actually have to learn the whole of the orchestral literature. And since there was no school in Tel Aviv with an orchestra, we would have to start one of our own!

So in Tel Aviv we started a music students' orchestra: we proudly called ourselves The Tel Aviv Music Students Symphony Orchestra. The players were all outstanding instrumentalists. Parts were something you could often find in the second hand bookstores. There was a wonderful one called Schreiber & Fromm, excellent people, who really knew their business. They didn't have enough money to have a store of their own and had gotten permission to set up shop selling music in the lobby of a building. And then of course there was Litauer's. I still have many scores with this name stamped on them. Herr Litauer was a wonderful human being, an exceptionally quiet and refined individual who liked me very much. There was everything to be had in the way of scores, since the emigrants had brought their music with them and then ended up with no place to put it. So they sold it for a ridiculously low price. You could actually buy the classics for five piasters: ten cents for all the Beethoven symphonies![44]

But we didn't always have enough money to buy parts. Once, when we wanted to play Haydn's D major symphony, Nr. 104, we copied the parts out of the Eulenburg pocket score: the oboist copied out the oboe

[44] That is, ten British pence (10d old style). The Palestine pound was pegged to the British pound sterling, and the piaster, a hold-over from the Ottoman Empire still in circulation, was worth about 2d, about 3¢ US at the time. Ten pence then would be worth about $2.67 today (2014).

part, the bassoonist the bassoon part, the first cellist the cello part, and I copied the part for the first violins – eventually every member of the orchestra had his assignment. Of course you get to know a piece very well if you write it out by hand. But my father objected that this was a complete waste of time. Surely we could borrow the parts from the Palestine Orchestra! He told me I should just go to Kestenberg and tell him that we'd like to borrow the parts.

Leo Kestenberg[45] had been in charge of the music, art, and theater department of the Prussian ministry of culture and had introduced a very important and very progressive reform of musical education in Prussia. He was also a participant in the founding of the very progressive Kroll Opera in Berlin. Besides which he was an outstanding pianist. Kestenberg was also known as the man who in 1925 had brought Schoenberg to Berlin as Ferruccio Busoni's successor at the Academy of Arts Music School; he also hired Artur Schnabel and Carl Flesch. Now he was the General Manager of the Palestine Orchestra in Tel Aviv. So I went to Leo Kestenberg and told him what I wanted, but in vain. All my negotiating skills were to no avail, he simply didn't want to do it. His position was that they didn't need any junior musicians for the Palestine Orchestra.

When I told my father that, he just said that couldn't be, that he'd speak with Kestenberg himself. My father was a tough negotiator and very energetic, he ended up roaring at Kestenberg, but that accomplished just as little: he didn't get the parts. Afterwards my father said we should just buy the music, he'd pay for it himself and also get us enough money to pay for a conductor. Along with Frank Pelleg, my piano teacher, we then had a number of conductors. One of them was Georg Singer,[46] a first rate Czech opera conductor who simply knew everything. A real operatic *Kapellmeister* who had already done a lot of conducting in Prague, knew the whole repertory, and could get along with young people. And then Chanan Eisenstadt, the one-armed conductor from Kibbutz Ben Shemen, he was another wonderful conductor. We rehearsed twice a week in the big studio in Frank Pelleg's house. We worked that way for a couple of years. From time to time we gave concerts in the Tel Aviv Museum, playing, for instance, the overture to *Don Giovanni*, the Mozart g minor

[45] Leo Kestenberg (1882–1962), pianist, man of letters, educator, and social activist, emigrated to Palestine in 1938, where he was General Manager of the Palestine Orchestra 1938–1945, after which he played a prominent role in the development of music education in Palestine/Israel.

[46] Georg Singer (1908–1980) studied piano with Franz Langer and Erwin Schulhoff at the Prague Academy of Music, and composition with Alexander Zemlinsky, afterwards conducting the opera in Prague, and , later, the Staatsoper in Hamburg. He emigrated to Palestine in 1939, conducting the Palestine Orchestra for the first time in December of that year, after which he was the orchestra's permanent guest conductor.

symphony, and the Beethoven first symphony. A beautiful program, some of it played from hand copied parts! We did everything ourselves, even getting the programs printed by a proper printer. I learned a great deal as the organizer of an orchestra. The hall was filled to overflowing and it was a huge success. You could do something like that in Tel Aviv, and there were people there who would support you.

RS Just like in America later on, really.

WL Exactly. To be fair though, I should really add that I also had just the opposite kind of experience with Kestenberg also, through my friend and colleague Max Pressler – later he called himself Menahem Pressler[47] – who was friends with Kestenberg as a pianist. He had an exceptionally high opinion of Kestenberg's pianistic abilities, which you could only hear privately, since Kestenberg didn't give concerts any more. Pressler arranged for Kestenberg to give lecture-recitals at home for our group of young music students. Those were wonderful afternoons in which he played and analyzed great works of the piano literature for us, for instance Beethoven's Diabelli Variations, one of the greatest of Beethoven's late works. I remember that one in particular very well, since I hadn't known that piece before then.

RS Had you already known Max Pressler in Berlin?

WL No, we first met one another in Tel Aviv. He arrived from Berlin the same year as I did and his father, like mine, had a men's store in Tel Aviv. He was studying piano and we got to be friends right away. He also belonged to this circle of young people who went around to wherever you could listen to records and who went to concerts together. He was an extraordinarily gifted pianist and from very early on a soloist with the orchestra. He went to America in the same year I did, in 1946, where he founded the Beaux Arts Trio along with Daniel Guilet and Bernard Greenhouse in 1954.

RS You've already mentioned your friends Herbert Brün and Wolf Rosenberg several times. How did you get to know them? Both of them were several years older than you.

WL I knew Herbert Brün so to speak from the day I was born. Brün's parents were among my parents' closest friends in Berlin. On the evening I was born, December 6, 1924, there was a costume ball at the home of

[47] Born in Germany, Menachem Pressler (1923–) emigrated to Palestine in 1939 and then to America right after the war. Since 1955 he has been on the faculty of the Indiana University School of Music.

an uncle of Herbert's to which my parents were invited. But my mother stayed home, because she felt that my birth was imminent. She called her gynecologist, Dr. Rosenberger, and brought me into the world. At that time Herbert was six years old. I cannot remember a time when I didn't know Herbert Brün. When I was six, I was already playing in the Children's Orchestra for which Herbert had written a children's symphony. We premiered it with Herbert at the piano and his cousin, Heinz Brün, conducting. He also wrote a wonderful Lied – both text and music – for the birthday of the director of the Jewish Kulturbund, Kurt Singer, whose daughter was friends with him at that time.

RS Was he actually composing already?

WL Yes indeed! He was practically born composing – he was unbelievably gifted. Herbert emigrated to Palestine in 1936, at the invitation of Emil Hauser,[48] the former first violinist of the Budapest Quartet. Hauser had founded a conservatory in Jerusalem, the only real conservatory in Palestine, as the one in Tel Aviv was dreadful. Herbert got a scholarship to study piano at the conservatory. Later on he had composition lessons with Stefan Wolpe: it doesn't get any better than that! And if you had a scholarship that paid room and board and everything else, then you could get a student visa from the English, who were extremely restrictive with visas. Otherwise it was practically impossible to get one. And that saved Herbert's life. His sister also got out of Germany, but his parents, Richard and Steffa, were murdered in a concentration camp. They were like an aunt and uncle to me. For my bar mitzvah they gave me the recording of the Brahms violin concerto with Joseph Szigeti and the Hallé Orchestra under Sir Hamilton Harty,[49] a wonderful recording. If you play it today, it's unbelievable how well-recorded it is, and with a single microphone!

RS Did you also already know Wolf Rosenberg in Berlin?

WL No, I first got to know Wolf Rosenberg in Palestine, through Herbert Brün. Like Herbert, Rosenberg – he was always 'Rosenberg,' never

[48] Emil Hauser (1893–1978) was a student of Jenö Hubay. He was a founding member of the Budapest Quartet and its first violin from 1917 to 1932. Hauser emigrated to Palestine in 1933, where he founded the Jerusalem Conservatory of Music and Dramatic Arts. Hauser travelled to Germany in the 1930s to arrange scholarships for young musicians and composers so that they could study in Jerusalem. His activities saved the lives of both Herbert Brün and Wolf Rosenberg, and many others as well.

[49] Hamilton Harty (1879–1941), Irish composer, conductor and pianist, conducted the Hallé Orchestra in Manchester 1920–1933, which he made into what was at that time probably the best orchestra in England. In 1930 he conducted the first performances in England of Mahler's Ninth Symphony as well as the first performances in Manchester of Mahler's *Lied von der Erde*. He also conducted the London Symphony Orchestra 1932–1934.

'Wolf' – was studying composition with Stefan Wolpe. Herbert was his best friend and both of them had jobs on the side playing piano in a bar. Herbert was an ideal jazz pianist. Rosenberg was dreadful at it, but he also had a job playing in a bar. Rosenberg was a wonderful human being, and such an inspiration for me! He had an incredible record collection, lots of pieces that I'd never heard yet. For instance the Ninth Symphony of Mahler, in the new – and first – recording, with Bruno Walter and the Vienna Philharmonic that was issued in 1938. These were 78s, you had to change the record in the middle of the Ländler, and then you got to hear a few of the same bars once again: when I listen to recent recordings now, in which of course there is no such duplication, I very much miss those extra bars, the piece as I know it is completely different! And I also heard the old *Aida* on Columbia at Rosenberg's place, a terrific recording! Rosenberg had nothing but recordings like that. He was an opera fanatic and had all the operas that had been recorded on 78s. It was incredible: I could spend hours and hours listening to them in the tiny room he was renting in Jerusalem. I learned more about musical interpretation from Rosenberg than I did from my instrumental teachers, since he knew a lot about things that I only heard of again at Juilliard or even later. For instance, he knew a lot about performance practice in Mozart's time, long before the authentic performance practice movement got started in the 1960s.

RS You also got to know Wolfgang Hildesheimer then.

WL Hildesheimer had already been a great friend of Rosenberg's in Germany, at the Odenwald School, an open and quite progressive institution.[50] Hildesheimer tells the story of how he met Rosenberg for the first time in 1932, when Rosenberg played a four-handed piano arrangement of Bruckner's Fourth Symphony with his chemistry teacher. You could write a whole book out of Hildesheimer's stories about Rosenberg in the Odenwald School. The two of them didn't bother themselves at all about the regular curriculum, since they already knew all of that. Hildesheimer emigrated to Palestine with his parents in 1933 and then studied painting and set design in London from 1937 to 1939. So he could speak English perfectly. As a result of that, after his return to Palestine he got a job right away as an English teacher at the British

[50] The Odenwaldschule in Heppenheim, just below Darmstadt south of Frankfurt, was founded in 1910 by Edith and Paul Geheeb as the first rural boarding school to embrace the principles of pedagogical reform that emerged in early 20th century Germany. The school aimed to develop the students' independence in thought and action, and promoted a radical equality of students and faculty, expressed at the simplest everyday level by the students' use of the familiar *Du* rather than the formal *Sie* when addressing their teachers.

Council in Tel Aviv and as an information officer for the English in Jerusalem. So I got to know Hildesheimer through Rosenberg. I was just fifteen going on sixteen, and they were already in their mid-twenties. But because I could play the violin, played Mozart and Beethoven violin sonatas with Herbert Brün at the piano, and knew something about music, I was accepted right away.

Hildesheimer got me interested in reading the German classics, he was constantly asking me things like whether I knew Kleist's 'On the Marionette Theater'[51] and had I read the *Marquise of O*? He insisted that Kleist's novels were wonderful and that I had to get to know them, and Lessing, too, and I don't know what else. I hadn't a clue about any of this. Of course we had all these books at home: in Berlin we'd had a library with thousands of books up in a gallery that went all around the living room. I inherited some of them, and we still have them: complete editions of Goethe, Schiller, Heine, and more, all bound in half leather.

But at that time I still hadn't read the classics yet! Now I wanted to own them all myself. In Tel Aviv I'd gotten a room of my own by now, with the attorney Ernst Markus and his wife Irene, just around the corner from my parents, who had found it annoying that I was always coming home so late. This was when I discovered that you could buy these books in the second hand bookstores in Tel Aviv ridiculously cheaply, because the immigrants had brought all their books with them and now didn't have space for them any more. So I did nothing but buy books, Kleist and Lessing, the whole of the classical German literature. I still have the three volume Heine edition with the blue covers. And I read all these books. My violin teacher Bergmann also used to ask me, over and over again, whether I knew this or that book. These people all simply took it for granted that you would read all night long and then work all day. You could sleep some other time.

RS In Palestine you also got to know Hermann Scherchen[52] personally. How did that happen?

WL Hermann Scherchen was a guest conductor of the Palestine Orchestra in 1939. He conducted a number of concerts, and I heard some of them because my teacher Bergmann was one of the concertmasters of the

[51] The marionette theater has a long history in German-speaking Europe – Karl Kraus wrote parts for marionettes in his *Last Days of Mankind* – and Kleist's 1810 essay was a particular favorite of the circle of friends around Rosenberg and Hildesheimer.

[52] Hermann Scherchen (1891–1966), German conductor, championed the music of Schoenberg, Berg, Webern, Varèse, and, later, Xenakis and Nono. His Mahler performances and recordings were exceptional and he was among the first to accept Kolisch's arguments for observing Beethoven's metronome marks for his symphonies.

Palestine Orchestra. That's how I heard an orchestral work of Arnold Schoenberg's for the first time, in the summer of 1939, namely his *Pelleas und Melisande*. Now that was a music that I knew nothing about. Then he also conducted his own arrangement of Bach's *Kunst der Fuge*.

My father worked in a big men's clothing business, five shops altogether in Palestine, one in Jerusalem, two in Tel Aviv, and two in Haifa. And all the musicians went there to have light-weight white summer jackets tailor-made, since the shop had a made-to-measure department. It went without saying that in Tel Aviv you went to OBG[53] and spoke German. My father always got the musicians who came into the shop to give me autographs. Bronislaw Huberman went there too, and one day Hermann Scherchen also came in to order a tailor-made white Palm Beach jacket. My father told Scherchen I was studying the violin with his concertmaster Bergmann and that I would very much like to meet him sometime and talk with him. Scherchen replied I should come to the beach he went to every morning and we would play medicine ball.

No sooner said than done! The next morning I went to the beach at 7 am, which was easy enough, since we lived right next to it, and there in fact was Hermann Scherchen! I walked back and forth up and down the beach with him while we played medicine ball, all the while asking him questions. That was very interesting. I asked him what documents he'd used in arranging Bach's *Kunst der Fuge*, and he told me that we only have the manuscript, which has no instrumentation – didn't I know that? I should have a look at it sometime: Litauer's, the music shop, would have it, I could get myself a copy. So I bought one, and also a copy of the Bach chorales.

And I didn't know Schoenberg? That was something I really did have to know! He invited me to the rehearsal for *Pelleas und Melisande* so I could hear it, it's a terrific piece! He told me all about Schoenberg and Webern; I never even heard of Webern! But he knew all of them personally! And he suggested that I read his book on conducting.[54] I still have it: a very interesting book, in my opinion utterly useless for learning how to conduct, but exceptionally interesting in regard to every other aspect of studying music. That was my summer on the beach in Tel Aviv in 1939, when I was fourteen going on fifteen years old. During the day it was very hot, but early in the morning it was really wonderful. The Mediterranean was still smooth at that hour, we went swimming and played medicine ball, and then he was there waiting for me again the next morning.

[53] The letters stood for '*Ofnat Bigdei Gevarim*' (fashion – clothes – men). They are also the first three letters of the Hebrew alphabet: א (aleph), ב (bet), ג (gimel); the 'o' vowel is understood as following the otherwise silent aleph).

[54] Hermann Scherchen, *Lehrbuch des Dirigierens* (Mainz, 1929); English, *Handbook of Conducting* (Oxford, 1989).

RS So in your experience Scherchen wasn't as unpleasant as one often hears.

WL No, not at all. My experience of him was marvelous! But I was very interested in what he was doing, and it's always very nice for a musician when someone takes an interest in what he knows, and asks intelligent questions.

RS With music teachers like Paul Ben-Haim, Frank Pelleg, and Rudolf Bergmann you certainly had an excellent musical education. What made you want to go to Juilliard in New York?

WL It was already my goal while I was studying music in Palestine to go to one of the great American music schools as soon as possible after the war and to begin studying really seriously there. At the time I had no idea at all what an extraordinary musical education I was getting from Rudolf Bergmann, Frank Pelleg, and Paul Ben-Haim, and how fortunate I was to be learning the fundamentals from exceptional and important musicians, that is, from teachers who as a young person you would never have access to in normal times. But as young musicians in Palestine we felt that we were cut off from the rest of the world and would have a lot to make up for later on. Our sense of isolation did lead us to make a special effort to hear as much music as possible. As music students we went with one another to all kinds of places where concerts of recordings were put on, we were intent on absorbing a whole lot of music. So I got to know a very broad spectrum of music this way, from recordings. And not only, as is often the case in music schools, listening to music for our own instruments, that is, only listening to violin music if you were a violinist, or piano music if you were a pianist. We also listened to vocal music, Lieder, operas, piano music, whatever was of interest to the people who had gotten together at the recordings concerts.

Nevertheless I always had the feeling that my real professional study of music would actually get underway only at one of the great American music schools, and so I worked very hard to prepare myself for admission to one of them. But once I'd gotten hold of a copy of the Sunday edition of the New York Times, and had seen how much music was played in New York in the way of concerts and operas in a single week, I was determined to go to school there. In the mid-1940s New York was the Mecca of music, it was where the greatest conductors were, the greatest orchestras, the greatest soloists and opera singers. It was a golden age and I was eager to experience it, since I thought we were very backwards in isolated Palestine. Of course there was a very decent musical life in Palestine, including chamber music concerts several times a week, but I had never experienced anything like what there was in New York. So in Palestine, after I had a serious look at the various music schools in America, what I wanted more than anything else was to go to Juilliard.

It had always been my intention to become a quartet player, which is another reason why I wanted to emigrate to America, since it seemed to me that only in such a big and rich country as America could you make a living playing string quartets. Which indeed proved to be the case. I applied to Juilliard and got a letter back confirming my provisional admission, based on the recommendations of my teachers, but it said that I still had to pass an entrance exam. It was towards the end of 1944 when I began to get my studying in America organized, and it took months to get everything in order administratively with Juilliard, since the mail went by ship and it was still wartime.

And then when the war was over, the next difficulty was to get a student visa. To get one I had to go to the American consulate in Jerusalem, where I told them I wanted to go to America and study at Juilliard. Their response was to ask me who was going to pay for that. I replied that it would be my father, whereupon they objected that my father was a citizen of the British Mandate and therefore subject to the sterling block, which meant that you couldn't just go and exchange any number of British pounds for U.S. dollars, there was a limit. First of all I would have to get a permit from the British administration's Foreign Exchange Controller, Mr. Hogben, here in Jerusalem.

Luckily I was staying with Dr. Rosenberger, who in Berlin had brought me into the world, and who was now a physician in Jerusalem. He knew Mr. Hogben and got an appointment with him for me. Mr. Hogben seemed very friendly while he listened to my request, but then he wanted to know why I wanted to go to New York of all places, and couldn't I just as well study in London, where they did indeed have very good conservatories! It wasn't easy for me to explain to him diplomatically that I found New York far more attractive than London. When I'd finished, he asked me how he would explain to the members of a kibbutz who needed a new tractor from America that, unfortunately, he didn't have the money for it, because he'd given it all to Walter Levin to go and study violin in America. I reported this negative response to my parents, and then my father had a better idea: he would discuss the matter with my uncle Paul Zivi in Brazil. In no time at all I got a confirmation that the necessary funds had been transferred to an American bank account. That satisfied the American embassy in Jerusalem and I finally got my student visa allowing me to go to America.

Now the problem was to find a way to get there. In the end I got a cabin on a Waterman Steamship Company freighter, together with three other music students. It was an incredible two-month odyssey getting to New York from Haifa by way of Limassol, Malta, Marseilles, Oran, and Casablanca, and then, finally and unexpectedly, Baltimore. That was February 10, 1946, a Sunday.

4 *En Route to America*

ROBERT SPRUYTENBURG: On this trip you made an intermediate stop in Paris. Was that because the ship was in port for some length of time?

WALTER LEVIN: Yes, we were in the port of Marseilles over Christmas and New Year's, and during the holidays they could neither load nor unload cargo. The captain said he would give us a pass that said we were crew members, that we would be Americans, who could do whatever we wanted in occupied France, we would have all the advantages and could buy whatever we needed cheaply at the army PX's, the army's stores for servicemen, which were everywhere. For a dollar we would be able to get a ten-pack carton of cigarettes and a box of Cadbury's chocolates, which would be enough to have a comfortable two weeks in Paris, the train trip included.

No sooner said than done! We really wanted to go to Paris. But first we had a look around Marseilles, since I had never been in France before. After that we went to the train station to find out how you got from Marseilles to Paris. Since it was Christmas, people were standing in long lines at the ticket windows. When we finally reached the head of the line, my friend told the ticket agent that we wanted to go to Paris. His response was to say that getting to Paris was hopeless, there was only one train, and it was already sold out and then some. Now the cigarettes came to the rescue. We told him we had Chesterfield cigarettes, that we were with the American occupation. Whereupon he told us to go down to the third ticket window and then shut his own.

The people standing in line muttered in protest. We went three windows further along, where he opened up and told us that if we had cigarettes and wanted to go to Paris we should give him a pack and he would give us round trip tickets. He would meet us in two hours at the far end of platform three, which was the freight platform. It was now about three o'clock in the afternoon and the train was supposed to leave at around eleven that evening. So we got to platform three at around five o'clock, and the ticket agent was already there. We walked a ways along the tracks with him, which he was allowed to do even though it was strictly forbidden, and arrived at a passenger car that belonged to the Paris train but hadn't yet been coupled to it. At that point he told us just sit ourselves down in one of the compartments and stay put: later on when the car rolled into the station with the rest of the train, people would just pour into it, but we would already have our seats.

We had to wait for six hours until the train left, and it was freezing. On the return trip I came down with a terrible cold. But that's how we got to Paris. Our captain had told us that there was a reception booth for arriving troops where we could get a place to stay. So we went there. They wanted to know whether we had any money and we said yes, we had money, and also cigarettes. They told us how to deal on the black market: not too many cigarettes at a time, at most five, we weren't to go offering a whole pack to begin with, that would be much too much. And likewise with the chocolate: always just a little at a time, so it would last. They told us to deal as much as we could in single cigarettes, for which you could get a great ticket to the Folies Bergère. Then they gave us directions to our room, which was in a beautiful private apartment, and where we were met by a very nice and good-looking woman and given very good accommodations. It seemed to be a kind of girls' hostel, since there were pretty girls in all the rooms. We only later found out that we had been put up in a very high-class bordello.

We went to the opera and to concerts with the orchestra conducted by Paul Paray.[1] At the opera I saw Saint-Saëns' *Samson and Delilah* in a performance led by Inghelbrecht,[2] a conductor who Toscanini thought highly of. As an encore he played Debussy's *L'Après-midi d'un faune* as a ballet – it was customary to present a ballet as an encore. But the staging was inconceivably awful: it was nothing but scraps of the old curtains! They simply had no money for a new production. But I was in a great opera house again!

On our last day in Paris I also went to Durand's, the music shop on the Madeleine – it's no longer there. They published Debussy and Stravinsky. I bought all my French editions of the Samuel Dushkin editions of Stravinsky's violin pieces there and then took the night train back to Marseilles. The next day I wanted to go to the opera in Marseilles, something I had missed out on before going to Paris. And what was on? *Samson and Delilah!* That opera really followed me around! It had been the very first opera I ever went to, in Berlin, in 1935, at the Kulturbund.

RS When did you arrive in New York? That has to have been in the middle of February.

[1] Paul Paray (1886–1979), French composer and conductor, was appointed conductor of the Monte Carlo Philharmonic in 1928 and of the Concerts Colonne in Paris in 1933, where he also conducted at the Paris Opera. During the Second World War he conducted in Marseilles and Monte Carlo, but returned to Paris after the liberation to reorganize the Concerts Colonne. He conducted the Detroit Symphony Orchestra, 1952–1963.

[2] Désiré-Emile Inghelbrecht (1880–1965), French composer and conductor, was a friend of Debussy and famous for his exemplary performances of Debussy, Ravel, Roussel, and Florent Schmitt. He conducted the first complete recording of Debussy's orchestral works. In 1934 he founded the Orchestre National de la Radiodiffusion Française, and he conducted at the Paris Opera 1945–1950.

WL The trip across the ocean was quite an adventure. First of all we headed for Algeria, to Oran, and I got sick on board the ship. In Marseilles I'd already come down with the flu and was running a fever, since we hadn't thought to reserve seats for our return trip from Paris and once again the train was completely sold out – we sat for fourteen hours in the drafty vestibule between two cars and it was ice cold. When we arrived in Oran, the ship's captain wanted to put me ashore; he was afraid I had pneumonia, which couldn't be treated on board. But luckily there were two kind women from Hadassah, a world-wide Zionist women's charity that among other things had founded hospitals in Palestine. The Hadassah hospital still exists in Jerusalem. When these women learned that I was sick and that the captain wanted to put me ashore, they intervened and had a French doctor come on board, who thoroughly examined me and told the captain that I didn't have pneumonia, just a cold with fever and flu, which would last four or five days. He would give me some medicine but with plenty of liquids and bed rest I would get well of my own accord. Whereupon the captain let me stay on board. One of the officers had been trained as a medic by the Red Cross and took care of me in the sick bay, and a week later I was well again. By then the ship had made it to Casablanca, but I wasn't allowed to disembark, otherwise I would have seen Casablanca too. And then the trip across the ocean got underway, and on such a small freighter, a Liberty ship.[3] And after four or five days there was a hurricane. I'd never experienced anything like it! We had to stay in our cabins, strapped into our beds, until it was over, and it was dreadfully frightening, since these little ships easily broke apart in such storms.

RS You have to proceed crosswise to the waves.

WL Exactly, that was what mattered. For about 48 hours the whole crew was busy with nothing else but keeping the ship headed into the wind. It went neither forwards nor backwards, only full steam ahead into the wind. But everything on deck, all the lifeboats, everything was washed overboard. And then it was absolutely still, the ocean was smooth as glass. That was really something to experience! But there was something else too: one of the mates whom I'd made friends with was a really fanatical racist, and some members of the crew were blacks. He hated them. And he was just as much an anti-Semite, but one of those who had never actually

[3] Liberty ships were a type of relatively small freighter built by the thousands in America during the Second World War. They were rather notorious for their supposed fragility, but although structural defects resulting in cracks were common, in fact only three out of the more than 2,700 built actually broke up at sea, apart from the 200 or so that sank as a result of enemy attacks. 'Liberty ship' became a somewhat generic term for any small and, in particular, decrepit freighter.

known anybody who was Jewish. I asked him what he meant by that, and told him I was a Jew! When he said that wasn't what he meant, I asked him what he did mean. He said he didn't mean any Jew in particular, he meant *the Jews*! That was the first time I ever realized what it means to have such insane prejudices.

Twelve hours before we were due to arrive in New York we learned that because of a strike there were no pilot boats and no pilots available to get us into port. We had to go south instead, to Baltimore. So that's how I got to America. It was February 10, 1946, a Sunday.

5 *New York*

ROBERT SPRUYTENBURG: When you finally got to New York, the spring semester at Juilliard had surely already begun.

WALTER LEVIN: Yes, and moreover it was too late to take the regular entrance exams, so I had to take them in a room all by myself. A woman brought me the exams, and as I finished each one she brought me the next one. The exams were easy enough to begin with but gradually they got more difficult, all the same there was nothing that I hadn't already learned long before in Tel Aviv. The exams took me from ten in the morning to half past five in the afternoon, and when I'd turned in the last of them, the woman came back again and asked me what I actually wanted to study at the Institute of Musical Art.[1] She told me that I'd just passed the final exams for graduation, so they had to send me to the graduate school, where I would have to pass the graduate school entrance exam. So thanks to my comprehensive musical education in Palestine I was able to skip the first four years at Juilliard.

RS Ivan Galamian became your violin teacher in New York. Was he at Juilliard too?

WL No, not to begin with. He only started at Juilliard in the fall of 1946. When I got to Juilliard in February he was still at the Curtis Institute in Philadelphia and only taught privately in New York.

RS Had you wanted to study with him or was that just how it worked out?

WL I didn't know anything at all about Galamian. I had wanted to go to Juilliard but since I arrived in the middle of the semester I had to be assigned to whatever violin teacher had an open slot in his schedule. The first teacher I had auditioned for was Edouard Déthier,[2] a very good Belgian violinist and very much a gentleman, but his schedule was full, and he recommended that I study with Hans Letz.[3] He meant well, since Letz

[1] The Institute of Musical Art was founded in New York in 1905. It merged with the Juilliard Graduate School in 1926 but the name remained in use for some time even after both were renamed the Juilliard Academy of Music in 1946.

[2] Edouard Déthier (1885–1962) came to America in 1905 and taught at Juilliard from 1907 until his death. Robert Mann of the Juilliard Quartet is among his best known students.

[3] Hans Letz (1887–1969) was a student of Joseph Joachim who was concertmaster of the Chicago Symphony Orchestra 1910–1912. He joined the Kneisel Quartet as second violin in 1910 and taught at Juilliard 1912–1920 and again 1925–1960. His students included Dorothy DeLay and Vittorio Giannini.

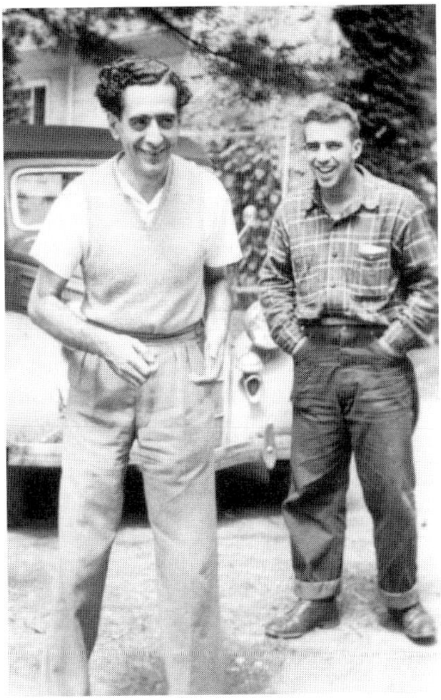

8 Ivan Galamian and Berl Sanofsky, Meadowmount, 1948

was from Strassburg, was an educated European, and had played second violin in the Kneisel Quartet.[4] The Kneisel Quartet was the first important American quartet, and was one of the very first ensembles in residence at the Institute of Musical Art, as Juilliard was called then. Letz had very good students, but was not the right violin teacher for me. He was of the old-fashioned German school, and Bergmann had taught me a much more modern school of violin playing: the Franco-Belgian school of Eugène Ysaÿe.

I was utterly miserable studying with Letz and I didn't know what to do about it. It was my first semester at Juilliard, it was already the end of February, and school would be over in June. Around this time there were chamber music evenings with violinists, violists, and cellists from Juilliard as well as from other schools, many of them very good violinists. That's how I got to know Berl Senofsky[5] and David Nadien,who was a phenomenal violinist who later won the Leventritt prize.[6] I asked them where they were studying and who they were studying with, and they told me they all studied with Galamian. I didn't know who Galamian was, which surprised them, but they assured me that he was *the* violin teacher in America. I wanted to know where he taught, and they told me he was at Curtis during the school year, at his own school at Meadowmount in upstate New York in the summer, and might be coming to Juilliard. I wanted to know how I could meet him and they gave me his address and telephone number in New York, telling me to call him and tell him I'd like to play for him.

[4] The Kneisel Quartet (active 1885– 1917) was founded by members of the Boston Symphony and became the Quartet in Residence at the Institute of Musical Art (later Juilliard) in 1905. It played an important role in promoting chamber music in America.

[5] Berl Senofsky (1926–2002) won the Naumburg Competition in 1946. He was deputy concertmaster in the Cleveland Orchestra under George Szell 1951–1955. In 1955 he won the Queen Elizabeth Competition in Brussels. He taught at the Peabody Conservatory in Baltimore 1965–1996.

[6] David Nadien (1926–) was concertmaster of the New York Philharmonic 1966–1970, but spent most of his career as a studio musician and a teacher. When Nadien won the Leventritt competition in 1966, Adolf Busch, Rudolf Serkin, Nathan Milstein, and Artur Toscanini were on the jury.

It also happened that by sheer good luck I got a room in the International House from a student who was just going on vacation, since otherwise there weren't any rooms available there. The International House was a student residence run by the Rockefeller Foundation at 500 Riverside Drive and Claremont, right across from the old Juilliard building, which is now the Manhattan School of Music. I practiced the violin in my room on the top floor, which wasn't at all permitted, and there was another violinist practicing just across the hall from me. I knocked on his door, which was opened by a man who was older than me, already in his late thirties. He was quite friendly, from India. He said he could hear that I also played the violin, and wanted to know who I studied with. I told him I was at Juilliard studying with Hans Letz, but what I'd really like would be to study with Galamian, because I'd heard so much about him. He told me he was a Galamian student and said that this coming summer I should just go up to Galamian's school at Meadowmount, nothing but the best violinists were there and I'd get a chance to study with him.

This Indian was Mehli Mehta,[7] and meeting him was a great stroke of luck. He had already been concertmaster in the Bombay Orchestra but wanted to study the violin even further. He was the hardest working violinist I've ever known, he practiced ten, twelve hours a day. Anyway, that's how I got to Galamian. I played for him at his apartment on 74th Street and then went to his school in Meadowmount the first summer I was in America, in 1946. I stayed in the same little cottage with Mehli Mehta. It was splendid meeting him, he was a charming and wonderful man. He lived to a ripe old age and led a youth orchestra in Los Angeles up until just a few years ago. He had two sons, Zubin[8] and Zarin,[9] and was always telling stories about them: they were still in India and were both very musical. And as it later turned out, they were indeed very musical: Zarin Mehta was the head of the Ravinia Festival for a number of years when I was there as the head of the Steans Institute for Young Artists and we saw quite a lot of one another then. I never got to know Zubin very well. Later on Zarin became the President of the New York Philharmonic.

[7] Mehli Mehta (1908–2002), violinist and conductor, founded the Bombay Symphony Orchestra in 1935 and the Bombay String Quartet in 1945. He studied with Galamian 1945–1950. He was concertmaster of the Hallé Orchestra 1955–1960, and was director of the orchestra department of the University of California at Los Angeles 1964–1976. In 1964 he organized the American Youth Symphony, which he led until 1998.

[8] Zubin Mehta (1936—), conducted the Los Angeles Philharmonic 1962–1978, the New York Philharmonic 1978–1991, and the Bavarian State Opera 1998–2006. His long association with the Israel Philharmonic dates back to 1969; he has been Music Director of the orchestra since 1977.

[9] Zarin Mehta (1938—) was Managing Director of the Montreal Symphony 1981–1990, Executive Director and then President and CEO of the Ravinia Festival 1990–2000, and Executive Director and then President and CEO of the New York Philharmonic 2000–2012.

RS Did Galamian turn your violin technique upside down?

WL When I played for him in New York he recognized that I knew something about playing the violin. But now I had to learn a whole new bowing technique. And he did turn my way of practicing upside down, and also overcame my resistance to working on pieces oriented to technique, that is, the violin virtuoso literature, which seemed to me to be less than first rate. He said I already knew how to play music, but violin playing is something you learn from pieces you can't play, and not by always playing only what you already can play. And for that you have to practice long and hard: no afternoon naps! He knew I always took an afternoon nap and he regularly called me up and demanded that I give him an A. So I had to keep my violin out of its case during my afternoon nap. He was strict with me and immediately recognized my weaknesses, which had to do with everything I thought I didn't need to know because what I wanted to do was to play quartets. But if I wanted to play quartets, he told me, I would have to be able to play the violin even better than the concert soloists.

RS Did the LaSalle Quartet also have lessons with Galamian?

WL After the LaSalle Quartet had been engaged at Colorado College, in 1949, we took lessons with him at Meadowmount for eight weeks every summer. But he didn't give us lessons together as a quartet, he gave each of us lessons individually.

RS Did Galamian otherwise teach violists and cellists as well as violinists?

WL At my insistence he agreed to teach not just me but also my colleagues, including Jackson Wiley, our original cellist. Otherwise I don't believe he ever taught a violist or a cellist. It seemed to me that Galamian's whole approach to technique, to bowing, was essential for a quartet that aimed at a homogeneity of execution, that it was essential for everyone to learn the same approach to articulation, to the different kinds of bowing, the problems of intonation, how to make the short notes of *spiccato* sound good, how to produce certain articulations and get them to sound, how to play expressively without becoming sentimental, how to use vibrato without exaggeration – you scarcely noticed that Caruso used vibrato, for instance. You have to learn how to do all these things and Galamian was terrific at teaching them.

RS So Galamian wasn't only interested in violinists.

WL No, he was very interested in quartet playing, he greatly admired his teacher Lucien Capet as a quartet player. And he was very supportive of our being so serious about quartet playing. We were the only students he had like that, otherwise everybody just wanted to learn how to become a violin virtuoso.

RS Was Galamian himself still concertizing?

WL No, he never played in public, other than possibly when he was a young man, not even when he was in Paris.

RS So Galamian, unlike Bergmann, was a violin teacher more than anything else.

WL Yes, that's right, but he had very good taste musically and he taught all his students nothing but first rate pieces, even though I didn't think much of the virtuoso literature to begin with. But he couldn't teach them how to be a good musician, that wasn't his specialty. Nevertheless, he was a fabulous teacher. He didn't just tell you to do something in such and such a way, he also showed you how to do it and explained why. There was never any mystery about anything. In less than thirty seconds he could show you how different something sounded if you held your elbow this way or the other way, if you put weight on the bow instead of pressure, and much more like that. And no matter what it was, he could demonstrate what he was talking about on the violin for you, and marvelously too.

RS In principle that's also your approach to teaching: you always explain just exactly what happens when you do something this way or that way technically, but you yourself always only explain it verbally, that is, without demonstrating it on the instrument.

WL I don't demonstrate what I mean on the instrument because I don't want the student just to imitate me, but rather to understand what the music itself is about and then to translate that into whatever is necessary in the way of technique to play it efficiently. Of course there are always various possibilities. Kreisler for example played the violin in a way that made a joke of any kind of theoretical efficiency, but it sounded fabulous! Certainly his technique was never as superior as Heifetz', that wasn't his thing. But it was a kind of bowing with which you actually shouldn't be able to play the violin at all.

RS What was Galamian's heritage as regards violin technique?

WL The French school of Lucien Capet, and also the Russian school. Capet must have been an excellent teacher, and, like Carl Flesch, he too wrote a violin method, albeit one that nobody uses anymore.[10] But as an Armenian Galamian had also studied in Moscow. And then he was in Paris for a long time, where he taught at the Russian school. He emigrated from Paris to America shortly before the war.

RS At Juilliard William Schuman[11] approved a string quartet curriculum for you. How did you manage that?

WL It was an extraordinary stroke of luck that in my first weeks of studying at Juilliard, I was approached right away by a violinist who told me that he was looking for a second violinist for the Charles Ives' second quartet, which they were going to play quite soon at the Ives Festival at Columbia University,[12] and would I be interested? To be honest I have to say that at that point I'd never even heard of Charles Ives, but all the same I said 'Quartet? Great! Any time!' The violinist who approached me turned out to be Robert Koff, at that time the second violinist in the Juilliard Quartet, so over the next few days I got to meet the other members of the Juilliard Quartet as well. Our ad hoc quartet played from handwritten manuscript parts, since the quartet, like most of Ives' work, hadn't been published yet. I was totally baffled by it, since I'd never seen anything like such a modern piece: rhythmically very difficult, practically without any phrasing indications, very few dynamic marks – you had to figure everything out yourself. The performance was a great success.

After the concert with the Ives quartet, I also got to know William Schuman, who had been appointed president of Juilliard shortly before I arrived there. Schuman was an exceptional individual, a composer and an organizer, a splendid musician and a real *mensch*. Under his direction the school was becoming a laboratory for new ideas, which suited me perfectly. He completely revised the curriculum, and established the so-called L&M system: Literature and Materials of Music. Instead of having separate subjects you would study music in the light of its his-

10 Lucien Capet (1873–1928): *La Technique Supérieure de l'Archet* (Paris, 1916); *Superior Bowing Technique* (New York, 2004).

11 As the school's president the American composer William Schuman (1910–1992) merged the Institute of Musical Art with the Juilliard Graduate School and established the Juilliard Quartet, which became a model for many quartets in residence at American universities.

12 The concert on May 11, 1946, at Columbia's MacMillan Theater included the first complete performance of Ive's second quartet, composed 1907–1913. The ad hoc quartet consisted of Robert Koff and Walter Levin, violins, Rena Robbins, viola, and Ala Goldberg, cello.

torical development, how it was composed throughout its history, you would analyze pieces, get to know their theoretical foundations, perform them, and learn something about the historical circumstances in which they were composed. It was a unified program of study and one that inherently demanded outstanding teachers, which Schuman succeeded in attracting.

So there was a revolutionary spirit at Juilliard and this ambient allowed me to do something that as far as I know had never been done before anywhere else. I wanted to major in string quartet. But there was no such major, you could only major in a specific instrument. However, I wanted my studies to emphasize quartet playing, so I could spend most of my time on that. After the Ives concert Schuman invited me to his office, because he was curious about my having come from Palestine. I took the opportunity to tell him that I would really like to have string quartet as my major at Juilliard. He thought this was an excellent idea, especially since he had just founded the Juilliard Quartet as the school's Quartet in Residence. And he did in fact establish a major in string quartet, and so for the next three years the quartet I'd started as soon as I got to Juilliard, early in 1946, and which came to be called the LaSalle Quartet, studied intensively with the Juilliard Quartet. That was exactly what I'd been looking for, and it was an exceptionally productive time in my studies.

RS I've often had the impression that your life consists of an unbelievable sequence of lucky accidents.

WL Yes, it really does. In hindsight, there are so many points at which things missed going wrong by just a hair's breadth and then it would have been all over. Maybe there's something like providence after all, combined with knowing exactly what it is you want to do, where you want to go.

RS Were you able to concentrate exclusively on quartet playing at Juilliard?

WL No, I couldn't, since it soon turned out that despite my string quartet major I was still supposed to take the subjects in the regular curriculum. I didn't want to do that, since I'd already taken those subjects in Palestine and moreover had passed them all in the Juilliard admissions exams without taking any of the courses. Worst of all was that I was also supposed to play in the Juilliard Orchestra. And I didn't want to do that either, since I'd already had enough orchestra experience playing in our student orchestra in Tel Aviv and in the Palestine Orchestra. All the same I did play in the orchestra for a whole semester, which is a story in itself.

When I had a room at the International House, two pianists, Richard Farrell and Leonard Hutcheson also lived there, a New Zealander and an Australian. I got to be good friends with them right away. They were really nice kids and excellent pianists. I was also a good pianist, and they were very impressed that a violinist could play the piano well enough to play Mozart piano concerti. One day at Juilliard we found a door open to a room in which there were two pianos, so we went in and played Mozart piano concerti: I was the soloist and they played the orchestra part four hands. It turned out that we were in Edgar Schenkman's[13] studio, the Juilliard orchestra conductor, which was strictly off-limits. That's how I met him, he came into his studio to get a couple of scores while we were still there and asked me who I was. He didn't know me at all, so he wanted to know who I was studying with, was it Madam Samaroff?[14] She was the great piano teacher at Juilliard. I said no, I was studying with Hans Letz. He objected that Hans Letz was a violin teacher, and I replied that yes, my major was violin. But then he wanted know why, if I was a violinist, wasn't I in his orchestra? So I walked right into the trap.

I became Schenkman's favorite in the orchestra, since I knew by heart practically all the pieces we played. But after a semester of playing in the orchestra I didn't want to do it anymore, it was too strenuous for me and for the most part the repertory didn't interest me, besides which I needed to spend my time practicing with the quartet. That's what I told the Dean, Norman Lloyd, who wasn't at all sympathetic, he told me he couldn't possibly exempt me from the orchestra. I could only be excused if I was sick and could get a note from my doctor. He could not have been more clear about what it was I had to do: I immediately went to my friend Doctor Brandstetter and asked him to examine me, saying that for weeks already I had been dead tired and had no energy. So he examined me and told me that I was over-stressed, which could really affect my health. I shouldn't go on being so stressed, couldn't I take a break for a semester? I told him no, it wouldn't do to take a semester off, but some relief would surely help me. He wanted to know what he could get me out of, and I asked him to write me a note saying that on account of my poor health I absolutely had to have my afternoons free so I could rest – that was when the orchestra rehearsed.

13 Edgar Schenkman (1908–1993) conducted the Depression-era WPA Federal Orchestra and other ensembles in New York prior to joining the Juilliard faculty in 1940. He conducted the Toledo, Ohio, Symphony Orchestra 1943–1946 and later founded both the Norfolk and the Richmond, Virginia, symphony orchestras, after leaving Juilliard in 1948.

14 Olga Samaroff (Lucy Mary Agnes Hickenlooper, 1880–1948) was the first American pianist to perform all 32 Beethoven piano sonatas as a cycle. In 1925 a shoulder injury ended her concert career, after which she taught at Juilliard and at the Philadelphia Conservatory. Among her best known students were William Kapell, Roslyn Tureck, and Alexis Weissenberg. She was married to Leopold Stokowski 1911–1923.

So the note went to the Dean, and from the Dean to Schenkman, who was furious and wrote me a letter saying that I was a selfish and undisciplined human being. I'd been far too transparent in getting my own way, which is not how you get anywhere in this world. You have to learn to compromise, you can't just stubbornly insist on getting everything you want. Schenkman even went so far as to inquire as to whether Brandstetter really was a certified physician, and then he called him up and asked him what was the matter with me. Brandstetter told him I was an exceptionally high-strung character, that I worked very hard and very intensely, which affected my nerves, and my body too. He said I was overworked, which was quite apparent from my irritability as well as my elevated blood pressure. I was very short-tempered, and this explosive condition wasn't healthy, and Schenkman had to do what he could to help me overcome my high stress level. There was nothing Schenkman could do in the face of such a diagnosis. That was the end of it, and I no longer had to play in the orchestra. It was a very uncomfortable situation all the way around. Schenkman wasn't mistaken, he'd seen right through me.

No sooner had I gotten this problem out of the way than the next one came along. Since I'd come to Juilliard, WQXR, the classical music radio station in New York, had decided to engage a Quartet in Residence. They had in mind Andrew Toth as first violin, an excellent violinist who also studied with Galamian, a crazy kid who I got along with exceptionally well. And the cellist was to be Madleine Foley, who later played with Pablo Casals. Who the violist was supposed to be I don't remember anymore. Anyway, they wanted to have me as their second violin. But since as a student I wasn't allowed to work in America – that was strictly forbidden – they asked me if I could get an immigration visa, and I said I thought I could. But to get one I would have to leave the United States, immigration visas were something you could only get abroad.

So over Christmas vacation, 1946, I flew to Brazil, to my uncle Paul Zivi, on a four engine propeller-driven DC-4, which was quite an undertaking.[15] But so soon after the war the U.S. had very strict quotas for immigration visas: in Venezuela only ten visas a month could be issued, in Uruguay seven, and in Argentina twenty-five – the numbers were completely arbitrary. The visas were issued based on the country of one's birth, but in Brazil they'd had scarcely a single request in the past four years for a visa from someone who'd been born in Germany and wanted to emigrate to the United States. They had lots and lots of visas available, whereas everywhere else people were waiting for

[15] The trip took about 48 hours each way, including stops for refueling.

years on end to get one! My uncle knew the American consul in Rio de Janeiro, he called him and said his nephew needed an immigration visa. The consul asked him when would he like to have it, tomorrow? A day later I had my U.S. immigration visa! The quartet for WQXR never got off the ground, but now I could work in America!

But then yet another problem popped up right after that one: now I was supposed to go into the army! The war was over, but the draft was still in effect, and I belonged to the age group that was being drafted for two or three years' service in the army. Just what I needed! Anyway, I got a summons to go to Brooklyn and report for induction. So I went to the induction center and saw all these military types I had nothing in common with. And then thank God it occurred to me that I knew a story about an army induction, it's in Thomas Mann's *Felix Krull.* I could assume that they didn't know this story. I'd read *Felix Krull* even before I went to America. In Haifa, while I was waiting for my ship, I had stayed with Walter and Leni Mendel, friends of my mother's since her childhood in Elberfeld. Walter Mendel had all the works of Thomas Mann, and he recommended the first part of *Felix Krull* – the second part hadn't been published yet. I was utterly taken with it. I read the story of the army induction so often that I almost knew it by heart. Krull also didn't want to go into the army and had studiously read up on the course of an epileptic fit, which he feigned while being examined by the military doctor.

From *Krull* I'd learned that the first thing I had to do on this occasion was to go in and before anyone on the induction committee could say a word announce that I was perfectly healthy, that I couldn't wait to get into the army, what I wanted more than anything else was to take part in the war effort and to defeat Hitler, that's what I wanted most of all! It was already nearly two years since the war had ended: they sat there thunderstruck. One of them wanted to know what was it I had just said? I very quietly repeated that I was absolutely fit, that I was desperate to join the army, that I wanted to do my part in defeating the Germans, that I couldn't wait to defeat the Nazis. And with a slight German accent too. Then they asked me where I was from and I said I was from Palestine, so they would know I wasn't a German, but a German Jew. And before that, they asked? From Berlin, I said. Whereupon they told me to wait a moment, they had to speak with the officer next door.

A guard led me into another room, to a very nice, apparently high ranking officer, who spoke with me very calmly, asked me about my past, and ascertained that I was exceptionally burdened psychologically and apparently had already been in a sanatorium in Palestine, namely Dr. Bodenheimer's sanatorium, the psychiatrist in Haifa. This was a well-known sanatorium in Palestine where you could also go on vacation.

My parents often spent their vacations there and I came to visit them now and then. It was a fabulous estate, like a big hotel with a magnificent park. The officer advised me to consult with a psychiatrist, as I'd obviously been through a lot. By this time I was in such a state of nerves that my hands were literally dripping with sweat. He went on to say that for the time being the army would be exactly the wrong thing for me. Of course I said I was very disappointed, but I went home, and a few weeks later got a postcard with the news: 4F – that was the draft category that meant absolutely unfit for military service. I happen to believe this was right: it was not in the army's best interest to have me. So this danger was also warded off: you just have to exploit your knowledge of literature a little bit and everything will turn out all right! But I was never able to shake the suspicion that this officer knew *Felix Krull*, which would have been perfectly marvelous. And it would have been the icing on the cake if he'd said he could see I was a fan of Thomas Mann. Unfortunately he didn't say any such thing, but maybe he'd figured it out anyway.

6 *Evi Marcov-Levin*

ROBERT SPRUYTENBURG: Frau Levin, you were born in Sofia, in Bulgaria.[1] Could you tell us a little bit about your parents and your childhood there?

EVI LEVIN: My father, Hugo Mayer, was from Bad Kreuznach in the Rhineland, where his family were vintners. He had six brothers and sisters. My mother, Rosel Kolski, was from a prominent family in Duisburg. My parents got married in Turkey, where from a very young age my father had worked in an export firm. But since my parents were German, they had to return to Germany even before the end of the First World War. So my sister Inge, three and a half years older than me, was born in Berlin in 1919. A year or two later my parents settled in Sofia, where my father and his friend Max Bachmann started an export business dealing in pelts and hides. We lived in a big house with many servants. For years my parents kept two horses in the stalls at the side of the house, and went out riding every morning. Now and then my sister and I would spend a night in the hay in these stalls, on account of the earthquakes in and around Sofia, which were frequent.

My mother led the life of a princess in Sofia: dinners for guests from abroad with caviar and champagne, daytime on the tennis courts and at the Diana Baths, and charity work. She took the children on vacation to Bled in Yugoslavia, to Velden on the Wörthersee, or to Istanbul-Bebek on the Sea of Marmara, but mostly to Warna, a favorite Bulgarian spa on the Black Sea. My parents often spent their own vacations – without their children, who were well taken care of by the servants at home – in Meran, Taormina, or on Lake Constance. We had a swimming pool in the yard in front of the house, and a lot of animals in the back yard: rabbits, chickens, a lamb, a goat, two cats – one for each child – and of course Kotti, the German shepherd. Inside the house there was also a big cage for two songbirds, canaries, along one whole wall of the greenhouse. They sang beautifully.

RS Was music important in your parents' home, as it was for the Levins?

EL Yes, there was always music at home: my mother took voice lessons, we had a big radio and a gramophone and listened to records together as a family: the usual stuff of the '*haute bourgeoisie*,' that is, Beethoven symphonies, excerpts from the Wagner operas, *Tannhäuser* or *Der Fliegende Holländer*, mostly performed by singers and conductors who came to visit

[1] Evi Levin, née Mayer (b. Sofia, March 4, 1923).

us. Actors and actresses also came to visit and also stayed with us, since there was a separate apartment in the house for guests, with its own servants and a chauffeur. My parents were always active in cultural affairs. They even arranged for internationally famous singers like Alexander Kipnis and Herbert Janssen[2] to come to Sofia, as well as actors like Hans Jaray,[3] all of whom signed the guest book at our house. Sadly, we lost that guest book when we emigrated, along with everything else. We also regularly went to the Nationaloper, which was very good: the performances were in Bulgarian, except when guest singers sang in an opera's original language – then it was a bilingual opera production. Our parents also took us along to many concerts with international guest soloists: the child prodigy Wolfgang Schneiderhan,[4] Elly Ney,[5] Fritz Kitzinger,[6] the conductor Issay Dobroven,[7] and many others.

I began to take piano lessons when I was five, because I already could play everything my sister played, just by ear. I remember that at six or seven I played something in a public concert in a big concert hall in Sofia at the *Voennen Klub* (Military Club);[8] I could only reach the pedals standing up. Then when I went to the German School in Sofia I always took part in the school productions, accompanying singers from the upper grades, also violinists. One of them was Fredy Ostrovsky:[9]

[2] Herbert Janssen (1892–1965) sang at the Berlin Staatsoper and at Bayreuth. Out of distaste for the Nazis he emigrated first to South America in 1938, where he sang at the Teatro Colón in Buenos Aires, and then to New York in 1939, where he was a mainstay of the German wing of the Metropolitan Opera from then until 1952.

[3] Hans Jaray (1906–1990) was an actor with the Neue Wiener Bühne, the Vienna Volkstheater, and Max Reinhardt's Theater in der Josefstadt. He emigrated to America in 1938, working in theaters in Hollywood and New York. He returned to Vienna in 1948.

[4] Wolfgang Schneiderhan (1915–2002), Austrian violinist and child prodigy, was concertmaster of the Vienna Symphony Orchestra 1933–1937 and Vienna Philharmonic 1937–1951. After 1948 he was the violinist in Edwin Fischer's trio with Enrico Mainardi. He performed extensively as a soloist and made numerous benchmark recordings, in particular of the Beethoven sonatas with pianist Wilhelm Kempff.

[5] Elly Ney (1882–1968), German pianist, won the Mendelssohn Prize in Berlin in 1901. After studies in Vienna with Theodor Leschitizky and Emil Sauer, she began her international career in 1908.

[6] Fritz Kitzinger (1904–1947), pianist and conductor, led the premiere of Aaron Copland's ballet *Billy the Kid* in New York in 1939.

[7] Issay Dobroven (1891–1953) conducted at the Moscow Opera and, after the Russian revolution, in Berlin and Dresden, and then later in Sofia, San Francisco, Budapest, and London. In 1949 he initiated a highly regarded series of Russian opera performances at La Scala.

[8] The Central Military Club in Sofia, built in 1895, has always been an important cultural center: Feodor Chaliapin, Nikolai Ghiaurov, and Boris Christoff, among many prominent singers, have sung in its great hall over the years.

[9] Fredy Ostrovsky (1922–2006) was himself a child prodigy; in 1939 he emigrated first to London and then to New York, where he played in the Radio City Orchestra, after which he played in the Boston Symphony for forty-some years.

when he was eleven and I was ten we appeared in recitals together as a duo. The two of us also played trios with a cellist from school, mostly at home, just for the fun of it. Fredy Ostrovsky later went to Vienna to study with Wolfgang Schneiderhan. The German School not only put on public recitals, they also did Humperdinck's *Hänsel und Gretel*: my sister sang Gretel and I was the orchestra – on the piano. Later on, 1938–1939, when I was at the American College in Sofia, I also performed regularly at musical events. And I used to play the accordion too: a year before the war my sister, who was studying art history in Grenoble, gave me a little accordion that she had brought home with her. Later on, in New York, I got a real, a wonderful accordion that I took everywhere with me.

RS What language did your family speak in Bulgaria?

EL I grew up bilingual: Bulgarian and German. When I was three, my parents got a French-Russian woman to come and play with us so that we would learn French. Later on I had French lessons at school, and weekly private lessons in French with Madame Fackler from Lausanne. From the fourth grade on I studied Latin and later on English, in order to be admitted to the American College in Sofia in 1938. After we emigrated I also learned Italian and Spanish. Learning languages has always been very easy for me.

RS The war broke out while you were at the American College.

EL Yes, and that changed our lives dramatically, from one day to the next. At home we had been brought up 'humanistically,' we had no religious instruction and knew almost nothing about Judaism. When I got my report card after my first or second year at the German School a friend of mine asked me what was meant by 'religious instruction: mos.' on my report card. I was taken aback and instantly replied 'mosamedanic'! I didn't know that 'mos.' stood for 'Mosaic,' and I wouldn't have known what that meant either. Later on, my friends and I used to pray in German at the German Protestant Church just before a German exam at school, just as we went to the French Catholic Church before a French exam, since we assumed that this way God would be more likely to answer our prayers for good grades, and before an exam in Bulgarian we of course went to pray at the Greek Orthodox Alexander Nevsky Cathedral.

Bulgaria was one of the few European countries that didn't obey the Nazi's orders to deport the Jews. But my father had never relinquished his German citizenship, since a German passport made his frequent travels as a businessman much easier than they would have been with a Bulgarian passport. But even though my parents had settled in Sofia before I was born, in 1939 German citizenship was a liability: a Bulgarian who wanted to take over my father's business filed a complaint against him which resulted in a deportation order. I never knew what he was accused of, but I now think it might have alleged that he was illegally holding foreign currencies. At first my father told the family nothing about this, he was certain he could get the deportation order revoked on the grounds that it was invalid. Only after several months, when his efforts had proved fruitless, did he tell us about our imminent deportation.

RS Wasn't there anyone among all the connections your parents had in Bulgaria who could block the deportation order?

EL Unfortunately not. Even their connection with King Boris, who my parents often met on their morning horseback rides, wasn't enough to get the deportation order lifted. When their further efforts also went nowhere, we had to leave the country within twenty-four hours, and my father had to apply for passports for the whole family at the German consulate right before our departure. But where were we to go? We finally got an Italian tourist visa, valid for three weeks, but Yugoslavia didn't allow those of us with German 'J' passports to take the short way through it to Italy. So we fled to Burgas, the Bulgarian port on the Black Sea, in order to embark on a tiny 2,000 ton Italian steamer to Naples. We had to leave behind everything we owned, including my father's valuable collection of Persian rugs. Everything was packed into moving vans by our friends and sent to an expediter in Trieste to await further instructions from us. That was in October, 1939. Later on, in New York, when we tried unsuccessfully to get in touch with the expediter, we were informed that our things were nowhere to be found – either they'd been destroyed in a bombing or else they'd been stolen at some time or other.

As it was already wartime when our ship left Burgas, the Mediterranean blockade was in force, and our journey to Naples turned into an unbelievable odyssey. In the middle of the night we were stopped in the Dardanelles by a British warship, our Italian registry ship was boarded on suspicion of smuggling for the Axis powers, and a British crew took command of it. Instead of going to Naples the ship went to Valletta on Malta and anchored just outside the port there – most of the British sailors and officers left the ship in little rowboats. But we weren't allowed to disembark. There were days and days of uncertainty until we got the official report that there was no contraband on board and we could proceed to Naples, where we arrived after a three week delay.

RS And where in any case you could only stay for three weeks!

EL Yes, and all through those three weeks my father tried desperately to use his good connections with the German consulate in Sofia to get us a visa for anywhere at all, but to no avail. Luckily the police in Naples made an exception and extended our temporary visa for another three weeks, but told us that under no circumstances would they extend it again. In the meantime we got an encouraging report from my uncle in Argentina: Dr. Kurt Mayer was my father's brother and a successful chemist who had been one of the people who developed Gelonida,[10] a drug for headaches. He would be able to arrange an immigration visa for Argentina. But no one knew how long that would take.

One day, as the end of our final three weeks was threatening, my father and I were out walking in Naples, along the *Passeggiata*, the Esplanade, and feeling utterly desperate, when all of a sudden my father ran up to an elderly gentleman shouting 'Monsieur Baton! Monsieur Baton!' They knew one another from when they had been together in Turkey, when they'd both worked there before the First World War. They embraced one another and my father told him about our desperate situation. To which Mr. Baton responded by assuring us that we didn't have to worry anymore, his son-in-law was the police prefect in Alassio, and he would be happy to issue us the papers we needed in order to stay longer. His mother had a little hotel in Alassio, L'Albergo Centrale, we would be able to stay there. And that's what happened: with the permission of the police prefect we spent six months in Alassio, an incredibly beautiful spa town, not far from San Remo on the Italian Riviera, at this charming little hotel. The police prefect and his mother were opposed to the fascists and gave us a lot of help.

While we were staying in Alassio an American business acquaintance of my father's came to visit us on his way to Sofia and promised to arrange an American immigration visa for us at the U.S. consulate there. He would also give them the necessary affidavit. But this could take some time. In the meantime we got a tourist visa for Spain that friends in Bulgaria had bought on the black market, but it came with an urgent warning not to use it except in an extreme emergency. Finally a telegram arrived from my uncle in Argentina, saying that our Argentine visa had been approved with no restrictions. So in a festive mood the four of us went to the Argentine consulate in Genoa and presented the telegram. The Argentinian official asked us for our passports, took one look at the big red 'J' printed on the first page, and informed us that he

[10] The prescription pain-reliever Gelonida combines paracetamol, caffeine, and a codeine-related compound. It is still marketed under that name in Germany.

couldn't issue the visa without a police certificate of good conduct. And he handed us back our passports.

You can't begin to imagine how incredibly disappointed we were. So we waited even longer in Alassio. My clever parents had my sister and I take Italian lessons every day from a retired professor. It was already the spring of 1940, and the war was taking a turn for the worse. Italian tanks and canons rolled through Alassio on their way to the French border, so we were afraid that Italy would also be entering the war before long. But then we got another telegram from Buenos Aires saying the visa had been sent to Genoa once again. Finally, after the certificate of good conduct had also arrived, my father went to the consulate in Genoa again, this time only taking my sister with him. 'Wonderful,' said the Argentinian official after he'd reviewed the Bulgarian police certificate, 'but we'll need a certificate like this for your children too.' By now it was the beginning of June, there was still no sign of the American visa from Sofia, and the Italian army was continuing to roll non-stop to the French border. Then and there my father decided to take the next ship to Spain.

It was just a short crossing from Genoa to Barcelona, which we reached on June 8, 1940. All the passengers disembarked except for us, we weren't allowed to go ashore, and we knew that the black market visa for Spain was to be used only in an extreme emergency. We sat on deck, on our luggage, totally defeated, and overheard the Italian crew saying they'd gotten orders to return to Genoa immediately. A classmate of my father's from Germany was waiting for us on the quay. My father shouted to him that the police wouldn't let us off the ship. We were absolutely desperate and totally discouraged, since what would become of us 'J' passport Germans in Mussolini's fascist Italy?

Then all of a sudden a highly decorated officer came on board the ship, extended his arm in the Falange salute, and shouted '*Eviva Franco! Eviva España!*' He came right up to my father and we were really terrified. The officer whispered in my father's ear, letting him know that he was really a Hungarian Jew, and ordered the four of us to come with him. He picked our four passports up off the police desk, let us go ashore to where my father's classmate was waiting for us, and disappeared. In a state of total shock over what had just happened to us, we asked my father's friend for an explanation about this turn of events. It turned out that my father's friend had found a Hungarian Jew who was rescuing Jews by wearing the uniform of an officer who had been killed in the civil war that had ended three years ago. On June 10 Italy declared war on Great Britain and France.

RS But even after this life-saving intervention you still found yourselves once again in highly tenuous circumstances. How long did you and your family have to hold out in Barcelona?

EL We were in Barcelona for five months, waiting day in and day out for the visa for the U.S. or for Argentina. Afternoons we hung around in the cafés for hours to catch whatever word was going around: someone might have heard that the Venezuélan consulate was issuing visas and everyone would run to the consulate. The next day it would be the Honduran consulate, or the Ecuadorian, nothing was out of the question. All of a sudden the Santo Domingan consulate surfaced, and my father was able to get a visa for the four of us for just a few thousand dollars! Now we had to book passage as quickly as possible. My father paid cash for that too, since we were in Spain illegally and were anxious to get away as soon as possible and settle down again somewhere else. But unfortunately it turned out that Cuba, like Yugoslavia, wouldn't issue us a transit visa, and in the meantime the Santo Domingo visa fell through, and because of the large sums of money that my father had laid out we were worse off than before.

But then all of a sudden one day – finally! – the unrestricted Argentinian visa was ready to be picked up, and then just two hours later we got a telegram saying that the American passport had also arrived. *Embarras du choix!* Should we go to Argentina now, where my father's brother was living, but about which one heard all sorts of terrible things about anti-Semitism, or should we go to the U.S., to the business acquaintance who had applied for the visa for us? Since after my year at the American College in Sofia I was an enthusiastic fan of the United States, and the rest of the family was too, we all decided to emigrate to the United States. A few days later, at the beginning of November, 1940, we embarked in Bilbao, and after stops in Santander, Lisbon, and Gibraltar, faced a perilous ocean crossing, since the war was already underway in the Atlantic, and passenger ships were routinely being torpedoed.

RS When did you and your family finally arrive in America?

EL We got to New York safe and sound at the end of November, 1940, just in time for the famous Thanksgiving Day Parade. Five days later I enrolled in the Julia Richman High School on Manhattan's Upper East Side. I was seventeen and a half and had missed a whole year of school during our forced emigration, but I convinced the school's administrators that in the next seven months I could master the work for graduation, for which I took the New York State Regents exams in English, French, German, Italian, and Latin, all of which I passed with the highest marks. In high school I took the required courses in English, American History, and so on. I was exempted from other required courses on the basis of my report cards from Sofia. I started a band on the side, playing piano, accordion, ukulele, and maracas, took part in school events, and earned pocket money by playing piano in a dance school, improvising whatever the dance teacher required. I even played piano at the opening of a new Woolworth's in Forest Hills, the neighborhood in Queens, in New York, where we were living: whatever hit tunes the crowds of customers wanted to hear. I graduated *cum laude* from Richman High in June 1941. The school's music teacher gave me a piano as a graduation present!

RS You once told me you worked as a free-lance translator in New York.

EL Yes, right after graduation I went to summer school at the Rhodes Business School in New York and learned touch-typing as well as stenography, book keeping, and the multi-lingual export business. I got my certificate in just three months and started looking for my first job in order to earn money and help support my father financially. In the fall of 1941 I took a job with a re-insurance company that did business mainly in South America. It was a big success, and I got a raise almost every month, until Alexander Marcov from the Bulgarian Division of the Voice of America began telephoning me day in and day out, nagging me about my patriotic duty to quit my job and join the Bulgarian desk at the State Department's Voice of America. Even my boss's offer to make me an agent wasn't enough to keep me holding out against Marcov's persistence, so in 1942 I went to work for the Voice of America.

There were only three of us in the Bulgarian department to begin with: Marcov was the chief, I was the translator, script-writer, and editor, and Ivan Petrov was the announcer. Later on the department got bigger. There was a period in which I had to listen to news broadcasts in various Slavic languages, for instance from Poland or Czechoslovakia, and translate them so that the censor would learn what was being said about the American broadcasts. It was interesting work. Marcov – stubborn, highly musical, a trained engineer, seven years older – married me in July, 1943. The marriage fell apart when he made the big mistake of going back to Bulgaria right after the war. Luckily my parents were able to persuade me not to go with him, since it would have interrupted my American naturalization process, without which I would never have gotten an American passport.

After the war was over I had free-lance positions with some very interesting businessmen, writers, and artists whose English wasn't so good. They wrote their business letters in their native language and I translated them into English and typed them up for them. At that time there weren't many people in New York who could translate Slavic languages into English, so I made rather a lot of money. I was just missing one thing: during the war years, after I had graduated from high school, I hadn't had anything more to do with music, since in my opinion music and war weren't at all compatible, but of course being away from music made me very unhappy. Then I happened to run into Fredy Ostrovsky again, on the street in New York, my violinist friend from my childhood in Sofia, who was now playing in the Radio City Orchestra in New York. He told me I was unhappy because I missed making music, what I had to do was to start playing the piano again! His advice was that I should go to Tanglewood and enroll in the International Summer Academy there.

But I couldn't go to Tanglewood as a pianist, where all those fabulously well-trained Juilliard graduates were that I couldn't compare myself to. But I thought I might be able to get into the chorus. It was true that I'd never sung in even a semi-professional chorus, but I signed up for an audition anyway. Aaron Copland, Serge Koussevitzky, Robert Shaw, and Leonard Bernstein were on the jury. They gave me a score – Bach's *St. Matthew Passion* – and between my *solfège* and my perfect pitch I sang in the right key.

WALTER LEVIN: The jury was very taken with the fact that someone could not only sing all the right pitches but that they could also sing with *solfège*, which wasn't all that common in America at that time. But people like Aaron Copland who had studied with Nadia Boulanger in Paris had to learn it.[11]

EL Copland asked me where I had learned to sing, and I told him it was in Bulgaria. But I'd had no training as a singer whatsoever! As a child in Sofia I had once listened when a music teacher who had just gotten back from Germany demonstrated his newly acquired *solfège* skills for the Bulgarian School Commission at our house. Since then I'd thought that you always sang 'do-re-mi' when you had music in front of you that had no text. And so I was accepted into the chorus, and sang the Brahms *Requiem*, Bach's *St. John Passion*, and Mahler's Second Symphony under Serge Koussevitzky, Leonard Bernstein, and Robert Shaw.

WL And when there weren't enough tenors in the chorus, the conductor asked you to sing along with the tenors.

[11] Bernstein learned *solfège* at school as a child. As a choral conductor, Shaw would have known it, and Koussevitzky surely also as a result of his studies in Moscow. *Solfège* was taught at the Curtis Institute of Music by Philadelphia Orchestra principal oboist Marcel Tabuteau from as early as 1924 up until his retirement in 1953. Tabuteau's course was taken by many instrumentalists, not only oboists, who went on to fine careers in major American orchestras.

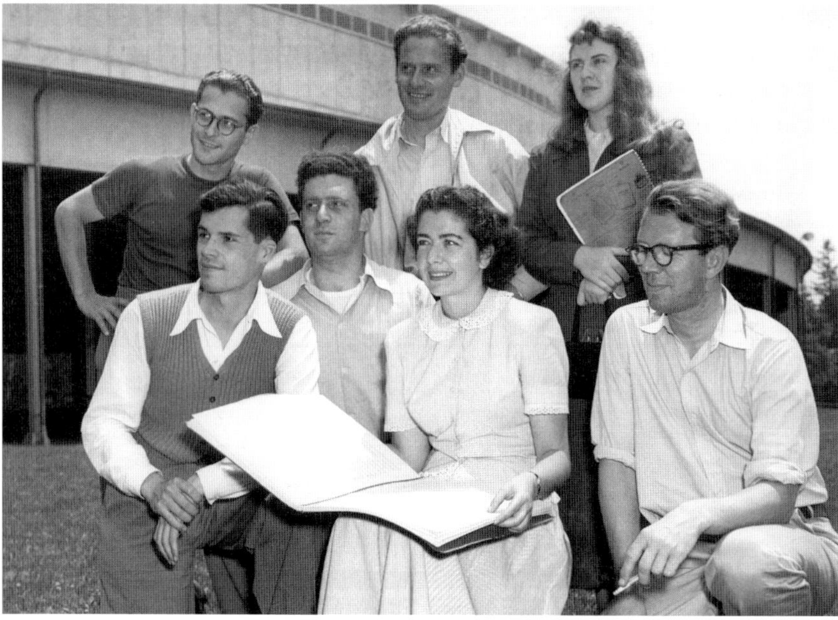

9 Herbert Brün (left, rear) and Evi Marcov (front, center), Tanglewood Summer School of Music, 1948

RS Were you at Tanglewood just the one time?

EL Yes, just this one summer, 1948. That was where I met Herbert Brün.

WL Herbert had gotten a scholarship to study with Aaron Copland at Tanglewood: it was a composition prize from the Jerusalem Conservatory. Just imagine, he played jazz four hands with Leonard Bernstein!

EL Herbert gave me piano lessons, completely different of course from what I was used to. For etudes he gave me Hindemith's *Ludus Tonalis*. At the end of that summer I brought Herbert home with me to Forest Hills, in Queens, New York, where my parents lived.

WL And I went there too, to see Herbert again. That's how I met Evi. After Tanglewood, Herbert studied at Columbia University for two semesters, thanks to a scholarship from the Esco Foundation in New York, so we saw a lot of one another.

EL A ballet of Herbert's[12] was performed at Columbia University, for which I played piano in the orchestra, and the LaSalle Quartet also played.

[12] *The Nightingale and the Rose*, Columbia Ballet Workshop, four performances, May 26–28, 1949, at the Brander Matthews Theater. Brün conducted the performances.

WL And for my graduate recital at Juilliard I prepared the Berg violin concerto, the Bach d minor Partita, and Herbert's Sonatina for violin solo, a hefty program,[13] which got the violin teacher Joe Fuchs to storm out of one of my rehearsals in a rage, shouting at us that he'd heard this 'screeching music' once before, in the recording sessions with Louis Krasner and the Cleveland Orchestra, and never wanted to have anything to do with it ever again. He then slammed the door shut behind him.[14]

[13] Brün's Sonatina, Opus 4, for violin solo was written in New York while he was a student at Columbia University in the fall of 1948; Levin's recital took place in May, 1949.

[14] Joseph Fuchs (1900–1997) was concertmaster of the Cleveland Orchestra 1926–1940. He began teaching at Juilliard in 1946. Krasner's recording of the Berg violin concerto with Artur Rodzinski conducting the Cleveland Orchestra took place on December 15, 1940. Krasner (1903–1995) commissioned Berg's violin concerto, which he premiered in 1936; he also premiered Schoenberg's violin concerto in 1940.

7 *Arturo Toscanini*

ROBERT SPRUYTENBURG: One of the reasons why you wanted to study music and violin in New York was to be able to attend the rehearsals and radio concerts of the NBC Symphony under Arturo Toscanini. But it was notoriously difficult to get into either of them. How did you manage that?

WALTER LEVIN: Richard Farrell and Leonard Hutcheson, my pianist friends from the Rockefeller House, and I all wanted to go to Toscanini's rehearsals, so I thought we should ask Samuel Chotzinoff, the director of NBC Music, for permission. Together with David Sarnoff, Chotzinoff had persuaded Toscanini to come to the orchestra that NBC was creating just for him. Chotzinoff was also a pianist,[1] and Jascha Heifetz' son-in-law. He was a notoriously high-handed individual, everybody was afraid of him. But I said to myself, he can't be that bad, let's just see. So I called up his secretary and told her that we would like to get an appointment with Mr. Chotzinoff. She asked me what it was about. I told her we wanted to go to Toscanini's rehearsals. She replied that this was absolutely impossible, Toscanini didn't allow anyone into his rehearsals. I wasn't about to give up, so I told her that was why we wanted to speak with Mr. Chotzinoff. We were three young music students at Juilliard and we would be very grateful if she could get us a brief meeting with Mr. Chotzinoff. I didn't let go until she had gotten us a half an hour with him.

So we went into Chotzinoff's office, and he asked us what it was we thought he could do for us. I explained to him that we were from three different countries: I was from Palestine, Leonard Hutcheson was from Australia, and Richard Farrell was from New Zealand, and one of the main reasons why we had come to New York to study was the Toscanini concerts: what we could learn from Toscanini's rehearsals was more important to us than many of the courses we had to take at Juilliard. I told him we knew about his relationship with Toscanini, we very much admired his success in engaging him here, we didn't want to miss this opportunity, and couldn't he please help us to get into the rehearsals? He said he would find out, and his secretary would call us.

Three days later the secretary actually called to tell me that Mr. Chotzinoff had made the arrangements and that we should get there an hour prior to the rehearsal, so Mr. Chotzinoff could tell us where

[1] Chotzinoff accompanied Heifetz in his recordings of Lensky's aria from Tchaikovsky's *Eugene Onegin*, Dvořák's Slavonic Dance in e minor, and Chopin's Nocturne Opus 27, Nr. 2. He also accompanied soprano Alma Gluck in her recording of Saint-Saëns' '*Le bonheur est chose légère.*'

we could sit and listen. Amazingly, we got permission to listen to Toscanini's rehearsals in David Sarnoff's loge – he was the General Manager of NBC. His glass-enclosed loge was behind the orchestra, so we could see Toscanini's face, which was of course ideal for observing the rehearsals. From then on we went regularly to hear Toscanini rehearse. David Sarnoff himself showed up occasionally, and when he did he asked us for permission to listen with us and offered us some whisky, which, however, we politely declined.

RS So that's how you got into the rehearsals! But how did you manage to get into the concerts?

WL Going to the rehearsals meant we were often at NBC at times when no one else was there except the regular employees, who knew we were always at the rehearsals and thought we had something to do with them. I always brought my violin with me, which made for a very good prop. Once they had gotten to know us, we asked them where the office was where they sent out the free tickets to the Toscanini concerts, and they told us it was Room 827. So we went to Room 827, where there were two girls working: we flirted with them and told them how important it would be for us to go to the Toscanini concerts, and after that we got free tickets sent to us every now and then. But we couldn't count on that, since these girls didn't have the authority to actually issue the tickets, and they could have lost their jobs if somebody found out they were sending us complimentary tickets on a regular basis. Their job was to send these complimentary tickets to the businessmen, investors, and others who advertised on NBC.

Toscanini's radio concerts were sponsored by General Motors, which was always mentioned by the announcer. Since the concerts were broadcast as a so-called public service, for tax reasons all the tickets had to be free, not just the complimentary tickets that were sent to NBC's special guests. The rest of the tickets were available to the public on request, but they were always gone long before the concert, as the demand for them was always much greater than the supply. But we learned from the girls in Room 827 that they regularly mailed not one but two complimentary tickets to each of the special guests. And then we had an incredible stroke of luck. One day I went to Rockefeller Center with Evi, who really wanted to go to the Toscanini radio concert, even though I told her that it made no sense at all to go there, we'd never get in!

EVI LEVIN: Which was all I needed to hear! I remembered what Walter told me about NBC's special guests each getting two complimentary tickets, so I asked the people going into the big RCA building with the NBC studios whether by any chance they had a ticket left over. And if someone would ask what I meant by that, I would ask them to have a look in their envelope: they would find two tickets in it, and did they need them both? They would be surprised, and sometimes said no, they didn't need them both, we could have one. But then, I believe it was the second time we went there, I had a fabulous bit of luck. Once again I was asking everyone as they went in whether by any chance they had a ticket left over. There was one man in particular for whom I invented a whole big fairy tale about why I was so anxious to get into just this concert, after which he said I should just come with him. I told him that wouldn't work at all, I wouldn't get past the ticket taker. He just said 'come along,' and so I walked past the queue with him and took the elevator to the eighth floor, which is where Studio 8-H was. He said I should just wait a minute, he would get a ticket for me. At which point I asked him whether he could possibly get me two tickets, as I was here with a violinist from Palestine.

WL And I was still standing downstairs without a ticket! I wasn't supposed to be there in the first place. They actually threw me out. There's a line incised in the middle of the sidewalk by Rockefeller center: inside the line it's private property, Rockefeller Center belongs to the Rockefellers, and they have their own security force, as they don't want to have any sort of riff-raff on their property who might bother the rich people. And you had to be inside this line, since the New York City police were on the other side of it, ready to charge you with 'loitering,' as they called it, 'making a public nuisance of yourself.' You always had to run away when you saw a policeman. But inside the line you were chased out by the security people if you didn't have a ticket.

EL Meanwhile the man who had taken me up to the eighth floor really did come back with two tickets for us. And he gave me his business card: it was Ben Grauer, the announcer for the Toscanini concerts on Saturday afternoons, who told me that whenever we wanted to go to a concert, I should call him and he would get tickets for both of us. We got to be friends with him and then also got to go to the dress rehearsals as well as the concerts. But that was later on. At the time, I just went back downstairs with the two tickets he'd given me, and there was Walter standing on the street, still desperately trying to get a ticket.

RS That really was an incredible stroke of luck! To have bumped into him of all people!

WL It was incredible, wasn't it? Just like in a fairy tale!

Part II

The LaSalle Quartet

8 *The Members of the Quartet*

ROBERT SPRUYTENBURG: In the first concert by the LaSalle Quartet for which there is extant documentation in the Paul Sacher Foundation's LaSalle Quartet archive in Basel, on December 13, 1947, the players are listed as you, Henry Nigrine, who played second violin, Max Felde, viola, and Jackson Wiley cello. Of the four, you are the only one to still be on the roster for the LaSalle Quartet's last concert, the concert in Bochum on May 21, 1987.

WALTER LEVIN: Well, such things were to be expected. A quartet as founded by four students while they're in school isn't necessarily what you'll end up with for a professional career. You start out with people who can help you get going and are interested in what you're doing, but once you start working together you begin to find out what sort of people they are. But actually we had astonishingly few personnel changes. Henry Nigrine was the first real second violin we had, right from the beginning. He was followed first by Isidore Cohen and then Henry Meyer, who was with us to the end. Max Felde was replaced by Peter Kamnitzer, who was also with us up to the end. We had more trouble with our cellists: Jackson Wiley was followed first by Paul Anderson and then by Richard Kapuscinski. Then came Jack Kirstein, who was with us for twenty years, and then Lee Fiser, who finished up with the rest of us.

RS Who was Henry Nigrine?

WL Henry Nigrine was a very nice man and someone I found very sympathetic. He was with the quartet for about two years, 1946–1948, but he wasn't so exclusively devoted to quartet playing, he wanted to have a career as a good violinist who could get somewhere in New York, and then he was hired by the New York Philharmonic, which was a big name orchestra, getting in there wasn't at all easy. The pay was relatively good and they made recordings and so on. He was a real New Yorker, born in Brooklyn, and that was his home turf. So to head off now to somewhere in the Wild West when this offer came from Colorado Springs, that just wasn't his thing.

RS There is a photo of you at Galamian's summer school in Meadowmount in 1948 that shows you and Mrs. Burpee, who owned the cottage you stayed in, together with Jackson Wiley, Max Felde, and Judith and Isidore Cohen,[1] as well as a dog, Fluffy.

[1] Isidore Cohen was second violin in the Juilliard Quartet from 1958 to 1966. In 1969 he succeeded Daniel Guilet in the Beaux Arts Trio, with whom he remained until 1992.

EVI LEVIN: That was the summer before Henry Meyer joined the quartet. I got to know Henry Meyer at Tanglewood in August, 1948. At that time Walter was at Galamian's summer school, and I hadn't met him yet.

RS So Isidore Cohen was with the quartet for only a few months?

WL Only for the summer of 1948. He was an excellent violinist, later on he played in the Juilliard Quartet and then he was with the Beaux Arts Trio for many years. He was concertmaster in the Juilliard Orchestra. But he was a bit of a bore, besides which Fluffy got on my nerves. My love of animals has its limits.

RS Ah! That was the Cohens' dog! I thought it was Mrs. Burpee's. But you yourself had a dog in Cincinnati.

WL We had a wonderful dog, only he was a little goofy.

EL He was not goofy! You hardly knew him!

WL And when Isidore Cohen left the quartet, we were very lucky that Evi had gotten to know Henry Meyer.[2]

EL When I was at Tanglewood in the summer of 1948, I sang in the chorus for the final concert, which was Mahler's second symphony. My sister came to hear the concert, and brought along with her a young musician who had just arrived from Paris: that was Henry Meyer. And at Tanglewood I'd gotten to know Herbert Brün,[3] who had just come from Israel and had a scholarship to study composition at Tanglewood with Aaron Copland. When I went back to New York again, Herbert told me I absolutely had to meet his friend Walter Levin, who was a violinist there. So Herbert called up Walter for me, and I told him that he really had to come out and join us at my parents' place in Queens, so Walter took the subway all the way out to Forest Hills. He was in a bad temper, he'd just lost his second violinist. He kept asking what he was supposed to do, school had already started again at Juilliard, so I told him about

[2] Henry Meyer (b. Heinz Wolfgang Meyer in Dresden, June 29, 1923; d. Cincinnati, December 18, 2006) was a child prodigy who made his debut with the Dresden Philharmonic. After the Nazis came to power in the 1930s he played in the Kulturbund orchestra in Berlin. When the orchestra was disbanded by the Nazis, he and his family were sent to concentration camps; he himself was interned at Sachenhausen, Birkenau, Buchenwald, Auschwitz, and Ohrdruf, from which he escaped in 1945. Immediately after the war he went to Paris, where he studied the violin with René Benedetti and George Enescu; he emigrated to America in 1948.

[3] About Herbert Brün see also pp. 41–42 and 287–289.

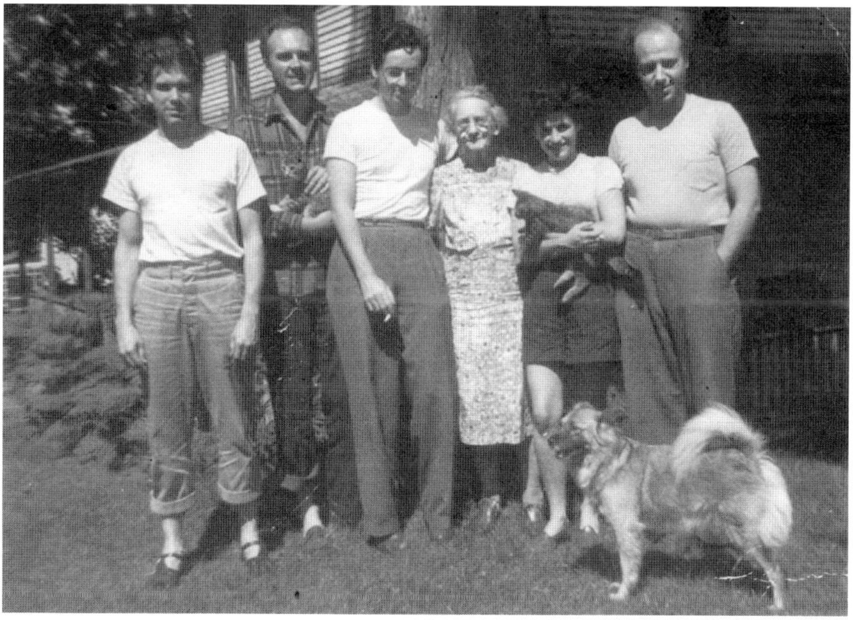

10 Jackson Wiley, Max Felde, Walter Levin, Mrs. Burpee, and Judith and Isidore Cohen with their dog Fluffy, Meadowmount, 1948

how I'd just met Henry Meyer. So we called Henry and that's how it came about that Henry Meyer became Henry Nigrine's successor after Isidore Cohen.

RS Apparently the second violinist of the LaSalle Quartet has to be called Henry.

WL Of course, that was the main criterion.

EL We, that is Walter and the other members of the quartet, took care of getting Henry a scholarship to Juilliard right away.

WL We infiltrated him into Juilliard, so to speak. By then we had gotten to be old hands at Juilliard, we knew everybody and everybody knew us, and so it was obvious that Henry would be accepted. Besides which, he was a very special case, he was one of the first students at Juilliard who came to America from out of the German concentration camps. Henry's emigration to America was organized at the highest level of the American army, by Eisenhower personally. Otherwise it would have been very difficult. Henry had been rescued from the concentration camps by the Americans, for whom he was an interesting case, since at the end of 1945, when the war had just barely come to end, there weren't all that many concentration camp survivors you could talk to. But there were a few such refugees that the Americans thought were credible, and Henry was one of them. He had a chance to talk to General George Patton, who then sent him, along with some other refugees, to Paris, where Eisenhower was headquartered. Henry told the people there that he wanted to come to America. They asked him whether he had friends or relatives there. He did: his uncle, his mother's brother, had emigrated to America with his children. But Henry hadn't a clue as to where he was. They told him to tell them everything he knew about his family, names and so on, and they would find him. But it took months and months before they found his uncle. I believe he was in Chicago. Eisenhower had also wanted to meet Henry, and he interceded personally on behalf of Henry's affidavit of financial support.[4] But in the meantime Henry was in Paris for a few years. We were even at the same concert at the Châtelet Theater early in 1946 without even knowing one another.

EL And of course after being in the concentration camps he no longer had a violin, but in Paris he got to know Nathan Milstein, who gave him one.

WL He also studied with some very good people in Paris, with René Benedetti and with George Enescu. So for him that was a great time. And then in 1948 he came to America and also wanted to study here. Juilliard and the LaSalle Quartet were a godsend for him, since from childhood on he was a very savvy chamber music player. He'd also played second violin in the Kulturbund Quartet in Berlin. There were outstanding people in that quartet.

RS And that's how Henry Meyer came to Berlin? He was after all originally from Dresden.

WL That's right, he went to Berlin from Dresden and joined the Kulturbund Orchestra as a very young man. He was sixteen or so then. The Kulturbund was an incredibly important organization,[5] and so Henry already had a lot of concert experience when he got to Juilliard. Of course new music was scarcely played then, practically speaking not at all. All the same, he already knew a lot of repertory and had known it since childhood. So it wasn't hard for him to fit in with us. But the Bartók quartets and the more recent repertory were completely new to him, he really had to work hard at them.

4 See also p. 11.

5 About the Kulturbund see pp. 12–14.

RS But once he had a taste of them...

WL Well yes and no. Henry always had a bit of a hard time with the new music. He learned to play it fabulously well, but it probably wasn't the direction he would have gone on his own, although in retrospect he was very enthusiastic about it once he had finally learned it. But I always ran into resistance in choosing such pieces, Henry would always ask, 'do we have to?' And it *is* difficult to learn such pieces from scratch.

RS What happened to your original violist, Max Felde?

WL Max Felde left us in the summer of 1949, shortly before our engagement in Colorado Springs. When we graduated from Juilliard in 1949 we had already been engaged as Quartet in Residence by Colorado College in Colorado Springs, and we wanted to prepare for that by working intensely on repertory. Every summer we went to our teacher, Ivan Galamian, at his summer residence in Meadowmount in upstate New York, northeast of Elizabethtown. We had room and board on a farm where we stayed every year and during the day we practiced and rehearsed in a barn. We'd already been there for several years as a quartet, and I'd been there prior to that as a violinist, so altogether I'd been there for seven years. The most important thing that summer was to prepare intensively for Colorado Springs.

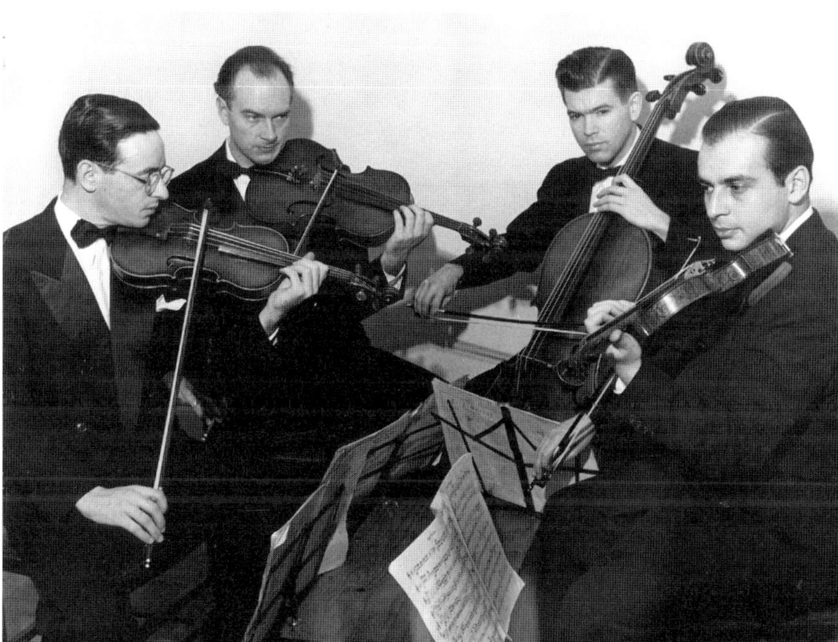

11 The LaSalle Quartet in 1949 (left to right): Walter Levin, Max Felde, Jackson Wiley, and Henry Meyer

And one day our violist, Max Felde, who we all liked a lot, disappeared, literally disappeared. We found a letter from him in which he said that he was dreadfully sorry to leave us in the lurch like that. But he had really considered it very carefully: he couldn't face it, it was too much for him, the work was too strenuous, too stressful, he just couldn't handle it.

RS Perhaps he was thinking of the tours as well?

WL I suppose he was, but I think that more than anything it was the intensity of our rehearsals. Max Felde was a particularly sensitive individual and the intensity with which we would be working was already very much in evidence. Apparently he'd never quite imagined it would be so intense. In any case, he threw in the towel and simply walked away from it, we had no idea where he went. We were totally dumbfounded: if you can imagine it, suddenly we had just six weeks before the end of the summer and the start of our engagement at Colorado College. Over the past few years we had worked up some repertory already, we had enough to make up two or three programs. But that wouldn't be enough if we were going to play three programs a year in Colorado, and how could we go on like that, year after year? Where was the repertory supposed to come from? So we had to work on repertory, urgently, and now all of a sudden we had to start all over again with a new violist – we certainly hadn't planned on that! So we had to rush to figure out where we could come up with a likely replacement here in the middle of nowhere in upstate New York – where on earth could we get somebody?

Fortunately Henry Meyer remembered someone he had played quartets with at a chamber music evening at someone's apartment in New York: Peter Kamnitzer,[6] who he said was a first rate chamber musician. But we had no idea how to reach him, so we called his father, a doctor who lived not far from Galamian in Midtown Manhattan, and asked him where Peter was. His father gave us Peter's phone number, so we called and told Peter the whole story, after which he said that of course he would be very interested, but when did we want him to start? I told him we needed him starting yesterday, it was now or never, we simply had to get started working on repertory, our first concert in Colorado Springs was just two months away, and we still had to move and get everything organized. And in the meantime we had to work up at least one program. We convinced him. He came

[6] Peter Kamnitzer (b. Free City of Danzig, November 22, 1922) started playing violin at an early age; he went to London in 1938 to study violin making, and was followed to London by his family prior to the outbreak of war in 1939. In 1941 he and his family emigrated to New York, where he began studying the viola with Nathan Gordon of the NBC Symphony and then with Julius Schaier, violist of the Manhattan Quartet (not the later, and still active, quartet of that name). He subsequently enrolled at Juilliard, where he studied with Milton Katims.

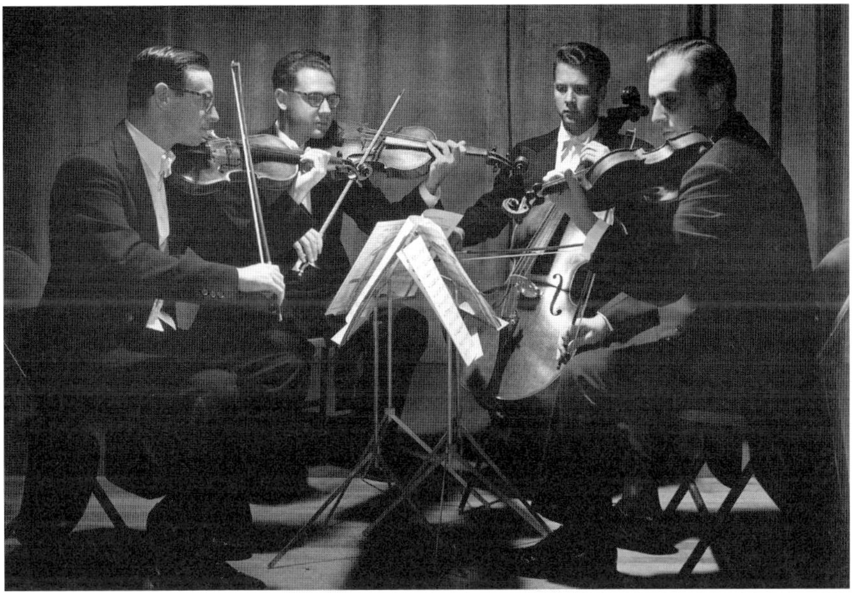

12 The LaSalle Quartet in 1951: Walter Levin, Peter Kamnitzer, Paul Anderson, and Henry Meyer, at Colorado College

to Meadowmount right away, and from that moment Peter Kamnitzer was the violist of the LaSalle Quartet, on down to our very last day.

RS Did Peter already know your repertory or did he have to learn everything from scratch?

WL He was an avid chamber music player, but students and young musicians seldom played the more recent repertory. So he knew neither the Bartók quartets nor Alban Berg's *Lyric Suite*, which we were just then learning, and which he didn't know at all. He knew this and that piece by Beethoven or Mozart, for instance, but not the ones we needed just then. For our first concert in Colorado Springs we were going to play Haydn's Opus 64, Nr. 6, Bartók's Nr. 6, and Schubert's d minor quartet, *Death and the Maiden*.[7] That was a really hefty program, for which we had to prepare thoroughly. And not only prepare those three pieces, since we were already working on future programs, although we did know some of the pieces already: Beethoven's Opus 59, Nr. 3, we had already played at Stefan Wolpe's apartment in New York, in February, 1949, and in concerts in New Jersey. And we'd also played Mozart's B♭ major quartet K. 589 and some other pieces in and around New York.

RS You mentioned Henry Meyer's initial difficulties with the new music

[7] The quartet's Colorado College debut took place on November 9, 1949.

you were playing when he joined the quartet. Was Peter Kamnitzer more open in this regard?

WL Yes, he was more open, his family had connections to modern art: his mother was a distant relative of Lyonel Feininger. Peter also had a completely different experience than Henry growing up, he and his family had emigrated in time, he had gone to Juilliard and was from an intellectual family. His father was a doctor and his uncle had been a member of the senate in Danzig.[8] Peter was a man who was interested in everything and he found new music intellectually stimulating. Henry you had to reach by way of feelings. But then that worked out very well too. There's no question that he was fully on board with us, otherwise it just wouldn't have worked.

RS How about the cellists? You had the most changes there.

WL Our first cellist was Jackson Wiley: he was a founding member of the LaSalle Quartet in 1946, he came with us to Colorado Springs in 1949, and was with the quartet until 1951.

RS What prompted him to leave the LaSalle Quartet?

WL He found a girlfriend he wanted to marry in Colorado Springs, a cello student, who told him in no uncertain terms that she didn't want a husband who was always on tour. Afterwards he taught at a little college in Indiana, and he was surely a very good teacher, as he had understood a lot about our way of making music.

And then we had Paul Anderson for a year, that is in the 1951–1952 season: a very nice kid from Chicago, a real sweetheart. We were too aggressive for him too, and it wasn't long before he too knew it wasn't going to work out. The last season in Colorado Springs, 1952–1953, we had Richard Kapuscinski. Kapuscinski was our great discovery! He was the cellist who should have stayed!

RS Had he also been to Juilliard?

WL No, he'd been at the Curtis Institute in Philadelphia, a student of Felix Salmond and Leonard Rose.

RS How did you happen to find him?

[8] After the First World War, Danzig (Gdansk) was a semi-autonomous protectorate of the League of Nations from 1920 until the German invasion in 1939, though its semi-autonomous status was effectively ended after the local Nazi party took over in 1933.

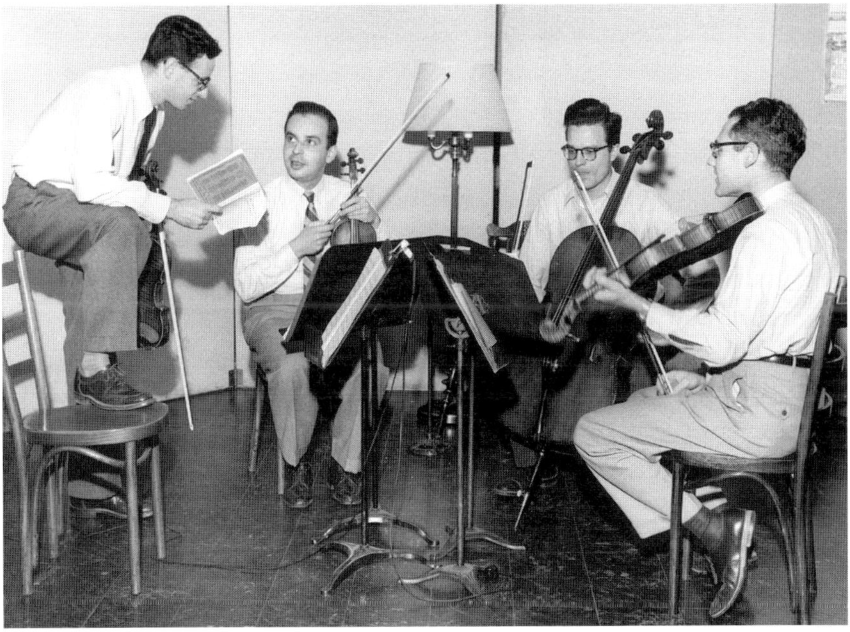

13 The LaSalle Quartet 1953: Walter Levin, Henry Meyer, Richard Kapuscinski, and Peter Kamnitzer

WL We sent out an alarm to everyone we knew, above all our teachers and the Juilliard Quartet, saying that we were looking for a cellist. In the meantime we had gotten a bit of a reputation and had a lot of contacts. So people were recommended to us, and we auditioned them. Kapuscinski was in the Baltimore Symphony. He was sensational: from the very first he played just like Lee Fiser did later on, a phenomenal cellist and a very funny guy. We were soul mates: he was a perfect match for us – what a pleasure!

RS And he had no problems with the repertory either, not even with the modern works?

WL None at all! He was game for every sacrilege, and he was a quick study.

RS Was he also an experienced chamber music player when he joined the LaSalle Quartet?

WL To some extent. He was one of those people who learn everything very quickly, he was very bright as well as a superb cellist. He was with us for our first European tour in 1954, the start of our career in Europe, he took part in the ISCM Festival in Israel and played a lot of new music.

That was sheer delight. Kapuscinski was a most congenial colleague, and a lot of fun to be with, too.

RS But he was with the quartet for only three years, until 1955?

WL Yes, the Kapuscinskis had children right away and at the time when they were expecting their third we simply didn't make enough money to support a family with three children.

EL They already had two children when he joined the quartet, and you, that is the other three of you, gave up some of your salaries, your already really low salaries, since with two children he of course needed more money than we did.

WL But I thought that was just the right thing to do. However, two years later, when his wife was expecting their third child, it was inevitable that he would throw in the towel. In 1955 he joined the Boston Symphony and wasn't happy there. He then went back to academic life, to Oberlin in Ohio, near Cleveland, as a teacher, and was much happier then. He also played a lot of chamber music there and taught people what he had learned and what he could do, he was also a wonderful teacher. Sadly he died much too young. He was barely 60, younger than us. That was a tragedy. After Kapuscinski we had a really hard time finding someone else.

RS So after Kapuscinski Jack Kirstein was a bit of a second choice.[9]

WL He wasn't like the rest of us, he was rather phlegmatic. But he played very well, no doubt about it, it's just that at first we had problems with him.

EL His wife[10] also had a lot to do with his being in the quartet, she was very enthusiastic about his playing in the quartet.

WL She was a phenomenal pianist and a very attentive wife. She was very helpful to him. In any case, Jack played with us for twenty years, from

[9] Jack Kirstein (1921–1996) was, like Kapuscinski, a student of Felix Salmond and Leonard Rose at the Curtis Institute of Music in Philadelphia. A World War II veteran, he joined the faculty of the College-Conservatory of Music in Cincinnati in 1953, two years prior to becoming a member of the LaSalle Quartet in 1955.

[10] Jeanne Rosenblum Kirstein was a concert pianist from New York who had won the Naumburg Prize and the Young Artists award. She was a passionate advocate of contemporary piano music and among other things gave the world premiere of Gunther Schuller's piano concerto with the Cincinnati Symphony under Max Rudolf in 1962.

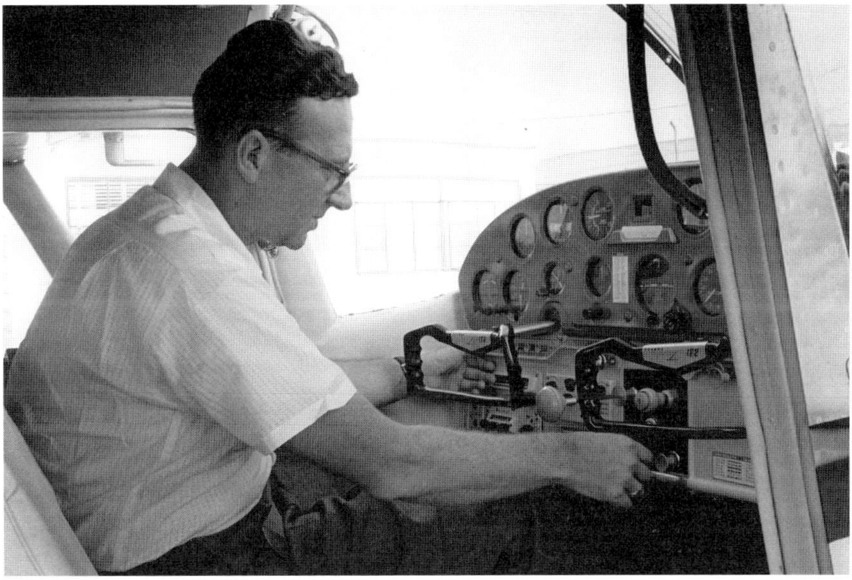

14 Jack Kirstein in his single engine airplane, Cincinnati, 1959

1955 to 1975, and that's not to be underestimated. He went along with everything, even modern works. But it was also an effort for him, and in the end he was happy to quit, he'd had enough. Eventually, sooner or later, they'd all had enough.

EL At the end of the 1973–1974 season he told us he would be leaving but would stay on until we'd found someone else.

RS That meant that you had enough time to find a replacement.

WL We did, but the problem was that we usually changed cellists at the same time as the Juilliard Quartet. That was already true in 1955, when Kapuscinski left us and Arthur Winograd left the Juilliard Quartet.[11] And then, just when Jack Kirstein announced his intention to quit, Claus Adam also left the Juilliard Quartet.[12] One of the cellists we found, Joel Krosnick, was snatched away from us by the Juilliards. We'd discovered Joel in Los Angeles. He came to Cincinnati and we agreed that he would join us in the quartet. But just then the Juilliard Quartet also had the brilliant idea to make him an offer.

[11] Arthur Winograd was a founding member of the Juilliard Quartet in 1946 and remained with them until 1955.

[12] Cellist Claus Adam, Winograd's successor, left the Juilliard Quartet at the end of the 1973–1974 season.

RS And highest bidder won.

WL Well, he wanted to go to New York rather than Cincinnati. We couldn't compete with that.

RS Too bad! What did Jack Kirstein do after he left the quartet?

WL He taught for a while longer, but in the end he wasn't at all well, he went into a nursing home and has since died.

RS How did you find Lee Fiser?[13]

WL It was easy to find Lee Fiser. He was a student of Lynn Harrell's in Cleveland, was in the orchestra there and in the circle of students around Jimmy Levine, who was conducting the student orchestra at the Cleveland Institute. Jimmy did a lot of fabulous things with this orchestra while he was George Szell's assistant in the Cleveland Orchestra. And Lynn Harrell was the principal cellist of the Cleveland Orchestra. But at the same time Lynn also taught the cello at the Cleveland Institute and played principal cello in the student orchestra, because he wanted to work with Jimmy Levine. A lot of players from the Cleveland Orchestra played in the student orchestra, which was a terrific ensemble! The concerts and opera performances with this student orchestra – you should have been there! What a standard of performance that was! And Lee Fiser was there as a young cellist. They also played a lot of chamber music at the Cleveland Institute – there's a recording of the Mendelssohn *Octet* with Lee Fiser and Lynn Harrell. Nothing but people like that! This whole approach to making music ultimately came from me by way of Jimmy Levine, who was brought up that way.[14] Which means that when Lee joined us in the quartet he already knew all about it. He knew how to work, he knew how to study a piece, he knew how to read a score, he could do all of it, so I didn't have to be concerned with any of it. On top of which he was a fabulous cellist.

RS I've made a list of everything the poor guy had to learn in his first year with you. It was pedagogically wonderful, you worked on pieces that were also new for the other members of the quartet. But for Lee Fiser there were twenty new works in his first season, 1975–1976, among them really difficult works, for instance the Lutosławski quartet,

13 Lee Fiser, b. Portland, Oregon, April 26, 1947, is on the faculty of the University of Cincinnati's College-Conservatory of Music.

14 James Levine had been a student of Levin's in Cincinnati since the age of ten; see also pp. 159–165.

the first and third Schoenberg quartets, Mozart's *Adagio and Fugue* K. 546, Beethoven's Opera 127, 132, 135, and the *Grosse Fuge* Opus 133, the Brahms quartet Opus 67, the second Zemlinsky quartet, the *Bagatelles* Opus 9 and the quartet Opus 28 by Webern, Stravinsky's *Three Pieces* for string quartet and, finally, Earle Brown's quartet. All of them difficult pieces. And in his second season, 1976–1977, there were eleven more new pieces, among them Beethoven's Opus 131, Schoenberg's fourth quartet, the Berg Opus 3, and Schubert's string quintet.

WL Well you know what? We didn't tell him about that in advance!

RS I should hope not! But how many months did it take him to learn all that?

WL We worked on one piece after another with him, starting already in the summer before his first season with us. And for Lee Fiser that was rather easy, since he was a quick study. And it wouldn't have worked otherwise. We couldn't take on anyone who wasn't a quick study, we were already too far along in our career. But don't forget, an orchestra player has to learn one or two new programs every week for thirty-six or more weeks a year! He simply must be able to do that! And some of those programs are insanely long and difficult! Professional musicians are used to that! Especially people who play in an orchestra! Unfortunately music students in Europe don't learn how to do that. This mollycoddling that everyone in Europe believes is a professional education is no such thing. That's why so often nothing comes of it.

EL Wasn't it the case that a cellist who auditioned for you had to be able to play Webern by heart?

WL No, he didn't have to, but if he was good, he could do it. Lee for instance sat down and played the *Bagatelles* Opus 9 and the *Five Pieces* Opus 5 by heart! He could do that, we couldn't!

RS Unbelievable! But for a non-musician, it all seems like an incredible mountain of repertory to have to learn!

WL And it is, too!

RS It wasn't just a matter of learning the pieces themselves, he also had to learn how the LaSalle Quartet wanted to play them.

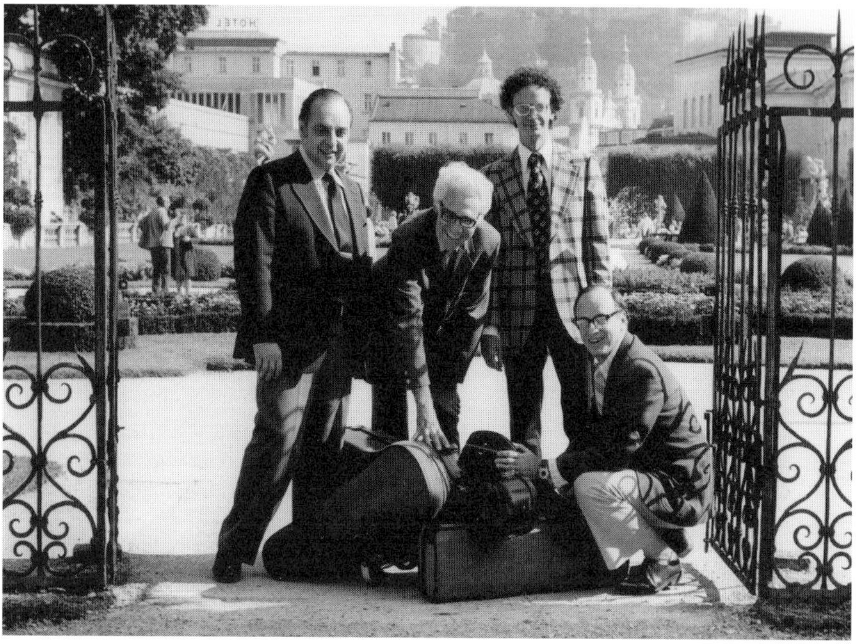

15 The LaSalle Quartet in Salzburg, 1976, Peter Kamnitzer and Walter Levin in front, Henry Meyer and Lee Fiser in back

WL That comes next! And of course that's something else entirely! But to be able to play the piece to begin with, that wasn't hard for him! He was a quick study and he was frustrated over and over again that we needed so much time to prepare something. When we learned new pieces, he came to the rehearsals and could already play them, and the rest of us still couldn't!

RS Would you say that the difference in generations had something to do with that?[15]

WL Yes, I would, that and an exceptional talent.

EL And something else too: Lee got from Jack Kirstein the parts with all the fingerings.

WL But he didn't use them very much! Lee didn't pay much attention to how Jack had played something. And he rarely marked fingerings in his own parts.

[15] Fiser was not yet thirty when he joined the LaSalle Quartet in 1976; the other members were already in their fifties.

RS Did he just make up his own fingerings on the spur of the moment?

WL Well, okay, for really difficult new works he made some notations. But if you look at his parts for Schoenberg's *Verklärte Nacht* or for the first Schoenberg quartet there are very few markings of his in them. He wasn't that type! And could he ever sight read! No matter what sort of part we put in front of him he could play it. That's the kind of musician he was, and for us that was ideal.

RS So in his case you didn't have to worry much about repertory?

WL No, not at all: zero. It just goes to show what a phenomenal musician Lee was and still is. For him our rehearsals were actually always too long! He didn't need that much rehearsal time. The rest of us did though!

9 The History of the LaSalle Quartet

Juilliard

ROBERT SPRUYTENBURG: After you got approval from William Schuman for a curriculum in string quartet as your major at Juilliard, your student quartet studied with the Juilliard Quartet. How did that work? Did the Juilliard Quartet teach as a group, that is, with all four members of the quartet present at your lessons, or were your quartet lessons with the members of the quartet individually?

WALTER LEVIN: Each member of the Juilliard Quartet taught a different piece. Initially we worked with one of the members on a Bartók quartet and with another member on Schubert's *Death and the Maiden*. And when we were far enough along to take on additional pieces, the other two members took over for the next two pieces. As we wanted to build up our repertory so as to be able to give concerts, new pieces were selected with an eye to what would make a good concert program.

RS Did the proposals for repertory come from you or from the Juilliard Quartet?

WL Both: we reviewed the choices together. I wanted to play Beethoven's Opus 59, Nr. 2, but they said it would probably be better to work on a quartet from Opus 18 to begin with, it wouldn't prevent us from getting to Opus 59, Nr. 2, later on. In any case I had already worked on Opus 59, Nr. 2, in Palestine, even though Gideon Strauss had advised me not to. So I knew the piece and had already marked up my part with fingerings and bowings, not very good ones, I must say, but all the same, you have to start somewhere.

RS You then used this method of instruction yourself: when young quartets came to you in Cincinnati, they were always taught by individual members of the LaSalle Quartet.

WL Yes, there's no other way to do it, in my opinion. There are quartets in which all four of the members teach jointly, together, but we never did that.

RS It seems that from the outset you were very taken with the incredible intensity with which the Juilliard Quartet played. Where did the Juilliard Quartet get this kind of intensity from, since there was no deep tradition of string quartet playing in America that was comparable to what had developed in 19th century Europe?[1]

WL It was their temperament. Both the cellist, Arthur Winograd, and the first violin, Robert Mann, were firebrands: they were incredibly intense individuals. It's hard to imagine another cellist as intense as Winograd, and so unrelenting – phenomenal! And also they'd studied with Eugene Lehner,[2] the violist of the Kolisch Quartet;[3] he added something of his

[1] The Kneisel Quartet (active 1885–1917) was the first professional string quartet of note in America; in 1912 they became the first ensemble in residence at the Institute of Musical Art (now Juilliard). The Flonzaley Quartet (1902–1928), the Zoellner Quartet (1903/4–1925), and the Berkshire Quartet (1916–1941) were prominent later American quartets. The Fine Arts Quartet and the Hollywood Quartet were formed in 1939, but string quartet playing in America only began to flourish after the Second World War. The Juilliard Quartet was founded in 1946; two of its members had prior connections to the European tradition: in the early 1940s Raphael Hillyer had played in the Stradivari Quartet alongside violist Eugene Lehner, who had been a member of the Kolisch Quartet, and cellist Arthur Winograd had played in Felix Galimir's second Galimir Quartet in New York, also in the early 1940s. The Juilliard Quartet was itself subsequently coached for a summer by Lehner. Hans Letz, with whom Levin initially studied at Juilliard, had played second violin in the Kneisel Quartet. For more on the history of the string quartet in America, see Levin's essay 'Immigrant Musicians and the American Chamber Music Scene 1930–1950,' in Reinhold Brinkmann and Christoph Wolff, eds., *Driven into Paradise: The Musical Migration from Nazi Germany to the United States* (Berkeley, 1999).

[2] Eugene Lehner (1906–1997) was a violin student of Jenö Hubay who also studied composition with Zoltán Kodály before joining the Kolisch Quartet as its violist in 1925. The quartet was stranded while on tour in the United States when war was declared on Germany on December 7, 1941; after the quartet disbanded in 1942, Lehner was invited by Koussevitzky to join the Boston Symphony, where he spent the remaining 39 years of his career.

[3] The Kolisch Quartet was originally founded in 1921 as the New Vienna String Quartet. Under the auspices of Schoenberg's Society for the Private Performances of Music the quartet dedicated itself equally to performing contemporary music as well as the classical quartet literature in accord with Schoenberg's theory of interpretation. Rudolf Kolisch and Fritz Rothschild alternated as first and second violins, Marcel Dick was the violist, and Joachim Stutschewsky the cellist. In 1927 the ensemble changed its name to the Kolisch Quartet; its members were Rudolf Kolisch, Felix Khuner (second violin), Eugene Lehner (viola), and Benar Heifetz (cello). Among the most important premieres given by the Kolisch Quartet were Bartók's fifth (April 8, 1935) and sixth (January 20, 1941) string quartets, Schoenberg's third (September 19, 1927) and fourth (January 8, 1937) string quartets, Alban Berg's *Lyric Suite* (January 8, 1927), and Webern's string quartet Opus 28 (September 22, 1938). The Kolisch Quartet was distinguished by the fact it played not only the classical repertory but also the modern works of the greatest degree of difficulty, like Berg's *Lyric Suite*, from memory. This was the result of their extremely thorough rehearsal work and had the advantage that the players could relate to one another much more spontaneously in performance. As part of their thorough rehearsal work the Kolisch Quartet always as a matter of principle studied its repertory as a whole, i.e., from the score and not from the parts. The Kolisch Quartet disbanded in 1942 in the United States. The Kolisch Quartet recorded Schoenberg's four quartets, the Schubert quartets in a minor, D. 804, and G major, and the *Quartettsatz* in c minor, D. 703, Mozart's string quartets K. 465, K. 575, K. 589, and 'Musical Joke' K. 522, Schumann's piano quartet Opus 47, and Hugo Wolf's 'Italian Serenade.' The Pro

own on top of that. And of course they studied the Schoenberg and Webern quartets via Lehner: they could never have come across these works by themselves. At their concert debut in Town Hall they played Webern's *Five Pieces* Opus 5, Beethoven's Opus 130 with the *Grosse Fuge*, and Haydn's Opus 77, Nr. 1 in G major. I was at the dress rehearsal and the concert. But the only real model for how the Juilliard Quartet played would have been the way Toscanini conducted orchestral music, but they had never heard him, since at that time they didn't go to concerts. Bobby Mann also didn't know a thing about opera, he didn't like operas. The first time Bobby ever heard *Don Giovanni* was when I took him with me to the opera. I had argued with him, asking him how he could possibly play Mozart without knowing his operas. So there was both give and take, he could learn something from me too. But the way the Juilliard Quartet played at that time was very important to us. You can still hear it in their early recordings of Bartók and Beethoven, when Winograd was their cellist.

RS Just when, exactly, was the LaSalle Quartet founded?

WL When I arrived in New York in February, 1946, I set about right away to start a quartet. The roster changed rather often while I was studying at Juilliard, but by 1947 we were already appearing as the LaSalle Quartet. Our official debut concert took place in December, 1947, at the Museum of the City of New York.[4] We gave some concerts in and around New York, also in New Jersey. Early in 1949 we played Beethoven's Opus 59, Nr. 3, and Bartók's sixth quartet at a house concert hosted by Stefan Wolpe in his apartment.[5] This was with Henry Meyer, who had joined us in the fall of 1948.

RS Did you already know Stefan Wolpe?

WL I met Stefan Wolpe by way of my friend Rosenberg. Wolpe had been his and Herbert Brün's teacher in Jerusalem but had already left for America when my family arrived in Palestine in December, 1938. When I left for New York seven years later, in December, 1945, Rosenberg gave me his string quartet, his first, to take to Wolpe in New York, which is how I met him. Rosenberg's quartet was lost in a fire in which Wolpe lost

Arte Quartet, already Quartet in Residence at the University of Wisconsin in Madison when Kolisch joined it as first violin in 1944 also recorded Berg's *Lyric Suite* in February, 1950.

4 On the program were Mozart's string quartets in D major, K. 155 and K. 575, as well as his c minor string quintet, K. 406.

5 The program also included Mozart's quartet in B♭ major, K. 589.

everything: all of his music, all of his own works, manuscripts, everything – terrible.[6] And Rosenberg didn't have another copy of his quartet, so it doesn't exist anymore. In the 1950s, we ran into Wolpe again in Darmstadt, where he was also teaching. But we never really had much contact with him, since we didn't play his pieces – it was only later on that we got interested in the direction his music was taking. But he was held in the highest regard as a musician and composer by people whose judgment I relied on, he was a very important reference for us, so we asked him if we could perhaps put on a house concert at his apartment, since he knew all the other musicians who you had to take seriously in New York as well.

RS So that was quite an elite audience.

WL It was a *very* elite audience: members of the NBC Symphony were there, and many quartet players, also Felix Galimir, and a few composers. It was a very important occasion for us. We had rehearsed the program with members of the Juilliard Quartet, and they were there too so they could judge the success of their teaching in an actual performance.

RS But this wasn't the occasion for which Robert Mann had to come up with a name for the quartet?

WL No, that had already happened. The Juilliard Quartet helped us get bookings in and around New York, since they couldn't always take on all the engagements they were offered. One day in 1946 Robert Mann got a message from the Juilliard office saying that a lady with a concert organization in New Jersey had called and wanted to invite the Juilliard Quartet to give a concert. Bobby was at home in his apartment on the corner of Broadway and LaSalle when he got the message from Juilliard and so he returned her call from there. He explained to her that the Juilliard Quartet was already booked on that date but that he could recommend a very good young quartet who would be delighted to play a concert for her. She wanted to know the name of this quartet. Bobby sensed that she wouldn't invite a no-name quartet, but at this point we still didn't have a name, so he would have to make one up on the spot. Desperate for inspiration, he looked out his window and saw the street signs on the opposite corner: Broadway and LaSalle, and promptly blurted out that we were the LaSalle Quartet. So that was that! It could

[6] Though the fire at Wolpe's Westbeth apartment in the winter of 1970 resulted in very substantial losses, including Wolpe's collection of paintings by his friends Willem de Kooning, Jackson Pollack, Mark Rothko, and others, a number of his manuscripts were subsequently salvaged.

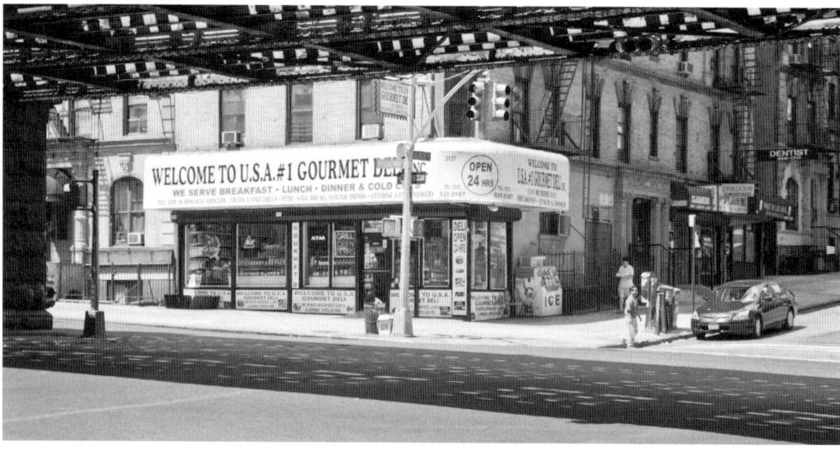

16 The southwest corner of Broadway and LaSalle Street in 2006; the store has changed hands many times since Robert Mann looked out the window of his apartment and saw the street sign for Broadway and LaSalle (on the pole near the center of the picture). The Juilliard School was at that time located just a block up the hill on the right.

have turned out badly though, as he might equally well have christened us the 'Broadway Quartet,' which wouldn't have been anywhere near as good a name for us!

Colorado College

RS How did it come about that after your studies at Juilliard you were engaged as the Quartet in Residence at Colorado College?

WL It was due to Carol Truax's initiative. Carol Truax was the head of the music department at Colorado College, a small liberal arts college in Colorado Springs with outstanding teachers and a music department that was tiny, but of the highest quality, of a caliber such as one can't even begin to imagine in Europe. And Carol Truax wasn't even a musician. She had come to Colorado decades ago because she had tuberculosis, just as in Europe one used to go to Davos. Colorado Springs is about 6,000 feet above sea-level and on account of its good, dry climate was a sanatorium for people with lung diseases. She came from New York, from the well-known Truax family. Her father was a famous jurist and judge and a great lover of music. They had one of those great New York households that cultivated the arts and where there were constantly dinner parties to which the likes of Caruso and Chaliapin were invited – all the great singers went there. So from childhood on Carol Truax knew lots of artists, had always been surrounded by artists, and had a flair for getting along with them. When she took over the music department at this school in Colorado she invited them to join her there. As an organizer she was absolutely peerless.

EVI LEVIN: She also wrote a cookbook full of nothing but anecdotes about Caruso and the other people she'd met at home: *The Sixty Minute Chef*– a best seller.

WL She was an incredible woman. Her faculty included the composer Roy Harris[7] and his wife Johana [sic], a great pianist.[8] When the two of them decided to leave the college Carol Truax said to herself that with the Harris' $10,000 salary she could engage a young string quartet, if she could find one. The four players could teach four courses at a minimum, they could play concerts and get the name of the college better known, and they could try out new works by the school's composition students. She then turned to her friend Thor Johnson,[9] who taught in the summers at Colorado College, and asked him whether he knew any young quartets. Thor Johnson was someone we already knew at Juilliard, where he conducted the orchestra along with Edgar Schenkman. Later on he was the conductor of the Cincinnati Symphony while we were there. He told her to come to New York and he and Virgil Thomson,[10] who they both knew, would help her to find such a quartet.

There was only one such quartet, namely us. We had always worked together very intensely, with the aim of one day getting positions for the four of us as a quartet. Shortly before graduating from Juilliard we played a concert for the League of Composers at Times Hall[11] in New York, a very progressive concert organization: every important composer in America was a member of it. At that time Aaron Copland was its director. We had been invited to play a piece for string quartet by Guido Turchi, an Italian composer, it was called *Concerto Breve (in*

7 Roy Harris (1898–1979) was an American composer who made a substantial contribution to the development of a specifically American style of symphonic music.

8 Beula Duffey was a young Canadian pianist whom Roy Harris met at summer school at Juilliard in 1934 and married in 1936. Thereafter he called her 'Johana.'

9 The American conductor Thor Johnson (1913–1975) studied conducting with Bruno Walter, Hermann Abendroth, and Serge Koussevitzky. He conducted the Juilliard school orchestra 1946–1947 and the Cincinnati Symphony 1947–1958. He conducted many lesser known works, and led a highly regarded performance of Schoenberg's *Gurre Lieder* in 1953. Johnson conducted the premieres of some 120 works, half of which he had commissioned himself.

10 Virgil Thomson (1896–1989) was an American composer and music critic.

11 The New York Times Hall on West 44th Street. Built in 1912 as The Little Theater, it was owned by the New York Times 1931–1958 and used primarily for conferences (the back of the old New York Times building is just across the street).

memoriam Béla Bartók).[12] That was a momentous concert for us, because Carol Truax was sitting in the audience. She did in fact engage us, and starting in September, 1949, we were the Quartet in Residence at Colorado College in Colorado Springs. Evi went there that summer to scout out just what this Colorado College was and whether she would really want go there with me. For my part, I was very much in favor of her coming along.

EVI LEVIN: But I was a New Yorker, and for me the idea of going to a resort and spa town in the mountains was simply dreadful![13]

WL But she did make the trip out there and discovered that the summer school faculty was simply incredible. Eduard Steuermann[14] was there, the pianist of the Schoenberg school and one of the best piano teachers in the world. Evi subsequently took lessons from him. And composition was being taught by a not wholly unknown composer by the name of Paul Hindemith. One of the violin and chamber music teachers was Louis Persinger, the famous teacher of the young Yehudi Menuhin. Musicology and music history was taught by the great musicologist from Indiana University, Willi Apel, who had previously been a professor at Harvard University,[15] a medievalist who had written the great textbooks on medieval music, all of them still in print, and who was also the editor of the Harvard Dictionary of Music, all in all a very famous man. After we had moved to Colorado Springs, we were at a school tea together once and I looked at him and thought to myself that I'd seen that man somewhere before. All of a sudden I realized he was my music teacher from the Theodor Herzl school in Berlin! He asked me whether I'd been one of those scoundrels who had gone out to play soccer, or had I stayed inside for his classes? I had stayed. The painter Mark Rothko was also in Colorado Springs, at the Fine Arts Center, but at that time none of us had any idea of the importance of what he and his contemporaries were about. So it was a phenomenal faculty at Colorado College, and even today it is one of the best small fine arts colleges in America. Evi thought it was terrific, so she came with me to Colorado Springs.

[12] The concert was on April 10, 1949. The piece by Guido Turchi was composed in 1947.

[13] At that time the population of Colorado Springs was about 45,000.

[14] Eduard Steuermann (1892–1964) was the pianist in Schoenberg's Society for Private Performance. He had played in the premiere of *Pierrot Lunaire* in 1912 and also in many of the premieres of Schoenberg's later works. He later taught at Darmstadt, Juilliard, and the Philadelphia Conservatory of Music.

[15] About Willi Apel see also p. 9.

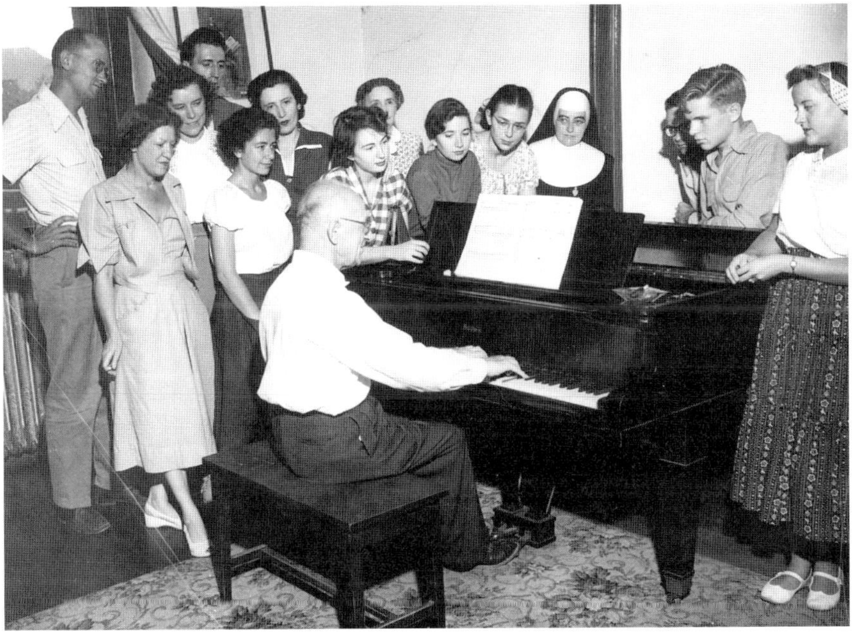

17 Piano class Eduard Steuermann, Colorado Springs Summer School, 1949 (Evi Levin standing to the left of Steuermann)

RS You weren't married yet?

WL No, but that happened rather quickly. The most important thing for Evi was the chance to do what she'd always wanted to do, namely to study at a college or university. And here was the opportunity.

EL When I went to register, I made my way through the various bureaucracies and finally got to the cashier. In front of me at the window was a student who was just about to pay her tuition when the cashier said to her she didn't need to pay, because she was the wife of a faculty member! Just what I needed to hear! I took my registration forms right home and told Walter straight out that we had to get married immediately so I could get free tuition! We rounded up Peter Kamnitzer and Henry Meyer as witnesses and went to the Colorado Springs City Hall, where I got a certificate with angels on it that changed my name from Marcov to Levin. I then happily registered for classes as Evi Levin.

RS What did you study?

EL Music history, music theory, piano, and all the subjects that were required for a Bachelor of Arts in music. I had the very good fortune that on Paul

Hindemith's recommendation David Kraehenbuehl[16] had been hired at Colorado College, he was my teacher in music history and theory.

RS Who was David Kraehenbuehl?

WL He was an exceptionally gifted composer who had studied with Hindemith at Yale – a fantastic teacher and a phenomenal, brilliant musician, a real genius. At Colorado College his approach to teaching music was just like William Schuman's approach in the 'literature and materials of music' curriculum he had instituted at Juilliard, broadly uniting study of the literature of music with the historical events surrounding its composition.

EL 'Integrated curriculum' is what this approach was called at Colorado College.

RS What was this curriculum like, actually?

EL For instance, when we were studying music in the middle ages and learned about Gregorian chant with its parallel fifths and its prohibition against most of the other intervals, we sang Gregorian chants and had to compose songs in the Gregorian manner ourselves. And we had to look for paintings, for instance, paintings of monks singing, from that period. We also studied its literature, looking for descriptions of society, how men and women dressed, whether nobles or their attendants, and what the political systems were in the different countries. We went through the whole history of music chronologically with reference to music theory, harmony, counterpoint, and the general history of each epoch.

So the integrated curriculum was a wide-ranging, multi-disciplinary system at Colorado College that unfortunately collapsed after a few years, for want of teachers who were qualified to teach it. David Kraehenbuehl was one of the few who had this breadth of knowledge and could teach it – and I was one of the lucky few who were able to profit from it for three whole years. I finished my studies *cum laude* with an academic Bachelor of Arts and a major in music. But I stayed on for another year while the quartet was engaged at Colorado Springs, and taught in the German department at Colorado College. And for the summer session in 1950 I was engaged by the University of Colorado in Boulder to play the accordion in outdoor classes, or to play German, French, Italian, and Spanish songs at foreign language events.

[16] David Kraehenbuehl (1923–1997), pianist and composer, was regarded by Hindemith as his most gifted student. In 1953, when Hindemith decided to return to Europe, he asked Kraehenbuehl to be his successor on the faculty at Yale. In 1960 Kraehenbuehl joined the faculty of the New School for Music in Princeton.

RS Didn't you also learn to play the viola at this time?

EL That's right. In my first year at Colorado College I began to take lessons with Peter Kamnitzer. I was eager to get to know first hand the problems that Walter was so intensely involved with in the quartet and that as a pianist I had very little inkling of. I got far enough along with my viola studies to be able to play in chamber music ensembles, which had really been my goal all along. Afterwards I gave up the viola.

RS How was the regular faculty, compared with the stellar summer school?

WL The regular music faculty at Colorado College consisted almost exclusively of remarkably young people in their late twenties and early thirties, all of them with all the élan and curiosity you could wish for. We were greeted as long lost friends and immediately integrated into the whole curriculum. We played in their classes, and an important function of our quartet was to perform pieces by David Kraehenbuehl's students.

RS In Colorado Springs you also performed a hilarious piece by Kraehenbuehl, his variations on *Pop goes the Weasel.*

WL We commissioned that piece from him for the children's concerts we gave in Colorado Springs. The theme is based on a well-known American folk song.

RS But what does the title mean: 'Pop goes the Weasel'?

WL Weasels emerge from underground all of a sudden, they 'pop up.'

RS Which is represented by the four instruments playing a unison pizzicato!

WL Exactly. We played the piece in a lecture-recital. But it's quite long and involved, and we only played a few parts of it.

RS I think it's an extremely witty piece, the variations in the styles of Bach, Haydn, Beethoven, Mendelssohn, Stravinsky, and Schoenberg are very clever parodies that really hit the nail on the head. And the audience is laughing all the time.[17]

WL Isn't it? It's simply brilliant!

[17] Kraehenbuehl had a special gift for parody: already at the age of twelve he composed a sonata for violin and piano with movements in the styles of Brahms, Chopin, Beethoven, and Debussy.

RS Absolutely. For instance how the theme of Schubert's *Military March*[18] transitions into the theme of *Pop goes the Weasel*, and the Schoenberg send-up which you tell me has all the notes in *Pop goes the Weasel.*

Speaking of Schoenberg, apparently the plan was to have him come to the Colorado Springs summer school as a member of the faculty in 1951. Was that your doing?

WL Yes, of course. In our very first season at Colorado College we had the third Schoenberg quartet on one of our concert programs, and I'd always wanted to meet Schoenberg and get to know him. Since Colorado College had such an advanced music department, I had the idea that this would be a wonderful opportunity to invite him. That's what we proposed to Carol Truax, and she thought it was a great idea. She wrote to him immediately, and he agreed to come. He would give a course on his quartets, and we would play them. I hadn't given much thought to what it would mean to learn the other three Schoenberg quartets in time for the following summer. God forbid, it would have been awful. But nothing came of it. He had confirmed that he was coming, he was listed in the course catalogue, but then he got sick and had to cancel. I'm sorry to say I never met Arnold Schoenberg.

RS In Colorado Springs you not only played quartet repertory but also took part in other concerts, some of which were recorded. For instance you have a recording of Haydn's *Sinfonia Concertante* for violin, cello, oboe, and bassoon.[19]

WL Yes, Peter Kamnitzer arranged it for string quartet. The orchestra is somewhat dilettantish, but the quartet played very beautifully. That was a real pleasure! I think it's a terrific piece, first class Haydn in high spirits! Toscanini also conducted it.

RS What orchestra did you play it with?

WL The Colorado Springs Symphony, conducted by Frederick Boothroyd, an Englishman who had come to Colorado Springs because he had tuberculosis. He had been a choral director, was the organist at a church in Colorado Springs, and had founded and conducted this orchestra. When we arrived in Colorado Springs they told us that we absolutely had to take over the first chair positions in the orchestra. But we only played with them in the beginning. We

[18] Nr. 1 in D major, D. 733, for piano four hands.

[19] The performance took place on March 8, 1951.

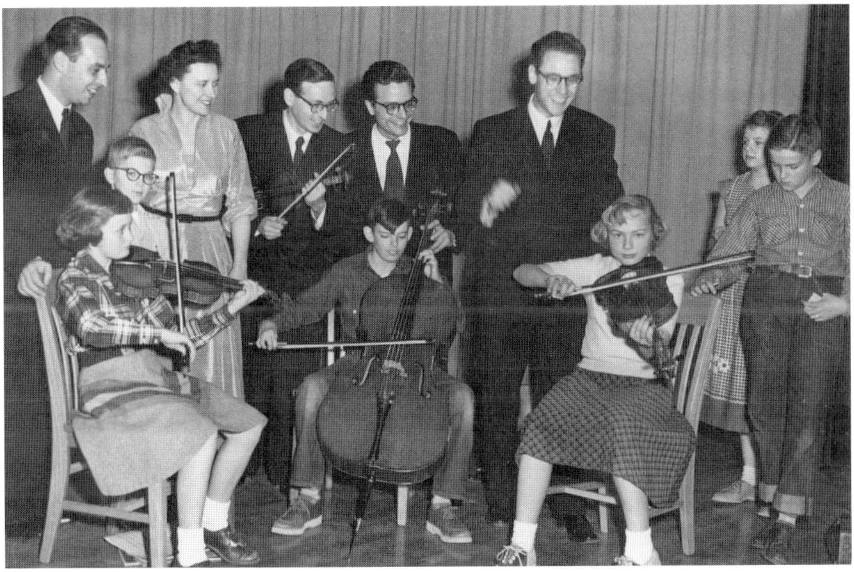

18 Frances Bible with the LaSalle Quartet at a children's concert in Colorado Springs, 1952

accompanied Kirsten Flagstad[20] in the *Liebestod* from *Tristan und Isolde*, and once we played with the pianist William Kapell.[21] But to have played on the same stage as Kirsten Flagstad, the greatest Wagner singer of the century, that was really something! In 1948 I was only twenty-four years old!

EL And with Rose Bampton.[22]

WL And with the mezzo-soprano Francis Bible.[23] The very best were only just good enough for the people in Colorado Springs.

RS You also have recordings of a Handel trio sonata and of Bartók's duets for two violins.

[20] Kirsten Flagstad (1895–1962), was regarded by many as the greatest dramatic soprano of the first half of the 20th century. In 1950 she gave the premiere of Richard Strauss' *Four Last Songs*.

[21] William Kapell (1922–1953) is held by many to be one of the most gifted pianists of his generation. Already famous in his twenties, he was killed in an airplane crash just south of San Francisco as he was returning from a tour of Australia.

[22] Rose Bampton (1907–2007), sang Leonore in *Fidelio* under Toscanini, among other roles. Schoenberg, in whose *Gurrelieder* she also appeared, called her three octave range a 'miracle.'

[23] Francis Bible (1919–2001) was a leading singer at New York City Opera 1948–1977. She was best known for her trouser roles: her breakthrough was as Octavian in Richard Strauss' *Rosenkavalier* in 1949.

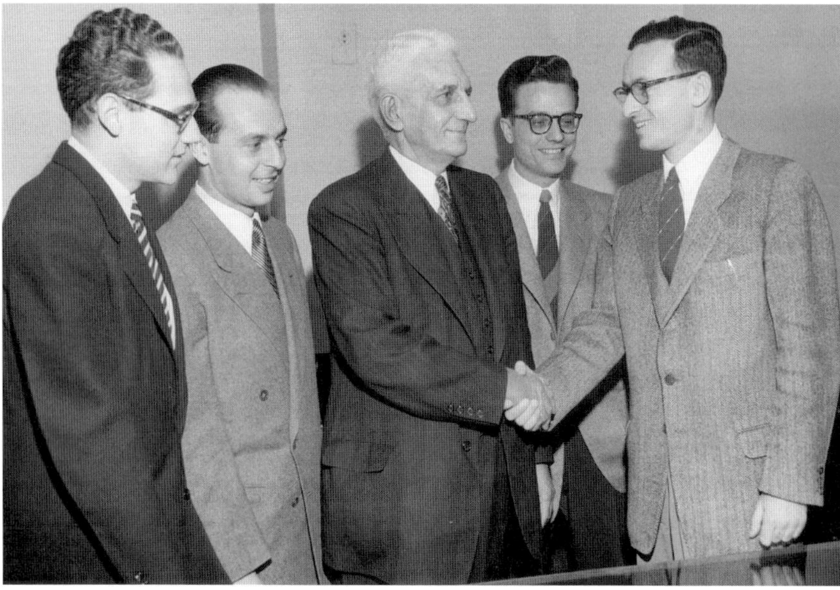

19 The LaSalle Quartet with Frederick Schmidt, President of the Cincinnati College of Music, March, 1953

WL Yes, Henry Meyer and I played them. David Kraehenbuehl played the piano in the Handel trio sonata.[24]

RS That must have been a very exciting time in Colorado Springs, since you were involved in so many different aspects of musical life there and could try out so many different things.

WL Indeed!

Cincinnati

RS In your last year at Colorado Springs you went on tour and played in two concerts in Cincinnati.[25] There's a photograph from March, 1953, of the LaSalle Quartet with Frederick Schmidt, who was the President of the College of Music. How did these concerts in Cincinnati come about?

WL Besides Frederick Schmidt, who was a wealthy real estate broker in Cincinnati, there was also a Fred Smith – no relation – at the College

[24] On March 21, 1951.

[25] On March 30 and 31, 1953. The programs included Haydn's Opus 77, Nr. 2, Tibor Serly's arrangements from Bartók's *Mikrokosmos* (March 30 concert only) and Robert Mann's *Five Pieces for String Quartet* (March 31 concert only).

of Music, a very famous pioneer in radio broadcasting[26] who at that time was also Director of the college and its chief adminstrator – what the English would call its managing director. Fred Smith's daughter wanted to study violin with Galamian, and for that reason he came with her to Meadowmount in the summer of 1952. All through our four years at Colorado Springs we took quartet lessons with Galamian every summer and worked on repertory for the next season. We always stayed in Mrs. Burpee's cottage and that summer Fred Smith stayed right across from us. Since Galamian didn't want to take Smith's daughter as a student, he recommended that she study with me instead. So Fred came over to our cottage to see me and asked me where I would be teaching. I told him that at present we were in Colorado Springs, and he asked me if I would like to come to Cincinnati, he had a college there.

RS Was your concert in Cincinnati actually the occasion on which you were offered a contract to become the Quartet in Residence at the College of Music?

WL It was. And I had to negotiate the contract with my jaw wired shut, I'd broken both sides of my jaw skiing in Aspen when the mountain was already iced over – I was determined to make one last run in spite of the ice, and a broken jaw was the result. In those days they wired your teeth together so that your jaw would stay put in exactly the right place – two whole months wired up like that! I couldn't eat properly, I could only drink fluids. Well, that at least was good for losing weight. And also good for teaching, I looked really ferocious, I didn't have to make any additional effort in that direction. And in this condition I went to Cincinnati with the quartet and also negotiated our contract.

RS There probably wasn't much to negotiate, since everyone would have been afraid of the 'Ironman.'

EL To give this long episode a happy ending, we said 'tomorrow we're going to celebrate your being able to eat normally again.' And I bought a huge steak, at least an inch and a half thick. So Walter went to the dentist, and when he got back home I cooked this magnificent steak, but he could scarcely open his mouth! After six weeks of being wired shut there were no muscles left in his jaw!

[26] David Frederick Smith (1888–1976) developed the hit radio program 'The March of Time' in the 1930s and later won an Academy Award for his 'March of Time' newsreels. In 1941 he was appointed Director of the College of Music in Cincinnati (which had launched the first college program in radio broadcasting in 1936), a position he held until 1956.

WL It was one of the few occasions when I didn't open my mouth . . .

RS And your family had rarely enjoyed a steak so much.

WL It really was a big disappointment, let me tell you. I've hardly ever looked forward so much to having a steak. It was another two weeks or so before I could open my mouth again, I had to exercise it!

RS What were the terms of your contract with the College of Music?

WL It stipulated that we teach our instruments and also teach chamber music, that we would give a series of concerts at the college, three per season to begin and later four. In addition we retained the freedom to go on tour. But I never gave Fred Smith's daughter lessons.

RS It's really a remarkable coincidence that the LaSalle Quartet settled down in Cincinnati, since the upper reaches of the Ohio River were discovered by Sieur de LaSalle.[27] Was this the same LaSalle that the quartet was named for?

WL We were named for LaSalle Street in New York. I don't know if it was the same LaSalle.[28] There was also once a beautiful General Motors car called the LaSalle.

RS When you took up your position as Quartet in Residence at the College of Music in Cincinnati in September, 1953, you were evidently welcomed with open arms, as there is a photograph of the LaSalle Quartet with Rembert Wurlitzer and William Albers, a patron of the LaSalle Quartet, and four Stradivarius instruments. Were these instruments literally waiting for you there when you got to Cincinnati?

WL Yes, they really were. Rembert Wurlitzer was an important stringed instrument dealer in New York and a friend of ours, we had gotten to know him while we were at Juilliard.[29] And now we were going to be in his hometown, Cincinnati. One of the great patrons of the College of Music where we were engaged was William Albers, the owner of a supermarket chain in Cincinnati. He invited us to make our formal debut at his immense villa, Alberly Manor, and he would invite everybody

[27] René Robert Cavelier, Sieur de LaSalle (1643–1687).

[28] LaSalle Street in Manhattan was named for Jean Baptiste de la Salle, the 17th century founder of the Christian Brothers, organizers of nearby Manhattan College.

[29] For more on Rembert Wurlitzer and the LaSalle Quartet's instruments, see pp. 139–143.

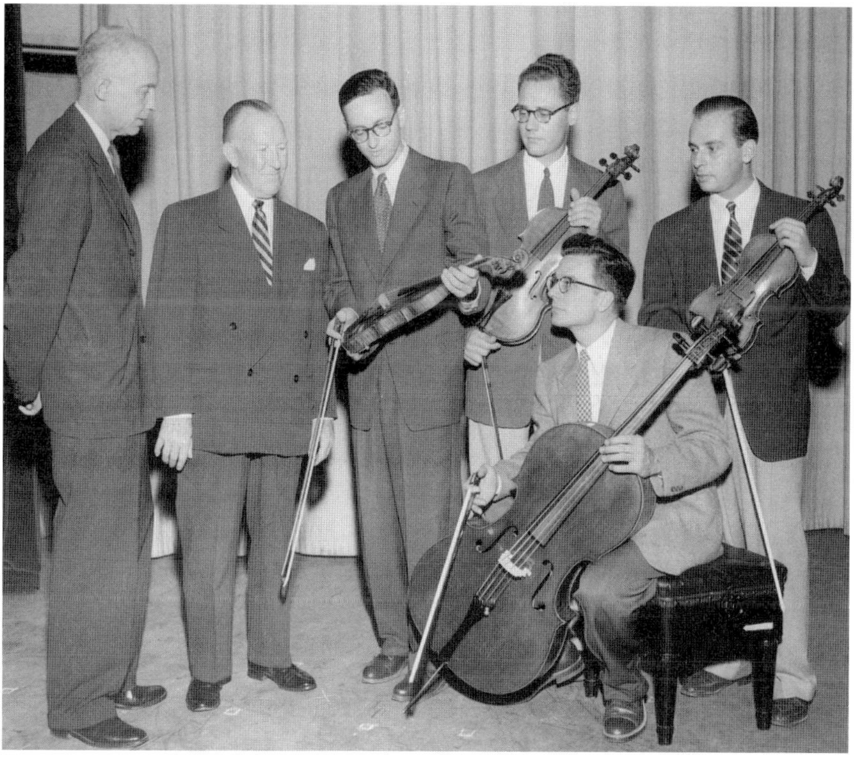

20 Rembert Wurlitzer, William Albers and the LaSalle Quartet with the Stradivarius instruments, Cincinnati, September, 1953

important in Cincinnati to come, so he could introduce us to them. Fred Smith, who was well-known as a broadcaster in New York, spoke with Rembert sometime prior to this event and told him that the LaSalle Quartet was going to be the Quartet in Residence at the college, they were having a big debut event for us here, and couldn't he come and bring along a couple of decent instruments? In response to which he brought us the quartet of Stradivarius instruments for our Cincinnati debut concert.[30]

RS That really was an incredible reception! Only in America!

WL Only in America. Our whole career, everything we are and everything we became was only possible in America.

RS Such generosity! But of course very high expectations come along with it!

[30] On September 20, 1953. Mozart's quartet in D major, K. 155, and the Ravel quartet were on the program.

WL Of course! And so later on we also got the Amati instruments, also with the help of the same Rembert Wurlitzer, who always kept us in mind until the moment arrived to put us in touch with Gerald Warburg.[31]

RS Who were the main sponsors of the LaSalle Quartet in Cincinnati?

WL The principal sponsors of the LaSalle Quartet were William Albers and Schmidt Real Estate – Frederick Schmidt was a successful real estate broker and President of the College of Music. We gradually got to know a lot of people who supported us in Cincinnati, descendants of the German-Jewish immigration of a hundred years before, not the emigration caused by the Nazis but the earlier one, which had gotten itself established by now. They were the great sponsors, and they weren't only Jewish: Albers and Schmidt weren't Jews but Catholics. There were two schools: the College of Music was purely Catholic and the Conservatory of Music was purely Protestant. The College of Music brought the LaSalle Quartet to Cincinnati when it was still a rather small and modest school.[32] Later the two schools merged and eventually were taken over by the University of Cincinnati as its music department – thus the rather complicated name: College-Conservatory of Music of the University of Cincinnati. But it became one of the most important schools in America for quartets. We were there for forty years, and we made good use of this time.

RS One of the LaSalle Quartet's patrons in Cincinnati was Ferdinand Donath.

WL Yes. When we arrived in Cincinnati we looked for a doctor and people recommended Ferdinand Donath, a wonderful human being. He came from Vienna and was a student of Sigmund Freud's. We became exceptionally good friends with him right away, as there weren't so many people like us in Cincinnati. In the first place he was a fanatical lover of music and literature, an expert on Karl Kraus, with a huge German library. And we spoke German, despite the fact that we were not all that much older than his children!

EL And his wife, Anni Schnitzler, was Arthur Schnitzler's niece.

WL Indeed, that was the milieu he came from in Vienna. He had also been a founding member of Schoenberg's Society for Private Performances. I inherited his membership card from his wife.

31 For Gerald Warburg see pp. 141–142.

32 In 1953–1954, the LaSalle Quartet's first year at the College of Music, the school's enrollment numbered about 500 students; ongoing financial difficulties led to the merger with the Cincinnati Conservatory in 1955, and then to the combined College-Conservatory of Music being absorbed by the University of Cincinnati in 1962.

RS But he was also a founding member of a Group for Private Performances in Cincinnati.

WL Yes, Donath started it in response to what happened with our first concert as the new Quartet in Residence at the College of Music in Cincinnati. Fred Smith had asked us what we were going to play, and I told him it would be Schubert's *Quartettsatz*, the fifth Bartók quartet, and Beethoven's quartet Opus 18, Nr. 5. His response was to say that this wouldn't work, we couldn't play Bartók here, nobody would come to the concert, nobody in Cincinnati was interested in modern music. I told him we weren't going to give a single concert without having such a piece on the program. We got our way, but we had to announce that on the Sunday afternoon two days before the concert we would give a lecture-recital on the Bartók quartet, an introductory lecture with excerpts and other musical examples played by us, after which we would play through the whole piece. As a matter of fact thirty or forty people came to this lecture and it was a big success. The news spread like wildfire that there was a young quartet that played new music brilliantly, and the concert two days later was practically sold out. Fred Smith was taken completely by surprise, and after that we could program whatever we wanted.

Ferdinand Donath also came to this concert and told us that an introduction like the one we gave for the fifth Bartók quartet was something we were going to have to do for all the new pieces we were going to play. He reminded us that this was what Schoenberg had done in Vienna and said it was what we had to do here in Cincinnati too. We started a private club, the 'Sunday Group,' and its members took turns hosting our introductory lecture-recitals in their homes on the Sundays before our Tuesday concerts. We gave these lecture-recitals for the Sunday Group all the way through to the very end of our career. Even today I'm still giving such lecture-recitals. Cincinnati had been a cultural center from very early on in its history, which is what made it possible to establish such a group, the members of which simply wanted to get to know new pieces of music, to learn something they hadn't known before.

And what a broad spectrum of interests it represented: businessmen, attorneys, university professors, doctors, on and on, not musicians, just residents of the city who were interested in music, something on the order of forty or fifty people. Year in and year out they listened to the new works that we presented in our lecture-recitals and got to know many pieces here in America long before they were ever played again in Europe. We played Adorno's music in America as early as 1986, and he's only now being rediscovered as a composer.[33] We also called attention to the English translations of Adorno's writings.

We presented not only new works but also complex works from the classical repertory, for instance the late Beethoven quartets, about which music lovers often have a lot of misconceptions and which sound very different from what one is used to hearing when played correctly. For instance, prior to our third concert at the College of Music we analyzed and played Beethoven's third Rasumovsky quartet, Opus 59, Nr. 3, in which Beethoven demands an extremely virtuosic tempo for the fugue in the finale, a tempo seldom taken in performance.[34] The Sunday Group also established a LaSalle Foundation, to which members of the group donated the money that for decades made it possible for us to undertake interesting projects and commission new works. Thanks to this foundation we were also able to invite composers to Cincinnati who weren't so well known in America in the 1950s: Karlheinz Stockhausen, Pierre Boulez, and John Cage all came to Cincinnati at our invitation.

RS How did Cincinnati become such an important center of culture?

WL Cincinnati is just one of many well-established cultural centers in the American Midwest. St. Louis, Cleveland, and of course Chicago are among the others. Those are big midwestern cities that were also important destinations for German immigrants in the 19th century. That's also why Cincinnati, like St. Louis and Milwaukee, is such a beer-drinking city. And of course the German immigrants brought their culture with them. On top of that, in all these cities there were big Jewish communities, especially in Cincinnati, which have always been particularly oriented to culture. When the new wave of immigrants arrived in the 1930s they were met with open arms by the established Jewish families who granted them the affidavit, the financial guarantee, so that they could start life over again. Even in our day Jewish immigrants were arriving from Russia, and they too were accepted just as readily. This sense of community, of responsibility, is very typical of the Jewish institutions that keep the Jewish people together, otherwise they couldn't have survived for as long as they have. That was very much the case as regards culture.

The Cincinnati May Festival,[35] the oldest regular choral festival in America, and one where German choral literature was performed,

[33] For Levin's discussion of Adorno as a composer, see pp. 322–326.

[34] The concert itself was on March 9, 1954. Mozart's quartet in D major, K. 499, and Leon Kirchner's first quartet were also on the program.

[35] Cincinnati's May Festival developed out of its choral festivals, which date back to the 1840s, and by the 1870s were the most important music festivals in the Midwest. They

was founded in 1873 by Theodore Thomas,[36] a great musician who had played in the world premiere of Brahms' Trio Opus 8.[37] He also wrote a very interesting autobiography.[38] Along with New York, Chicago, and San Francisco, Cincinnati had one of the first great symphony orchestras in America. And you can see the kind of conductors they engaged. Both Leopold Stokowski's and Fritz Reiner's first engagements were in Cincinnati, also Eugène Ysaÿe conducted in Cincinnati for many years.[39] And really great conductors were constantly invited, for instance Richard Strauss and Arturo Toscanini. Cincinnati also has the second oldest opera company in the United States.[40] And the first musicians' union in North America was founded in Cincinnati.[41]

So there were people in Cincinnati for whom culture was important. There were also very well-to-do industrial families who were also very taken with culture: the Wurlitzers for instance were a native Cincinnati family who financed chamber music. Chamber music in America was not a business, it was organized by private organizations, that is by chamber music lovers, in private homes. The Wurlitzer concert series is to this day a private business that invites quartets from all over the world. So Cincinnati was a cultural center for music from very early on.

were permanently established as the May Festival in 1873, with Theodore Thomas as their first music director. Originally held every two years, the May Festival has been an annual event since 1967.

36 The German-born conductor Theodore Thomas (1835–1905) was the first American conductor of real stature. He co-founded an important chamber music ensemble in New York in 1855; he also played in the New York Philharmonic. In 1862 he founded his own orchestra, which toured extensively in the United States and Canada. He conducted the New York Philharmonic from 1877–1891, the year in which he founded the Chicago Symphony Orchestra, of which he was Music Director until his death.

37 In New York, on November 17, 1855, with William Mason, piano, and Carl Bergmann, cello. The work as Brahms originally composed it when he was twenty was not a success, neither with the critics nor with Brahms himself; in 1889 he revised it so extensively that the work as we know it today is an almost entirely new piece.

38 Theodore Thomas, *A Musical Autobiography* (New York, 1964).

39 The Cincinnati Symphony Orchestra was organized in 1895 as the successor to the Cincinnati Orchestra, which had been founded in 1872. Leopold Stokowski conducted the orchestra 1909–1912; he invited both Busoni and Rachmaninoff to perform as soloists. Eugène Ysaÿe conducted the orchestra 1918–1922, and Fritz Reiner 1922–1931; in Cincinnati Reiner premiered Bartók's first piano concerto with the composer as soloist.

40 The Cincinnati Opera was organized in 1920, New York's Metropolitan Opera was founded in 1880.

41 The American Federation of Musicians Local 1 was founded in Cincinnati in 1881 as the Cincinnati Musicians Association. All four members of the LaSalle Quartet belonged to it.

RS But not only for music, also for other art forms.

WL Yes, it's still that today. Recently we went to the new Contemporary Arts Center, a very avant-garde building by the architect Zaha Hadid. The Cincinnati Art Museum is still a private institution, even today.

EL In 2004 we were in Riehen, at the Beyeler Foundation, where the Cincinnati Mural by Joan Miró was on exhibit. That was the first time it had left Cincinnati.

WL That's another typical example. The Emerys, whose children we knew quite well and who gave us a lot of support, had many properties in Cincinnati and among others had built the Hotel Terrace Plaza and invited Miró and Calder to decorate it. In 1947 that was quite out of the ordinary, as it would have been in Europe too. But the European view of American culture is marked by an arrogance that is scarcely to be believed. You have to have been there, you have to have seen for yourself what all is possible in America, and you have to have experienced the extraordinarily high level of the great American universities and the generosity of the people and their openness to good ideas.

RS It really is the land of infinite possibilities.

WL Yes, and it still is! In America if you have a good idea, you can always make something of it, and you'll find people who will support you: the LaSalle Quartet is the best example of that. And this is as true today as it was back then. We had no trouble at all getting financial support for the ensembles that the LaSalle Quartet wanted to invite to Cincinnati, nobody said that they had to talk to so and so first. It's taken for granted that if you see someone who knows what they're about and is achieving something in their field then you have to support them without a lot of questioning. In Europe this attitude is all too rare. I also get very upset about the notion that America is backwards and naive. For instance, during the war a group of people lived in Los Angeles that you could scarcely imagine being in Europe at that time: Thomas Mann, Franz Werfel, Theodor Adorno, Lion Feuchtwanger, and composers like Stravinsky, Schoenberg, Eisler, and Ernst Toch. And they got together in the evenings to discuss things. Jascha Heifetz, Emanuel Feuermann, Artur Rubinstein, and Gregor Piatigorsky lived there too.

You have to really know America, and you have to have lived there for a good while, to know what all is possible there. You've seen it yourself: The Steans Institute for Young Artists at Ravinia is a typical example. That was Edward Gordon's idea,[42] and he was able to get sponsors enthusiastic about it, including some big bankers, so that there were unlimited funds for establishing the Institute along the lines of the most up to date knowledge: you just can't imagine anything better. And what Evi experienced at Tanglewood: unbelievable, how they supported young people with scholarships there! I simply must say that in this respect I was then and I am now still an ardent American, and the prejudices against America upset me a lot. Of course there are negatives, that goes without saying, you run into that everywhere. But I do find it very important also to say what there is that's positive about America.

A career like the LaSalle's would not have been possible in Europe. And why did the Alban Berg Quartet and Pražak Quartet and all the other younger quartets have to come to Cincinnati for their education in quartet playing? Because there was nobody in Europe who could do that! That's why we're so closely associated with America and with Cincinnati in particular. To engage a young quartet like us, right out of school, to teach at a progressive school like Colorado College: who would ever have such an idea in Europe? We had no experience at all! Carol Truax had only her instinct to rely on when she engaged us. We were just four students from a famous school, nothing more than that.

RS That's the American pioneering attitude: Give them a chance!

WL Exactly, really well put!

RS And of course for a young quartet these expectations were a great challenge!

WL Of course! Even today this kind of generosity is still a part of American life, for instance as regards donations. We experienced that ourselves at the College-Conservatory of Music. One day the director, Jack Watson, got a call from an oil millionaire in Texas, Frank M. Starling. His wife had just died and she had taken violin lessons for a few years at the College of Music. He wanted to make a donation in her memory – a large amount.[43]

[42] Edward Gordon (1930–1996), pianist, child prodigy, and performing arts administrator, was Executive Director of the Ravinia Festival, the summer home of the Chicago Symphony Orchestra, 1968–1989. In 1971 he engaged the then unknown James Levine as Music Director, a position Levine held for 23 years. In 1988, Gordon founded the Steans Institute for Young Artists as the summer conservatory of the Ravinia Festival. The Steans Institute was led by Walter Levin 1989–1993.

[43] Dorothy Richard Starling had studied violin with Eugène Ysaÿe at the Cincinnati Conservatory of music, graduating *cum laude* in 1921. Starling's donation established the Dorothy Richard Starling Foundation, which still funds the Dorothy Richard Starling violin professorship at the College-Conservatory of Music.

Evi and I then worked up so to speak overnight a big plan for how to use this money. We had three goals in mind. In the first place, we wanted to engage an absolutely first rate violin teacher at the school. We asked Dorothy DeLay,[44] who we knew from when we were students – she was also a student of Galamian's and had been his assistant for more than twenty years. She asked us why she should come to Cincinnati, and I answered: unlimited funds! She said in that case she would come. I knew Dorothy. She conducted a master class in violin in Cincinnati for almost thirty years, starting in 1974.

We also wanted to establish a school of violin-making at the College-Conservatory and also an Artist Management curriculum, so that young musicians can learn how to prepare for a career and everything that goes along with that. The violin-making school never got off the ground but today Artist Management is a big department that was able to develop to an incredible extent, thanks to the Starling Foundation. The Starling Foundation is led now by Kurt Sassmannshaus and he really does have virtually unlimited funds. He also teaches in the children's division, phenomenal.

RS You mentioned that Cincinnati has an excellent public library.

WL Yes, it's incredible. If I needed some obscure book in German that I couldn't find anywhere I would just call Alice Plaut, the director of the Public Library Music Division, a highly educated graduate of Harvard University. And she would say that she'd look for it and if they didn't have it, she would order it and we'd have it within three weeks. A public library! And the university in Cincinnati had a better German library than most German cities: there was practically nothing you couldn't find there, in part because nothing was ever destroyed or thrown out as happened in the German university libraries in the Nazi time.

The Cincinnati Public Library was simply unbelievable. There's the great story of Beethoven's quartet Opus 14, Nr. 1, the arrangement of the piano sonata. When we first learned of its existence, we looked everywhere for the music and on our European tours asked in all the music shops. But nobody had ever heard of it, so we were rather disappointed, coming back to Cincinnati after one of these tours. But at a party hosted by Alice Plaut we told her how we couldn't find the music, whereupon she asked us if we'd ever tried the Cincinnati Public Library. We asked her why and she told us that if such a thing ever existed, it

44 Dorothy DeLay (1917–2002) was one of the most important violin teachers in America in the latter part of the 20th century. Her students included Itzhak Perlman, Midori, Sarah Chang, Kurt Sassmannshaus, Nadja Salerno-Sonnenberg, Nigel Kennedy, Shlomo Mintz, and Gil Shaham, among many others. Her student Kurt Sassmannshaus is now the College-Conservatory's Starling professor of violin.

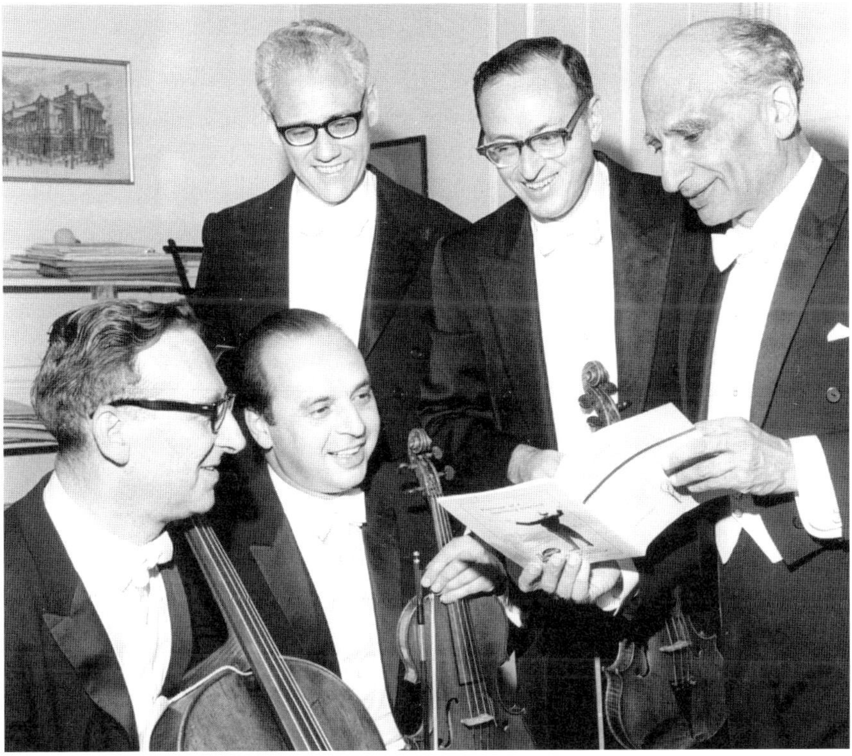

21 The LaSalle Quartet with Max Rudolf, Cincinnati, April, 1966

was certain they would have it. They were always getting bequests from quartet lovers, especially of old scores, so they have thousands upon thousands of them that no one ever uses. She said she would ask about it, and on the very next day she called and said we could pick up the music. The parts, the score, they had everything, in the old Peters edition. We studied the piece for the first time using these materials.[45]

RS Incredible! That's a real center of culture! The conductor Max Rudolf[46] was also in Cincinnati, a highly educated musician. It seems to me that the two of you would have had some real intellectual affinities. Weren't you also in close contact with him?

[45] The LaSalle Quartet recorded Beethoven's string quartet arrangement of his piano sonata Opus 14, Nr. 1, for Deutsche Grammophon in 1987; the recording was released with pianist Stefan Litwin playing the original, solo piano, version as well. See also pp. 206–208.

[46] Max Rudolf (1902–1995) was Music Director of the Cincinnati Symphony 1958–1970. He conducted at the Metropolitan Opera 1946–1960, and after 1981 led the opera and conducting departments at the Curtis Institute in Philadelphia.

WL Of course, because we had the same friends, we ran into one another again and again at parties. And we played Louis Spohr's Concerto for String Quartet with him.[47] He also came to our concerts, for instance, he came to our concert in the 'little' Carnegie hall.[48] He was very enthusiastic about it. We were very much of the same musical and intellectual persuasion.

RS Yes, absolutely, I've read his essays and letters with great enthusiasm. When he was 90 he was still very active and among other things was working on the third edition of his book on conducting.[49]

WL He was indeed a phenomenal musician, a real professional of great abilities, and an intelligent, educated, and refined gentleman. Afterwards he went to the Curtis Institute in Philadelphia. There are many recordings with him at the Metropolitan Opera from the 1940s and 1950s. We had people of that caliber in Cincinnati, and later on we had Michael Gielen[50] too, for seven years.

RS Thanks to you!

WL Well, we had some influence, and the people on the orchestra's board of directors listened to us.

Darmstadt

RS An experience with great ramifications for your future and the future of the LaSalle Quartet was no doubt your involvement with the Darmstadt Summer Courses for New Music. How did that come about?

WL It was the result of our participation in the ISCM Festival that took place in Israel in 1954, to which we had been invited by Peter Gradenwitz, who played an important role in new music in Israel. I had known

[47] Spohr's Concerto for String Quartet in a minor, Opus 131 (1845), was performed by the LaSalle Quartet with the Cincinnati Symphony on April 28 and 29, 1966. See also pp. 181–182.

[48] Now the Weill recital hall at Carnegie Hall. The concert on February 7, 1959, included Mozart's quartet in B♭, K. 458, Webern's Opus 5, 9, and 28, as well as Schubert's d minor quartet, *Der Tod und das Mädchen*.

[49] The two books are *A Musical Life, Writings and Letters*, ed. Michael Stern (New York, 2001), and *The Grammar of Conducting. A Comprehensive Guide to Baton Technique and Interpretation* (New York, 1995).

[50] For more about Michael Gielen, see pp. 292–298.

him ever since I was fourteen years old and had gone to the concerts of recordings on the roof of his house in Tel Aviv. He also knew Evi from Tanglewood. He proposed that the LaSalle Quartet play the American quartets that had been chosen for the festival program: Roger Sessions' second quartet and Leon Kirchner's first.[51] So we went to Israel and on the way made our debuts in various European cities,[52] since you had to go through Europe anyway to fly to Israel. In Israel we got to know and appreciate the music critic from *Die Welt*, Heinz Joachim. He had been invited to Israel as the first representative of a German newspaper to report on the ISCM Festival.

Following the festival in Israel we visited my uncle in Gstaad and drove his car to Salzburg to hear this and that, and while we were there we ran into Heinz Joachim again, as well as Michael Gielen and his uncle Eduard Steuermann. We'd already been friends with Steuermann and his wife Clara Silvers, a student of Schoenberg's, at Colorado Springs. At the end of our stay in Salzburg Joachim and Gielen told us that they were now going on to Darmstadt, to the International Summer Courses in New Music. I'd never heard of it. So they told us what was going on there, and we thought it sounded like something we'd want to go and hear for ourselves. Evi had never been to Germany, this was a good reason to go there, and we had a car. So we offered to take everybody in our car and drive together from Salzburg to Darmstadt. A most enjoyable trip, with Michael Gielen, Heinz Joachim, Evi, and me in a Plymouth Cabriolet convertible. We didn't take the autobahn, we took the back roads, stopping along the way at some marvelous country inns and having some great meals. I don't think I've ever seen Gielen laugh so much, he was in such a good mood! It was a wonderful trip. We arrived at Darmstadt in high spirits, and the first thing on the program for that afternoon was a tape recording of the premiere of Schoenberg's *Moses und Aaron*, which had just been given in Hamburg under Hans Rosbaud.[53] Gertrud Schoenberg was there too, together with her daughter Nuria, who was just 22 then, and pretty as a picture.[54]

[51] See pp. 330 and 334.

[52] These debut concerts took place between May 18 and May 26, 1954, in London, Amsterdam, the Hague, Copenhagen, and Zurich. On the program were Mozart's D major quartet, K. 499, Bartók's third quartet, and Beethoven's Opus 59, Nr. 3.

[53] Hans Rosbaud (1895–1962), pianist and conductor, was noted for his performances of contemporary music during his tenure as Chief Conductor of the Southwest German Radio (SWF) in Baden-Baden 1948–1962. In 1932 he conducted the premieres of Schoenberg's *Four Songs with Orchestra* and Bartók's second piano concerto with Bartók as the soloist. Rosbaud was also known for his performances of Mahler and for the Mozart operas he conducted in the 1950s at the Aix-en-Provence Summer Festival.

[54] Nuria Schoenberg married the Italian composer Luigi Nono in 1955, whom she had met at the Hamburg premiere of *Moses und Aaron*.

So that was in 1954. At Darmstadt we got to know all the people who would be important for our later career: Luigi Nono, György Ligeti, Henri Pousseur, Krzysztof Penderecki, Franco Evangelisti, Mauricio Kagel, Giuseppe Englert, Pierre Boulez, Karlheinz Stockhausen, they were all there.[55] And René Leibowitz,[56] Adorno, and Stefan Wolpe were teaching there. It was a kind of potpourri and of course we were utterly taken with it. We also met the director, Wolfgang Steinecke.[57] He was interested in us, he had already heard of the LaSalle Quartet. But we still had never played in Germany, and Herr Steinecke told us that we absolutely had to come to Germany and play there. Henry Meyer had great reservations as to whether he was willing to do that, but Steinecke was able to persuade him, and so at Steinecke's invitation on our next European tour, in the fall of 1956, we played our first concert in Germany, a private concert at the Kranichstein Institute of Music in Darmstadt.[58]

Our acquaintance with Darmstadt continued to develop, as did our relationships with the young composers of the post-war avant-garde. We told them we were surprised that although there were wonderful concerts, there weren't any new string quartets. When we asked why not, the answer was always the same: who would play them? We were told that there wasn't a single quartet that would be interested, but we said that we, at least, would be very interested! We were told that in that case we should arrange for some commissions, and that's just what we did, with the help of the Sunday Group in Cincinnati, after we told them about our experiences at Darmstadt, and who were very interested. And so starting around 1960 we began to get new pieces that we learned in due course and then played, one after the other.

RS There was a concert in Darmstadt in September, 1958, on the occasion of Anton Webern's 75th birthday, at which Rudolf Kolisch[59] also played,

[55] For all these composers see Chapter 17, 'Commissions and Premieres.'

[56] René Leibowitz (1913–1972), composer, conductor, theorist, and teacher, was an early champion of the Second Viennese School in France and a major figure in the early years of Darmstadt. Himself a student of Webern, he authored an important study, *Schoenberg and his School* (Paris, 1947; English New York, 1949); his students included Jacques Monod and Pierre Boulez. Along with Hermann Scherchen, he was the first to observe Beethoven's metronome marks in performing the symphonies.

[57] Wolfgang Steinecke (1910–1961) founded the Darmstadt International Summer Courses for New Music in 1946 and directed the festival until his death.

[58] The concert took place on October 23, 1956. On the program were Webern's Opus 28, Leon Kirchner's first quartet, and Arnold Schoenberg's third quartet.

[59] Rudolf Kolisch (1896–1978) studied with Otakar Ševčik at the Vienna Academy of Music and studied composition with Franz Schreker and Arnold Schoenberg. He played a leading role in Schoenberg's Society for Private Performances of Music. In 1924, Schoenberg married Kolisch's sister Gertrude; it was his second marriage.

who was a very important person for you in many respects. Did you get to know him personally?

WL Of course. I ran into him many times as he was frequently in Darmstadt, but we'd already met him prior to that in Boston on one of our tours. We went to see him then on account of his recordings of the Beethoven quartets that he had just recorded with the Pro Arte quartet, but which were never released. I really wanted to have copies of them, but I never did get them. And then in the fall of 1961 Kolisch was supposed to give a course on the Second Viennese School at Darmstadt, analyzing them and playing examples from them based on his first hand experience. Unfortunately he had an automobile accident shortly before the summer course began and had to cancel. Whereupon Wolfgang Steinecke called me at Schönried in Switzerland, where we were spending the summer, and asked me if I could take over the course. He had a hard time convincing me to do it, I really didn't want to, I couldn't possibly replace Kolisch. I did know the repertory, but not as well as Kolisch. Besides which I simply hadn't had his experience of sitting together with Schoenberg and working through everything with him. So I was a poor replacement. But Steinecke quite rightly told me that there wasn't anybody else who knew this repertory, and he certainly didn't want to cancel the course, as they already had people registered for it.

So we went to Darmstadt, got to our hotel, unpacked, and then ran into Heinz-Klaus Metzger[60] sitting in the lobby and talking with Adorno. He called me over and introduced me to Adorno as Walter Levin of the LaSalle Quartet. Adorno just said something like 'nice meeting you.' And then Metzger asked me what I was doing here already, he thought I wasn't coming for another two weeks. I told him that Steinecke had called me up because Kolisch had an accident and asked me to take over Kolisch's course on the Second Viennese School string quartets. Adorno looked at me thoughtfully and rather skeptically, and said to me, 'Young man, if you believe you can replace Rudolf Kolisch here you are very much mistaken.' That was the end of the conversation, and that was my introduction to Adorno. But I didn't reject Adorno on that account, I wasn't at all put off by what he said – I could have said the same thing myself! In any event the course went quite well. I taught some quartets and gave some lectures on the Second Viennese School, using LaSalle Quartet recordings as examples.

60 Heinz-Klaus Metzger (1932–2009) was a German music critic and theorist. In 1977 Metzger and the composer and conductor Rainer Riehn founded the journal *Musik-Konzepte*, which they edited and for which they researched and provided texts criticism till 2002. *Musik-Konzepte* was and remains widely recognized as one of the most important organs of the later 20th century musical avant-garde, a position akin to that held previously by the Darmstadt School's *Die Reihe*, though broader in scope.

RS Did you also discuss Kolisch's researches into Beethoven's tempi with him?[61]

WL No, I'd already become familiar with his work on that while I was at Juilliard. I was so convinced by it that I didn't see anything more to discuss. And I only realized that he had done more work on the subject after his death. I greatly admired the scope of Kolisch's interests and works, a large part of which is in the Houghton Library at Harvard University and still unpublished. When we went there, it was all still in cardboard cartons and not at all organized, just the way it had been when they got it. No one was the least bit concerned about it.

RS Wasn't Kolisch's assistant David Satz, who was working with him on revising his essay 'Tempo and Character in Beethoven's Music,' concerned about this legacy either?

WL David Satz withdrew from this work after Kolisch's death in 1978. It was difficult to work with Kolisch, as it was with the whole Schoenberg school, who were authoritarian and headstrong, apodictic and by no means always straightforward. But it's quite remarkable how these people stopped developing at some point, they got just so far and no further. And nothing that came after that was of much interest to them, they didn't want to bother with it. So the new music, that is the post-war avant-garde, meant nothing to them, not even for Eugene Lehner, the violist of the Kolisch quartet. When we were playing the second Ligeti quartet, Lehner wanted to know what we thought of it, whether it was a good piece or not. I think it's a splendid piece. Or also Lutosławski: the older generation around Schoenberg didn't want to know anything about this kind of new music. They were the avant-garde of their time and had fought their battles, committing themselves to that music and risking everything for it, but as is so often the case, for them that was the end of the avant-garde. They didn't want to acknowledge that there could be yet another avant-garde after theirs. The new music so to speak shoved them into second place, it historicized them, and nobody really likes to have that happen. But it was a somewhat shocking insight to realize that you have to be extremely careful never to draw an arbitrary line under something, never to get stuck in whatever discoveries you've made, no matter how interesting

[61] See Rudolf Kolisch, 'Tempo and Character in Beethoven's Music,' in the *Musical Quarterly*, vol. 29, Nr. 2 (April, 1943), pp. 169–187 (part 1); vol. 29 Nr. 3 (July 1943), pp. 291–312 (part 2). Expanded German version in *Musik-Konzepte* 76/77 (Munich, 1992). An English translation of the expanded version was published in the *Musical Quarterly*, vol. 77 (1993), with an introduction by Thomas Y. Levin. See also pp. 341–345.

they might be. In time they too will become part of history, which continues to develop and change.

Tours

RS In the course of your career with the LaSalle Quartet you made 67 tours. In the beginning it surely wasn't easy to get bookings. How did your first tours come about? Apparently you got a letter of recommendation from Joseph Szigeti.

WL Szigeti was visiting Galamian at the summer school in Meadowmount, where we took lessons every summer. There were student concerts every Sunday that we sometimes took part in, so he heard us play. I was a great admirer of Szigeti ever since I'd gotten the Brahms Concerto with Hamilton Harty for my bar mitzvah, and I'd gone to many Szigeti concerts while I was studying in New York, including the chamber music concerts at the Frick, where he played trios with Artur Schnabel and Pierre Fournier and sonatas with Schnabel. So at Meadowmount I asked him whether he could write a short recommendation for us. And he gave us a wonderful letter.[62] We also got a recommendation from Samuel Dushkin, the violinist who premiered various works of Stravinsky's.[63] He also came to visit Galamian in Meadowmount. We often had very nice dinners together with him in Lewis, the village near us, and asked him about his work with Stravinsky. We were very interested in hearing about that. He'd given the world premiere of the violin concerto in Berlin, and there are some recordings with him, including a performance of the violin concerto. We could have learned a lot about Bartók from Szigeti, but our personal relationship with him didn't go that far. So those were important musicians who wrote recommendations for us. To help get concert bookings when we were starting out, at Colorado Springs, we printed a promotional brochure with Szigeti's and Dushkin's recommendations, and sent it to all the concert managers whose names and addresses we could get from our friends, acquaintances, and teachers. Evi did all that.

[62] Szigeti wrote that 'The perfection and the coherence of the LaSalle Quartet's playing were an extraordinary pleasure for me. It is of the greatest significance for the decentralization of chamber music that they are now the Quartet in Residence at Colorado College.'

[63] Samuel Dushkin (1891–1976) was a friend of Stravinsky's for whom he wrote his violin concerto (1931) and his Duo Concertant for violin and piano (1932). When Dushkin heard the LaSalle Quartet in Meadowmount, he wrote, by hand, and quite spontaneously, 'I had the great pleasure of hearing the LaSalle Quartet play classical and contemporary music. Wonderful music, brilliantly played with enthusiasm and conviction: truly gifted musicians.'

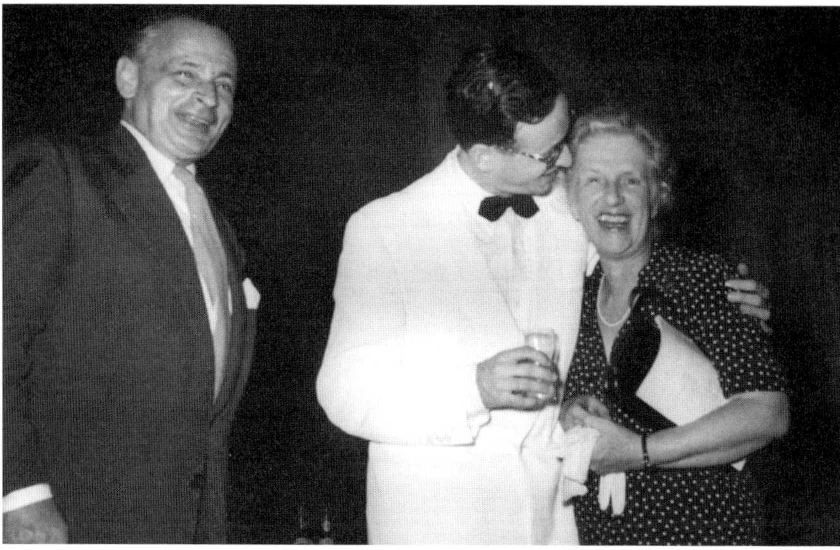

22 Walter Levin with his parents after a concert in Tel Aviv, 1954

EL My music studies at Colorado College and my business training at the Rhodes Business School in New York turned out to be the perfect combination for launching the career of the LaSalle Quartet. We got a copy of Lovejoy's Colleges Guide and looked up 500 college and university music departments. We sent each of them a letter along with our brochure. We got about fifty responses, out of which we got something like five or ten bookings.

WL It's absolutely essential that you look after your own career yourself. People nowadays seem to believe that bookings are just manna from heaven. On the contrary! You have to do everything yourself.

RS You were invited to Israel in 1954 for the ISCM Festival, but you combined this tour with concerts in Europe. How did that come about?

WL We had a friend, Theodor Ranan, originally Rosenzweig, an artistically gifted man, you can't imagine anyone more wonderful: highly intelligent, educated, musically informed, incredible! He lived in Israel and we were very good friends with him. When we were invited to participate in the 1954 ISCM Festival in Israel, he arranged a tour of Israel for us. We'd consulted with him already the year before about how to get a foothold in Europe. Ranan was a friend of Peter Diamand, who was originally Artur Schnabel's secretary in Tremezzo on Lake Como and

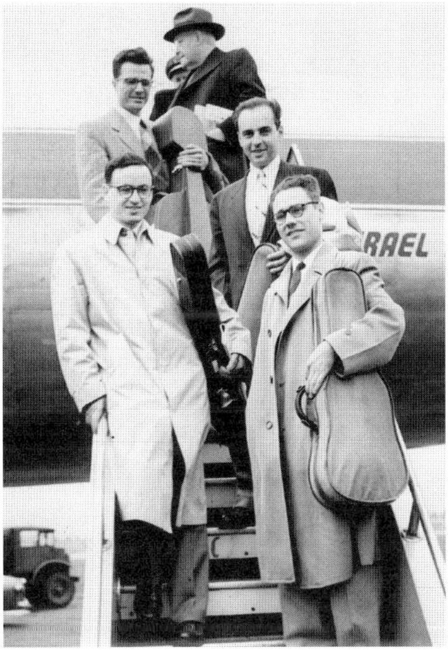

23 The LaSalle Quartet arriving in London after their concert in Israel, 1954

in the meantime had become the director of the Edinburgh Festival. Ranan admired Schnabel and visited him in the summer, so he knew Peter Diamand from that. Ranan said that since Peter Diamand was the director of the Edinburgh Festival he would know lots of managers, and we would need a manager to launch us in Europe, and he would speak with Diamand about this. The three of us met in Amsterdam in the summer of 1953. Peter Diamand was Dutch and knew everybody who was anybody in his own country. He recommended a manager in the Hague, Mevrouw van Beek, and wrote her a letter recommending us. So I drove to the Hague, and she suggested organizing a European debut tour with concerts in London, the Hague, Amsterdam, Copenhagen, and Zurich. I wanted to know how you did that. She said it was really very simple: you rent a hall, advertise, and hope that the public and the critics come, and then see if anything comes of it. I wanted to know how much all this would cost, and she said about $200 per concert, so I said we'd do it. She contacted the concert agents and organized our debut tour. That's how we got our first European manager.

EL And on the tour itself we even got a couple of bookings for radio broadcasts, in Athens and Paris, and they even paid us for them!

RS When you played in Amsterdam on your debut tour, you were approached by a representative of the Society of Arts Clubs of Indonesia.

WL Yes, Mevrouw Hilfman van Dam. She asked us if we would be willing to make a tour of Indonesia. Of course there was no question but what we would be willing to do that! She not only organized concerts for us in Indonesia but also arranged contacts for us with music organizations in other countries in the South Pacific. We were on the road for almost four months starting in mid-May, 1956, going from Hawaii and the Fiji Islands to New Zealand and Australia, and then, after spending July and August in Indonesia, on to Bombay and Bangkok.

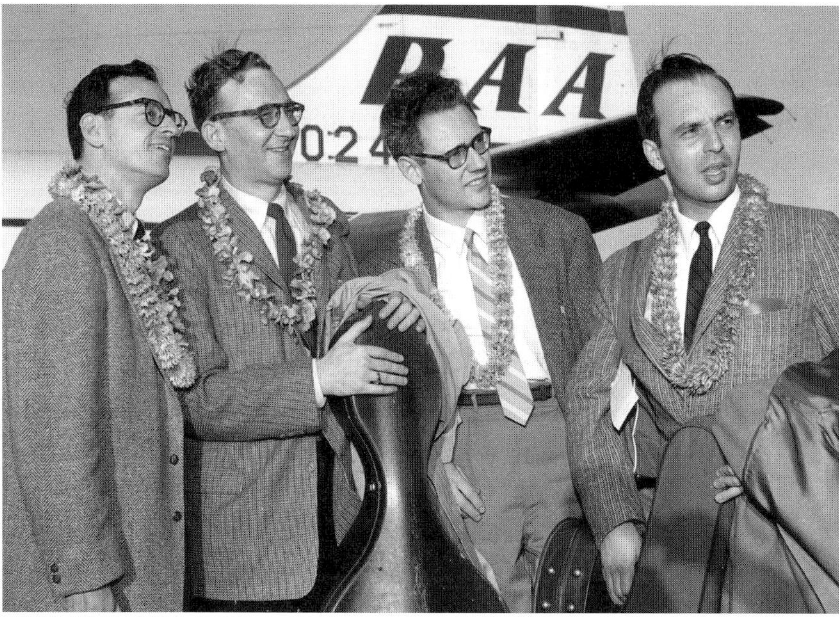

24 The LaSalle Quartet arriving in Hawaii on their world tour, 1956

RS And at the end of the Asian tour there was yet another extended European tour of Switzerland, Austria, Germany, Denmark, Sweden, Holland, and, finally, London.

WL Yes, and from then on we regularly went on tour in Europe, as a result of these first concerts. Our success in Holland, for instance, was sensational, even with the critics, and as a result concert organizations in various other cities got in touch with us, and so our career gradually developed from one recommendation to the next, and engagements followed. Your first concerts simply must be successful if you're to have a career, and people have to know about them! What's crucial is both to play well and to get further bookings, which of course you mustn't decline. That's still true even now for young musicians who win a competition. If the competition is a really good one, it arranges a concert tour for the winner. But that first tour has to be a real hit, since you don't get a second tour pre-arranged for you. You only get a second tour if your first tour was so successful that the agents want to engage you again. You also have to answer letters, you may even have to go to the trouble of writing a thank you letter if someone has done something particularly nice for you. Nowadays it's no longer taken for granted that you have to do that. But if you don't, some people will think twice before doing something for you again.

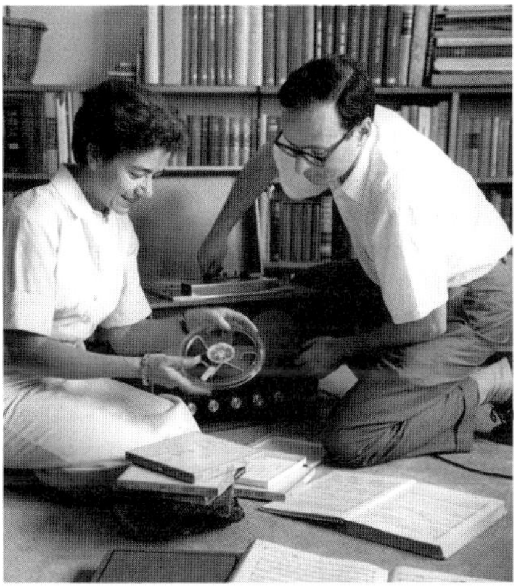

25 Evi and Walter Levin organizing tapes of the LaSalle Quartet's concerts, Cincinnati, 1959

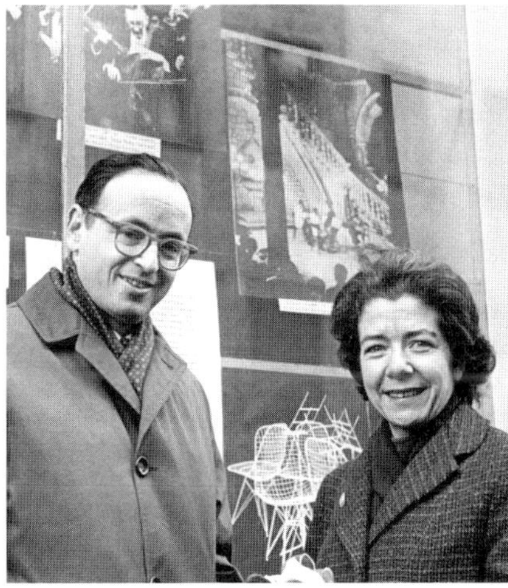

26 Walter and Evi Levin in Sofia, 1965 (in back the Eames wire chairs logo of the LaSalle Quartet)

RS Evidently the LaSalle Quartet didn't have a permanent concert agent, you organized everything yourself. Did you always do that?

WL Evi started managing the quartet already in Colorado Springs and was our General Manager up until the end.

EL What that means is that I always took care of all the coordination between the quartet and the local managements, everywhere, also in America. We tried using an outside manager several times and we always gave up on it.

WL Evi was also the manager of our first European tour. At that time we had no general manager in Europe. Once one has a bit of renown, the managers get to be more interested, but then you don't need them anymore and we politely declined. In America you pay 20% or more of your gross fee per concert to the manager. And on top of that all the expenses, every postage stamp, every telephone conversation, everything: awful! You can assume that you'll be giving a third of your fee to your manager, and in advance, too. Most of the managers demand that you guarantee them a certain sum and pay them every month, so that they have at least a minimum income from any ensemble that they take on. We preferred to pay Evi a small salary. So Evi was the manager of the LaSalle Quartet all through our career, and since we disbanded she manages my lecture-recitals and chamber music courses.

Disbanding

RS How did it come about that in 1987, after forty years, the LaSalle Quartet disbanded?

WL In November, 1986, I was suddenly very sick and had to go to the hospital. I was really very ill, ill like I'd never been before. I came to realize then that it couldn't go on like this forever: this season and the next and the season after that and so on. There comes a moment when you have to think about when to make an end to all this stress. For it really was stressful, living like that: teaching, going on tour, giving concerts. And I came to the conclusion that after forty years it was time to disband the quartet. We had already agreed that the following year, 1987–1988, all four of us would take a so-called sabbatical, a year off, for the first time in our career. At the university you're granted a sabbatical leave every seven years, but we'd always put it off, because if we hadn't, the music school would have been short four teachers for a whole year. It seemed to me that the sabbatical offered a perfect way to bring the quartet's career to an end. We would use our sabbatical to take a break not only from teaching but also from quartet work, which meant that we wouldn't be giving any concerts the next year either, because we wouldn't have anything prepared. So altogether two years with no concerts. While we were on sabbatical I informed my colleagues that I would be happy to give up the quartet. This came as a shock to them and they were very upset and confused about it.

RS That's perfectly understandable when you've worked with one another so long and so intensely, rehearsing and giving concerts, going on tour 67 times and making records. And for Henry especially, as a bachelor, the quartet was a kind of family.

WL Yes, of course. It's always difficult for musicians to decide to end their active concert careers – rehearsing, touring, and concertizing have become an integral part of their lives. It's difficult to decide to really stop. But with the passing years it had become more and more difficult to work up the very demanding programs we continued to play right up until the end. Eventually my colleagues were no longer so enthusiastic about taking new works into our repertory, for instance Michael Gielen's quartet. And it became harder and harder to maintain the standard of performance we had so arduously achieved: no one's technique improves after sixty. And more and more I had to deal with the quartet's resistance to my keeping the quartet working the way I had always insisted on. I much preferred to have people saying it was a shame we'd stopped while we were still playing so well than to hear them saying it was really about time we gave it up.

RS What's particularly striking is that the LaSalle Quartet simply disappeared from the scene without any fuss or bother. No one but you knew that the concert in Bochum on May 21, 1987,[64] would be the last concert by the LaSalle Quartet. Most prominent artists and chamber music ensembles mark their retirement from the world's stage with a farewell tour.

WL Yes, well of course we talked about doing that too, and opinions differed in that regard. But that didn't sit well with me, I find it a sentimental way of being celebrated, which was something I didn't want under any circumstances. Of course that's simply a matter of personal taste.

[64] This final concert by the LaSalle Quartet included three Purcell *Fantasies*, Webern's 1906 *Rondo*, Beethoven's *Grosse Fuge*, Opus. 133, and the sixth Bartók quartet.

10 *Working Together*

ROBERT SPRUYTENBURG: Going through the LaSalle Quartet's concert programs, I'm struck by how often in the first concert in Cincinnati following a tour a piece was performed that was not previously in your repertory. Does this mean that you worked on new repertory even while you were touring? Or did you only rehearse the pieces you were performing on the tour?

WALTER LEVIN: It all depends. It might be that on tour we would work on a piece that we didn't need until the tour was over. But in that case it was usually something we'd worked on the summer before.

RS So those were working vacations.

WL They were partly vacations, I would say 25% vacation and 75% working vacation, in the sense that we rehearsed in the morning and then had the rest of the day free to practice and afterwards to do whatever we wanted.

RS So the whole quartet came to Schönried or Flims.

WL We all lived in Flims or Fidaz, so we could rehearse in the skiing school.

EVI LEVIN: We also spent a summer with the quartet in Grand Lake, Colorado.

WL That was when Jack Kirstein was new to the quartet, in the summer of 1955, before we started going to Flims. But throughout our whole career, from beginning to end, every year, we used our summers to prepare the new repertory for the coming season. That's how we were able to continually learn new pieces, we had built these regular work sessions into our schedule. Even when we were at Colorado College we worked on new repertory every summer while continuing our quartet studies with Galamian in New York. We kept to a very precise daily schedule: in the morning each of us practiced his part by himself for something like an hour and a half, after which we had a two and a half hour quartet rehearsal, followed by lunch and a short midday break. Then each of us practiced alone for another hour or so, and then we had another two hour quartet rehearsal. Afterwards we went to Elizabethtown to play tennis: two against two. And after an hour of tennis doubles we went swimming in Split Rock, where there was a magnificent waterfall. Then it was back to Mrs. Burpee's with a big appetite for dinner. The quartet kept to this rehearsal schedule for years and years.

RS That's what I thought, that you would probably never be able to find the time to learn new repertory while you were on tour.

WL No. But we always rehearsed the concert programs on tour: that's another way in which we differed from most other quartets. On tour we had a very clever system. The morning after a concert we rehearsed from ten till twelve. We had a list of what had to be worked on, since right after the concert or early the next morning each of us made notes about what in his opinion hadn't gone well or what we needed to take care of for the next concert. We never just played a piece straight through. Instead, one of us would say, for example, that in bars 17 to 29, such and such wasn't right, and we would start right in on those measures. We could get through a huge amount of work in two hours, since each of us had his list.

We arranged everything so that after the rehearsal we would catch a train with a dining car to take us to the next concert. The trip never took more than three or four hours, we didn't accept bookings further apart than that. We had lunch on the train, and when we got to our destination we went to our hotel, where everyone could do whatever he wanted. I took a nap, practiced for another hour, from six till seven, and then it was time for the concert. Unlike many other quartets we didn't rehearse on stage in an empty hall, since the acoustics will be completely different with the audience present. We didn't have dinner until after the concert.

RS And you didn't practice in the dining car....

WL No, and we didn't sit together either.

RS Seriously?

WL Yes of course! If you want peace and quiet you don't want to have to carry on a conversation! But that wasn't true for all of us: my colleagues enjoyed sitting together, I didn't. Henry Meyer usually had a couple of friends who travelled with us: he was our man about town, he always had friends with him. We had a rule that you could never sit down at a colleague's table without asking permission first. And with me you needn't even bother asking. We also always stayed on different floors of our hotel, and in different parts of it, so that we wouldn't hear one another. None of us wanted to know whether the others were practicing or not, and least of all did anyone want to hear what they were practicing. For instance, the very first thing Lee Fiser would do when we got to our rooms would be to start practicing the Elgar Cello Concerto, which was the last thing in the world I wanted to hear just then.

RS As regards practicing: the earliest newspaper articles about the quartet say that you routinely practiced from seven in the morning until twelve o'clock noon. That seems almost inhuman.

WL When we were first in Cincinnati we started our rehearsals very early in the morning so we could still teach for two hours before lunch. We rehearsed from seven to ten, taught from ten to twelve or one, and then we went home and had the afternoon free: it was ideal!

RS You really had to be a morning person!

WL No doubt! A couple of my colleagues weren't at all morning people, but they got used to it. Once they realized that this gave us the whole afternoon and evening free they could see how marvelous it was to have half the day open. Otherwise we'd have to drive to school and back home again. When would we practice? This schedule allowed me, for instance, to insist that we rehearse an entire movement once again the next day, and moreover to rehearse it thoroughly. If you're at school at that hour, you're fresh, and there's nobody to disturb you, because no one else is there yet! Later on, when we said, okay, we'll start rehearsing at nine, I taught for the two hours before that, so I would be done just as early as before. When my students protested about violin lessons starting at seven in the morning, I asked them if they would rather start at six.

RS Had it been different in Colorado?

WL It had. In Colorado we had practically no instrumental students, we taught classes instead. So we rehearsed for three or four hours in the morning and then taught from eleven o'clock to one or twelve. Our schedule in Colorado was still very congenial.

RS It was characteristic of the LaSalle Quartet to work through each new piece at great length and in great depth. When you played a difficult piece for the first time, like the second Ligeti quartet or Nono's quartet or any other piece that was new to you, as Berg's *Lyric Suite* was to begin with, did you ever suffer from stage fright? Or were you just so well prepared that you only had the normal adrenalin rush?

WL Of course we had the normal adrenalin rush, but we never had stage fright on account of a premiere or a new performance of a piece. We always tried new pieces out beforehand in a lecture-recital, so we'd already performed them once, and when we played them in concert afterwards we already knew them, so there was no more cause for stage fright than with a Beethoven quartet or one by Schubert or Mozart. In any case you're never completely relaxed when appearing in public, but not so nervous that it gets in the way of your playing. No, I wasn't the type to get stage fright, never. And neither were the others. If you listen to our premieres, they don't suffer from stage fright.

RS No, but it's not something to take for granted.

WL No, not at all.

RS But of course because of the way you worked together you were always so well prepared that everything about a piece had become deeply absorbed into your playing, both mentally and physically, long before you went on stage to perform it in public.

WL Indeed. If we couldn't play a new piece yet, we postponed the premiere, as we did with the second Ligeti quartet. We were quite rigorous about that. It doesn't work to perform a piece you can't really play yet, you have to let it go.

RS When you teach the classical-romantic repertory here in Basel and bring your own parts along, it's obvious that they're often from the old Peters editions, which you so often disparage today.

WL When we were starting out there wasn't much else to be had.

RS I understand that, but did you really use the old editions of this repertory on through to the end?

WL As time went on we got the new editions. We used the parts and scores from Alfred Einstein's *Neue Mozart Ausgabe* (New Mozart Edition), published by Novello. We always used the best of the new editions, including, for instance, the Henle and the Doblinger urtext editions of Haydn. And wherever possible we also got copies of the autographs. That was difficult at first. But little by little we got more and more of them. So we did what the musicologists should have done long ago: we looked in the original manuscripts to see what the composers had actually written. The differences between that and what's in the old editions is often hair raising. Irregular periods in Haydn and Schubert were 'improved' by the early publishers, since for them it went without saying that a period had to have eight bars and not seven, five, or nine. So the traditional editions are full of mistakes and arbitrary changes and, moreover, wrong notes that are still played very bravely by some interpreters today even though they're obviously total nonsense. The new Haydn editions from Henle and Doblinger were a big step forward. But now Peters is issuing a critical edition prepared by English musicologists which is really excellent. It was obvious to us from the outset that the old Eulenburg editions were unusable.

RS And there's still no complete urtext edition of Brahms.

WL And only very recently one for Schumann. What's to be done? But we based the fingerings and bowings in the parts we used on our copies of the autograph scores. I still have most of these parts and I always bring them with me to Lübeck and Basel, there's more than a little worthwhile still in them.

RS There are some pieces you played only in certain phases of your career, that is, after playing them for a while you dropped them and then took them up again, sometimes after as much as ten years or more. Did you have to work through these pieces all over again as regards fingerings and bowings?

WL Yes, in general we did. But there was also much that didn't change. I played Beethoven's Opus 59, Nr. 2, in Palestine, and we worked on Opus 135 very early on. And when I listen to the recordings of our performances of them over the years…

RS … they are mostly distinguishable only by the technical quality of the recording.

WL Yes, that, and in a few details. In principle, though, nothing changed. And that had nothing to do with my being rigid and inflexible. Once you've worked through a piece properly and thoroughly scrutinized every aspect of it, you know exactly how it should be played, so what is there to change?

RS There are two parallels worth mentioning between the Kolisch Quartet and the LaSalle Quartet, in the first place that you both usually played from scores and not from parts, and secondly, that from the very beginning you both used equal temperament. Was that just happenstance, or does the fact that both ensembles worked that way have a common origin?

WL I don't believe we got the idea of playing from scores from the Kolisch Quartet, since we never had any contact with the Kolisch Quartet. I got the idea from Gideon Strauss in Palestine. It's a necessary consequence of the fact that you can't learn a piece if you don't have the score in front of you, or rather you can learn it, but only much more slowly. So you might as well learn the piece as a whole to begin with, and not just your own part. But since that's only possible if you work from the score, we began playing from scores very early on. It helped that the Webern pieces were only available as scores, never as parts, so when we first worked on them we could see right away how much better it is to play from scores, and then we began to play other pieces that were new to us from scores too, like the Schoenberg quartets. Trying to learn a piece from the parts is almost as hopeless as an actor trying to learn his lines without reading the whole play: imagine coming to the first rehearsal and saying: 'I'm supposed to play a guy called Othello. And you? Who are you? Desdemona! Who's that? I don't know the piece, I've just learned my own part!'

RS If you need to cheer yourself up sometime, you should have a look at Hans Keller's book on the Haydn string quartets.[1] In it he says that he immediately shows the door to ensembles that come to him and play from scores. For him one only plays from parts.

WL Well, what can I say? At times he's very advanced and at other times he's equally reactionary! He hated Kolisch, for instance.

RS Sometimes he's something of a blind hot head and then sometimes very lucid.

WL Yes, that's what I think too. But now and then I get really furious about some of the things he says. On the other hand he's very knowledgeable, and he's often right about things.

RS And what about equal temperament?

WL I also don't believe that's something we got from Kolisch either, it's something I'd already gotten from my teacher Bergmann in Palestine. It was only afterwards that I learned that Kolisch also used equal temperament.

[1] Hans Keller, *The Great Haydn Quartets. Their Interpretation* (London 1986).

It was already common practice in the 1930s.

RS But apparently not everywhere, as it's still a matter of contention among string players.[2]

WL Not for all of them! Some of them are very proud of playing out of tune!

RS As I understand it, there was a division of labor in the LaSalle Quartet, every member of the quartet had his own job to do in addition to playing his instrument. So, for instance, Jack Kirstein wrote the program notes.

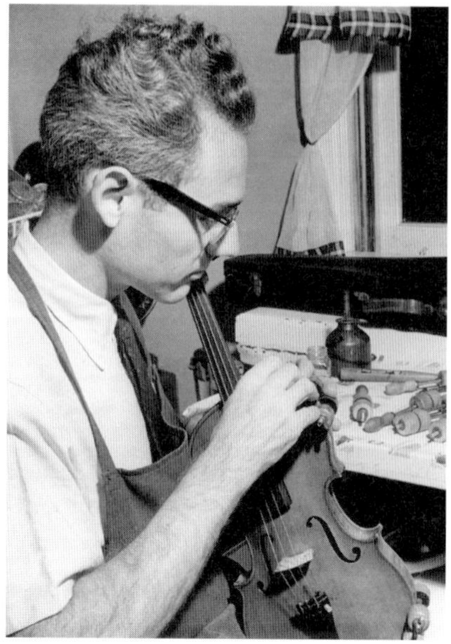

27 Peter Kamnitzer as a violin maker, Cincinnati, 1959

WL Well, that's how we originally intended it. But Jack's program notes didn't match up with my ideas about what they should be like. In and of itself it was a good idea, but it didn't work out, so Evi and I ended up writing them ourselves.

RS What was Peter Kamnitzer's job?

WL Peter was responsible for the library, that is, he maintained an archive that had all our parts in it. Each of us had his own part for every piece, and these had to be kept somewhere, not by each individual, but gathered together by him. When we went on tour, he got the parts out of his archive and gave them to each of us. He also bound the individual parts very beautifully himself.

RS I've always associated the scores and parts with you, so I was surprised to learn that Peter kept them.

WL I have my parts here with me because I need them all the time.

EL When we wanted to donate the LaSalle Quartet archive to the Paul Sacher Foundation, Henry Meyer sent his parts, which he'd kept or gotten back from Peter, to them. What's awful is that when we told Peter

[2] See Rudolf Kolisch, *'Religion der Streicher,'* in *Musik-Konzepte* 29/30: *Rudolf Kolisch, Zur Theorie der Aufführung* (Munich, 1983).

that we wanted him to send the other parts to the Sacher Foundation, he replied, 'Gosh, I just threw them out with the trash last week. They're gone.' So we're missing the cello and viola parts.

RS That's really unbelievable! Did he just want to make an end to it?

EL No, they needed the space after they'd sold their house and moved into their apartment.

RS But it didn't occur to him to ask you first? To have so little sense of history, even after a forty year professional career!

WL He was certain that no one would ever be interested! If I hadn't kept my own parts, and Henry hadn't sent his to the Sacher archive, they would have been thrown out too. But I have my parts here, nearly complete: I took everything I could use with me, everything that was of some value to me.

EL Peter was also responsible for repairing the instruments, at least to begin with.

WL To a certain extent. He was a trained violin maker and when we were starting out he took care of the simple repairs, like repositioning a bridge or even regluing, and he could rehair our bows: he had all the tools. But later on, when we had the Amati instruments, he didn't do any of that anymore.

RS What was Henry's job with the quartet?

WL He was the quartet's treasurer when we were on tour. He paid the hotel bills, he collected the honoraria. There's a great story about that. In Warsaw we were paid exclusively in złotys, which could not be exchanged for other currencies. We got piles and piles of złotys, all in cash, after every concert. And Henry had to somehow get them into his violin case or put them in his pockets and then into the safe at the hotel – it was dreadful. And what were we to do with them? We could only spend them in Poland. We went to the bookstores and the music stores, where there were wonderful German books from East Germany that cost next to nothing.

I bought whole bookcases of music from East Germany and still had złotys left over. Then one day we were in Kraców for a concert for which we had been paid in advance, so Henry packed the złotys in his violin case in a red velvet bag. We were in a Green Room that had only two exits: one to the stage and one to the corridor, where there was a soldier on guard. We went out onto the stage and played the first part of our program. When we came back for the intermission the money was gone! How could that be? We had been on stage, the soldier was still standing by the other door, but the money was gone. We threw a fit! The only response we got was to be told that we were, after all, in Poland.

When we got back home to Cincinnati there was a big party for us. Our insurance agent was there, an old friend of ours, Fritz Rauh. We were telling everyone this amazing story about how our money had been stolen from us in Poland. But Fritz interrupted and told us that we were insured against such thefts up to so and so many thousands of dollars, we should just report the loss. I was skeptical about filing a claim for złotys, but he said it didn't matter what the currency was. I objected that the złotys were worthless to begin with, but he asked me what it was I meant by 'worthless,' I should have a look in the New York Times for the official exchange rate, they had to be worth at least something. On the black market the dollar was then worth 400 złotys, but Fritz got the stolen money valued at the official rate of four złotys to the dollar. We never earned so much in Poland ever again! Whenever we were in Poland after that we always looked for someone who could steal the złotys from us!

11 *The Instruments*

ROBERT SPRUYTENBURG: For the LaSalle Quartet's debut concert in Cincinnati in September, 1953, Rembert Wurlitzer[1] brought you four Stradivarius instruments, and in 1958 he arranged for the LaSalle Quartet to have the Amati instruments. How important were these instruments to you?

WALTER LEVIN: If you're used to driving a used Chevrolet and all of a sudden you get a Cadillac with all its comforts, it's wonderful! But both cars will get you from here to there. Which is to say that the instruments that we had up until then would have worked too. They weren't bad, but they weren't anything special. I had what I thought was a Ceruti[2] violin, though it turned out not to be. Henry Meyer still had Nathan Milstein's Stradivarius replica, that is, a modern instrument. Peter Kamnitzer had a French viola, and the cello, whatever it was, it was good enough. These were all middling instruments that a student could afford, but nothing more than that. Still, we launched our whole career, including our European career, using them. And people were always talking about those lucky Americans with their fabulous Italian instruments! Nonsense! What you do with your instrument is also of some importance, or so I would think. Again and again, this fixation on the instruments! If you can play a stringed instrument at all well, you can play just as well on a mediocre instrument, so well in fact that people can't hear the difference – okay, so I'm exaggerating a little. But by now people have been saying for a long time that there are contemporary violin makers making phenomenal instruments. There were such violin makers already in the 1950s: Carl Berger in Chicago was making fabulous instruments at that time. Nothing about their sound betrayed the fact that they were modern instruments. Christian Tetzlaff prefers his Greiner violin[3] to his Stradivarius, and Günter Pichler does too.

1 Rembert Wurlitzer (1904–1963) was the grandson of Franz Rudolf Wurlitzer, Cincinnati-based founder of the piano and organ company that bears his name. Rembert Wurlitzter studied violin making with Amédée Dieudonné and learned the technical fundamentals of the business under Alfred Hill, of W. E. Hill & Sons, in London. In 1937 he joined the stringed instruments department of the Wurlitzer family business in New York, which he set up as an independent company in 1949, and which became one of the most distinguished firms in the trade, patronized by many of the world's leading violinists, with a first rate workshop and an important collection of rare and fine instruments. The business was closed in 1974.

2 Giovanni Battista Ceruti (1756–1817), Cremonese violin maker.

3 Along with Tetzlaff and Pichler (who was the first violinist in the Alban Berg Quartet), Kim Kashkashian, Isabelle van Keulen, and members of the Hagen Quartet play instruments made by Stefan-Peter Greiner; Anne-Sophie Mutter and Vadim Repin have also commissioned instruments from him.

RS Heinrich Schiff once said in an interview that his students often came to him saying that they don't like the sound of their instrument, they've got to take it back to the shop and have the bridge adjusted, and so on, and his response was always to ask them whether they'd tried fixing it by practicing.

WL Indeed, exactly, that's just it. String players very often impute far too much importance to their instruments, and so much of what concerns them is extrinsic to making music, superficialities that don't mean a thing to me. Of course it helps to have a good tool. Of course there are subtleties that are easier to produce on a Stradivarius or Guarneri or Amati, and more difficult on most others: dynamic and timbral differences are more differentiated on such instruments, and they respond more reliably. But the great 17th century instruments are also very fragile, you're constantly having to go back to the shop to keep them in good working order. Peter Kamnitzer never dared to work on the Amatis: when we were on tour we had to go to Zurich to have the instruments adjusted, to Paul Bänziger.

RS How did you get to know Rembert Wurlitzer?

WL At first, after I arrived in New York in 1946, I would go to Emil Herrmann's shop on 57th Street to have my violin serviced, which is also where I first bought a violin myself and was cheated right away: what he sold me as a Ceruti violin wasn't one. But once I realized I'd been cheated I started going instead to Rembert Wurlitzer's shop on 42nd Street. Afterwards the whole quartet always went to Wurlitzer to have their instruments cared for. He was from the famous Wurlitzer family in Cincinnati, the Wurlitzers of the Wurlitzer organs, the theater organs. Their son Rembert had opened a stringed instrument shop in New York, in a building that belonged to the Wurlitzers. He had a whole floor, and it was more fantastic than you can possibly imagine. He had all the money in the world and was quite knowledgeable, actually incredibly knowledgeable about stringed instruments, and he'd hired the best people to repair instruments and maintain them. Simone Sacconi, who was a great violin maker, went to Wurlitzer's when Herrmann gave up his business.[4] At Wurlitzer's you met everybody who was anybody. Whenever you were there, Nathan Milstein might be playing in the

[4] Simone Fernando Sacconi (1895–1973) became an assistant in Giuseppe Rossi's violin making workshop in Rome while he was still a student. By the time he was sixteen years old he had a clientele of his own. In 1931 he joined Emil Herrmann's firm in New York, and when Herrmann's closed in 1951 he went to Wurlitzer's, where he established a first class workshop. In 1972 he published *I 'segreti' di Stradivari*, in which he describes Stradivari's working methods in detail.

back room, or Szigeti would be there – all the great violinists brought their instruments to him and tried out this one and that one or had their violins looked at to see if they were in good shape. Wurlitzer was a wonderful person, quiet, great, refined: a real gentleman. We totally understood one another, right from the beginning, and he always lent me decent instruments.

So it happened once that I came back from Brazil with an instrument that Wurlitzer had lent me; I had spent the Christmas holidays in 1947 visiting my uncle there. In those days they were still flying the DC-4 propeller aircraft that didn't have pressurized cabins. And after the insanely hot summer in Brazil, well over 100° every day without air conditioning and with incredible humidity, we flew north over the equator and arrived in New York in a mammoth snow storm, one of the biggest, one of the worst snow storms ever, we couldn't even land in New York, the airport was closed, we were redirected to Bermuda. We flew to New York the following day, and I walked through the most incredible snow drifts to get to Wurlitzer's and return the borrowed violin. I opened the case, and there were 88 pieces of wood: I've never been so shocked in all my life, I must have turned as pale as chalk. And Wurlitzer just laughed and said, oh, I must have just come back from the tropics! Thank God violins are made with a glue that gets soft when something like this happens, otherwise the wood would crack and we'd have to throw the violin away. But it looks like all the pieces are there, so all we have to do is glue it back together! He put me right at ease, I found that so touching: not a single word of reproach. Wurlitzer was always very nice to us, and he always kept in mind that we were looking for instruments.

One day I was with Wurlitzer in his shop, having some repair work done on my violin, and I spoke with him once again about how we were still looking for instruments, he said, he thought he had an idea about that: Gerald Warburg just happened to be sitting in his office in the back, did I know him? I didn't know him. So he took me back to his office and introduced me to Gerald Warburg. Warburg was a cellist and conductor from the family that owned the Warburg Bank. He was a passionate chamber music player and could afford to own very beautiful instruments and to have famous musicians from in and around New York come to his house to play chamber music on these splendid instruments.

He had a Stradivarius quartet, a Guarneri quartet, and an Amati quartet. And he was on the verge of buying the Stradivarius cello that had belonged to Emanuel Feuermann, but his wife told him that she was not having that in her house. If he was going to buy another cello, then he would first have to sell some of the instruments he already had: he didn't need to have three quartets standing around! And he told

Wurlitzer that, who responded by reminding him of the Amati quartet[5] that he had brought to us for repair and adjustment. Why didn't he sell it? There was someone in the shop just then who was looking for a quartet of stringed instruments.

And so Gerald Warburg invited me to come to his apartment on Fifth Avenue that very evening, where they were going to be playing music. It was an unbelievably exciting evening, the most fantastic musicians were there, and at dinner later he asked me if we were interested in this Amati quartet. I told him that if Rembert Wurlitzer said they would suit us, then 'interested' wouldn't be the word for it! But we could never afford them, we didn't have that kind of money! But, Warburg said to me, since we were in Cincinnati, we needn't worry about the money, his cousin Alfi Friedlander was there, he'd speak to him about it and make some arrangement. Alfred Friedlander was one of our best friends in Cincinnati, and he was Gerald Warburg's cousin! We didn't know that. When I asked Gerald Warburg how much the instruments would cost, he replied that he didn't know, the price would be booked as income and so it couldn't go beyond a certain level, since otherwise the tax on all his earnings would be in a higher bracket and that could cost him a fortune.[6] So his tax advisor would have to establish the price. And Alfi Friedlander referred us to a bank in Cincinnati for the financing.

When I got back to Cincinnati I asked them how we could finance the purchase of these instruments. They told me they would give me the money now, so that I can pay for the instruments, and I could pay them back later. I wanted to know how much that would cost us in the meantime. He just smiled and explained to me that they weren't interested in making money off the great musicians of the city! They were happy to be able to help us acquire these beautiful instruments and they would make money from their other business! The guarantee for the money was our friend Friedlander. But we only found out about that much later, he didn't want us to have to thank him for it. But we were able to pay off the loan in just three or four years, since after Gerald Warburg's discussion with his tax advisor the price was ridiculously low, it had nothing at all to do with the real value of the instruments. Besides

[5] The two violins (1648 and 1682) and the cello (1670–1684) were made by Nicolò Amati, the viola (1619) was made by his father Girolamo Amati and Girolamo's half-brother Antonio Amati.

[6] The four instruments were sold to the LaSalle Quartet, not to its individual members, for a total of around $37,500 (which would be roughly ten times that amount in today's dollars). It is likely that Warburg sold them at a loss relative to what he had paid for them and used the loss to offset other income, whereas had he sold them at market-value he would have been liable for about 90% (the top bracket in those years was 91%) of the difference between what he netted from such a sale and what he had originally paid for them. Warburg's 'tax bracket' story was no doubt a simplification for Levin's benefit of what was a rather complex accounting situation.

which we already were getting rather a lot of concert engagements and we regularly turned over about half of our honoraria to the bank.

So we came to possess this splendid Amati quartet, and to this day the instruments belong to the members of the LaSalle Quartet. Later on we dissolved our joint possession of them and each member got his instrument as his own personal property. That was a good investment, since shortly thereafter the value of the instruments began to rise. It's amazing enough just to have an Amati violin from 1648, a large and relatively rare Stradivarius model – phenomenal! The only drawback to this violin is its highly arched top plate, which makes it easy for the sound post to slip out. My violin, by the way, had been in Cincinnati once before, when it belonged to Eugène Ysaÿe, who conducted the Cincinnati Symphony for four years and taught violin at the Cincinnati Conservatory. There's a famous picture of Ysaÿe with the violin that I now have. Peter Kamnitzer's instrument was the world famous 'Medici' viola made by Girolamo Amati. The cello had belonged to Gregor Piatigorsky and for a long time was thought to be a Stradivarius instrument. But Rembert Wurlitzer discovered that it was an Amati cello that Stradivarius had worked on.

RS People are always talking to you about the Amati instruments, but nobody ever talks to you about your bows. What bows did the LaSalle Quartet have?

WL Well, that's a sorry chapter in our history. We were never as fortunate with bows as we were with instruments. It's also a difficult matter, you have to be extremely careful to find one that suits you, and even with a very good bow you have to get used to it and to some extent adapt your technique to it.

RS And not every bow is right for everything.

WL No, not necessarily. I never made a fetish of instruments and I was never all that concerned with bows either. That was probably a big mistake. I should have been more interested in getting a really first class bow, or several of them, but even at that time the price of bows was going up very fast. On top of which they were often sold under fraudulent names, which made them much too expensive. I was no expert in this field and didn't feel at all sure of myself. On the other hand, Günther Pichler of the Alban Berg Quartet knows an enormous amount about bows and is constantly trying them out. It was a sheer stroke of luck to have gotten the Amati instruments. Otherwise I might have played my Ceruti violin for the rest of my life.

RS Couldn't Rembert Wurlitzer also help you out with bows?

WL He could have helped, but you had to show you were interested in them, and I really wasn't.

RS It wasn't any different for your colleagues?

WL Henry Meyer had several good bows and was always more interested in them than I was. The other two weren't interested in them at all, not even Peter Kamnitzer, who was a trained violin maker.

RS Apparently Jack Kirstein wanted to keep the Amati cello after he left the LaSalle Quartet in 1975.

WL Yes, that was an unpleasant business. He violated our contract, under which at that time the instruments were still the common property of the LaSalle Quartet. That's when I learned for the first time that contracts don't mean a thing if people don't honor them. But we got it back, and since then Lee Fiser plays the Amati cello.

RS Recently my wife and I have listened to several different tapes of the LaSalle Quartet performing Mozart's last quartet, K. 590, in F major. My wife has a good ear and as we were listening to the second recording she said that the cello was not the same instrument as the one being played in the first recording. And then listening to the third recording she said that this time it was the cello from the first recording again. I looked it up: the first recording was from October, 1967, with Jack Kirstein, the second was from 1976 with Lee Fiser, apparently playing his own cello, and the third was from October, 1986, with him playing the Amati cello.

WL Yes, right, at close listening there is of course a difference. Bravo!

RS How long did it take you to get the Amati cello back?

WL It took a year or two. We ended up going to court, where the judge said we were completely out of our minds. He told us to kindly come to some agreement among ourselves, that something like this doesn't belong in court. So we eventually settled out of court.

RS There's an early photo that shows the LaSalle Quartet seated in a very unusual arrangement: the first and second violins are sitting opposite one another, that is, the arrangement is, going clock-wise, first violin, viola, cello, second violin.[7] I found that rather illuminating, since so much music, for instance by Haydn, Mozart, and Beethoven, is composed antiphonally. Did you really play in this seating arrangement to begin with?

WL No, we never played seated like that! It was probably just the photographer wanting us to sit that way for the picture. Seating was never an issue for us.

RS So you always sat with the viola on the outside, that is, opposite the first violin, and the cello inside?

WL Always, from the very beginning. I don't think it really matters much, how a quartet seats itself. That's a personal preference – though of course the balances have to work. But all the same I find seating the cello outside inferior, not only visually but also with respect to the balance and coherence of the group, which a quartet has also to exemplify. People argue that when the viola is seated on the outside its sound projects backwards into the stage instead of out into the hall. But even if the violist is seated inside its sound isn't projected directly to the audience. And with the cello on the outside you're forced to sit in a rather open semi-circle in order for its sound to project into the hall, since the sound radiating from the back of the instrument is somewhat muffled by the body of the player. It's never been proven that stringed instruments sound better when they're played with the f-holes facing into the hall: the back of the instrument is also vibrating and projecting its sound.

RS But in symphonic music the antiphonal seating with the first violins on the left and the seconds on the right does make sense.

WL In symphonic music I find it better, just as Toscanini did, and as was common prior to that.[8] Then you can really hear the 'stereo effect,' but for a string quartet the circle is just much too small for that. But I really don't think it's all that important.

[7] See figure 11, p. 83.

[8] The most widely used orchestral seating arrangement, with the first and second violins to the left of the conductor and the violas and cellos to the right, goes back to Leopold Stokowski, who for acoustic reasons experimented with various seating arrangements during his tenure as conductor of the Philadelphia Orchestra (1912–1936). The argument for the seating arrangement that he came to prefer was that it allowed the sound of all the violins to project directly into the hall.

12 *Recording*

ROBERT SPRUYTENBURG: For a long time the LaSalle Quartet didn't have a contract with a record company. How did it come about that in 1967 you signed up with Deutsche Grammophon?

WALTER LEVIN: That's another one of those chains of coincidences. That Deutsche Grammophon took an interest in us was due to one of their producers, Karl Faust. Karl Faust was the son of a master craftsman in my uncle's knife and steel works in Brazil. When my uncle Zivi started this business he hired people who were working at home, people who had come from the Rhineland, Wupperthal, Solingen, and all around there, people who were masters of their craft, and who became the master craftsmen in his factory. They were relatively young Germans with families who had gone to Brazil, to Porto Alegre, after 1933. One of them was a certain Herr Faust, whose son Karl became a musician. Karl Faust was a violist and a composer who went back to Germany after the war, in 1946–1947, and got a job not as a violist but as a producer at Deutsche Grammophon, which at that time still needed people who knew something about music. He was also someone who knew how to get along with people, someone who had a certain flair about him. So he was obviously someone they could use. I didn't know him then. But he knew about us from the newspapers, since we also played in Hamburg, where Deutsche Grammophon had its offices, and he knew that I was a nephew of Paul Zivi, with whom his father worked, so he'd already heard of me.

One day we got a letter or a call from Karl Faust saying that he wanted to meet with me in Schönried near Gstaad. He met with me and told me that he'd heard that we had a very good quartet – and would we possibly be interested in recording something for Deutsche Grammophon? I replied that we would of course be interested, the question was only what we would record. He said we would have to talk about that, but that in the meanwhile I should make a list for him of what we were prepared to record and what would be of interest to us, so he could think through how they might go about it.

So I sat down one afternoon and thought about what I would like to record. We found this list again recently: in the coming years we recorded virtually everything on it, from A to Z. Of course I would have liked to record a couple of Mozart quartets too, but other things had priority, since I could never see the point of duplicating what had already been recorded any number of times. I didn't even need to do all the Beethoven quartets. The late quartets, though, that's something else again, there are different ways of approaching them, so that appealed to me. The Schoenberg school also appealed to me, and the New Music, the post-war music.

We got along very well together, Karl Faust and I, and at some point we got word from Deutsche Grammophon that we should come and make a recording with them. That's how our first recordings came about: Hugo Wolf's d minor quartet and the Lutosławski and Penderecki quartets.[1] We made them at Tempelhof, the old airport in Berlin that has since been closed, in an old airplane hangar that had once been used as a film studio and was now empty. The roof leaked, so every now and then we had to shift a little to one side or the other to get out of the way of the drips. You can't begin to imagine how primitive it was. That's where we made our first records for Deutsche Grammophon.

RS Didn't Deutsche Grammophon have studios of its own?

WL No, never. We often made our recordings in the auditorium of a school in Hamburg-Harburg. We had to interrupt the recording sessions during recess, since the children were yelling and screaming in the yard. In Munich the recordings took place in a hall in the Residenz – the old palace – beautiful!

RS Did you have a five year contract to begin with?

WL Yes, an exclusive contract. It was very favorable for them, we got almost nothing, only a very small percentage. In the beginning they paid our expenses, and then we waited for the records to be issued, from which we got a very small percentage of the sales. At first it wasn't even ten percent.

RS Did the contract also stipulate what you were to record?

WL Again, never. From time to time we discussed what we would record, and when. The recording sessions had to coincide with our tours, and the pieces to be recorded had to be in our active repertory. It seemed self-evident to us that you needed a long time to prepare a piece for recording, that if possible you would have already played it for several years at least. For instance, we didn't record the Nono quartet for Deutsche Grammophon until three and a half years after we'd premiered it. We always scheduled our recording dates for the end of a tour, by which time we'd played these pieces repeatedly in concert, and

[1] These recordings were made in December, 1967.

could thoroughly rehearse them once again. You have to be able to concentrate on a piece in order for it to go well in the recording session.

EVI LEVIN: But then in the later contracts there was a lot that you insisted on, for instance, you had to approve the photographs.

WL What the record covers would look like, what would be in the liner notes, everything had to be sent to us for review and approval.

EL There were some offers from other record companies before Deutsche Grammophon.

WL Yes, for instance after Gunther Schuller was with us in Cincinnati the second time we played his quartet, his first quartet – incidentally a very beautiful piece which we played rather often.[2] Since then he's written more quartets, but I don't know them. Anyway he came to Cincinnati, and was very pleased with our concert. Afterwards he asked us why we hadn't made any recordings. At home I played him some of the live recordings of our concerts, about which he said that they were better than anything else out there. He told me that he had made recordings with Columbia Records in New York and that he would speak to them and tell them they should listen to us sometime.

So I got a call from someone in New York, from Columbia Records, informing me that Gunther Schuller had indeed said that we were a good quartet, and asking me if I could drop by sometime with something they could listen to. So I gathered up my records, a whole suitcase full of them, took a plane to New York, and went to the office of the man Gunther Schuller had spoken with at Columbia Records. A huge office with a magnificent view of New York – beautiful. He was on the telephone. He had two telephones, and when he was finished with a call on one of them, the next call came in on the other. I sat there and waited and waited while the telephones rang and rang. After a while I stood up and was on the point of leaving when he asked me whether I was waiting for him. I said that yes, I was, but I wouldn't be for very much longer. He apologized, saying he didn't know about this, and told his secretary that he didn't want to be disturbed for the next 15 minutes.

He wanted to know what he could do for me, and I reminded him that it was he who had called me, that I was Walter Levin from the LaSalle Quartet. Then he remembered that I was someone Gunther Schuller had recommended. He wanted to know what I had in mind, and I told him that we would like to make some recordings: we were a

2 Gunther Schuller (1925–), American horn player and composer. For his quartets, see pp. 334–336.

young quartet, we were good, and we had a large repertory. I mentioned that I'd brought some live recordings of our concerts with me so that he could hear us playing all kinds of things, including Gunther Schuller's quartet, and also earlier music, and the classical and romantic repertory. I thought that among them there might be some pieces that Columbia hadn't already recorded with another group. His response was to say that they already had the Juilliard Quartet, which of course was one of the best quartets in the country, and however good we might be, he wouldn't want to have another quartet working in the same kind of repertory.

But he had another idea, he said, something he thought would be of interest to us, an idea for a great recording that would probably sell a lot. Columbia wanted to make a recording of Strauss waltzes, with Alexander Schneider as the violin soloist in a kind of Schrammel Quartet, like they had in the wine gardens, the outdoors garden restaurants in Vienna a century ago, with double bass and string quartet.[3] Would that be of interest to us? I told him no, that wasn't what we had in mind at all, neither something I thought we would like to do nor even anything we ought to do. A recording like that would introduce us in the wrong way, it would give people a mistaken impression of us, and it would be very difficult for us to overcome that later on. So no, it wasn't a good idea at all, although, I told him, I would be honored to be asked even to unpack my instrument for Columbia. But if he thought that our repertory was of no interest to Columbia, or that we would be in competition with the Juilliard Quartet, then he was asking the wrong person. Thank you very much, good bye. That was my experience with Columbia Records.

RS But didn't Deutsche Grammophon have concerns about the Amadeus Quartet that were similar to the concerns Columbia had about the Juilliard Quartet? That is, since the Amadeus Quartet already covered the classical repertory for them, wasn't there some agreement to the effect that the LaSalle Quartet would record a different repertory?

WL No, never. The Amadeus Quartet were friends of ours, and there was never any competition between us: we played a repertory that they never played, and there was quite a lot that they didn't play. And it wasn't long before we had a huge success with the boxed set of the complete Second

[3] *Schrammelmusik* is a strain of Viennese popular music dating back to the late 19th century; it takes its name from the violinist-composer brothers Johann Schrammel (1850–1893) and Josef Schrammel (1852–1895.) Together with their bass guitar playing friend Anton Strohmayer (1848–1937), they formed a phenomenally successful trio in 1878, playing in wine gardens, inns, outdoor restaurants, and similar venues in and around Vienna. The trio became a quartet a year later, in 1879, with addition of clarinetist Georg Dänzer (1848–1893).

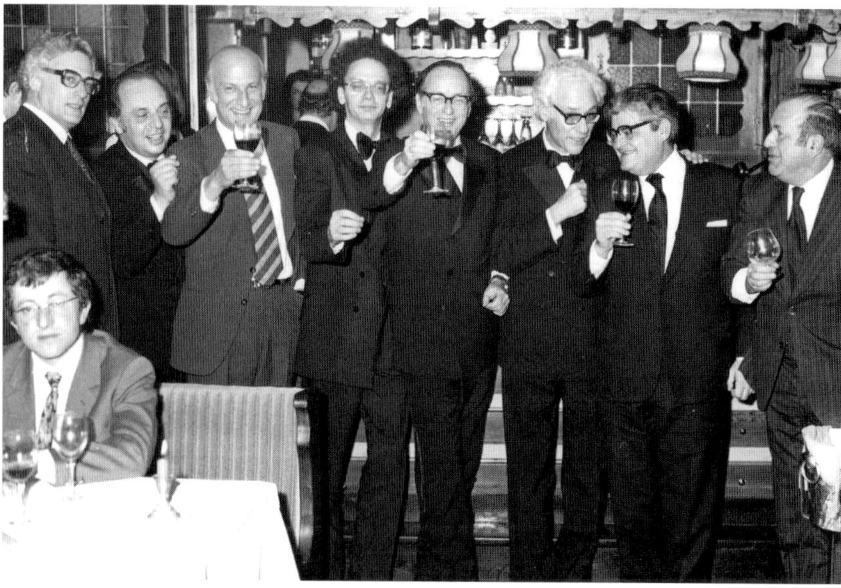

28 The LaSalle Quartet with the Amadeus Quartet, Hamburg, 1976

Viennese School quartets.[4] It was Karl Faust who wanted to produce this set. But Deutsche Grammophon rejected the idea at first. They told us we wouldn't sell even thirty copies, the project was total nonsense, it would be a complete waste of money! But Faust got his way, we made the recordings, the set was listed among the new releases announced for Christmas, 1971, and the relatively small initial pressing sold out completely within just a few days. It was self-evident that Deutsche Grammophon had completely misjudged the market, so they had something on the order of another 200 copies pressed, which sold out just as quickly. Then they were in a frenzy to get another 1,000 copies pressed. Crazy! They finally realized that they had a best seller on their hands and had it produced in huge quantities, which sold like hot cakes.

RS And it's still in print!

WL Even now. There's nothing else like it. As far as I can tell, it's the only quartet recording that's been in the catalogue non-stop for more than forty years and is still selling. It was a colossal hit. After that the people at Deutsche Grammophon realized what it was they had with us. And the reviews of it were just sensational, it made our whole career in Europe.

[4] The five quartets by Arnold Schoenberg, Alban Berg's two quartets, and Anton Webern's *Fünf Stücke* Opus 5, *Bagatelles* Opus 9, and quartet Opus 28 were recorded between March 1968 and March 1970.

RS Then came the *Deutscher Schallplattenpreis* and the *Grand Prix du Disque.*

WL Yes, all of that, and it made the press worldwide, even the German and Austrian press, you can't begin to imagine the reviews it got. A huge article by Joachim Kaiser in *Die Welt*, in the recordings section of the Christmas edition. After that we could do any crazy thing we wanted at Deutsche Grammophon. All we had to do was to say what we wanted to record and they did it. Right up until the very end. Who else would have made recordings of Michael Gielen's quartet and a Schnabel quartet? But I wanted to have them, as documentation, and so Deutsche Grammophon recorded them.

RS Did you generally have a good working relationship with Deutsche Grammophon for the recording sessions themselves?

WL A phenomenal relationship, actually, we had the best team you could possibly imagine. We always had the same producer, Rainer Brock, a wonderful man who then, sadly, died in 1986. He was an absolutely marvelous human being, cultivated, level-headed, with a comprehensive musical education and infallibly good taste. He'd studied conducting with Hans Swarowski in Vienna, in the same class with Claudio Abbado and Zubin Mehta. He put himself completely at our disposal and really loved working with us. He only had three artists with whom he worked on a regular basis: Claudio Abbado, Maurizio Pollini, and ourselves. It all went exceedingly well. Deutsche Grammophon produced outstanding recordings, and in my opinion their technical quality was equally good. We always had not only the same producer but also the same recording engineers, Klaus Scheibe, and later Wolfgang Mitlehner – with them you practically didn't need to listen to the sound checks. Later on we didn't even check the microphone placements: Rainer Brock knew exactly what it was we wanted. He came to our concerts and brought the recording engineers with him so they could all hear just how we played the pieces in concert. They wanted to record us in such a way that the pieces would sound exactly as we had conceived of them in the concert. Which means in such a way that you can hear everything and can hear all four instruments, and that our balances and dynamics can be heard as we played them and not overridden by the sound technicians.

RS Did you always play each movement of a piece all the way through when you were recording it?

WL Always. And then after we had recorded two or three complete versions of a movement, Rainer Brock would say that for safety's sake he needed to have us play a few little sections again and could we please start again at bar 5 and just play as far as bar 20, and so on. Then before we went on to the next movement, he would suggest that we take a break and get something to drink. Then we would play through the next movement, as many as three times or more, and if that went well he would say 'okay.' And if it didn't go so well, then we either played it through once again or else played little bits of it. Usually he asked us to play it all the way through, he thought it was better for us to play everything all the way through. Our recording sessions generally went very smoothly, and never lasted as long as we had planned for. We always booked the studio for more time than we needed, intentionally, so we wouldn't be under any pressure to finish up.

But strange things sometimes happened in the studio. For instance, it sometimes happened that Lee Fiser interrupted a take, and not just once! During a take! That was strictly forbidden. He would interrupt to say that something was no good and that we had to start over again from the beginning, that we weren't together. We all fell silent, and then started over again from the beginning, but shortly he would interrupt again, saying that we still weren't together or that he simply couldn't accept how he had played something. You could just throw out all these takes. After maybe half an hour of this we would hear the voice of our imperturbable Rainer Brock suggesting that we take a short break and come up to the recording booth, have some juice and cookies, and to listen to one or another of the takes. Great, marvelous. We were all overjoyed to be taking a break, to get away from this.

So we all went upstairs, and Rainer said he'd very much like to play us something. He began to play the first take, up to where Lee Fiser had interrupted, at which point he stopped and said, 'So that's that,' and gave Lee a good hard look before going on to the next take. He played us all the takes, and nothing Lee had said was true. It was all just a figment of his imagination. Maybe he wasn't feeling well. As Rainer went on, Lee grew more and more silent and withdrawn. Finally Rainer said he would like to remind us once again that we had an agreement that none of us would interrupt a take, that if anyone was to interrupt, it would be him. He asked us to please go back downstairs and play a complete take of the movement, just as we'd always done, and if something wasn't right, he would ask us to make a second or even a third complete take, and if there was still something that wasn't right, we would make some short takes, as always – we really ought to know by now that we could rely on him. And then we went back and resumed working the way we always had.

It's terrible when people become contentious, even mulish, as Lee sometimes did. When that happened then as far as he was concerned nobody could do anything right. And vice-versa too: nobody was doing anything wrong. I was the one who was always criticizing everything, and if that got on his nerves, he would argue vehemently that there was absolutely nothing wrong with how we had just played something, no matter how dreadful it had just been. It's difficult when someone has a personal conflict with someone else in a quartet and allows that to affect how they work together on something that has nothing at all to do with the conflict at all.

Listening to recordings you've made but haven't heard for years or decades is something else again: they always sound as if someone else were playing. You can't even recall how the recording came about. At first all you hear is everything that didn't work, that is, everything that isn't the way you wanted it, or the way you would want it now. You don't even hear what's good about it. Do you know the story of our recording Schumann's F major quartet for Radio Zurich? We recorded it at the end of a season, after a tour of Japan. We went to Zurich and in the morning we had a recording session[5] with Radio Zurich that included this quartet. It was the last thing on our schedule before we went on vacation, and we weren't looking forward to it at all.

We went to the studio, where we were met by a very nice elderly gentleman who was to be our producer. We began to play, and the first movement was – well, I've heard better kazoos. And Lee Fiser, who was always self-critical, said we couldn't let that be, we had to do it again. So okay, we play the movement once again. Beautiful, said the producer, could we go on to the second movement now? Lee said it wasn't all that beautiful, but nevertheless, we played the second movement. This time Lee said that what we had done was no good at all, we would have to play it again, at which point the producer asked us why we played everything twice when it was already fabulous the way we played it the first time. One of my colleagues replied that it was safer if we recorded everything twice, since if something happened to one of the takes while it was being edited, he would have the other one to fall back on.

So we played the movement again, and after this take, which we weren't at all happy with either, Peter Kamnitzer said to me that what we were doing didn't make any sense, because this producer was clueless, a complete idiot. We should just play the rest of the piece straight through and then get out of here and go on vacation. What else could we do? The producer wasn't going to do any editing, he'd use the first takes as is, just as they were, so there was no point in our playing everything twice. No sooner said than done. We played the rest of the piece with our vacations firmly in mind and devil take the hindmost, packed up our

[5] On July 15, 1983.

instruments, and left the studio swearing to one another that we would never ever listen to this recording. The producer asked us whether we didn't want to have a listen and Peter told him 'no way!' Peter was like that. We just wanted to get out of there. So we left, and as far as we were concerned the recording was over and done with.

Fifteen or twenty years later we were in Flims, just sitting around doing nothing in particular, when we heard the Schumann F major quartet on the radio. 'Ah,' I said, 'what a lovely piece, I really like that piece.' I said to Evi, 'Just listen to that, they play really well, these people, I've scarcely ever heard this piece played so well. My god but I'd like to know who it is.' We listened through to the end and then heard the announcer say it was our recording! You could have knocked me down with a feather. I have no idea what was going on with us in the studio when we made the recording. It had been at the end of the season, nothing seemed to go right, we were hyper-critical, we were irritable, we didn't want to be there, everything about it was awful. We were just in a bad mood.

13 *Teaching*

ROBERT SPRUYTENBURG: The LaSalle Quartet was always a teaching quartet as well as a performing quartet. When did you begin teaching?

WALTER LEVIN: We began to teach systematically at Colorado College, where we were on the music faculty. Since it was just a small liberal arts college, there weren't very many instrumentalists, which kept our instrumental and chamber music teaching load within bounds. But we were supposed to teach various subjects in the music department, each of us according to his own interests. Peter Kamnitzer, for instance, gave a course on 'music for the layman' and also a course in musical analysis. I gave a course on the Mozart operas, because I was always a big Mozart opera fan and had been ever since I first heard them as a child at the Staatsoper in Berlin – I remember when I was only twelve years old I took the piano reduction of *Die Entführung aus dem Serail* with me to England on vacation, to Swansea, and played it for myself. In New York, while I was at Juilliard, I bought all the Mozart opera scores, and in Colorado I finally had a chance to study them more closely and to play recordings of them for people: the Glyndebourne recordings with Fritz Busch were available by then. I really enjoyed doing that.

Some of the students at Colorado Springs were a bit older than us, war veterans, both men and women, whose college education was being paid for by the federal government under the so-called 'GI-bill.' So they were in their early to mid-thirties, and exceptionally highly motivated. We'd never met such students before: adults who were eager to make up for what they'd missed out on because of the war, and their enthusiasm was highly motivating for us, too. I took these students with me to Denver, where a live transmission of Carmen from the Metropolitan Opera was being shown in a movie theater – that was in the early 1950s! Of course back then it was still in black and white, but for people who had never seen an opera before it was an incredible experience.

RS You once mentioned that you put on a Mozart opera at Colorado College.

WL Well, part of one. Some of the students in my course on the Mozart operas were studying voice, so we had soloists, we could put together a small chorus, and there were a couple of good wind players. The string students at Colorado College weren't good enough, so the LaSalle Quartet played the string parts. We presented the whole first act of Mozart's *Zauberflöte* for one of the regular Sunday concerts at Colorado College. I have a recording of it.

RS Did the individual members of the LaSalle Quartet also teach their instruments in Cincinnati?

WL Yes, it was a much bigger conservatory, with a great many more instrumentalists. Some of them went on to have good professional careers.

RS In Cincinnati, did you also continue to give special courses on subjects like the Mozart operas?

WL No, in Cincinnati we no longer taught any courses, we had enough to do with teaching our instruments and teaching chamber music – a subject that developed to an extraordinary extent after 1962, when the College-Conservatory was merged into the University of Cincinnati, which hadn't had a music department before then. My main interest was in teaching quartets. By that time, our Sunday Group had not only established a LaSalle Foundation but also a Friedlander Chamber Music Fellowship fund, the earnings of which made it possible for us to invite a gifted young quartet to come and study with us in Cincinnati every year. The College-Conservatory offered a stipend on top of that and waived tuition for them. The first to come to Cincinnati on a Friedlander Fellowship was the Alban Berg Quartet. In the course of the following years many quartets came to Cincinnati on Friedlander Fellowships: the Brahms Quartet from Hamburg with Uwe Haiberg as first violin, the Pražák Quartet from Prague, the Artis Quartet from Vienna, the Buchberger Quartet from Frankfurt, the Ponche Quartet from Germany, and in 1989, shortly before the reunification of East and West Germany, the Vogler Quartet came to us from East Berlin. We had met the Vogler Quartet in 1986 at the Evian Competition, where the whole LaSalle Quartet was on the jury. They played the second Ligeti quartet and a Mozart quartet so extraordinarily well that they won the competition with multiple prizes. They had been very well prepared by Eberhard Feltz, their quartet teacher at the Hanns Eisler Academy of Music in Berlin.

RS You once mentioned that you considered teaching to be a way for the LaSalle Quartet to reflect on its own approach to performance.

WL When you're teaching, you really have to be able to explain what it is that you're trying to get across, you really have to be able to give reasons for it. But since we'd all had very good and systematic instruction from Galamian, and I'd also had much the same thing from Bergmann even before that, we had no problem with knowing how to teach our instruments. But when you want to convey to an ensemble what it means to interpret something, that is, if you're to teach a quartet how to play, for instance, Haydn, Mozart, or Beethoven, then you have to come to some clarity yourself about what it is that a string quartet is actually supposed to render in sound, that is, what the music itself demands: what are the characteristics of the classical quartet composition?

Usually you begin with the classical style, since you begin by teaching Haydn, Mozart, Beethoven, Schubert, and Brahms. More recent and difficult pieces already presuppose a very high level of both technical facility and musicianship. First of all there's the purely technical issue of playing together. Secondly there are the issues of balance and tone color: should the quartet sound like one single instrument or not? And then you have to think about what decisions have to be made with respect to a composition, what questions must be asked of it, the answers to which are ultimately represented by the interpretation, by the performance. It always has to do with asking questions about a composition, about its particular style, and about what was taken for granted by musicians in the period in which it was written. 'Because that's the way I like it,' is no criterion at all.

For instance, you have to learn – and learn for yourself – that in the classical period when there's no dynamic marked in the score the piece is supposed to begin *forte* – this and a whole lot more. In time we acquired books that deal with such issues: Leopold Mozart's treatise on violin playing,[1] for example, and Czerny's writings on interpreting Beethoven's piano works,[2] and any other such historical sources that tell us something about these matters of interpretation. We had to learn a lot of this by ourselves, that, to take another example, if the first bar of a piece is marked *piano* and a bar later a *forte* is written, it means that there is to be a continuous crescendo across the two bars. We didn't know that when we were just starting out on our career and so we didn't do it: if you listen to our early recording of Mozart's F major quartet K. 590, we play a *subito forte* in the second bar. So you yourself end up learning a lot when you teach. Unfortunately most teachers do just the opposite: they have their own ideas about how the music should be played and aren't interested in what's in the score.

RS Did you first read these sources with a view to teaching or were they already known to you?

WL I knew some but by no means all of them, as in many cases I didn't even know they existed. You come to learn an enormous amount over the

[1] Leopold Mozart, *Versuch einer gründlichen Violinschule* (Wiesbaden,1991). English translation, *A Treatise on the Fundamental Principles of Violin Playing* (Oxford, 1985).

[2] Carl Czerny, *Über den richtigen Vortrag der sämtlichen Beethoven'schen Klavierwerke* (Vienna, 1963). English translation, *On the proper performance of all Beethoven's works for the piano* (Bryn Mawr, 1970).

years. Your education isn't finished when you're twenty-four, and when are you ever really finished with it? I've always been a reader, always getting new books, and I've always been surprised at how much I didn't know. For instance, I wanted to get the analysis of Berg's *Lyric Suite* in Willi Reich's book, which at that time was the only available biography of Berg,[3] but I couldn't find it anywhere. When Evi was in Colorado Springs the summer before our engagement at Colorado College checking out the college, she found the book in the library and made me a typewritten copy of the chapter on the *Lyric Suite*. When I first read it, I really found myself wondering what sort of German *that* was supposed to be. This was the first time I was confronted with a text by Adorno. But it was only much later that I found out that it was by Adorno, since although the book of course indicates which chapters are by Adorno, I only had Evi's typescript of this one chapter, so I didn't know that then. And what a brilliant analysis it is! But I can understand it only now, having analyzed the piece myself.

RS After the LaSalle Quartet disbanded in 1987, you might also have said to yourself that you were finished with teaching and now you were going to travel.

WL And that's just what I said!

RS But you nevertheless went on to concentrate on teaching and you've being doing that for more than twenty years already! That wasn't something you'd planned on doing?

WL No, it wasn't, not at all. I didn't have the least intention of teaching! We wanted to go on vacation! First of all we spent four weeks in Florence, relaxing and taking our time to see the city. On tour we went to many cities, but just for one evening, not really seeing them at all. We went everywhere, but we never had any time. After the Lasalle Quartet disbanded, we took over Stefan Litwin's apartment in Basel, where we still live, and from Basel we had in mind travelling all over Europe, going to museums and concerts, going to La Scala in Milan, we wanted to go to Vienna and Paris and to see Italy and Spain. But what actually happened was that Rudolf Kelterborn, who was then the director of the Academy of Music in Basel, asked me whether I would be willing, now that I was free, to teach chamber music in the winter term, just as I'd done with the quartet in the summers, but this time for the regular students at the Academy of Music. In the summers it had always been mostly students

[3] Willi Reich, *Alban Berg* (Vienna, 1937). English translation, *Alban Berg* (New York, 1965).

from elsewhere who got the benefit of the school's having invited us to give a course, since their own students were mostly gone during the summer vacation. So I agreed to do it, just once. That was more than twenty years ago, but it didn't stop at that, since then I've given the chamber music course every year.

The first year I taught here the Swiss music school directors' annual conference happened to be held in Basel. Kelterborn asked me to give a lecture-recital at the conference, with a student quartet from the school. Right afterwards the director of the Paris Conservatory approached me and asked me if I wouldn't also come to Paris to teach for a week, and then came Friedhelm Döhl, the director of the Academy of Music in Lübeck, who asked me if I wouldn't come to Lübeck sometime. And so one thing led to another, but not a bit of it was planned in advance. And then we were at a concert in Vienna and ran into Robert Mann and his wife Lucy, who told about the Steans Institute in Ravinia, which had just been established, and they asked me if I wouldn't also like to teach in Ravinia. So for five years I led the summer academy there.

RS The fruit of this twenty years of teaching is that by now a whole new quartet culture has arisen.

WL I do believe one can say that.

RS Without question your most prominent student is James Levine. How did you happen to meet him?

WL When we arrived at the College of Music in Cincinnati in September, 1953, to be the college's Quartet in Residence, I got a call right away from a lady who told me that her name was Helen Levine, that she was the mother of a boy who was musically very gifted, and that she wanted to know whether I might be willing to give him music lessons. I asked her what instrument he played, and when she said he was a pianist, I said that I thought she had called the wrong person, since I was a violinist and taught violin, not piano. She said that wasn't what she meant, that she and her husband had taken their son to Juilliard for an evaluation where they were advised that he should be given a general instruction in all aspects of music. I wanted to know how old the boy was. When she told me he was ten, I replied that I taught seventeen and eighteen year old students at a music school who are studying with the intention of having a professional career in music, and that I didn't teach prodigies or very young children. But she insisted that her son was a special case. I was unable to get rid of her, despite all my best efforts to do so. Finally she suggested that rather than go on talking about this on the telephone, I should just come and have dinner with them, then I could meet James, and maybe I would change my mind. So Evi and I accepted her invitation, went to the Levine's, and met Helen and her husband Lawrence and their oldest son, Jimmy.

It was an incredible visit. The first thing we noticed was that with James at the table nobody could get a word in edgewise: he was bursting with conversation and had a temperament that was simply overwhelming. And as a matter of fact, we didn't have much to say, and neither did his parents. They had just been in New York to have Jimmy evaluated at Juilliard and while they were there they went to the Metropolitan Opera, which is right across the street from Juilliard. It turned out that Jimmy was a big opera fanatic. He'd been allowed to look for a birthday present at F.A.O. Schwarz, the biggest toy store in New York, and had asked for a toy theater, which he showed us – he staged operas in his toy theater! After dinner he performed the first act of Mozart's *Figaro* for us, moving the toy figures around, playing the orchestra part on the piano, and singing the vocal parts in Italian, all of it by heart. It was absolutely incredible! Afterwards we talked a lot about opera, and he recounted a scene from *Aida*, which he said was from the second act. I told him he was mistaken, the scene he was telling us about is in the third act, not the second act. And then for the first time in the entire evening he stopped talking and just looked at me. He had an expression of complete surprise on his face, and then something happened that turned out to be very typical of Jimmy: his whole face lit up and he laughed and said, 'Yes! You're right, you're right!' It wasn't often that he ran into someone who knew more than he did, and evidently this made quite an impression on him.

His mother called us the next day and told us that later the same evening he had asked if she couldn't make arrangements for him to have lessons with this Walter Levin – that was Jimmy's doing, not mine. So that's how my relationship with James Levine came about. Afterwards I got a letter from Mark Schubart, the deputy dean of the Juilliard School, who had heard about James' evaluation and had urged his parents to find someone who could give him a general education in music. It occurred to him that the LaSalle Quartet was now in Cincinnati, that all four of us had been Juilliard students, and that in his opinion Walter Levin would be ideally suited to take on the responsibility of educating James in all the subjects that go along with becoming a musician.[4] I gave this idea some very careful consideration, and discussed it with the

[4] Mark Schubart's March, 1954, letter to Walter Levin includes the following: 'Today Mr. and Mrs. Levine brought their son James to Juilliard to play for our advisory committee. The jury was extremely impressed with his playing and it was obvious from their reaction that this young man was to be supported in every respect. After

Levines after I had gotten to know James a little better. He went to New York twice a month for piano lessons with Rosina Lhévinne,[5] who had been Van Cliburn's teacher and had taught many other great pianists as well. She was a wonderful woman and musician. Later on he studied with Rudolf Serkin at Marlboro. Evi and I took on everything else: Evi undertook to teach him languages and I taught him music theory.

EVI LEVIN: When he was in high school, he was excused from his afternoon classes so he could take language lessons with me privately and take the exams at the end of the year. We used opera libretti in French, German, and Italian.

RS Had your reputation as a pedagogue and mentor preceded you even then?

WL Yes, by then we'd already taught at Colorado College for four years, and word about us had gotten around a little.

RS How had James acquired such an astounding knowledge of music at such a young age?

WL He very quickly learned to play the piano quite well, the way all prodigies learn everything very quickly, also music.

EL When he was about three, his parents consulted a pediatrician because James stuttered. The doctor recommended having him play the piano, so that his excessive tension would pass through his hands and into the piano. So he began to play the piano, and his stuttering actually did vanish.

he played, Mr. and Mrs. Levine met with me to discuss their son's future. He appears to have a competent piano teacher, but the jury was of the opinion that it was time for him to begin studying the related musical subjects. I told the Levines that in my opinion they should put James in the hands of the best possible musician who would understand how to present the material to him clearly and vividly. From all that I've heard, that's what he needs most of all just now. His parents reminded me that you were now in Cincinnati, that they knew you and thought highly of you, so I had the idea that you might be willing and able to take on this interesting task. It may be that this is somewhat remote from your normal activities, but it seems to me that you would be just the right medicine for this young man. In any case I proposed to the Levines that they get in touch with you, which they will surely do within a few days. I'll be very curious to hear what comes of this.'

[5] Rosina Lhévinne (1880–1976) studied with both Alexander Scriabin and Sergei Prokofieff at the Moscow Conservatory. In 1898 she became the youngest woman ever to graduate with a gold medal. In the same year she married the pianist Joseph Lhévinne. From 1924 until shortly before her death she taught at Juilliard. Van Cliburn, John Browning, James Levine, and Misha Dichter are among her most famous students.

WL He discovered the piano all by himself and immediately taught himself how to play, playing everything by ear. Jimmy's father was a violinist and had a band, but he had a lot of opera recordings, and Jimmy spent hours listening to them and then playing them by ear on the piano: it was obvious that he was prodigiously gifted. His parents took him to the Cincinnati Summer Opera, which played in the zoo, where there was a pavilion-theater – during the performances you could hear the tigers and elephants roaring and braying. The Summer Opera put on very good performances with excellent conductors, for instance with Fausto Cleva, one of the outstanding Italian conductors at the Metropolitan Opera in New York.[6] As a six and seven year old Jimmy went backstage with his piano reductions, listened to the operas, got to know the singers, and gave them their cues for when they had to go on stage. So he was the manager behind the scenes, and that was accepted as perfectly natural.

Once when the director of the chorus wasn't there, someone said to Fausto Cleva that Jimmy Levine could give the cues. Fausto Cleva didn't know who Jimmy was, but he agreed to it anyway. So Jimmy gave the chorus their cues, and of course it all worked out perfectly. When the chorus director returned for the next rehearsal, nothing worked, and Fausto Cleva yelled, 'Go get the boy! Where is the boy!' So Jimmy was a de facto chorus director even before we got to know him. He was at every opera performance and knew the operas from beginning to end, with some of the top singers from the Metropolitan Opera: Richard Tucker, who had sung Radames with Toscanini just a few years before, and Roberta Peters, the phenomenal coloratura soprano!

When Jimmy started studying with me, one of his first assignments was to get ready for a concert with the Cincinnati Symphony. He'd already played Mendelssohn's second piano concerto with them under Thor Johnson, and now he was to play the Mozart 'Jeunehomme' concerto, K. 271, which had to be thoroughly prepared for the orchestra rehearsals. At this point his piano teacher in Cincinnati told us that she wouldn't continue as his teacher if he was going to go on having lessons with me, since we would be in competition with one another. Of course what she was really thinking was that this threat would provide her with enough leverage to get me out of the way, since she thought that without her he wouldn't be able to play the concert. But instead Jimmy came to us an extra two or three times a week just to work on the 'Jeunehomme' concerto, with Evi accompanying him on a second piano that we had set up in our apartment for this purpose.

[6] Fausto Cleva (1902–1971) became the chorus director of the Metropolitan Opera at the age of eighteen. He was one of the Met's house conductors 1950–1971 and was Music Director of the Cincinnati Summer Opera 1934–1963.

The concert with the Cincinnati Symphony was a huge success, since everything was much more thoroughly prepared than anyone else ever bothered with. He still plays that concerto today, conducting from the piano and using the same music we'd used then, in which we'd made all the annotations he would need for the performance. This was when he first grasped what it means to really work on a piece, and what it means to interpret something. Later on we often played with him, for instance, in Mozart's g minor piano quartet, K. 478, and, then, when he was fifteen or sixteen, we went on tour with him playing Schumann's piano quintet, which we played in New York and at Yale University and eventually recorded for Deutsche Grammophon. So it became a very intense collaboration: we worked our way systematically through orchestration, analysis, Schoenberg's *Harmonielehre*, and also score-reading, for instance the Bach chorales in the old C clefs.

But there was one time when he came for a lesson and went on and on about everything he had to do, but I interrupted and told him to just show me his homework! Evidently he had wanted to talk his way out of it. He said that was just what he was about to tell me, he hadn't had time to do it. I showed him the door and told him he could come back when he'd finished it. But his mother had dropped him off at our place and driven on into town, so he had to sit on the steps outside our apartment building and when his mother came to get him two and a half hours later, he was still sitting there, completely downcast. He never forgot that, and today, when he has his own students, he tells them this story in order to emphasize to them that there's no such thing as undisciplined musicianship. He never did that again.

The next thing for Jimmy was for him to systematically learn to play the Haydn quartets at the piano, from the scores, which have an alto clef in the viola part. Then the Mozart quartets, and then a Beethoven quartet – that was much more difficult. And after that a Haydn symphony, where you also have to deal with the transposing wind instruments. If you're going to sight read symphony scores at the piano, you have to learn to distinguish between melodic lines and accompanying lines, since at the piano you have to reduce the orchestra score to its essentials. Since he was a gifted pianist and very quickly learned how to read a score, he made very rapid progress. We even worked our way through some of the Mahler symphonies.

As an exercise in orchestration I gave him an assignment to arrange a Beethoven piano sonata for string quartet, the sonata Opus 14, Nr. 1. This was something he really had to sink his teeth into, since it's quite difficult to do. The main problem is that the sonata is in E major, the dominant of which, B major, is used frequently. But the low B natural is outside the range of the viola and the cello, their lowest note is their open C string.

That's why Beethoven transposed the sonata into F major when he made a string quartet version of the piece. In this key the viola and the cello can play the dominant, namely C, on their open C string. Jimmy insisted that he wanted the cello to tune the C string down to B natural, as it does in Berg's *Lyric Suite*,[7] but I didn't let him off that easily. He ground away at this assignment for weeks and weeks before he was ready to show it to me. And when he did I went to my bookcase and pulled out Beethoven's own arrangement: Jimmy could have killed me! But such an exercise can teach you something about how the master himself handled the problem.

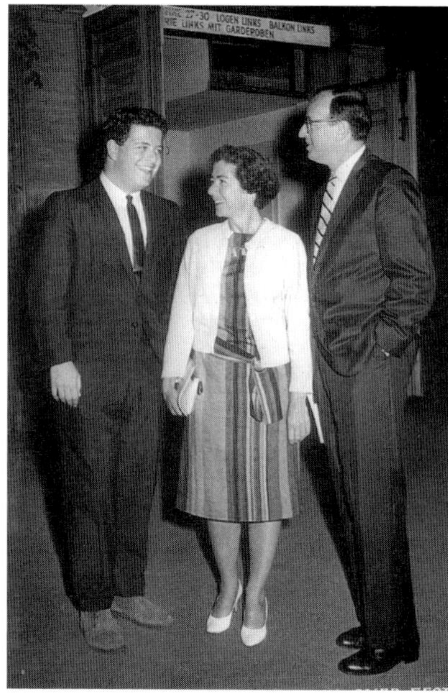

29 James Levine with Evi and Walter Levin, Bayreuth, 1966

After he'd had lessons with us for six or seven years, he had also finished school in Cincinnati and wanted to go to New York, to Juilliard, where it turned out that he already knew all the material in the basic curriculum. So he was accepted immediately as a graduate student and only had to take conducting, which saved him an enormous amount of time, just as I had, and for the same reason. After Juilliard he studied with Alfred Wallenstein,[8] Max Rudolf, and Fausto Cleva, in Baltimore, at the American Conductors Project with the Baltimore Symphony, where Jimmy entered a competition for young conductors put on by the Symphony League in Baltimore. George Szell was on the jury. Apparently Jimmy was by far the best and won the prize.

After the competition Szell wanted to discuss something with Jimmy and invited him to his apartment in New York, where he told Jimmy that he needed an assistant for the Cleveland Orchestra and would like to see if he was suitable for the job. Could Jimmy play something for him from this score? What he gave Jimmy was one of the Haydn symphonies he'd already worked on with me, but Jimmy kept mum about that and acted

[7] In the sixth movement of the *Lyric Suite*, the *Largo desolato*, Berg directs the cellist to lower the C string to B natural.

[8] Alfred Wallenstein (1898–1983) was principal cello of the New York Philharmonic. Toscanini advised him to become a conductor. He conducted the Hollywood Bowl Orchestra and was Music Director of the Los Angeles Philharmonic 1943–1956 and made a number of recordings with prominent soloists including Artur Rubinstein and Jascha Heifetz. He taught at Juilliard from 1968 until shortly before his death in 1983.

as if he'd never seen it before. Then Szell asked him whether he could also read the old clefs, for instance in the Bach chorales, and Jimmy responded, yes, certainly! 'My god,' Szell said, 'wherever did you learn to do that?' And Jimmy told him in Cincinnati, from Walter Levin of the LaSalle Quartet. After he'd had Jimmy play a couple of other pieces for him, Szell asked him if he would be interested in the position in Cleveland. That's how Jimmy got the assistant conductor job with the Cleveland Orchestra.

EL When Jimmy was maybe twelve or thirteen, he went to a studio in Cincinnati and recorded the Webern *Variations*, Opus 27, and the Schoenberg *Klavierstücke*, Opus 19, and had a disk made which he gave to Walter for his birthday.

WL I still have it. Opus 19 was the first piece of Schoenberg's Jimmy ever played. Before then he had no clue about new music. For instance, we studied Berg's *Wozzeck* with him and together we went to Karl Böhm's performance in New York. The whole Second Viennese School was new to him at that time, as was the 'New Music' altogether. Even today he'll still tell you that it was the LaSalle Quartet that opened up new music for him. He always came to our concerts, and we played all these pieces by composers he'd never heard of. So for instance in 1962 he played the Schumann piano quintet with us in the concert in which we premiered Herbert Brün's third string quartet.[9]

RS James Levine is surely your most prominent student, but there were surely others as well.

WL Linda Sharon was also a student of mine. I played the Bach double concerto with her, and we have a lovely recording of our performance.[10] Linda was in a children's trio along with Jimmy and Robert Martin. There's also a recording of them playing at the College-Conservatory of Music,[11] on which you can hear how nicely these children played. Linda came to me at Galamian's suggestion, she had already worked with him in the summer, and she had already been the soloist in the Prokofieff concerto with the Philadelphia Orchestra: she was a fantastic violinist. She's the wife of David Cerone, the director of the Cleveland Institute of Music, and is still teaching there today.

About fifteen years ago, when I was still directing the Steans Institute in Ravinia, both Linda and Robert Martin, who was on the faculty

9 On May 20, 1962, in Cincinnati, when Levine was eighteen years old.

10 On April 4, 1955, in Cincinnati.

11 On March 18, 1956, in Cincinnati.

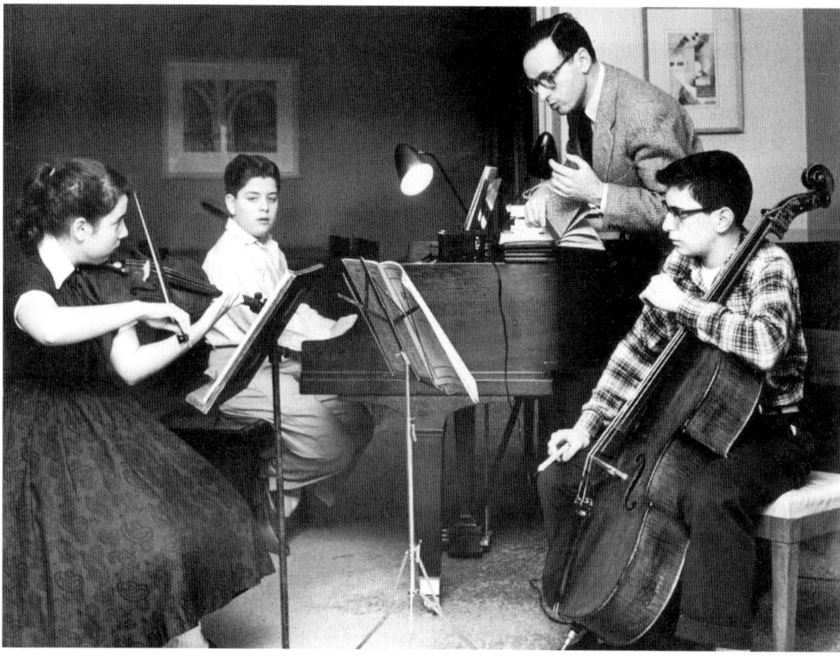

30 Walter Levin with the children's trio: Linda Sharon, James Levine, and Robert Martin, Cincinnati, 1955

of the Steans Institute teaching cello and chamber music, were with us and we took a picture of them with Jimmy, who at that time was the music director of the Ravinia Festival: the children's trio almost forty years later. Every one of these three made their mark in the world: Bob Martin studied music at the Curtis Institute in Philadelphia while at the same time studying philosophy at Haverford College. He got a Ph.D. in philosophy from Yale and is now the dean of graduate studies and a professor of music at Bard College in upstate New York. They were all exceptionally gifted people, and all of them went to Walnut Hills High School in Cincinnati, which our children also attended later on. It was an outstanding public school then, and still is today. People who criticize the American educational system, claiming that they don't teach anybody anything, are simply wrong: there are fantastic public schools in America, and many young people who attended Walnut Hills have gone on to study at the best universities.

Jenny Wagner from Lexington, Kentucky, also came to me as a very young girl and studied violin and chamber music with me for many years. Her story is interesting because it shows that if you get a comprehensive musical education and study the violin intensely at a conservatory where orchestra music and chamber music are taken seriously, so that you learn the whole literature, then you can have a professional

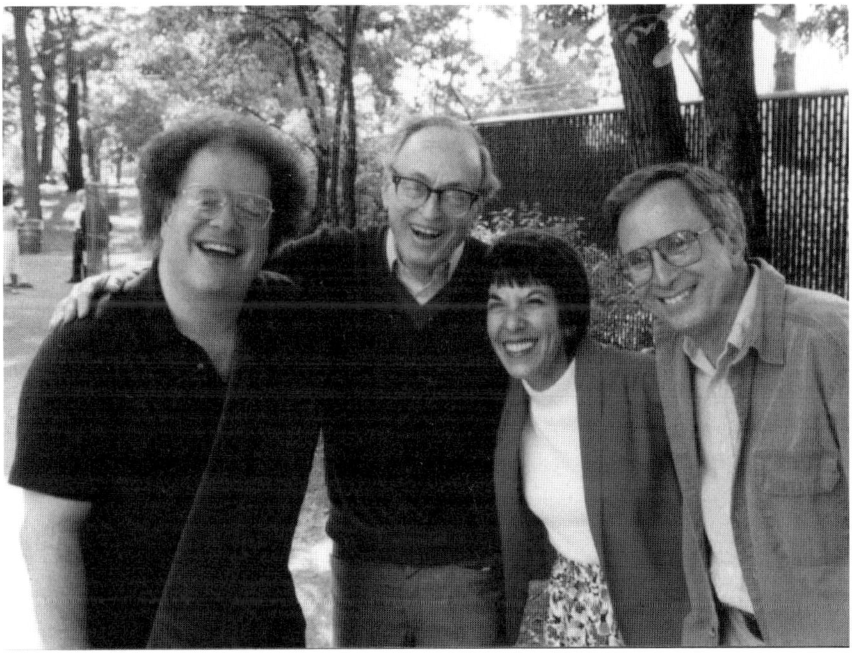

31 The children's trio 38 years later: James Levine, Walter Levin, Linda Sharon, and Robert Martin, Ravinia Festival, 1993

career of a kind that otherwise would be just a pipe dream. Jenny Wagner not only studied with me but was also a soloist with the conservatory orchestra and was learning literature like the Mozart concertos. When she graduated, she wanted to audition for an orchestra job. She looked around for openings and when she found out that the Chicago Symphony was looking for a second violinist she signed up for the auditions. When she told me that, I told her I thought that was more than just a little crazy, it was one of the very best orchestras in America, under Georg Solti, and she wanted to play her very first audition there? There would be a hundred violinists auditioning, all of them playing virtuoso pieces, and a lot of them would already have professional orchestra experience. 'So what?' she said, she'd just see how it went, it was after all just another kind of experience she could have. Why not start out with a good orchestra? Then she'd see right away what the competition was like. Okay then, I told her, as long as she wasn't disappointed afterwards!

So she went to the audition, and what happened? They went through the first round of auditions, which eliminated half the candidates, but Jenny was one of those who survived. The second round brought the number of candidates down to three, and Jenny had played all the orchestra excerpts so well that out of over a hundred people who had come to the auditions she was among the finalists. The auditions were blind, so the committee didn't know who was playing, but Jenny played the violin very well. And then came the last round, for which Solti announced that he'd like to take part himself, since after all whoever was selected had to be somebody he could work with. So he sat down at the piano and accompanied the three candidates. One of them played the Tchaikovsky concerto, another one played a Paganini concerto, and then it was Jenny's turn and Solti asked her what she wanted to play. She said Mozart's A major concerto. Whereupon, she told me, he turned to her and said he was astonished by her choice, but she should go ahead and play. So he accompanied her, and she played the A major concerto very beautifully. Afterwards he asked her where she had studied, and she told him it had been in Cincinnati, at the College-Conservatory, with Walter Levin of the LaSalle Quartet. Evidently he knew of us. Then he wanted to know if she also knew the orchestral literature, and she replied that she did, at least up to a point.

Jenny had a fabulous memory: she practically knew by heart all the pieces she had learned in the College-Conservatory orchestra under Gerhard Samuel, an outstanding conductor.[12] Solti told her that at the next concert he wanted her to sit next to the principal second violin. The concert was on a Sunday and by now it was Wednesday, there were three pieces she knew on the program and one she didn't know. But she learned that one in a hurry. Then came the rehearsals, and here's what happened – I heard about this from someone else in the orchestra who knew both of us – Solti conducted, and every time he looked at the second violins, she was always looking up at him, never at the music. This happened a couple of times, and each time there she was, looking back at him, and the third time he looked at her he had a smile on his face, which was very unusual for him. During the rehearsal break he asked her into the Green Room and told her she got the job. Her first audition ever, and she got a job in the Chicago Symphony! That's what a conservatory training should do!

Jorja Fleezanis also studied violin with me. She was from Cleveland, from the group of people around Jimmy. She came to Cincinnati at the same time as Lynn Harrell. She studied chamber music with us – her quartet was the first group to play Webern's *Bagatelles* Opus 9 from memory: Jorja could play almost anything by heart, for which we all envied her. After graduating she got one of the concertmaster positions in San Francisco: what an orchestra! By now she's been the concertmaster of the Minnesota Orchestra for a long time and is much appreciated because she knows how to work with a group of musicians. Education is decisive for a young musician, and many young gifts are squandered because they're not developed properly.

[12] See also pp. 303–306.

RS Christian Tetzlaff, Stefan Litwin, and Rainer Schmidt also studied with you. How long were they each in Cincinnati?

WL Stefan Litwin and Christian Tetzlaff were each in Cincinnati for a year, Stefan in the academic year 1984–1985 and Christian in 1985–1986. I knew Tetzlaff's teacher, Uwe Haiberg, quite well, since he'd been with us in Cincinnati 1978–1979 as the first violinist of the Brahms Quartet. He taught Tetzlaff in Lübeck, and when he was eighteen sent him to me for a year in Cincinnati. We worked intensely on the Beethoven concerto, the Schoenberg concerto, and Artur Schnabel's solo sonata for violin as well as his sonata for violin and piano, Stefan Litwin playing the piano. The solo sonata is a huge piece, about 45 minutes long, and hardly anyone ever plays it. I got to know it through Carl Flesch's *Art of Violin Playing*. In volume two, *Artistic Realization and Instruction*, there is an appendix with twelve examples of music in different styles. The next to the last example is the third part of Schnabel's solo sonata.[13] I've never played it myself, but I've looked at it again and again. Tetzlaff was the first person I found who was really interested in learning this piece, and he really did learn to play it quite wonderfully.

Rainer Schmidt was with me in Cincinnati for chamber music and with Dorothy DeLay for violin, also for a year. The Hagen Quartet auditioned him for second violin while he was still in Cincinnati. When he came back from Salzburg, I asked him how the audition went. The Hagen Quartet had hired him!

RS Another musician who has developed a career is Gordan Nikolić, who studied chamber music with you in Basel.

WL Yes, we often listen to his performances on the radio, most recently the Beethoven violin concerto, and now he's conducting too. Gordan Nikolić took my quartet course here in Basel around 1989–1990. He arrived for his first lesson with me with a new ensemble and announced that they would play the sixth Bartók quartet. I was amazed that a new ensemble would start out with such a piece. So I asked them whether they had already worked on it, and they assured me that indeed they had. They began to play, and it was incredibly awful, absolutely nothing was right! I let them go on for a while and then stopped them and asked them how long they'd been working on it. They told me that they'd already had two rehearsals, and I replied that it was perfectly obvious that two rehearsals weren't nearly enough. Do they have the score? Each of them? No, only one of them. And where was it? It was in his violin case. I told them that it was impossible to learn a quartet the way they

13 See pp. 318–319.

were going about it, that they had to play from the score and not from the parts and then work their way through the piece very slowly and carefully. They could come back after they'd worked through the first page of the score. And I sent them away.

I later learned that they went to Herr Hildenbrandt, at that time the director of the school, and told him that they had enrolled in Walter Levin's quartet course and that he had just thrown them out. Hildenbrandt inquired what had happened. They told him they had played the sixth Bartók quartet for me, and I had said that they had to study it much more thoroughly, that they were completely unprepared, but it wasn't true, they'd already had two rehearsals. Hildenbrandt told them he was certain that I had my reasons for saying that, and that apparently two rehearsals weren't nearly enough for such a difficult piece. They protested that they had gone to the lesson so that I would show them how to play it, they wouldn't need me if they already could play it. Hildenbrandt told them that they really were mistaken about that. What he would suggest is that they go back to me and apologize and tell me that it was a misunderstanding on their part, that they didn't know how to prepare for such a lesson, and that they would do everything they could to be better prepared next time.

A few days later Gordan Nikolić came to my class and told me that his quartet had broken up, that the others didn't want to work that hard, but that in the meantime he'd prepared one of the Mozart Duos with a violist and would I listen to them. I told him I would be happy to listen to them if they were properly prepared, were using a decent edition, and had really worked on the piece, otherwise no, I wouldn't. He said he understood. So they came and played the Duo for me, quite decently: it was something else entirely. It turned out that he was a very good violinist, very gifted and very musical, and that he'd understood exactly what I was up to as a teacher. He began to study seriously with me, with a newly formed ensemble, and frequently also came to listen when I was teaching other ensembles, and always had the score with him.

On one such occasion, when I criticized an ensemble and asked them what the first thing you have to do is when you start to work on a new piece, he looked at me and asked if he might say something. He turned to the quartet and asked them whether they had a score to the piece. And then he began to teach them, just as I would have done: I didn't need to say another word. He had understood exactly what I had meant and had learned how to do it, he became one of my greatest admirers, and we got along famously together. He subsequently worked on a number of pieces with me, the Lutosławski quartet among them, and became a really respectable musician and violinist. He studied the violin with Jean-Jacques Kantorow, who took him along to be concertmaster

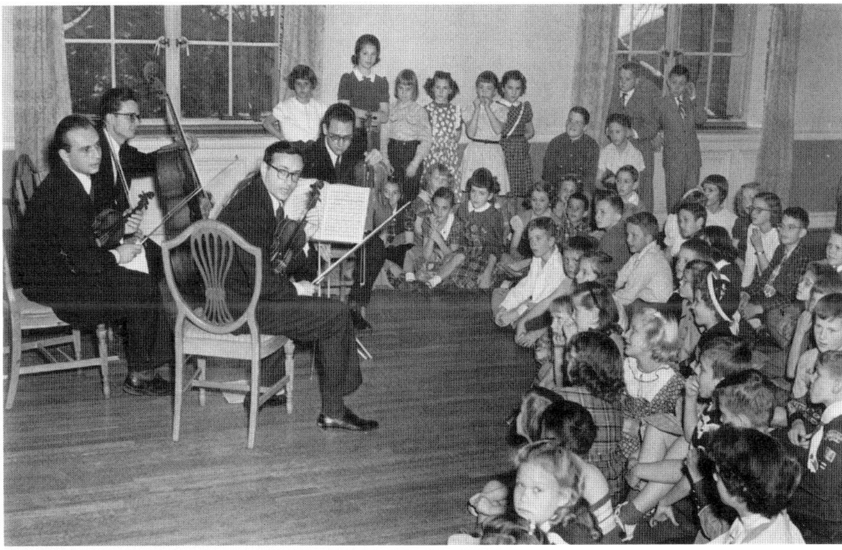

32 Children's concert with the LaSalle Quartet, Boulder, Colorado, 1952

in southern France. Later on he was engaged as concertmaster in London, and now he's a great soloist and a conductor too.

RS He's now conducting the Amsterdam Chamber Orchestra.

WL You can see once again how crucial it is: how one goes about teaching. You most certainly shouldn't just accept whatever the students do and 'make nice' about it. Sometimes it's better to tell people the truth.

RS Another central aspect of the LaSalle's teaching activities was the children's concerts. You've often said that you gave hundreds of children's concerts. When did you begin doing that?

WL At Colorado College, so to speak out of an instinct for self-preservation. We said to ourselves, we have to create a new public. You hear the complaint all the time that young people don't go to concerts anymore, and what will come of that? Music will gradually die out. At some point it's the next generation that will have to support music and they won't do that unless they're interested in it. If they aren't, there soon won't be any more chamber music, nor any symphony orchestras, nor any opera. But there are still any number of conservatories. Where's the public for which their students are learning their profession? So we wanted to get children interested in music as early as possible, and maybe a couple of them would even learn to play an instrument. So we put on children's concerts in the schools, went to the first and second grade class rooms, and played string quartets for six and seven year olds. They sat in a circle around us and we played short, contrasting pieces for them and explained in simple terms what was going on in them: this was very successful, and we had a great relationship with these children.

RS These concerts were originally only in Colorado Springs?

WL Yes, but then in Boulder and other cities in Colorado also. In 1953 there was an article in *Time* magazine reporting how the LaSalle Quartet was giving children's concerts.[14] That was a huge advertisement for these children's concerts all over America. Young Audiences heard about us, a national movement for children's concerts in America that had just been established by Rosalie Leventritt,[15] and we were invited to the various cities where Young Audiences concerts were being organized, to demonstrate what we had been doing and how we did it. We played a lot of these 'demonstration' concerts for Young Audiences all over America, which gave us a great deal of experience in playing for school children.

RS Did you make special trips for these concerts, or did you combine them with your concert tours?

WL Insofar as possible we combined them with our concert engagements. And the works we played were from our tour repertory. There was a big article in the *Los Angeles Times* after we had become the Quartet in Residence in Cincinnati describing the pieces we played in our children's concerts: movements from Haydn quartets, from the Ravel quartet, from the great G major quartet by Schubert, the 'Dancing Bear' from Stravinsky's *Three Pieces* for string quartet, or some pieces from Bartók's *Mikrokosmos*.[16]

In Cincinnati the children's concerts grew to be a big organization. Horace Stewart, a well-known pediatrician, was a music fanatic. He didn't have an office, he only made house calls, since he believed that in a doctor's office the children would only infect one another. He was also the Levine's pediatrician, and when one of their children was sick, he sent the parents off to bed and sat with the child himself the whole night through to make sure nothing bad happened. He never billed for his services, an injection was simply 98 cents. He was a Cincinnati institution and everyone loved him. We also got to be good friends with

[14] 'Music: Argument for Strings,' in *Time*, August 3, 1953.

[15] She later also founded the Leventritt Competition for young musicians.

[16] As arranged for string quartet by Tibor Serly.

him. When he died, people wanted to know what could be done in his memory, and we proposed that they establish a 'Horace Stewart Children's Concerts Society.' And that's what happened. All these ladies who were eternally grateful to him for taking such good care of their children joined forces and organized children's concerts in the Cincinnati schools, and we played them by the dozen.

RS You also once told a terrifying story about being in schools in some of the worst neighborhoods in New York …

WL … where the students had to hand in their knives before they were allowed into the concerts and the principal was afraid they would smash our instruments. We took that into consideration in choosing what music we would play, and we invited the students to take part by asking us questions. We succeeded in getting them really interested, so much so that the teachers were absolutely fascinated, they had never seen these really dangerous kids as transformed as they were for us. Juilliard also organized and financed young people's concerts in those kinds of schools with the idea of demonstrating that it was possible to get even those kids interested in music, which would be very important for young people. People are doing that again today: Simon Rattle has performed Stravinsky in Berlin with young people like that.

RS Did you also teach as a young person in Palestine?

WL Yes, I did. As a young man I taught music students who had no money and wanted lessons in music theory. I did this because it interested me and because I enjoyed teaching. I've always taught, I find it endlessly fascinating, besides which it's a very gratifying activity. I also gave private violin lessons while I was studying in New York. I never charged for them, not even later on.

Part III
The Music

Repertory, Commissions, Premieres

14 *Ideas and Repertory*

Basic Principles

ROBERT SPRUYTENBURG: The LaSalle Quartet is famous for championing modern and contemporary music, for its performances of the works of the Second Viennese School and for its many commissions, which resulted in the creation of a whole new string quartet repertory over the course of your career. At the same time works from the standard classical and romantic repertory account for nearly half of all your performances. You also performed quite a number of forgotten or out of the way pieces, and yet there are a number of significant omissions, for instance you played very little from the Slavic repertory. Do these choices of repertory reflect the various preferences of all the members of the LaSalle Quartet, or did you yourself make most of the proposals regarding repertory?

WALTER LEVIN: Most of them came from me, virtually the whole direction of the quartet came from me. I was, after all, the founder, it was my quartet.

RS Or should we differentiate a little and say that the proposals for contemporary works came mostly from you and the proposals for works from the classical-romantic repertory tended to come from the other members?

WL No, in the classical-romantic repertory also the choices of what we did and didn't play had to do with my interests and with my likes and dislikes. You mentioned the Slavic repertory, which on the whole doesn't much interest me: why else did we play so little Dvořák, and nothing at all by Tchaikovsky or Shostakovich?[1]

RS So was Smetana a concession?

WL No, absolutely not! I've always been a great fan of Smetana's music. I think his opera *The Bartered Bride* is marvelous, I heard it for the first time in 1936 at the State Opera in Berlin under Leo Blech, it was the second opera I ever heard. To this day I can tell you who was in the cast. We played Smetana's first quartet, *From My Life*, rather often and with great enthusiasm, it's a really good piece. Unfortunately we never got around to playing his second quartet, which Schoenberg thought was the better of the two. I'd still like to convince one of my younger quartets

[1] Levin's quartet in Palestine did, however, play Tchaikovsky's quartet Opus 11.

to play it. And we did play Dvořák's 'American' quartet, three times, in 1957: once in Cincinnati, once in Richmond, Virginia, and once in Nazareth, Kentucky – outside Louisville, there's a college there – and then never again!

RS Yes, I listened to the live recording from Cincinnati, it's absolutely thrilling. You also played it very differently from what one usually hears: it's extremely energetic and has an incredible rhythmical élan.

WL Yes, I think the Cincinnati concert was very good. But for me it's enough if you've once learned a piece well enough to do it justice, for me that meant we were done with it. It's more important to champion music that's just as good as well-known works like the Dvořák but that nobody bothers with. It was always important to me to play pieces that weren't so famous, for instance Hugo Wolf's great quartet in d minor.

RS Despite some omissions, your repertory ranged over the whole of the string quartet literature, even prior to Haydn: all the way back to Henry Purcell in the 17th century. How did it happen that you played his *Fantasies in Four Parts*?

WL The Purcell *Fantasies* were included in the music library that I got as a bar mitzvah present, so I got to know them when I was only thirteen, when we were still in Berlin. They're short pieces of very contrasting character and tempo. We found them attractive because of their range, from contrapuntal to homophonic, and they're very modern for such old music. So they made ideal program openers for us.

RS At first you always played all four of them, later on only three.

WL After a certain point we settled on the same three. Four was a little too much of the same style.

RS I would say that your individual programs reflect a similar concern with contrast. The LaSalle Quartet's programs are a wonderful guide for how to structure a string quartet concert.

WL We never repeated our programs: there was never anything routine about how we put them together, about our choice of pieces. Of course there were certain emphases, that is, we wanted to offer mixed programs with contrasting pieces: the greater the contrast the better, and these contrasts included those between different periods and styles of music. I always wanted to play works that our experience of contemporary music could shed a new light on and that, conversely, could reveal something about where more recent works came from. Indeed, I very rarely wanted us to play anything else! A typical LaSalle Quartet program would be the Purcell *Fantasies*, Beethoven's *Grosse Fuge*, and the first Schoenberg quartet.

RS Or a Haydn quartet followed by Lutosławski and then Ravel.

WL Yes, or Mozart, Zemlinsky, and Brahms.

RS In the course of 40 years you played 158 different works by 60 different composers, which amounts to adding four new works and between one and two new composers to your overall repertory every year. And I remember your saying that building up your repertory was a major concern during the four years you were at Colorado Springs.

WL Yes, we had to learn new repertory for every concert then.

RS How many concerts did you usually have in a season at Colorado College?

WL To begin with, when we were first in Colorado Springs, we played three concerts per season, but that was shortly increased to four, where it remained for the rest of our career: we gave four concerts per season at the College-Conservatory in Cincinnati also. We couldn't have handled more than four, given our tours and our teaching load. But even four concerts with as much new repertory as possible meant having to learn several new pieces each season. Starting out of course everything was new for us and we had to build up our repertory gradually. That meant that we didn't repeat pieces from one season to the next, since in the meantime we'd rehearsed new ones. On top of that, in our early years, up until 1955, we had to deal with the turnover in cellists, which was always a setback in terms of repertory, since the new cellists had first of all to learn the pieces we already knew.

RS So by the time you left Colorado Springs you had built up a repertory of around 35 pieces, including the works you had studied at Juilliard. Didn't that suffice as a stock to draw from later on?

WL No, it was only much later on that we'd accumulated enough of a repertory stock to be able to offer pieces on our tours that we didn't need to rehearse so much. And we would also play some pieces more often than others, pieces that were particularly well-suited to us and that we enjoyed playing. But even so we continued to learn new pieces, to the despair of my colleagues. Eventually they really didn't want to learn any more new pieces, for instance, the Gielen quartet, or to take up and rehearse other pieces again prior to our recording sessions with Deutsche Grammophon. For Deutsche Grammophon we had to work through even the pieces we already knew and thoroughly polish them up. For instance, we worked through the late Beethoven quartets all over again, and played them in concerts, before we recorded them. Another example would be Mendelssohn's Opus 12, which we'd played very early on, in 1954, but only took back into our active repertory in 1968, when we wanted to record it along with Opus 13.

RS And Alban Berg's *Lyric Suite*? That's another piece that became part of your bread and butter repertory, but not until twelve years after you first played it in Colorado Springs in 1950.

WL The *Lyric Suite* is an extremely difficult piece that requires too much effort to learn over and over again with a new cellist. It can't simply be conjured up again as if by magic, at least we couldn't do that! We were never a gifted quartet in the sense that we could learn such pieces in our sleep. We worked very hard on all the pieces, and so they got better as time went on.

Revivals: Wolf, Spohr, Donizetti, Verdi

RS A moment ago you said that it was important to you to champion music that nobody bothers with, to play pieces that weren't so famous, like the d minor quartet by Hugo Wolf.[2] And indeed one of the ongoing themes of the LaSalle Quartet's career was your revival of forgotten string quartets by otherwise well-known, and even not so well-known, 19th century composers, among them Louis Spohr, Donizetti, and Verdi, and of course, in the 20th century, Alexander Zemlinsky. But to begin with, how did you come across Hugo Wolf's d minor quartet?

WL I came across it on a recording by the New Music Quartet[3] with Claus Adam as the cellist that had been made by Columbia: an excellent

[2] Hugo Wolf (1860–1903) composed the first three movements of his d minor quartet 1878–1880, the fourth movement was composed in 1884. The work was premiered by Karl Prill and his quartet in Vienna in February, 1903, shortly before Wolf's death.

[3] The New Music Quartet was founded in 1948 by Claus Adam, who had studied cello with Emanuel Feuermann and composition with Stefan Wolpe in New York. He was the Juilliard Quartet's cellist 1955–1974.

recording. The New Music Quartet made fabulous recordings, for instance, of Beethoven's Opus 59, Nr. 3, and the third Bartók quartet. I heard the Wolf d minor quartet at our friend Samuel Rosenfeld's in Akron, whose wife had organized the children's concerts there. He was a fanatical quartet lover and had a huge record collection, including the Wolf d minor quartet, which I'd never heard. However, the New Music Quartet still used the old Peters edition, which was all that was available at that time. The editor, Joseph Hellmesberger, had partially revised the quartet when he published it in 1903. After the autograph score, which was thought to have been lost, was rediscovered in 1955 and acquired by the Austrian National Library, the International Hugo Wolf Society in Vienna published a new edition, which we at first studied just out of curiosity. But when we got the contract with Deutsche Grammophon, we immediately proposed it as one of the works to be recorded.

RS It was highly indicative of what your collaboration with Deutsche Grammophon was going to be like that you proposed a work so far off the beaten track as the very first piece to be recorded.

WL Deutsche Grammophon was often floored by our proposals. But the Wolf d minor quartet really is an astonishingly mature work of the greatest intensity, you would never guess it had been written by a composer who was barely twenty years old. He'd obviously delved into the late Beethoven quartets very deeply, and the Scherzo is reminiscent of the third movement of Beethoven's f minor quartet, Opus 95, in its many syncopated accents.

RS Another piece that had fallen by the wayside was the concerto for string quartet by Louis Spohr.

WL Yes, and it was exceedingly expensive to perform, both in terms of the effort required and because of the orchestra.

RS How did you come across it, and what prompted you to take it up in the first place?

WL I don't remember exactly anymore, but I would assume that Max Rudolf, who at that time was the conductor of the Cincinnati Symphony, approached us as to whether, after all the years the LaSalle Quartet had been in residence in Cincinnati, we wouldn't play a concerto for string quartet and orchestra. So we thought about what the possibilities might be. We hadn't yet studied Schoenberg's concerto for string quartet, but it is so extraordinarily difficult that at that time it was out of the question. Then the Spohr concerto occurred to me. I didn't know it, but Spohr was a good composer who knew what he was doing, and I myself had often played his a minor violin concerto 'In the form of a vocal scene,'[4] which I always had my students learn too. And I knew his concertant-style string quartets.

Spohr had been an itinerant virtuoso going from town to town, wherever he was playing he always tried to find three other people with whom he could present quartet evenings of his own works. They were so to speak violin concertos accompanied by three strings, whose 'oom pah-pah oom pah-pah' was occasionally interrupted by a scale passage. You could almost sight read these pieces in performance, but for a professional string quartet they really are somewhat too banal. But the concerto for string quartet is really beautiful, and our performance of it with Max Rudolf was very good, since he was an excellent conductor. We also recorded it for WDR radio in Cologne, with Othmar Mága conducting. But we almost skipped out on this recording session. I've seldom seen my colleagues as angry as they were then. The orchestra was totally uninterested in the piece and the conductor didn't care either, so that's what it sounded like too. My colleagues would rather have dropped the whole thing.

Recently, by the way, a funny thing happened. About two weeks ago the young Ullmann Quartet wrote to tell me that lately they'd been preparing to perform the Spohr concerto for string quartet, and by chance had discovered a tape of an 'ancient' performance of it by us. Isn't that amazing? 'Ancient,' meaning before they were born! That really is a bit of an exaggeration, don't you think?

RS Yes, but even so, it's astonishing that they would look for it, and find it too!

WL And the first violinist added that it was an enormous help to them to be able to hear the piece! They really had no idea how it went at all!

RS Yet another quartet composer you resurrected is Gaetano Donizetti, who composed eighteen string quartets between 1817 and 1836. The LaSalle Quartet played the fifth one, in e minor, from 1818, several times. How did you know about Donizetti's quartets?

[4] This work, which Louis Spohr (1789–1859) composed in 1816, became famous on account of its unique structure, in which the opera composer Spohr so to speak translates an operatic scene into a wordless *recitativ*, *arioso*, and *aria* for the violin. Carl Flesch included the *recitativ* as one of the musical examples in the appendix to volume two of his violin method.

WL I've always been interested in out of the way pieces and sometime or other, I no longer remember when, I discovered that there was a complete edition of the eighteen quartets published in 1948 by Francisco Prati,[5] an industrialist of Italian extraction in Buenos Aires, but I could never find it anywhere. As always in such cases we looked for it in all the big city music shops when we were on tour, but in vain. Then after many years, one day early in 1972, a package arrived out of the blue from Switzerland: it was the complete edition that we'd been looking for! One of the many music dealers we had spoken with had actually been able to chase it down, and he remembered us. So of course we immediately set about to learn one of the quartets, namely the fifth one, and we performed it the next season.

RS You also played the Verdi string quartet quite often and with great pleasure, even very early on, in 1953, and then again in the mid-1970s. How did you come to know about it? Was it also included in the Peters music anthology that you got for your bar mitzvah?

WL No, but as I was a Verdi fan forever I took an interest in what else Verdi had done besides his operas. When he was staying in Naples for the rehearsals of *Aida* in 1872, the rehearsals were interrupted by the Aida's being sick. And so he composed this quartet in three weeks, so to speak for relaxation, which is pretty rare for composers of string quartets. So I said to myself I'd like to hear it sometime.

RS Was it already being played by other quartets at that time?

WL Indeed, there were already some quartets who played it then, for instance, the Quartetto Italiano, but I don't believe I ever heard it before we played it ourselves. Probably there were even recordings of it already. But I've never liked to listen to recordings of pieces I didn't know yet, since if the recordings of a piece were like the recordings of the Beethoven quartets I'd heard, I would never have wanted to play Beethoven! But I did buy the score, an old Eulenburg score that I still have. In the meantime I've also gotten the original Ricordi score, and now the Verdi Society is supposedly about to release a new urtext edition. I can hardly wait!

But I have to tell you something else too. Once when I was teaching quartets at the Paul Hindemith Foundation in Blonay, I was in Hindemith's house, where they had the recordings he made with the Amar Quartet when he played viola with them. I made copies of some

[5] Gaetano Donizetti: *Diciotto Quartetti, a cura dell'Istituto Italiano per la Storia della Musica* (Rome and Buenos Aires, 1948).

of these recordings, including the last movement of the Verdi quartet. Now then, Verdi gave a metronome mark for every movement, but the way the Amar Quartet plays the last movement is not to be believed: way too fast![6] It sounds like electronic music played backwards.

While we're on the subject of the Verdi quartet, by the way, Eduard Steuermann once told me, right after the Quartetto Italiano had played the Verdi quartet, that he found it to be superficial music that wasn't to be taken seriously. This was when we were driving with him from Salzburg to Mondsee after the ISCM Festival in Israel in 1954. Astonishing! I don't find it to be any such thing. Actually, the musicians in Schoenberg's circle didn't like the Verdi operas either.[7]

RS Apparently there had been a plan to record the Verdi quartet and the fifth Donizetti quartet with Deutsche Grammophon in December 1974.

WL There was, but unfortunately it had to be cancelled because I had a nail-bed infection. But prior to this recording date, and in spite of my bandaged finger, we played the Verdi quartet on a concert in Frankfurt. Shortly after that I had to go to the hospital to have the abscess that had developed lanced, otherwise I would have run the risk of blood poisoning. And of course I was then forbidden to play the violin.

RS Couldn't those recordings have been rescheduled for later?

WL We'd just played the Verdi many times on tour with a view to making the recording. As usual, we'd planned something else for the following year, there simply wasn't enough time to prepare the Verdi quartet the way we ordinarily would for a recording.

RS Too bad!

WL I think so too. It's just about the only thing I really wanted to record, along with a couple of Mozart quartets, that we didn't get to do. We also wanted to record the Brahms piano quintet with James Levine, but by then his schedule wouldn't permit it.

[6] Verdi's metronome mark for the last movement is half note = 100; the Amar Quartet takes it at half note = 126.

[7] Schoenberg himself considered Verdi's last opera, *Falstaff*, to be 'the sort of rubbish that a senile old man would just barely be able to write.' Recollected by Edward J. Dent in William Glock's 'Schnabel und Berlin' in *Artur Schnabel – Musiker/Musician* (Berlin, 2001).

Zemlinsky

RS You made a substantial contribution to the revival of interest in the music of Alexander Zemlinsky, who had been banned by the Nazis and who died, virtually unknown, in exile in America in 1942. How did you come across his music?

WL It was by way of Alban Berg's *Lyric Suite*, which we had begun playing a long time ago, in 1951, and the *Lyric Suite* is dedicated to Zemlinsky: the dedication is right at the front of the score. And of course I also knew the *Lyric Suite's* quotation from Zemlinsky's *Lyric Symphony*.[8]

RS Does it say in the score that it's a quotation and where it comes from?

WL Certainly! In the score the notes quoted are even in quotation marks, just as they would be in a text. In the whole literature of music I don't know anything else like it: a score in which the quotation of a theme has been notated so explicitly with quotation marks. There is also a note at the bottom of the page saying that the theme is a quotation from Zemlinsky's *Lyric Symphony*: '*Du bist mein eigen, mein eigen*,' you are my own, my own. In 1951 of course I had no idea what was so special about the quotation. The whole story about Berg and Hanna Fuchs only came to light in the 1970s.[9] I had wanted to get to know Zemlinsky's *Lyric Symphony* as soon as we began working on the *Lyric Suite*, but in the 1950s it wasn't so easy to find, and it was quite a while before I got hold of a score. When I did I could see right away that it was a work to rank with Mahler's *Lied von der Erde*: it absolutely had to be performed. From that moment on I never wearied of trying to interest people in this work.

RS You told James Levine about the *Lyric Symphony*.

WL Yes, and also my colleague on the College-Conservatory faculty, Gerhard Samuel, who conducted it with the student orchestra in June, 1979: it was the first American performance of the *Lyric Symphony*, 55 years after its world premiere in Prague! Later that same year James Levine performed it with the New York Philharmonic.

RS But your rediscovery of Zemlinsky's string quartets actually began earlier, in the early 1960s. How did that come about?

WL When I was in New York I always went to Frank's Music, which was

[8] Fourth movement, bars 32–33 in the viola and 46–50 in the second violin.

[9] On 'the secret program of the *Lyric Suite*' see Perle 1977.

then on 46th Street. It was a little shop on one of the upper floors that had the most marvelous things. It was always chock full of antiquarian parts and scores. It's also where I first saw Adorno's *Philosophie der neuen Musik*, which I bought because I wanted to know what that could possibly mean, 'philosophy of new music'? When first I tried to read it I didn't understand a single word of it. Frank's was also where I first saw a score of Zemlinsky's third string quartet, a Philharmonia score, and I recognized the name: he was the one Alban Berg had quoted in his *Lyric Suite*, and I knew he was Schoenberg's teacher. So I bought it, and on the flight back to Cincinnati I began to browse in the score and saw that it was a really beautiful piece, something we really had to play.

RS You learned the third string quartet in 1963, but twelve whole years passed before you learned the second string quartet!

WL The second quartet is a very difficult, and a very long, piece, though in my opinion it is altogether one of Zemlinsky's greatest works. But to begin with I had to overcome the resistance of some of my quartet colleagues who thought it was a bad piece and didn't want to play it. Besides which no one would let us program Zemlinsky on our tours: in the season after we had learned the Zemlinsky third quartet we played it only three times in Europe, one of which was for a recording session at the SWF broadcasting studio in Baden-Baden.[10] No one wanted it!

What was I supposed to do if nobody wanted to hear the piece? Deutsche Grammophon also didn't want it. Deutsche Grammophon wasn't willing to record Zemlinsky until after we'd made the boxed set of the Second Viennese School quartets, which was a huge success against the predictions of all the experts. After that it began to dawn on some people, including Deutsche Grammophon's producers, that we might have a better idea than the experts as to what was good music and what was worth putting out on records. We told Deutsche Grammophon we wanted to record the Zemlinsky second quartet and had learned it precisely in order to perform it and record it. And that recording had the success we'd hoped for. But we could never have imagined just how successful it would be. It was a sensation!

The success began in America, where the second quartet was released against the opposition of the American representative of Deutsche Grammophon. Our contract required him to distribute all our recordings, because we were an American quartet. But his response to the Zemlinsky was, 'over my dead body.' He said that if he released the record in America he wouldn't be able to sell even ten copies, and when

[10] The LaSalle Quartet first played Zemlinsky's third quartet in Cincinnati on March 17, 1964; the studio recording for SWF was made a year later, on March 25, 1965.

that happened we could have his whole stock back as is and distribute it ourselves: he wasn't going to pay for it.

And then within a few weeks of its release it became a best seller. It was on the *Billboard* charts, the trade magazine for jazz and all branches of music – they compile statistics of the ten best selling jazz and classical records, and there we were at number two, just below Pavarotti's '*O Sole Mio*'! Number two among the ten best selling records in the USA! A string quartet? And right next to these *Billboard* statistics there was a review headed 'Who is Zemlinsky?' They didn't know. The recording sold like hot cakes, even today nobody knows why. In Chicago you could go into record stores that otherwise only sold jazz and there would be a whole wall plastered with the covers of our Zemlinsky recording with its beautiful sepia-brown photograph of Zemlinsky as a young man – amazing! And the jazz fans bought it, and Zemlinsky's second quartet was in the juke boxes!

We never again sold as many copies of any recording as we did of this quartet. The press picked up on it too. *The New Yorker* published a big article, a fabulous article, about Zemlinsky, who almost no one had ever heard of.[11] And now all of a sudden he was a famous composer, which inspired Peter Dannenberg[12] at the Hamburg State Opera to revive Zemlinsky's operas, which he championed vigorously. Dannenberg was also quoted as saying that the Zemlinsky renaissance had been pioneered among others by the LaSalle Quartet with its recording of his second string quartet. All of a sudden there began to be interest in Zemlinsky, and we could program his music, even his third quartet. Later on we were able to record his other quartets as well, one after the other.

RS Why were people so opposed to programming Zemlinsky's music?

WL It was because nobody knew Zemlinsky and no one was interested in him. He was an unknown composer, he had been banned by the Nazis and his name eradicated in Germany and Austria, where his operas had formerly been famous. He wasn't actually murdered by the Nazis, but he was totally silenced by them and had to emigrate to America, where he died during the war, in 1942, by and large unknown. So Zemlinsky had no presence after the war, he had vanished, and no one bothered about him until we did. After our big success with his second quartet it became painfully obvious that the Nazis had succeeded in completely eliminating a composer. Not only had they murdered the composers in

11 Andrew Porter, 'A Great Composer,' in *The New Yorker*, January 14, 1980, p. 84.

12 Peter Dannenberg was Chief Dramaturg and Director of the Hamburg Opera 1977–1987. Since 1989 he has been Chairman of the Alexander Zemlinsky Foundation at the Gesellschaft der Musikfreunde in Vienna.

Theresienstadt and Auschwitz but they had totally silenced other composers simply by banning them.

The same thing happened to Webern. If Webern hadn't been killed in that terrible accident, it's likely that no one would have been interested in him twenty years later. We were very receptive to composers whom the Nazis had branded as 'degenerate.' And people like Zemlinsky, I knew, were close to my heart, we owed him an effort to revive his name and his music, to give him the prominence he deserved and that was taken from him. And then we got to know Frau Zemlinsky and got more and more interested in Zemlinsky as a human being. His correspondence[13] for instance was only published because of us. We were interested because we all had good reason to want to restore something that had been criminally destroyed by the Nazi atrocities. Zemlinsky was part of that effort, as was Webern, whose suspect attitude to National Socialism and Hitler I didn't know about then, otherwise I might have had second thoughts about him. But maybe the music still has to come first, in spite of all that.

RS But to return to the question again, what was the reason for this resistance to programming Zemlinsky's music?

WL It was because his music had been banned in Nazi Germany, so that it wasn't possible to hear it until the Second World War had ended. And after the war contemporary music rather quickly turned towards Webern and post-Webernian serialism, and during this period it seemed uninteresting to be concerned with music that was fundamentally post-romantic, like Mahler, Strauss, and Reger. So Zemlinsky was a composer who was of no interest to the younger generation: they had first of all to catch up with everything that had been denied them. Above all they wanted to catch up with Schoenberg and Webern, and Stravinsky too, which is why there was no Zemlinsky renaissance after the war.

RS In an interview about Zemlinsky with Gerhard Samuel and Ann Santen[14] in Cincinnati you said you anticipated that Zemlinsky's operas in particular would boost his renaissance. That was at the beginning of the 1980s. How do you assess the situation today, almost 30 years later? Did the renaissance of Zemlinsky's operas actually happen?

WL Absolutely! Other than Strauss and Puccini there are hardly any operas

[13] *Briefwechsel mit Schönberg, Webern, Berg und Schreker* (Mainz, 1995).

[14] Ann Santen was the director of the University of Cincinnati's radio station WGUC; a friend of the Levins; she frequently introduced the LaSalle Quartet's broadcasts and hosted interviews with Levin, Gerhard Samuel, and other music faculty.

from the turn of the 20th century that are on par with the Zemlinsky operas. So they are an important addition to the repertory. Zemlinsky has certainly not become another Puccini in the world of opera, but nevertheless his operas are performed everywhere today, particularly in Europe, and some of them quite often. *Der König Kandaules* was premiered in 1996 at the Hamburg State Opera, and then produced at the Salzburg Festival in 2002 as well.[15] And Peter Dannenberg in Hamburg was the first to program the two one act operas *Eine florentisische Tragödie* and *Der Zwerg* as a pair on a single evening – we saw them this way a year ago in Frankfurt – he also pioneered a revival of *Der Kreidekreis.* James Conlon recorded most of the Zemlinsky operas; he performed them all in Cologne and now is doing them in Los Angeles too. That's an enormous renaissance in and of itself when you consider it was starting from absolute zero. For example, *Der Traumgörge* had its world premiere in Nuremberg in 1980.[16] Mahler had scheduled *Der Traumgörge* for the Hofoper, now the Vienna State Opera, but then Mahler left and his successor Weingartner immediately dropped the work again.[17] So *Der Traumgörge* was never performed. Mahler also premiered the opera *Es war einmal* at the Hofoper.[18] He was a great believer in Zemlinsky.

Zemlinsky's principal interest was opera. He got his start as an opera conductor, as an operetta conductor, actually, in the Volkstheater in Vienna, and in his lifetime he was the greatest opera conductor of them all. We have none other than Stravinsky as witness for that. In a conversation we had many years ago in Cincinnati he asked us what we were playing in our next concert, which he was hoping to attend. We mentioned that we were playing the third quartet of Zemlinsky. Stravinsky went into ecstasy at the sound of this name, exclaiming that Zemlinsky was the greatest conductor he'd ever heard, and then he told us about a performance of *The Marriage of Figaro* conducted by Zemlinsky in Prague. Stravinsky was adamant that it was the greatest performance of anything he had ever heard conducted by anybody in his whole life. And that really is saying something, Stravinsky was very critical of conductors!

15 Owing to the Anschluss (the annexation of Austria by Hitler) in 1938, Zemlinsky had to break off the orchestration of *Der König Kandaules*; it was completed in 1991–1994 by Antony Beaumont on assignment from the Hamburg State Opera. Gerd Albrecht conducted the premiere, which was recorded for commercial release, as was the later Salzburg performance under Kent Nagano.

16 On October 11, 1980.

17 The premiere planned by the Vienna State Opera for the 1907–1908 season did not take place, owing to Mahler's dismissal. Zemlinsky himself scheduled it for the 1914–1915 season of the New German Theater in Prague, where he was Music Director, but it had to be dropped owing to the outbreak of the war.

18 Mahler's premiere of *Es war einmal*… took place on January 22, 1900.

RS You also had access to some recordings on which Zemlinsky conducted the Kroll Opera orchestra in Berlin.

WL Yes, he was a conductor there, along with Otto Klemperer, and made some recordings with the orchestra. Mediocre, I would say. In recording sessions at that time they had to play a piece straight through, once and once only, and that was that, there wasn't any way to edit takes. And the Kroll was no virtuoso orchestra like we're accustomed to today. The best example of how bad the orchestra could be is the recording of Mozart's g minor symphony conducted by Richard Strauss. Fortunately Frau Zemlinsky gave a few recordings her husband had made with the Berlin Philharmonic to the Yale University Archives: Mozart's overture to *Così fan tutte*, Smetana's *Moldau*, Beethoven's overture to *Fidelio*. But those were just test disks, not proper pressings, and you had to be very careful not to break them. Later on they were available on LPs. These recordings give some idea of Zemlinsky's tremendous intensity as a conductor, of his classical, unromanticized approach to music, and of his love of great dynamic contrasts.

RS It's astounding how a renaissance sometimes arises simultaneously in different places. At the Frankfurt Opera there was recently an exhibit called 'The Rediscovery of Zemlinsky under Adorno's Sponsorship' which mentioned that Adorno had given a lecture on the radio in 1959 in which he had made the case for Zemlinsky as a composer.[19] But Adorno's lecture was only two or three years before you found the score to the third string quartet at Frank's Music in New York.

WL I know the lecture, but I didn't know it in 1959. At that time I had no interest in Zemlinsky at all. You have to come across such things for the first time somehow! But Adorno had always known Zemlinsky, he had been in Vienna in the 1920s, and in Prague he had been the go-between for Alban Berg and Hanna Fuchs, so he knew Zemlinsky in Prague as a conductor of Schoenberg's and Berg's works. So it doesn't surprise me that Adorno was interested in Zemlinsky. He'd already written various things about Zemlinsky before that.

RS You got to know Frau Zemlinsky[20] personally. How did that happen?

[19] See Adorno's *Quasi una Fantasia: Essays on Modern Music (*London, 2012).

[20] Luise ('Louise') Sachsel (1900–1992) met Zemlinsky in Prague in 1915 when she auditioned for the Prague Theater chorus; he subsequently gave her a few singing lessons, after which she studied singing at the Vienna Academy of Music and painting at the Prague Academy of Art. She auditioned for Zemlinsky in Prague again, this time as a soloist, in 1924, and was engaged for minor parts. They were married in January, 1930, a year after the death of Zemlinsky's first wife.

WL We met in June, 1965, while the LaSalle Quartet was in New York to tape a segment for 'The Today Show,' a daily television show to which all kinds of people were invited for interviews. It was a two hour show that began at an ungodly hour in the morning. For many years the anchor was Barbara Walters, who later became very famous. The LaSalle Quartet was invited to be on this show. We had to get up at 4 am in order to be there at 5 am and get made up for the cameras: horrible. We taped our segment at around 6 or 6:30 am; we even have a recording of it.

RS Were you playing a quartet by Zemlinsky?

WL I believe we played Lutosławski. In any case we were done by 7 am and had the whole day ahead of us: what to do with the rest of the day? One couldn't just go back to bed! So first of all we had a big breakfast, and then Evi and I went to the movies and saw *Zorba the Greek* – a wonderful film. By then it was about 11 am. It was a long day, and sometime in the afternoon we went to the Russian Tea Room, on 57th Street next to Carnegie Hall. At that time it was a real artists' cafe, everyone went there if they didn't go to the Carnegie Delicatessen. So we went to the Russian Tea Room to have an elegant tea and enjoy their wonderful pastries. And there we ran into Lotte Klemperer, the daughter of Otto Klemperer, who we'd known for a long time. We sat together and talked and then at some point a man we didn't know at all joined us and Lotte introduced us to him, he was a rehearsal pianist at the Metropolitan Opera, Hans Brück. He wanted to know what we were playing and I told him that at the moment we were working on Zemlinsky – I believe it might have been the third quartet, which we had in repertory then. He was surprised by that, he found it really interesting and told me I should let Zemlinsky's wife know, it would give her a lot of pleasure.

I couldn't believe it, it was 1965 and Zemlinsky had been dead for more than twenty years, and even if his wife were younger than he, it seemed unlikely that she'd still be alive! But he told me that yes, she was indeed much younger than Zemlinsky, and that she was very much alive and teaching voice here in New York, living on West End Avenue. He went to the phone booth, got the Manhattan telephone directory, opened it, and pointed out Louise Zemlinsky, telling me to call her, she'd be ecstatic.

So there was nothing for it but to go to the telephone booth and call her right then and there. And lo and behold Louise Zemlinsky herself answered, and I told her that Mr. Brück had told me that I could call her, my name was Walter Levin, we were a string quartet, the LaSalle Quartet, we were playing a piece by her husband that we thought was really terrific and we wondered whether she might not like to come and visit us sometime in Cincinnati, and also whether I might come and visit her sometime. She wanted to know where I was calling from and I told her that at the moment I was in New York. Whereupon she invited me to come the next afternoon and have tea with her.

And so I went to have tea with Frau Zemlinsky. That was an astonishing visit. A quiet, attractive woman, very modest. A beautiful apartment with a grand piano and a living room with old-fashioned furniture. The walls were covered with pictures of the most incredible musicians, incredible for me of course, all inscribed to Alexander Zemlinsky personally and autographed by Brahms, Mahler, Berg, Webern, all the great composers and instrumentalists of his time. The whole musical history of Zemlinsky's Vienna was hanging there on the walls, and of Austria, Prague, and Bohemia also. She went out to the kitchen to make tea, and when she opened the door, a gust of wind came in from the balcony and blew some letters onto the floor that had been piled up on the grand piano lid. I picked them up, and they were letters from Brahms, from Schoenberg … I couldn't believe my eyes: every one of them an autograph, an original! I laid them carefully back down on the piano again, and when she came back, I asked her why she left all these letters just lying around on the piano. 'Well,' she said, 'why not? No one's at all interested in them.' I asked her if she'd tried the Library of Congress and she said, no, she'd already offered them to the Library of Congress and they weren't at all interested. So that's how I got to know Frau Zemlinsky.

A rather intense acquaintanceship developed from there, as a result of which she bequeathed royalties from Zemlinsky's works and recordings to the University of Cincinnati to fund an Alexander Zemlinsky Prize for Composition, to be awarded every six years: the first competition took place in 1999 with Henry Meyer as the coordinator.[21] My relationship with Frau Zemlinsky was really very strange. She was somewhat inclined to mysticism:[22] she believed I was the reincarnation of Zemlinsky, that my personality and my whole being was the reincarnation of Zemlinsky.

RS That really is bizarre!

WL Indeed!

[21] The prize results in a commission for a new piece, to be premiered by the University of Cincinnati College-Conservatory of Music (CCM). The 1999 competition resulted in Katsuji Maeda's 'Reflections' for orchestra with two pianos, premiered by the CCM orchestra in 2000; the 2005 prize went to Enrico Chapela for his concerto for percussion trio and orchestra, 'Encrypted Poetry (after Poe),' premiered by the CCM's Percussion Group Cincinnati and the CCM orchestra in 2007. The 2011 prize went to Ulrich Kreppein for his *Spiel der Schatten* (*The Play of the Shadows*). Second and third prizes are also awarded.

[22] When Frau Zemlinsky gave up singing, she devoted herself entirely to painting and to the anthroposophy of Rudolf Steiner.

Marginal Works and French Repertory

RS At the other extreme from your experience in resuscitating Zemlinsky, there were a number of works that you played only once, or only a few times, or only in one or two seasons and then never again. Since I worked for so long in private industry, it's only natural that for me the question of return on investment is never far away. To what extent was it worthwhile for you to invest in learning a piece and then play it just once or only a few times?

WL It's not worthwhile at all, but sometimes you have to do it, for instance when you're invited as a young quartet to give a concert in the Coolidge Auditorium of the Library of Congress, where the Budapest Quartet performed for decades as the house quartet, and later the Juilliard Quartet too. It was practically impossible to get an engagement there. But one day we got an inquiry as to whether we would come and perform a quartet by Mary Howe,[23] one of the sponsors of the Library of Congress who was also a composer. So we learned the piece, played it there once, and never played it again.

The same thing happened to us once in Cincinnati, when there was a celebration in honor of Martin Dumler.[24] Dumler was one of the sponsors of the College of Music as well as its Vice President, a businessman with a lot of money who had helped make it possible for the LaSalle Quartet to come to Cincinnati. He was president of the Bruckner Society in America, a man with a good head for the arts, who also composed, and we were asked to perform his string quartet at this celebration. On the same concert we also played Mozart's sonatas for organ and string quartet and Bach's double concerto. The Dumler quartet is more or less in the Bruckner mold, if my memory is right. We had to learn it, our position at the school depended on it, and we certainly wanted to remain the Quartet in Residence there, so we just learned it and played it the one time.

RS Dumler also convinced you to play the early Bruckner quartet.[25]

WL Yes, and we took it with us on tour to Australia. Martin Dumler was a big Bruckner and Mahler fan. That was pretty impressive in and of itself: a

[23] Mary Howe (1882–1964), pianist and composer in a conservative style. The quartet had been composed in 1939. The concert took place on February 11, 1955.

[24] Martin Dumler (1868–1958). The concert was on April 5, 1955.

[25] Bruckner composed the c minor quartet in 1862 as a student assignment from his teacher Otto Kitzler in Linz. The work was rediscovered around 1950 and had its premiere in modern times by the Koeckert Quartet in 1951.

musical dilettante, someone who was really a businessman through and through, who championed Bruckner and Mahler at a time when these two composers were still scarcely known in America.

RS A newspaper article about this quartet said that it had recently been discovered by the Bruckner Society. Apparently Dumler presented the first printed score to the LaSalle Quartet so that Cincinnati would hear the first American performance.

WL Yes, this early Bruckner quartet was a novelty at that time. Whether we were heroes for playing it is something else entirely. I wouldn't have gone looking for it myself, to say the least.

RS Before we go on to discuss the mainstays of your repertory, that is, the classical and romantic literature, the Second Viennese School, and your role in the creation of a new literature for the string quartet by contemporary composers, I want to mention that I can't help noticing that of all the French quartet literature you only played the Debussy and Ravel quartets. The LaSalle Quartet also paired them on a single recording, as most ensembles do. But you would never guess from this pairing how differently they figured in your repertory: after Webern's *Bagatelles* Opus 9, the Ravel quartet is the work you played the most, with just under 200 performances distributed more or less evenly across your whole career. Whereas you played the Debussy quartet just 21 times, in two phases, starting in 1955, and then after 1972 never again.

WL The Ravel quartet was one of our repertory pieces, it was something we could so to speak play in our sleep. It's easier than the Debussy quartet by a wide margin, whereas the Debussy is a difficult piece, you have to work hard on it again and again. It would probably have been possible to make it into a repertory piece, but we never got that far. We weren't that enthusiastic about the French impressionists. We also never played either Gabriel Fauré or César Frank. We weren't so crazy about the French quartet literature, although I do consider the Debussy quartet to be an outstanding piece. But even the Debussy isn't exactly my cup of tea. We played the Ravel quartet so to speak in self-defense, it satisfied the need to deal with the French quartet literature without our having to put any effort into it, since the Ravel quartet was easy for us.

15 *Classical and Romantic Composers*

Haydn

ROBERT SPRUYTENBURG: If you look through the collection of LaSalle Quartet programs, the 'classical' string quartets by Haydn, Mozart, and Beethoven, together with those by Schubert, Mendelssohn, Schumann, and Brahms in the later, 'romantic' period, account for nearly half of all the LaSalle Quartet's 4,725 documented performances of individual works. Even so, it may be surprising that Haydn, with over 500 performances, was one of the most frequently performed composers in your repertory, after Beethoven, Mozart, and Webern.

WALTER LEVIN: Haydn was an important composer for me even before I began in earnest to establish a professional quartet in America. I had also played Haydn's piano pieces – there are a large number of marvelous piano pieces by Haydn that, like so much of his music, are neglected. From the outset it was important to me to play Haydn quartets. The first piece on the program in our debut concert in Colorado Springs was Haydn's quartet Opus 64, Nr. 6. Haydn was the first to treat the four instruments in the quartet as equals. His mature quartets have nothing more to do with pieces for solo violin accompanied by three instruments. All four instruments have an equal part in the musical proceedings: that's the conversation among four intelligent people that Goethe so famously described. And the Haydn quartets are so incredibly diverse: in every one of them he posed a different problem for himself and found a new solution, he never repeated himself.

So once you've played ten or twenty Haydn quartets you know more about the basics of the quartet style than you'd learn from the whole of the literature that followed. And actually you can only learn that literature on the basis of knowing Haydn's quartets, since he was the one who first established everything the composers after him developed. In that sense the Haydn quartets are the absolute foundation of quartet playing. When I'm teaching now, I require all the ensembles to learn a new Haydn quartet practically every season they work with me. And we repeatedly took new Haydn quartets up into our repertory, on account of the multitude of musical problems that Haydn quite consciously posed for himself, in order to solve them.

RS Haydn composed altogether 68 string quartets.[1] I assume it wasn't your intention to play all of them, but that you made a selection of them.

[1] And not, as was long thought, and is still sometimes mistakenly held, 83 quartets. The quartet formerly known as Opus 1, Nr. 5, has been shown to be an arrangement by some

WL Exactly. I believe we played about twenty Haydn quartets.

RS Yes, it's exactly twenty. In making your selection did you rely on the Peters edition of the 'thirty famous quartets' that you got as a present for your bar mitzvah?

WL I didn't have much choice to begin with, as there were scarcely any alternatives.

RS Had you previously known the Haydn quartets that you played with the LaSalle Quartet?

WL Not all of them. When I was studying at Juilliard in New York I got the others, the 'not famous' Haydn quartets, also in the old Peters edition. They were never reprinted, since nobody ever bought them. Publication of the later, and better, editions of the Haydn quartets only began in 1968. The Doblinger edition scores are quite decent, but they never published the text-critical reports, and, unfortunately, the parts are unusable because the publisher added dynamic marks and phrasings that aren't in the score. Now both Peters and Henle are publishing complete urtext editions of the Haydn quartets. I think the new Peters edition is particularly outstanding, in part thanks to its excellent text-critical reports.

RS I've compiled a set of performance statistics from the LaSalle's concert programs which makes it obvious that for the most part each of the Haydn quartets that you played was in repertory at just one point in your career: Opus 20, Nr. 2, for instance, in 1975–1977, Opus 20, Nr. 4, in 1978–1982, and Opus 20, Nr. 3, in 1982–1985, though there are some that you later returned to, such as Opus 33, Nr. 5, which you played in the 1957–1958 season and then again in 1979–1981, or Opus 50, Nr. 2, in 1961–1963 and 1969–1972, and Opus 76, Nr. 6, in 1963–1965 and 1981–1983.

WL We were never interested in playing the same thing over and over again. In order to stay fresh you have to put a piece aside and then take it up and work on it again, otherwise you fall into a routine with it, and for

other hand of a symphony, Nr. 107, and the quartets Opus 2, Nr. 3 and 5, have been shown to be arrangements, again by an unknown hand, of two of his six-part divertimenti. The six quartets Opus 3 have been shown to be not by Haydn but by Roman Hofstetter. Together, these nine bring the total down to 74. The traditional list also counted the *Seven Last Words*, Opus 51, as seven separate quartets; although the string quartet arrangement is by Haydn himself, the piece was not composed as a quartet. So this brings the total further on down to 67. In 1931, however, a hitherto unknown quartet was discovered, now known as Opus 0 or, sometimes, as Opus 1, Nr. 0, which brings the total up to 68.

us the Haydn quartets were just too good to let that happen. Besides which, we always wanted to learn new ones, though not all 68, as we weren't such quick studies. There are ensembles that learn six Haydn quartets in a single season. I admire that, if they can really do it: we certainly couldn't. And we certainly didn't offer all the Haydn quartets we ever worked on, we never played twenty Haydn quartets in a single season, at most just two or three. Also, we always played mixed programs, so we never played three Haydn quartets in a single concert,[2] we would play, for instance, a Haydn quartet, then a romantic quartet, and then a contemporary piece. And it takes a great deal of time to learn contemporary pieces, which leaves less time for the others.

RS There's one Haydn quartet that you played again and again from the beginning of your career to the end, and more frequently than any other, by a wide margin, which is his Opus 71, Nr. 2, which you played altogether 80 times, more than half again as many times as the next most frequent, Opus 9, Nr. 4, which you played 51 times.

WL Opus 71, Nr. 2 was in fact our favorite quartet.

RS Something else that's striking about the selection of Haydn quartets in the LaSalle's repertory is that with very few exceptions you concentrated on the pieces that are seldom played: who was playing the A major quartet Opus 55, Nr. 1, in the 1950s, or the C major quartet Opus 50, Nr. 2, and the d minor quartet Opus 9, Nr. 4, in the 1960s? Also the C major quartet Opus 64, Nr. 1, and the E♭ major quartet Opus 76, Nr. 6, are among the rarely performed works.

WL That's right: it was always our intention to play pieces that nobody else was playing. Today the players prefer the named quartets, like the 'Bird,' the 'Joke,' the 'Lark,' or the 'Rider,' so that out of 68 Haydn quartets there are at most twenty that are played regularly, and always the same ones. Even the young quartets want to play these same pieces over and over again. With us it was just the opposite: we consciously set out to play the pieces by Haydn that were seldom played and that exhibit a highly unconventional structure. These include the very best of his string quartets, which scarcely anybody knows, and among them, for instance, is the Opus 76, Nr. 6, a wholly unconventional piece that against all the 'rules' starts with a variations movement. All four movements break with the conventional rules: the second movement is

[2] An exception was the concert in Sydney, Australia, on September 10, 1982, on the 250th anniversary of Haydn's birth, for which the LaSalle Quartet played his Opus 20, Nr. 3, Opus 64, Nr. 1, and Opus 76, Nr. 6.

astonishingly futuristic in that the first part of it has no key signature, something that otherwise doesn't appear until at the beginning of the 20th century, at the end of tonal music. And the last movement is so difficult rhythmically that even a very savvy quartet player has to pay close attention not to get tripped up by it.

Mozart

RS When I look at my performance statistics from the LaSalle Quartet concert programs, it's apparent that you also have some unambiguous preferences among the Mozart quartets: you played the d minor quartet, K. 421, over 100 times and at many points in your career; the A major quartet, K. 464, is a close second with 95 performances. And evidently the D major quartet, K. 499, with a good 60 performances, was also one of your favorite pieces. On the other hand, I was surprised to find that you played the G major quartet, K. 387, only relatively infrequently, and practically speaking only at the end of the 1960s, despite its highly polyphonic finale. You made an exceptionally wide detour around the famous 'Dissonant' quartet, K. 465: there are only three performances of it, two of them in Cincinnati and one for the Swedish radio, which means that you never played it on tour.

WL I'm happy to concede that the G major quartet is a lovely piece, but it didn't suit us, and neither did the 'Dissonant' quartet, which we had a lot of trouble with. As you said, we played the d minor and A major quartets quite often, and with great pleasure, as they were particularly well suited to us. For me the d minor quartet is among the most emotionally mature and expressive of all of Mozart's last ten quartets. The key of d minor had a very special meaning for Mozart: for him it was virtually a key of mourning, of funereal grief, which you can also hear in the d minor piano concerto, K. 466, and the last of his works, the *Requiem*, K. 626, which is also in d minor. The d minor quartet expresses a deep, serene, and poignant sadness in all its movements, both minor and major. We played it so often because in our opinion its tempi were usually misunderstood by performers, they played some movements too fast, others too slow, and on the whole without enough contrast and drama, even though the most dramatic of Mozart's keys is g minor, not d minor. But the d minor quartet actually encompasses all the musical characters. That's what drew us to it, and we never tired of it. It's a piece we could play again and again, and one that bears listening to again and again. But we also played the F major quartet, K. 590, the E♭ quartet, K. 428, and the B♭ major quartet, K. 458, the so-called 'Hunt' quartet, repeatedly and with pleasure from time to time in our career. I had enough of the D major quartet, K. 575, after we played it so many times on our Southeast Asian tour in 1956.

RS The second 'Prussian' quartet in B♭ major, K. 589, is also conspicuously underrepresented in the performance statistics.

WL Indeed! It's an extremely difficult piece for the cello and for that reason it takes a lot of effort to keep it in repertory.

RS But when you were teaching the last ten Mozart quartets at the Academy of Music in Basel you didn't show any favoritism, you treated all the works with the same love and respect.

WL When I'm teaching a piece it's the best piece in the world! Otherwise you shouldn't do it. I don't teach any pieces I don't like or have no connection with. Recently I came to an agreement with a young quartet that they would play a Mendelssohn quartet, either one of the Opus 44 quartets or else Opus 80, and I told them what edition they should use. They said that was great, they'd do it. But two days ago I got an e-mail saying they'd decided they'd rather play Borodin. That's not an alternative as far as I'm concerned. I don't teach Borodin.

RS But just now you have to teach Mozart's 'Dissonant' quartet, K. 465.

WL And I'm happy to do that too.

RS But not to play it?

WL It wasn't my favorite Mozart quartet. At first glance it seems slick and somewhat banal, and it is too, to a certain extent. But there's more to it than meets the eye, and you have to get beyond that. And I learned something about it too. For sure there are better, that is, more complicated Mozart quartets, and I'm interested in complex structures like the A major quartet, the d minor quartet, or the *Adagio and Fugue* in c minor, K. 546,[3] although the introduction to the 'Dissonant' quartet is one of the most daring things Mozart ever wrote. Today I'm also interested in other things than I was when we had the LaSalle Quartet. When I teach a piece now what interests me is the challenge of discovering something that had previously escaped me. Mozart didn't write any bad quartets, so there's always more to learn from them.

[3] The LaSalle Quartet played the arrangement of K. 546 for string quartet and contrabass a total of 38 times.

RS We know that in 1782 Mozart arranged four fugues from Bach's *Well Tempered Clavier* for the circle of people around Baron Gottfried van Swieten; they're listed in the catalogue of his works as K. 405. But in the early 1980s you succeeded in finding the previously unpublished preludes that Mozart had composed for these fugues. How did you happen to come across them?

WL For a long time the manuscript of Mozart's fugue transcriptions was owned by the famous cellist Gregor Piatigorsky in Los Angeles, where the musicologist Warren Kirkendale examined them and then described them in the 1962–1963 *Mozart Yearbook*. He also copied the four fugues by hand, and in the early 1970s the Swiss branch of Eulenburg published the parts to these fugue transcriptions. But Kirkendale and Eulenburg had only the fugues, not the preludes, which is surprising because Bach composed a prelude for each of them. In the meantime it turned out that Baron van Swieten's copy of the fugues evidently didn't have Bach's preludes either, so Mozart couldn't have known what the original preludes looked like. But he did know, probably because van Swieten told him, that usually there were introductions to the fugues, and so he composed new ones. Unfortunately the manuscript has been lost, we only have a copy from 1796 that doesn't give Mozart as the composer. This copy was mentioned by Kirkendale in his article and is in the National Library in Vienna.

We followed up on this and eventually, after some back and forth, we got a microfilm of the parts for the four preludes. I assembled a score from the parts and then we played the preludes together with the fugue transcriptions,[4] and recorded them for Deutsche Grammophon. For a long time before we found out about the preludes we were reluctant to play the fugues without them. I was of the opinion that it didn't do justice to the fugues to play the four of them one after the other, it would get to be monotonous. It's not for nothing that Bach wrote an introduction to every fugue, and in a completely different, that is, homophonic style, so that the listener can relax after the strict counterpoint of the fugues. And Mozart's preludes accomplish this perfectly, they're wonderful, artful, and ambitious pieces in his mature style, which despite all their complexity appear to be simplicity itself, as is so often the case with Mozart.

RS It's very unusual for there to still be unpublished material by a composer as well known as Mozart.

[4] The LaSalle Quartet first performed the fugues together with the preludes on September 2, 1984, at the Academy of Music in Basel, and subsequently played them more than 40 times, up to and including their last concert in May, 1987.

WL Indeed! But evidently nobody had bothered to take a closer look at these manuscripts before then, probably because Mozart's name isn't on them, and apparently nobody before us had taken the trouble to follow up on Kirkendale's source references. At least nobody had written about them after seeing them except Kirkendale. I also don't know whether there had been a performance of the preludes before ours, at least in recent times. In any case it was an extraordinary experience to assemble the score from the microfilmed parts, to see a piece by Mozart take shape so to speak before my very eyes. I'd never experienced anything like that before, we're not musicologists, for whom discovering music is part and parcel of their profession. At most we'd now and again exhume contemporary music.

RS In the meantime some musicologists have questioned Mozart's authorship of the two preludes in E major and D major.

WL Of course the ultimate proof is lacking, since we don't have the 'smoking gun,' which in this case would be an autograph, a manuscript in Mozart's own hand. But when you've played the preludes as often as we did, doubts like that completely disappear.

Beethoven

RS A number of years ago, when you made copies for us of the tapes of the LaSalle Quartet's live performances of the Beethoven quartets, I was astonished to discover that the recordings of Opus 18, Nr. 2, and Opus 95 were from the year 1956, the recording of Opus 18, Nr. 1, was from 1958, and the recording of Opus 18, Nr. 5, was from 1962. So I asked myself whether there weren't any more recent recordings of these quartets? And then a couple of years ago I made some inquiries about the radio network archives of LaSalle Quartet performances, with the same result: they had only old tapes of some of the early Beethoven quartets. After you donated the LaSalle Quartet archive to the Paul Sacher Foundation in Basel, in 2003, I began to do some research into this, which confirmed that beyond a certain point in time, there are no more recordings of the early quartets Opus 18 from Colorado or Cincinnati, except for Nr. 3 and Nr. 6. On the other hand, there are scarcely any early recordings of the late quartets. In addition to that, there is often a substantial interval between when you first studied a piece and when you began a regular series of performances of it. Take for instance Beethoven's Opus 59, Nr. 2, which you had already been so anxious to play when you were in Palestine: in the LaSalle Quartet's first season in Colorado, 1949–1950, you played it just once, then in 1956–1957 you played it four times, and it was actually only in the 1960s that you began to play it really often.

WL But surely you can make sense of that! The LaSalle Quartet worked on the Beethoven quartets throughout its career, and after we had played one or the other of them on tour for a while, we wanted to study one of them that we didn't know so well. We also didn't work on them in chronological order. In addition, we were slow learners, that's one of the explanations for our repertory. I'm a great admirer of the Arditti Quartet, and their ability to learn a new piece overnight, so to speak before the composer has even finished writing it, is totally incomprehensible to me. There's a young American quartet today, the Pacifica Quartet, that has played and recorded all five of Elliott Carter's quartets. It wasn't like that for us, every piece was difficult, and it took us a long time to learn each of them, often longer than we'd expected. Also, we didn't keep pieces in our repertory forever, on tours we only offered a very limited repertory, twelve pieces or so. We constructed our programs very carefully, and we never allowed a manager or a concert organizer to make up a program themselves out of our repertory. Whereas the Amadeus Quartet had a list of about 40 quartets that were always on offer, from which the promoter could choose whatever he wanted.

RS Getting back to the Beethoven quartets: the performance statistics I compiled from the records of your concert programs clearly show that you played most of the early and middle quartets at the beginning of your career and the late quartets mostly in its second half. The performance statistics also clearly reveal some preferences. For instance, you only played Opus 18, Nr. 1, twice, both times in 1958, and also played Opus 18, Nr. 2, in just one season, in 1956.

WL At that time I wasn't particularly interested in Opus 18, Nr. 1. Opus 18, Nr. 2, had been in our Southeast Asian tour repertory, and after we'd played this piece on tour for seven months I never wanted to play it again – it and a few others too!

RS You also played Opus 18, Nr. 4, only in the 1961–1963 seasons, and then never again.

WL I don't regard Opus 18, Nr. 4, as one of Beethoven's best quartets, I find it rather banal in places, and compared to Beethoven's other c minor pieces it's definitely inferior. Also I played the piece much too soon in Palestine, which spoiled it for me. You should never play a piece too soon! But you do have to start somewhere.

RS But quite surprisingly you also didn't play Opus 18, Nr. 5 and 6, very often either, and they're such beautiful pieces!

WL We played Opus 18, Nr. 5, at the very beginning in Cincinnati and now and then later on. I think it's a very beautiful piece, I agree with you about that. Whereas Opus 18, Nr. 6, is in every respect an extremely difficult work, both technically and musically, and hard to keep in the repertory, since you have to work through it over and over again.[5] But we liked it a lot and, in my opinion, we also played it very well. Of the quartets Opus 18 we played Nr. 3 the most, since this piece suited us particularly well. But I was never concerned with whether we'd played a piece often or not. We played what we had in repertory, what fit into our programs, and what we wanted to record. That's how it was with the late Beethoven quartets. We didn't play the quartets Opus 18 so often because it was never our intention to record the complete cycle of Beethoven quartets: there are enough of those already.

RS Of the middle quartets you played Opus 59, Nr. 2, the e minor quartet, the most often, and you played it throughout your entire career.

WL The e minor quartet Opus 59, Nr. 2, and the quartet Opus 127 were on the program together when I first heard the Beethoven cycle played by a professional quartet, the French Calvet Quartet, in Berlin, in 1936. That made an extraordinarily strong impression on me at the time. Since then I always endeavored to play these two pieces, both later on, when I had my own quartet, and also very early, in Palestine.

You can still hear how the Calvet Quartet played Opus 59, Nr. 2, their recording is still available. When I listen to their very cultivated but also very genial way of playing this piece, I can't help wondering about it, since Beethoven prescribed exact metronome marks for his quartets up through Opus 95, and for his symphonies too, and they are very different from the tempi chosen by the Calvet Quartet. Evidently the Calvet Quartet didn't take these metronome marks seriously, at that time it would have been very unusual to do so.

Few conductors and few ensembles have paid attention to Beethoven's tempi, but we did. At Schoenberg's insistence the Kolisch Quartet, which was closely associated with him, became the first quartet to observe Beethoven's metronome marks precisely. And in this respect we were very much influenced, albeit indirectly, by the former violist of the Kolisch Quartet, Eugene Lehner, who had taught the Juilliard Quartet. The Juilliard Quartet in turn taught us, so for us it went without saying that you took Beethoven's metronome marks

[5] For more on Opus 18, Nr. 6, see p. 345.

seriously.[6] And when you do that, the character of a piece changes radically. Whenever it was clear to us on the basis of completely objective criteria that a piece was traditionally interpreted wrongly, we were always concerned to put it right, and it was perfectly clear that Opus 59, Nr. 2, was in this category.

RS The other two quartets of Opus 59 you played relatively less often, the F major quartet Opus 59, Nr. 1, only in the years 1959–1961, and the C major quartet Opus 59, Nr. 3, mostly at the beginning of your career. The tempi usually taken in these two pieces are also too slow. Didn't you feel the need to put them to right also?

WL Not to the same extent as the much more radical e minor quartet, though of course we also observed Beethoven's metronome marks in the F major quartet and the C major quartet. As you said, we played Opus 59, Nr. 3, mostly at the beginning of our career, and the fugue in the last movement was one of our bread and butter pieces: we always played it when we were on tour.

RS That's right, you often tell the story about the open air concert in Athens in 1954.

WL Right in the middle of the fugue the wind blew the music off our stands, but we played the piece to the end from memory, stoically, while the audience held its breath.

RS Apparently Opus 74 was not one of your favorite middle quartets.

WL I like the piece a lot, but not the last movement, which is by no means one of Beethoven's great variation movements – even the master falls short sometimes.

RS The f minor quartet Opus 95 is the middle quartet you played the most: almost 120 performances, distributed over the whole course of your career!

WL That's because it's one of those pieces you can shock the public with.

RS It's as radical as the *Grosse Fuge*, Opus 133.

WL Exactly. Along with Opus 59, Nr. 2, Opus 95 is one of the pieces that is

6 For more on Beethoven's metronome marks and Kolisch's investigations of tempo in Beethoven see pp. 341–345.

ordinarily totally misunderstood, as a result of tempi that are too slow. Whenever it turned out that people had a completely mistaken idea of a piece, we were always attracted to it. Kolisch had the same experience as we did with Opus 95: 'everything too fast' is what people said about their interpretation.[7] You only have to listen to most of the recordings to know what I'm talking about, except for the Busch Quartet's: they were also playing this piece at the proper tempi in the 1930s.

RS The other Beethoven quartet that you'd wanted to play from early on, as soon as you'd heard the Calvet Quartet concert in 1936, was Opus 127. It was in fact the first of the late Beethoven quartets that you worked on.

WL That's right, we played it a few times in Colorado Springs in 1950, in our very first season, but we only took it up again much later, in 1976, when we wanted to record it for Deutsche Grammophon.

RS Opus 135 is the other late quartet that you were already playing in Colorado Springs. But evidently you didn't particularly like it, since you only played it there three times, in 1952, and then not again until 1970, when you played it just once, and afterwards a few times on tour before recording it for Deutsche Grammophon in 1976.

WL Opus 135 was a difficult case, because I've always been very ambivalent about it. I find the first and last movements rather banal.

RS The last movement is like a children's song.

WL Both movements are like a potpourri of children's songs, whereas the middle movements, the Scherzo and the slow movement, are great. Toscanini thought so too.

RS Yes, he conducted those two movements in an arrangement for string orchestra, but not the other two.

WL Of course! He knew what was good and what wasn't! Incidentally it was through his recording of these two movements with the strings of the NBC Symphony that I first got to know Opus 135.

7 Levin is referring to Kolisch's anecdote: 'I happily recall an occasion in Paris when after a performance of Opus 95 in which I took the prescribed tempi a professor at the conservatory, a true keeper of the holy grail of tradition, burst out with "*Tout ça trop vite!*" before the last note had even finished dying away. The ensuing dispute turned into a real brawl.' See Kolisch, *Tempo and Character in Beethoven's Music* (Munich, 1992).

RS When you started playing Opus 130, in 1959, you played it with the alternative finale, and only after a long interval, in 1969, did you begin to play it with the *Grosse Fuge*. What led to this change?

WL We had to learn the *Grosse Fuge* first! It was simply too difficult for us to learn all the movements all at once, learning the *Grosse Fuge* is a big job in and of itself.

RS Only Webern's *Bagatelles* Opus 9 and the Ravel quartet were played more often by the LaSalle Quartet.[8]

WL The *Grosse Fuge* is radical and visionary to such a degree, and makes such demands on the interpreters, that it suited us perfectly. When he was 80 years old Stravinsky called it the most contemporary piece he knew, perpetually contemporary, scarcely showing its age, rhythmically more subtle than any music of his century.

RS Something like that also holds for the a minor quartet, Opus 132, which you played quite often from 1963 on through to the very end of your career, as well as for the c-sharp minor quartet Opus 131, which appears in your repertory starting in 1964.

WL Opus 132 was one of our favorite quartets, and both it and Opus 131 are extremely complex pieces that make the greatest demands on their interpreters. On account of their structural complexity, and also in part their rhythmic complexity, they have affinities with Bartók's string quartets as well as with some of the contemporary pieces we played. Our engagement with 20th century works had a very fruitful retroactive effect on our interpretation of the late Beethoven quartets, in particular our deliberate use of tone color to make complex textures in them audibly transparent.

RS A typically unusual work in the LaSalle Quartet's repertory is Beethoven's transcription of his piano sonata Opus 14, Nr. 1, for string quartet, which entered your repertory in 1957, once you were able, after chasing after many dead-ends, to unearth the score and parts in Cincinnati, of all places. This work is still not usually included in the canon of Beethoven's string quartets and isn't even mentioned in most of the monographs on them.

WL That's just why we were interested in it! It's a very beautiful piece and

[8] The LaSalle Quartet played the *Grosse Fuge* 148 times, Webern's *Bagatelles* 243 times, and the Ravel Quartet 199 times.

as an extra Beethoven quartet so to speak it's a real gift. And it's fascinating to see how the master himself arranged a piano sonata for string quartet, since he didn't just simply distribute the piano music among the four voices of a string quartet but partly recomposed it from a string quartet point of view. Transcriptions of all sorts were very much the fashion then, and in this piece Beethoven meant to demonstrate how a truly creative composer goes about it.[9] A comparison of the two versions also offers a rare opportunity to follow the development of a composer in just three years, which among other things shows a marked intensification of expression. No wonder, since after composing the piano sonata in 1799 Beethoven had in the meantime composed the six string quartets Opus 18, the septet Opus 20, the first symphony Opus 21, and the first two piano concerti. In 1802 he was a completely different composer than what he'd been three years previously.

As we've already seen, the first major change that Beethoven made in the quartet arrangement was to transpose the key of the piano sonata, E major, to F major, so as to make the dominant, C, playable as the bass on the viola's and cello's open C strings. The quartet version is also distinguished by an enormous increase in the number of dynamic changes. The most frequent, which occurs eighteen times in all, is that Beethoven added the mark *sforzato*, his so typical dynamic accent on a note or a chord. In addition he constantly makes use of the stringed instruments' ability to make *crescendi* on long held notes, whereas on the piano, as everyone knows, long held notes inevitably decay. There are thirteen places in the quartet version where he added such crescendi, and nine of those places are followed immediately by a *piano*: this instruction is also typical of Beethoven's middle years.

And then he also added rhythmically more incisive counterpoint, altered some pianistic accompaniment figures that don't lie well for the strings, and in the first movement coda composed an additional violin part. Both the original, piano solo, and the quartet arrangement are printed, one above the other, in the Eulenburg pocket score, so you can quite easily track the differences. We played both versions in the same concert several times with Stefan Litwin, and demonstrated the

[9] In a letter to his publisher Breitkopf & Härtel dated July 13, 1802, Beethoven wrote that 'it would be good if the insane rage for transcribing even piano music for strings, instruments that are such opposites in every respect, were to stop. I firmly assert that only Mozart himself could transcribe his piano music for other instruments, and the same holds for Haydn too; and without meaning to put myself on the same level as these two great men, I assert the same for my piano music also, since one not only has to completely cut out or rewrite entire sections but also to add to them, which is the miserable stumbling block, for the overcoming of which one must either be the master himself or at least have the same deftness and inventiveness. I have transformed just one sonata of mine into a string quartet ... and so I know for certain how hard it would be for someone else to do that.' Cited in Wilhelm Altmann's preface to the 1910 Eulenburg pocket score.

differences in a lecture-recital with examples. We also recorded both versions with Stefan for Deutsche Grammophon.

Romantics: Schubert, Schumann, Brahms

RS The composers in the LaSalle Quartet's repertory who are traditionally considered 'romantic' account for about only twelve percent of all the LaSalle Quartet's documented performances, and over two-thirds of these are works by Schubert, with 202 performances, and Brahms, with 173. And of the remaining third, half were performances of works by Mendelssohn, with 54 performances, and Schumann, with 41. While Brahms wrote only three quartets, Schubert wrote 16 quartets, and yet over half of your Schubert performances were of the *Quartettsatz* in c minor, D. 703, and the a minor quartet, D. 804, with 57 performances each, while his great quintet in C major, D. 956, received only a dozen performances by the LaSalle Quartet.

WL Well, the quintet requires a second cello, and it wasn't easy to find a second cellist who understood how we worked and had both the time and the willingness to work with us that way. We were very fortunate to be able to record the quintet for Deutsche Grammophon with Lynn Harrell, who had been Lee Fiser's teacher and who had worked with Jimmy Levine in Cleveland and therefore already knew what we were about, besides being a fabulous cellist and musician himself. We had played it with Lynn a number of times before we recorded it, and indeed we never played it with anyone else.

RS The LaSalle Quartet performed all the late quartets of Schubert, that is, the d minor quartet, *Death and the Maiden*, D. 810, as well as the great G major quartet, D. 887, but also two of his early quartets, the g minor quartet, D. 173, and the E major quartet, D. 373, of which you played the first mentioned even quite often. I find it a real shame that you didn't record any of the Schubert quartets for Deutsche Grammophon, since your perspective on these works really is distinctly different from that of most of the other string quartet ensembles.

WL It was the same as with the early and middle Beethoven quartets, I felt that there were already enough recordings of the Schubert quartets, though later on the live recording of our 1976 Salzburg Festival performance of the *Quartettsatz* was released on the Orfeo label.

RS You've often emphasized the importance of singing for your conception of violin playing and of string playing generally, starting with your first experiences with opera and Lieder as a child in Berlin in the 1930s, and you've constantly urged your students to become acquainted with the vocal repertory and in particular the art of *bel canto*, as a model for instrumentalists also.

WL Absolutely, it's indispensable, it's where the rhetoric of music comes from.

RS And the 'romantic' composers you played the most were the very greatest and most prolific contributors to the development of the Lied: Schubert, Schumann, Hugo Wolf, and Brahms. And among the 19th century byways of the quartet literature you explored, Donizetti, Verdi, and Smetana, to say nothing of Zemlinsky, were above all else opera composers. So the obvious question for the romantic string quartet repertory is the extent to which you would characterize these works as, in Mendelssohn's phrase, 'songs without words.'

WL Well, certainly not only that, but yes, of course, what is probably most characteristic of the romantic composers, starting with Schubert, is their emphasis on rhetoric. Schubert is a rhetorical composer, even more so than Haydn and Mozart, who are also rhetorical composers. In performing Schubert the question is always, how would you sing it. Forget about Schubert's notes: sing! Of course I'm exaggerating here, but it's a mistake to play Schubert too literally, to cling too closely to the printed page: Schubert isn't Beethoven, he's not an instrumental composer, he's a writer of songs, even when he's writing for instruments, as in the symphonies and the string quartets.

Schubert's instrumental pieces are really sequences of song writing separated by recitatives and punctuated by dramatic events, and so the music must breathe the way a singer breathes, and have the continuity of a dancer's movements from one gesture to the next, in this case from one rhetorical gesture to the next, which is where all those techniques of *bel canto* come in: *legato*, *portato*, *portamento*, and *messa di voce*, and so on. Of course this isn't only true for Schubert, and to some extent it's true for every music except for perhaps some post-war composers who deliberately set about to work against it, which was one of the aims of some of the more radical serialists at Darmstadt.

Singers at least have the advantage of having the words as a guide to the rhetoric, but instrumentalists must so to speak invent the words for the rhetoric. Schubert's music simply cannot be played metronomically, you don't have to feel guilty about that, on the contrary, you should feel guilty if you do play it metronomically.

RS Doesn't this contradict what you say about fidelity to the score, to the composer's intentions, for instance, in performing Beethoven?

WL Actually, no, it doesn't. What you have to realize, as a performer, is the extent to which composers take for granted the common performance practices of their time, something that we've become familiar with in regard to baroque music and now in the classical period too but which is still in the process of being recovered for the romantic composers. So you do indeed have to follow the score in Schubert or Schumann as closely as you do in Haydn or Mozart or Beethoven, but you also have to realize that what Schubert's or Schumann's notation means is different from those earlier composers. And of course you first of all have to learn what those changes are and what they mean.

And precisely because this is music of such great enthusiasm, of such extraordinary intensity, rhythmic precision is all the more crucial as a means for concentrating its expressive energies: every note must be clear and distinct if it's also to be alive and expressive, which can only happen if the music is played with great precision as well as great flexibility. Much the same holds for Schumann too, and Brahms. Schoenberg too, for that matter, and Berg and Webern also.

RS To stay with Schumann for a moment, you've told us the story about your recording the Schumann quartet Opus 41, Nr. 2, for Radio Zurich. At two different times in your career you played this piece quite often, and in between you also played the A major quartet, Opus 41, Nr. 3, a couple of times, but never the first quartet, Opus 41, Nr. 1. So here too there's a marked preference.

WL I like the F major quartet a lot and think it's a very good piece. The first movement is a good example of how Schumann sought to fuse the romantic idea of 'endless melody' with his very different impulse to write a continuously propulsive and very energetic music. But to be honest with you, I'm not such a Schumann fanatic. Schumann never really escaped being a pianist and a song writer: he wanted to write counterpoint, he wanted to write instrumental music, but he only partly succeeds, which means that interpreters have to help him out in this respect, not necessarily by the kind of rewriting that Mahler and others undertook, but at least in translating his phrases into bowings and fingerings that bring out his counterpoint and allow this music to sound like it was conceived for four different, individual, instruments and not just one.

You have something of this problem in Schubert too, though of course there are exceptions where the music really is lyrically homophonic, for instance, the slow movement of the d minor quartet, the *Death and the Maiden*. You have those exceptions in Schumann too of course. Romanticism was never just one thing, it was a whole complex of impulses. But what it was above all was expressive, rhetorical, and the difficulty for interpreters is not to confuse emotion and its expression with subjectivity and arbitrariness. It takes work to do this, so people don't do it. I love the Schumann F major quartet, but if it's up to me, I'd rather play Brahms, or occasionally also Mendelssohn. I think the Mendelssohn quartets are very good pieces too. It's a shame that we never played Mendelssohn's e minor quartet Opus 44, Nr. 2. But all the same we played his two early quartets rather often, the one in E♭ major Opus 12 and the a minor quartet Opus 13.

RS You also enjoyed playing Schumann's piano quintet Opus 44, and your interpretation is unusual in that you have an extremely energetic conception of the piece.

WL I do indeed! Which is also why we could only play it with James Levine, he was my student, and with him I could work on it the way I wanted to. We tried a few times to play it with someone else. Twice with Richard Goode, who has since become a famous pianist, but not my type. And then we played it once with Pierre Barbizet, Christian Ferras' accompanist, and once with Michel Béroff. We also tried working on it with John Browning in New York. But all this only showed us how impossible

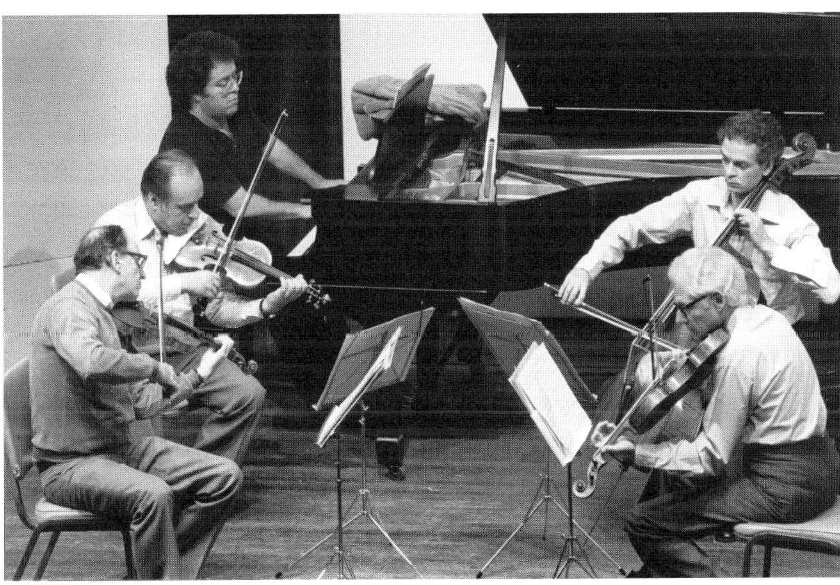

33 Schumann quintet with James Levine, Cincinnati, September, 1980

it was for someone to play with the LaSalle Quartet as a fifth member of the ensemble, though it did work out with James Levine in the Schumann, and with Lynn Harrell in the Schubert string quintet.

John Browning was one of New York's favorites, he gave a lot of concerts there, and the management of Columbia Concerts was eager for us to play the Schumann quintet with him in New York. So we met for a rehearsal at his immense apartment, all full of parrots and exotic plants, two Bösendorfer pianos and a Steinway. He began the first movement at what Schoenberg would have called a 'first performance' tempo. My cellist stopped playing immediately, and then the others stopped as well. Browning looked at us in confusion and asked what the trouble was, and we asked him if he were playing the piece for the first time? He responded that he'd played it many times already, also with the Guarneri Quartet. But, we informed him, we had a completely different conception of the Schumann quintet, for which his tempo was much too slow. 'Ah,' he said, 'you want it faster?' And he began to play again, in the same tempo as before. At that point one of my colleagues got impatient and announced that this simply wasn't going to work. As far as he was concerned it was anemic, the way Browning was playing it, and he proceeded to demonstrate the way we played it. Browning's response was that this was impossible, that you just couldn't play Schumann like that! He proposed to play it once for us the way he imagined it.

After we had heard him, I told him that if that's how he wanted to play it, then we were the wrong quartet for him. But my cellist was already packing up his instrument. I really didn't need to say another word, it was hopeless, we just left. Of course that was the end of our reputation with the Chamber Music Society of Lincoln Center. They played chamber music just like everybody else, albeit at an exalted level of virtuosity that had nothing whatsoever to do with our conception of chamber music. So that's why we never played quintets, it didn't make any sense. Nobody wanted to work that hard, and we didn't want to play the way they did.

RS As we've seen, Brahms is the composer of the romantic period whom you played the most frequently after Schubert. I believe the Brahms quartet Opus 67 was a real repertory piece for you, one that you played in several phases throughout almost your entire career. You also played it 98 times, altogether half again as many as the other two Brahms quartets put together.

WL Opus 67 is a piece that attracted me from the very beginning and that we learned very early on, while we were still in Colorado Springs. I always found it to be an exceptionally good piece and more interesting than his previous two quartets, although they are also very good.

RS What made this piece so attractive for you?

WL It's a metrically and structurally complex work, which is something that has always interested me. For instance, the time signature of the first movement is 6/8, and right from the beginning two meters oppose one another: the division of the bar into two groups of three eighths each is confronted with a division into three groups of two eighths each, what we call 'hemiola' in music and which is very common in Brahms. But if you have six notes, a division into two groups of three is only audibly apparent if the three notes that make up these groups are played fast enough. This is comparable to how the eye resolves the sequence of individual frames in a film: at less than about sixteen frames per second the eye perceives the individual frames instead of a continuous motion. There's a similar phenomenon in hearing: below a certain tempo you hear the individual elements and not the larger relationship that holds them together. In the case of Brahms Opus 67, a first movement tempo that is too slow results in hearing only the individual eighth notes, whereas at a quicker tempo the three eighths can be perceived as a metrical unit in opposition to the pairs of eighths of Brahms' hemiola.

There is yet another, very important aspect that enters into the choice of a basic tempo for the first movement: the last movement is a theme and variations, and in the last variation the themes of the first and last movements are combined. Of course when the theme of the first movement returns it has to be in the same tempo as at the beginning of the piece: that's the meaning of the cyclical structure.

RS So what that means is that you have to define a tempo that is appropriate for both the theme of the first movement and the theme of the last movement.

WL Yes, exactly, that's just the kind of complex relationship that interests me, and that interpreters should bring out and make audible.

RS But it doesn't seem trivial at all to me to find a tempo common to both movements, since the first movement is in 6/8 and marked *vivace*, while the last movement begins in 2/4 and is marked *poco allegretto.*

WL That's right, the two movements are markedly different in character. But *poco allegretto* is a rather vague indication that allows for a relatively wide range of tempi. The theme of the variations has the character of a simple folk song that mustn't be played too slowly, since otherwise the four rather than the two of the 2/4 will predominate. So there's a question of meter here similar to the one in the first movement's 6/8, and in both places what is required is a fluid tempo. The seventh variation, in which the theme of the first movement returns, is also written in 6/8, and Brahms prescribes a *doppio movimento* for it, that is, it's to be taken in two, in the same tempo as the preceding variations in 2/4.

RS Expressed in metronome marks, what tempo would you recommend for the first and last movements?

WL I think something like quarter note equals 104 works very well for both of them.

RS But does this tempo hold equally for all the variations in the last movement?

WL No, clearly in such a movement the different variations each have their own specific character, which makes certain tempo adjustments necessary, but they have to remain in some relationship to the basic tempo. That's the particular danger in the sixth variation, the last one prior to the return of the first movement theme. Here Brahms has already composed the relaxation of the tempo into the score itself. But many interpreters add a *ritardando* on top of that, which results in a redundancy, and unnecessary exaggeration of the music.

RS This concern with the whole is a central element in the clarity of interpretation and performance that was a hallmark of the LaSalle Quartet.

WL All things considered, yes, you could say that. As I see it one of the principal aims of the interpreter has to be to ensure that the listener doesn't lose the thread that holds the music together, whether in some part of a movement, in a whole movement, or even across all the movements in a whole piece. The element bearing the meaning of a composition that propels its progress must be clearly audible at all times. The task of the interpreter is to work out the relationships in a movement, and in the whole work, and to make these relationships audible to the listener. Tempo is certainly one of the means of achieving this, but articulation and phrasing, which aren't precisely captured by our musical notation, are also decisive for making the linguistic elements of music clear. A lot of interpreters prefer instead to substitute subjective judgments, for example, arbitrary *ritardandi* that actually contradict the composer's intentions.

RS That's what is usually called 'playing with expression.'

WL Yes, unfortunately, what is usually called 'expression' is what the interpreter, with or without any justification, adds to the music, whereas in my view expression is already one of the elements, a category, of composition: expression is composed by the composer, and very often it's just that expression that the composer intended that is spoiled when you add 'expression' to it, especially by using *rubati* that destroy the rhythmical figures or metrical precision and momentum.

RS Another criterion for clarity of interpretation and performance is of course the balance among the four instruments.

WL Yes, that's obvious. What balance is about is ensuring that the sense of the principal material is always clearly audible. But often the whole sense of a piece has to do with the changes that the principal material undergoes. In most of the really good compositions there are no literal repetitions, it is so to speak the fate of the theme, the changes it experiences in the course of the composition, that are decisive as it recurs again and again.

RS Can one say that this conception of the task of the interpreter that you've just presented is a result of your engagement with new music?

WL The idea that a musical work can only come alive in performance if it is interpreted from the standpoint of the present, interpreted with a consciousness of what is important in the music of the present, in the music of contemporary composers, has always been fundamental to my conception of the task of the interpreter. In our time one of the leading ideas is structure, we live in an age of structural thinking, both in general as well as in the most varied approaches to composition. What this means for the interpreter of music is that the individual elements and details of a piece all reflect the structure of the whole, so that every element and every detail must be interpreted in its relationship to the whole, just as, conversely, the sense of the whole arises out of the interplay of the elements and details.

That, I believe, is the central task of the interpreter today, and applies as much to music of the past like Haydn or Beethoven or Brahms as it does to the music of Lutosławski or Ligeti or Nono or any of the other contemporary composers from who we commissioned new quartets or whose quartets we premiered. The issues raised by the highly complex music of the present have a retroactive effect on how we hear earlier music, our understanding of new music sheds a new light on older pieces that otherwise appear unproblematical to performers and listeners alike. That's what's so fascinating about music, how at every level of comprehension it continuously reveals new facets, opens up new points of view.

16 Modern Classics

ROBERT SPRUYTENBURG: The LaSalle Quartet was founded by you, at Juilliard, less than two years after Bartók's and Webern's deaths, both of them in September, 1945. Berg had died in 1935, but Schoenberg was still alive and, moreover, living in America, in Los Angeles. Bartók's music was still little known, and his string quartets were virtually unknown, while the music of the Second Viennese School, especially the later twelve-tone works, was almost unheard of at the time. So both of these otherwise very different musics were still, in the late 1940s, 'new music,' radical, challenging, and often disdained by performers and audiences alike.

WALTER LEVIN: Yes that's right, and that's what interested me about Bartók's quartets and the Second Viennese School quartets, and not only their difficulty and complexity but also how they rubbed audiences the wrong way. *Epater le bourgeois* was something I was always interested in, even then. Of course Bartók and the Second Viennese School represent two very different directions in what was then called 'modern music,' but in this respect they had much in common, and it was something that appealed to me equally, despite their other differences.

Bartók

RS What specifically prompted you to play Bartók's music after you got to New York, since you'd mostly dealt with the classical-romantic repertory while you were in Palestine? Did the impulse come from the Juilliard Quartet?

WL No, I'd already played Bartók's duets for two violins with my friend Werner Torkanowsky in Palestine, who was also a violinist and later on became the conductor of the New Orleans Symphony. We thought they were a lot of fun, and they're also very good pieces. We very much liked playing them in house concerts, but we also played them in small auditoriums in Tel Aviv. That's how I first became acquainted with Bartók's music.

RS How did you stumble onto the duets?

WL I was always finding music I didn't know at Litauer's marvelous little music shop on Ben Yehuda Street in Tel Aviv.

RS Did you also get to hear Bartók's orchestral works in Palestine?

WL As far as I remember, Bartók's orchestra pieces weren't played there, in any event I never heard them, nor did I hear the violin concertos. I only got to know these pieces later on in America.

RS And the quartets weren't played there at all.

WL No, they weren't played by the string quartets in Palestine. And my own quartet in Palestine wouldn't have been able to play them either, they were too hard for us. Even in the early years of the LaSalle Quartet this was still new music, which we learned only with the greatest difficulty. The Bartók quartets were what really got us properly started learning advanced new music, even before we got to the Schoenberg school.

RS When you arrived in New York in early 1946, the Juilliard Quartet was in the midst of preparing its legendary cycle of all the Bartók quartets. Did you get to hear them?

WL Yes, certainly. Evi heard their Bartók cycle in 1948 at the Summer School of Music at Tanglewood, and then in 1949 we went together to the two concerts with the cycle of all six quartets at Times Hall in New York.[1] Dmitri Shostakovich was at the second of these concerts, he was staying in New York then as part of a Soviet peace conference delegation, and he was enormously enthusiastic about this music.[2] These two concerts were my introduction to live performances of the Bartók quartets. Afterwards the Juilliard Quartet recorded them for Columbia, still one of the outstanding benchmark recordings.

RS But it was surely a big step, going from Bartók's violin duets to his quartets. How did the quartets strike you the first time you heard them? Was it a shock for you?

WL It was a huge surprise, since the duets are simpler and more playful, whereas the quartets are so concentrated and advanced that in their

[1] The first concert, on February 28, presented Bartók's second, third, and fifth quartets; the second concert, on March 28, presented the first, fourth, and sixth quartets.

[2] The Soviet-sponsored 'Cultural and Scientific Conference for World Peace,' held at New York's Waldorf-Astoria Hotel, March 25–27, 1949, was a signal event in the opening of the 'cultural cold war' in America. Stalin ordered Shostakovich to attend the conference and to give a speech; it is unlikely that Shostakovich had written a word of it himself, and his discomfiture while it was read by an interpreter was obvious to those present. Shostakovich's enthusiasm for Bartók's quartets is manifestly apparent in his own later quartets.

own way they can only remind you of the late Beethoven quartets. So that was totally new to me. I thought I already knew something about Bartók, but I was mistaken about that. I had also hoped to be able to meet Bartók in New York, but he died before I got there: that was a huge disappointment. One of the first pieces by Bartók that I got to know in New York was the Concerto for Orchestra, which he composed on commission for Serge Koussevitzky in 1943. It was completely new to me when we rehearsed and played it in the Juilliard Orchestra under Edgar Schenkman. That was also a shock for me: it's a difficult piece and we all had to work very hard at it. I'd never played anything like it. It's an extraordinarily effective and brilliant orchestra piece. That's how I first got to know an orchestra piece by Bartók.

RS How did you find your way into the quartets? Did you first get the scores and work your way through them, or did you first hear the music when it was played by the Juilliard Quartet?

WL It's hard for me to say now. I would assume I heard some of them done by the Juilliard Quartet, but for me scores were always what I started with. Scores weren't hard to get in New York then. At Juilliard I also studied the second violin concerto, and I played it on my final recital.[3] At that time I was already interested not only in Bartók's quartets and his second violin concerto but also in his orchestra works. I went to wherever I could hear Bartók. Joseph Szigeti, who I very much respected and admired, played the violin sonatas. So bit by bit I got to know Bartók, both by listening and by studying the scores. And we began to study the sixth quartet with the Juilliard Quartet right away, and then the third quartet. The sixth we played already in early 1949 at the house concert at Stefan Wolpe's apartment – the first time we ever played a whole concert for friends, including the Juilliard Quartet.

RS That was bold, starting with the sixth quartet, at that time it was only just ten years old. What prompted you to study this one first?

WL That's always a good question: what pieces to start out with, and for what reasons? I can't altogether remember why anymore. I was drawn to the sixth quartet by its form: this *mesto* – it means 'sad' – that returns in a new form before every movement, and then the contrasting movements themselves. For me it's always been an extraordinarily attractive piece of music.

3 In May, 1949.

RS Although it's actually very depressing, on account of the sadness, the *mesto.*

WL Well yes, a lot of music isn't exactly happy: Schubert can also be depressing. The idea that music should have a particular character or a particular quality was never of much interest to me. I found Bartók's sixth quartet extraordinarily fascinating, rich in contrasts, a very demanding piece technically, rhythmically, and acoustically. I was totally fascinated by the construction of this piece, and I was eager to play it. We also played it on our debut concert in Colorado Springs.

RS And on the LaSalle's last concert, in Bochum, on the 21st of May, 1987.

WL Yes, we played it quite often, and with great pleasure.

RS Would you say that the sixth was the most advanced of Bartók's quartets, technically, rhythmically, and conceptually?

WL No, you can't say that. It is perhaps the most mature of his quartets. It has many of the qualities that are characteristic of Bartók, without overly accentuating any of them, they are all fully integrated into the music. It's in every respect a classical piece, whereas in some of the other quartets the contrasts are extreme, they are extremely avant-garde. The third quartet, for instance, is much more advanced, much more concise. It's the shortest, in a single through-composed movement. That's what we found attractive about it. It was also perhaps the most modern piece we could possibly have learned when we were starting out. It's also extraordinarily demanding in every respect, and when we first played it, in Colorado Springs, Henry Meyer had to work hard to learn it. It's still a difficult piece for young quartets to play, even today. When they want to learn to play Bartók, I always suggest starting with the third quartet, since it has everything in it that is found in the other quartets, albeit greatly compressed. The others are not so extreme and not so concentrated. After we'd learned the sixth quartet, the next one we studied was the third, and over the years the other four, the first quartet last of all.[4]

RS You had no special affinity for the first quartet? You played it mostly in just one season, in 1965, and altogether only eight times.

WL No, I wouldn't say that. It was just that in the meantime we'd gotten to know the young composers at Darmstadt, so we suddenly had a big-

[4] The LaSalle Quartet's first public performances of the Bartók quartets, in chronological order: Nr. 6: March 13, 1949; Nr. 3: March 22, 1950; Nr. 5: November 17, 1953; Nr. 2: January 8, 1957; Nr. 4: October 6, 1959; Nr. 1: May 14, 1963.

ger selection of new pieces. Besides which we'd also learned the Second Viennese School quartets by then, and people were asking us to play Webern, Berg, and Schoenberg more and more often, and Bartók rather less often. And if they did request Bartók, they didn't request the first quartet, which is still rather conventional compared to the later ones. Nevertheless I think it's a very good piece. I'm amazed that we played it so infrequently. That can only be because we were so late learning it.

RS And the second quartet? You played it scarcely more often than the first one.

WL I think the second is an absolutely terrific piece, but difficult, extremely demanding technically.

RS But I got the impression from your chamber music courses that the fifth quartet is the most difficult.

WL The fourth and the fifth. In both of them Bartók uses a symmetrical, five movement form with a central slow movement. The fifth quartet is very long, and after you've survived the first four movements, there comes the enormously demanding finale, which is almost as long as the first movement.

RS A concept of movement proportions similar to Beethoven's Opus 130 with the *Grosse Fuge* as the finale.

WL Yes, that's correct. The fifth quartet is a huge, massive work, and really very difficult. The fourth quartet is a fabulous piece, also very demanding and hard to play, but completely different from the fifth and from the point of view of string quartet technique no easier, but it's much more concentrated and not as long as the fifth.[5] It's unfortunate that the Bartók quartets aren't played all that often anymore. In the meantime people have gotten interested in other things, but at the time the Bartók quartets were much more advanced musically than they are today.

RS The sixth and the third quartets were the two that you played most often, and by a wide margin. Would you say they were in your regular active repertory?

[5] In the interpretations by the LaSalle Quartet and the Juilliard Quartet the fourth quartet lasts 22–23 minutes, the fifth quartet 30 minutes.

WL Yes, absolutely, we could always just play them without having to invest much more effort in them. The others had to be thoroughly worked through again every time we took them up.[6]

RS And then there are the pieces for string quartet from *Mikrokosmos*: how did you come across them? Were they at all known?

WL No, Tibor Serly[7] had arranged the original piano pieces for string quartet. When we were in Colorado Springs I thought they would be ideal for children's concerts, and so we learned them.

RS They're actually very appealing.

WL Very! And humorous too!

RS It's astonishing, how the Bartók quartets accompanied the whole career of the LaSalle Quartet, from beginning to end. Not quite from the very first concert, but nevertheless from 1949 on and then up until the very last concert.

WL The Bartók quartets don't get worn out by being played and they never become boring. Whereas there are pieces we played a few times and then never again, for instance Paul Hindemith's third quartet or Walter Piston's first quartet.[8] And there were a few American pieces we had to learn when we were starting out that we then got bored with. That never happened with the Bartók quartets. They are really great music, among the very best compositions of the 20th century.

RS I have the impression that everyone loves playing these pieces.

WL Absolutely! They're brilliantly written for our instruments, even when they're difficult. The sound is simply phenomenal. Bartók knew how to write for strings like scarcely anyone else.

RS Astonishing for a pianist! Did he have somebody to rely on for string music like Brahms had in Joseph Joachim?

[6] There are 78 documented performances of Bartók's third quartet by the LaSalle Quartet, 56 of the sixth, 36 of the third, ten of the second, and eight of the first.

[7] Tibor Serly (1901–1978), Hungarian violist, violinist, and composer, was Bartók's assistant and an important promoter of his work.

[8] The LaSalle Quartet played Piston's first quartet 25 times in the course of its 1956 world tour but never again after that.

WL Yes, Imre Waldbauer. The Waldbauer Quartet also premiered Bartók's first four quartets.[9] In Budapest there were very good string players with whom Bartók worked very closely.

The Second Viennese School

RS There is no doubt about the importance of the LaSalle Quartet as a proponent of contemporary music, which was a third center of gravity in your repertory throughout your career, along with the classical and the romantic works. The extent to which this emphasis was prominent from the very outset has perhaps been forgotten today. As we've already seen, Bartók's sixth quartet was only ten years old when the LaSalle Quartet played it in 1949 – it was the first modern piece in your repertory – and Bartók's fifth quartet was not yet twenty years old in 1953 when you first played it, as was also the case with Webern's quartet Opus 28 when you first played it in 1956.[10] One of the first works of the 20th century which the LaSalle Quartet was already working on in 1949 was Schoenberg's third quartet, Opus 30, a scant twenty years old at the time, and Berg's *Lyric Suite* was just twenty-five years old when the LaSalle Quartet began working on it in 1950.[11] Along with the premieres of works you commissioned from contemporary composers, you were an exceptionally forceful proponent of the composers of the Second Viennese School. How did you come to have such a marked interest in these composers?

WL It began in Palestine already, when my friends Herbert Brün and Wolf Rosenberg tried to acquaint me with twelve-tone music. They had studied composition with Webern student Stefan Wolpe in Jerusalem, but I wasn't much interested in it to begin with.

RS But then you had the opportunity to hear the Kolisch Quartet recordings of Schoenberg's third and fourth quartets at one of Peter Gradenwitz's recordings concerts on the roof of his house in Tel Aviv.

WL And I didn't understand a single note in them! But I was enormously

[9] Imre Waldbauer (1892–1945), first violinist of the Waldbauer Quartet (active from 1910–1945). He had a close relationship with Bartók and Kodály, whose works he premiered at a time when their music was still met with indifference or even hostility.

[10] On April 3, in Cincinnati.

[11] The LaSalle Quartet first played Schoenberg's third quartet on February 23, 1950, in Colorado Springs; their first performance of Berg's *Lyric Suite* was on February 11, 1951, also in Colorado Springs.

impressed by the fact that the Kolisch Quartet played these pieces from memory! They were totally incomprehensible to me.

RS You played all the Second Viennese School works for string quartet, and for that reason there's an air of authenticity to your performances. But on a closer look, the question does arise as to where, ultimately, this claim comes from. There's no direct line of descent from Schoenberg to you at all.

WL No, there isn't any. This so-called authenticity is a myth. Just because you're interested in something and learn as much about it as you possibly can and this learning helps you to get to some kind of breakthrough doesn't make what you do authentic. To me the whole concept of authenticity is anyway suspect. Who's to say what's authentic? Is Brahms playing Brahms authentic?

RS That is indeed the question. So you didn't study this repertory with the Juilliard Quartet, who had worked with Eugene Lehner, the violist of the Kolisch Quartet, and who in turn was close to Schoenberg?

WL No, we didn't work with Lehner, nor did we ever work on music of the Second Viennese School with the Juilliard Quartet.

RS So you undertook to learn these pieces on your own.

WL Yes we did. Of course I knew the Juilliard Quartet's performance of Berg's *Lyric Suite*, and the recording of it that the Pro Arte Quartet in Wisconsin made after Kolisch had joined it as first violin. And in Colorado Springs we'd gotten to know Eduard Steuermann, the Schoenberg school pianist, with whom Evi studied piano. But is that enough reason to claim authenticity? There is, however, another kind of authenticity, an authenticity of feeling, of sympathy, that results from having a felt affinity for a person or his work or his writings. I always felt myself in sympathy with Schoenberg, which is actually rather unusual: most people are quite the opposite. What I'm sympathetic to is just exactly what everyone else finds unsympathetic: his sharp, critical manner, the stand he takes against anything and everything that is muddled or compromised, how he advocates everything that everyone else rejects. This contrariness and abrasiveness is something I find marvelous, and both these traits have always appealed to me.

RS And these sympathies carried over to your interest in his music?

WL Indeed, because his music is very much like that. Schoenberg wrote music that he knew for certain would get on everyone's nerves. What interested me was why everyone was so angry with Schoenberg, since he was actually a very insightful person! What he writes makes total sense! His *Harmonielehre* and the ideas in it are terrific. I read everything in it with the greatest possible pleasure and said to myself his pieces really ought to be played! All in all I was very much influenced by the whole Schoenberg school and their milieu. But at that time, when I read his *Harmonielehre*, I didn't know the works themselves, I only got to know them as the years went by, and today I'm still of the opinion that relatively speaking I still don't know Schoenberg very well at all. To really know the works well you ultimately have to play them. But unfortunately I can't play *Moses und Aron* by myself, nor the orchestra works either: *Pelleas und Melisande*, a huge piece, and *Erwartung* – what phenomenal pieces they are, even today they are scarcely analyzable: they are freely atonal but nevertheless completely convincing musically, and nobody can tell you why. What sort of principles did he use in composing these pieces? The same thing is true of Artur Schnabel's third string quartet:[12] what kind of music is this, so completely different from every other kind of music and nevertheless so immensely strong? And no one can actually say why.

So as far as authenticity is concerned, you can only go so far as to say that I was genuinely enthusiastic about the music of the Second Viennese School, that I had so to speak an elective affinity for it, nothing more than that. So that's a different kind of authenticity, which I assume entails an intellectual affinity. And we studied and rehearsed these works zealously, so much so that we could really play them in such a way that allowed them to come across with a real presence of their own. The recordings for Deutsche Grammophon were such a success just for that reason: it was the first time these works could really be heard, were really transparent, and a few critics recognized that. When I listen to those recordings again now, I still think they're very good. And sonically, as recordings, they're all representative of Deutsche Grammophon at its best: they sound good and you can hear everything.

But as to whether that amounts to authenticity? I have no idea what Schoenberg might have said about that. Maybe exactly what he said to the Hollywood Quartet when they played *Verklärte Nacht* for him. It was on a terribly hot day, and Schoenberg interrupted them right away after just a couple of bars. They asked him to please just let them play through it once, after which he could say whatever he wanted to. So they played it all the way through, and afterwards he said that it was

[12] For Schnabel's quartets, see pp. 318–321.

very good, even excellent, he had nothing to say about it, they shouldn't change a thing. Maybe he would have said the same thing to us as well.

We played *Verklärte Nacht* somewhat differently than the Kolisch Quartet played it, but then again actually not all that much differently. We played the tempi indicated, the Kolisch Quartet often played perhaps a little bit faster. I believe our tempi are rather more advantageous for transparency and precision, but fundamentally we played it the same way they did. The claim to authenticity now being made by some of the interpreters of older music is something I find questionable, always: there's no such thing, we simply weren't there to know!

After 1953 we also began to play Webern, but at that time I didn't have much of a clue about how the pieces were composed. Eventually books on Webern were published and I got them and read them with interest: for instance, the big monograph by Hans Moldenhauer.[13]

EVI LEVIN: Moldenhauer also asked you to give the premiere of one of Webern's student compositions.[14]

WL It was an early composition of Webern's, a rondo that he wrote as a homework assignment for Schoenberg in 1906, and we did play it quite a few times, and we recorded it, too. It's not just simply a student piece, as the obvious models have been worked over to an astonishing degree and have been developed in a wholly personal manner. Now the marvelous complete edition of Berg is also publishing all his early works, some of them apparently not without interest, for instance, a fugue for string quintet. I don't know anything about it. Now that they're being published, people will probably start to play these early pieces. There's still a lot left that one could learn and play. It was the same with Schoenberg's early quartet from the year 1897. He was quite fond of it, but he never published it. After it had been discovered among the things in his estate it was published by Faber Music in London in 1966 – all of a sudden there was a new piece by Schoenberg! I bought the score immediately, and we learned it and played it for the first time not long afterwards.[15] It was only after the war that musicologists could publish such things, especially in Europe. Before then they couldn't: who could publish anything about Webern, whose music was considered *entartete Kunst*, degenerate art? Everything that interested me was *entartete Kunst* in Europe. And the musicologists had been banished as well, they were all in America. So it took some time after

[13] *Anton von Webern: A Chronicle of his Life and Work* (New York, 1978).

[14] Webern's *Rondo* for string quartet was discovered by Moldenhauer in 1965.

[15] On May 21, 1968, in Cincinnati.

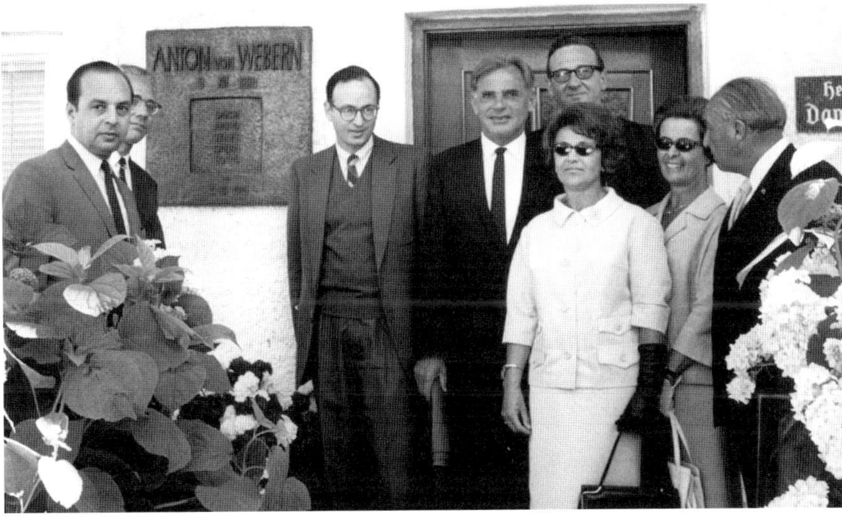

34 The LaSalle Quartet with Hans Moldenhauer (center), Webern's daughters Amalie Waller and Maria Halbich, and Ernst Krenek, in front of the Webern memorial in Mittersill, August, 1965. The memorial plaque next to Walter Levin is a gift of Anna Mahler, the daughter of Gustav Mahler. It displays the Latin magic square: SATOR AREPO TENET OPERA ROTAS.

the war was over for books on this music to be published. I bought them just as soon as they came out.

In the mid-1960s we made a recording for the Polish label Musica that included the Lutosławski quartet, the Penderecki quartet, and Webern's *Five Pieces* Opus 5, *Bagatelles* Opus 9, and string quartet Opus 28. The *Bagatelles* were never released, which is a pity, as it was a fabulous recording. I have a rehearsal tape of those recordings. When we were on form, we played these Webern pieces devilishly well in concert, as if there was nothing to it at all. Far better than I remember. Time and again we would take our places on stage and play the opening of Opus 5 straight away without any fuss or bother, as if we were one single instrument, which really is very hard to do. At that time no one else could match our performance of it, we were famous for it, it made our career. And our performance of Opus 5 at the Webern memorial concert in Salzburg[16] gave our career such a boost that you just couldn't ask for more: the critics outdid one another with superlatives! But even so it was also a very good concert.

RS I believe all three works: Opus 9, Opus 5, and Opus 28, are equally close to your heart.

[16] On August 3, 1965, the twentieth anniversary of Webern's death. The program included his 1905 quartet, his trio Opus 20, the *Five Pieces* Opus 5, the *Bagatelles* Opus 9, and the quartet Opus 28.

WL I would say Opus 9 and Opus 5 more than Opus 28.

RS But you played Opus 28 somewhat more often than Opus 5, 125 times vs. 96, though you did play Opus 9 some 243 times, more often in fact than any other work in your entire repertory!

WL In part that was because at the time there was hardly anyone at all playing Opus 28. It was also important for us to have a work by Webern in our repertory that could represent the whole of Webern, and Opus 28 is radically different from Opus 9 and Opus 5 in its complexity. As is his string trio Opus 20, which again represents something totally different: a twelve-tone work of surpassing difficulty and complexity. These are all pieces that scarcely anyone was playing. We had to transcribe Opus 5 by hand in order to have copies to play from, since we only had the pocket score, and photocopying and enlarging weren't commonly available back then.

EL You also sometimes got letters asking why you played Webern, since he was after all a Nazi?

WL Yes, at the time that was held against me by people who were already in the know about it. When the Moldenhauer biography appeared some people had already read the chapter on this, but I hadn't yet. Afterwards we were severely reproached by some people for performing the music of a man who in his letters had expressed such admiration for Hitler. A difficult question: to what extent can you allow yourself to be influenced by such things in judging music written much earlier – and the man actually was ambivalent, that's not just a euphemism. Even now I can scarcely understand the contradictions in him. But we did make an effort to revive the Second Viennese School, first in America and then in Europe also. There was no other quartet that had all of these works in its repertory. To some extent the Juilliard Quartet, but even so not all of them. And when the Vienna Festival needed a quartet to play all the Second Viennese School quartets, we were the only quartet that could do it. That had a lot to do with our choice of repertory – and likewise with Zemlinsky too, the fact that we had stumbled onto a composer who didn't really exist any more. We were very receptive to composers who the Nazis had branded as 'degenerate.' If Webern hadn't been killed in that terrible accident, it's likely that no one would have been interested in him twenty years later.[17]

RS And how was it with the two quartets by Alban Berg: did you have any special preference?

[17] Webern was shot and killed by an American soldier on September 15, 1945.

WL Both quartets were always favorites of ours.

RS I had the impression that you preferred the *Lyric Suite* rather more, on account of its being so extraordinarily multi-layered and demanding.

WL Which it really is. However, Opus 3 – Berg wrote it for Schoenberg as a homework assignment – is already of a quality and complexity for a young composer that surprised even Schoenberg. And it's also extraordinarily difficult on account of how it's notated: the quartet is so to speak an explicitly composed *rubato*.[18]

RS Because the LaSalle Quartet played all Second Viennese School works for string quartet, it's considered to be expert in this music . . .

WL But that didn't happen overnight. What was decisive for our reputation was surely the Second Viennese School cycle we played at the Vienna Festival in 1969.[19]

RS How did that come about?

WL In December, 1967, after a concert on which we played the d minor quartet by Hugo Wolf, there was a big party at the Schweizer restaurant next to the Four Seasons hotel in Munich. A lot of very interesting people were there, including Fritz Kortner. And while we were unwinding, Peter Weiser also came in, the General Secretary of the *Wiener Konzerthaus*, a real character. He regaled us with wicked stories about the most famous people, with a dryly sarcastic humor, a genially Viennese slander that finished them off with the most delectable scurrility. He and Kortner, another great Viennese raconteur, outdid one another telling stories, we were all rolling on the floor with laughter.

And then, after we'd been drinking wine and carrying on for two hours, Weiser said to me, that's what he'd been meaning to ask me, he'd like us to play all the Second Viennese School quartets next June at the Vienna Festival. 'Come again?' I asked. 'The quartets by Schoenberg, Berg, and Webern!' 'But,' I said, 'we don't have them all in our repertory.' 'Of course you do!' he said, 'You've played them all.' He'd found out all about us; I didn't even know myself that we'd played them all:

[18] See also pp. 347–350.

[19] The 1969 Vienna Festival presented performances not only of the complete string quartets of Schoenberg, Berg, and Webern, but also all the other works of theirs that had been published by then: the operas, orchestral and orchestral-choral works (conducted by Pierre Boulez), and works for mixed ensemble, as well as the piano music and the songs.

we'd simply worked on one piece after the other, now one by Webern, now one by Schoenberg, but never with the thought of playing them all together in a cycle. But in time our Second Viennese School repertory had grown to the point that by the end of the 1960s it was complete, at least as regards the principal works.

The process was a gradual one, it took us almost twenty years to learn all the works of the Second Viennese School. A few years earlier we couldn't have done the whole cycle. It's also the only cycle we ever played, and we only did it because Peter Weiser pushed us into it. He originally wanted us to play the whole cycle in the span of a single week, but we told him that was absolutely out of the question. We arranged the programs so that we could play all the pieces in four concerts, but with a four day interval between them, even though we had all the pieces in our repertory. And that was how we did it: he had no choice, there wasn't anyone else who could do it. That was in June, 1969. But if you want to say that the LaSalle Quartet were Second Viennese School experts, then yes, as we did in time play all the pieces and we recorded them for Deutsche Grammophon, albeit against their will to begin with.

RS It was a whole process.

WL And a slow, slow process at that, we really were very slow. That's something I try to teach the young quartets: there's nothing special about learning pieces quickly and superficially. I think it's better to take the time to learn them slowly, inside out. And if you haven't mastered a piece, then you shouldn't play it. We weren't able to learn the second Ligeti quartet by the date set for the world premiere in Baden-Baden and we had to postpone it for a year. And if the organizers had found that unacceptable, we would have said okay, then we won't do it at all. We only worked in a way that made sense to us. And sometimes things went faster, sometimes slower, but for the most part slower. Maybe other people could work faster – how nice for them! But our slowness enabled us to learn pieces that others never even attempted.

RS The Second Viennese School cycle that you gave in Vienna in 1969 was apparently repeated the following year in Cleveland.[20] How did that come about?

WL It was due to the efforts of John Gidwitz when Jimmy Levine was

[20] On April 8 and 15 and May 3 and 6, 1970. The Second Viennese School cycle was subsequently performed in Düsseldorf and Hannover (November–December, 1971), Ravinia (July, 1972), New York (Alice Tully Hall, January and April, 1975) and finally in Amsterdam and London (February–March 1978).

conducting the student orchestra at the Cleveland Institute of Music. Gidwitz was one of the principal heirs to Helene Curtis, the famous American cosmetics firm, and had unlimited funds at his disposal. But he was very modest, he was part of the circle around Jimmy Levine, he organized opera performances with the Cleveland Institute student orchestra for Jimmy, with the greatest singers of the time, for instance, Renata Tebaldi, Richard Tucker, and Ezio Flagello.[21] By the way, in his autobiography, the tenor Jan Peerce tells the story of how the year before he had been invited to the Meadowbrook Summer Festival near Detroit to sing *Rigoletto* with a student orchestra.[22] When he arrived he could hear the orchestra rehearsing, without being able to see who was conducting. And he said he thought he wasn't hearing right, all he could think of was Toscanini, for whom he'd sung the part in the 1940s, but it turned out to be Jimmy Levine. Anyway, John Gidwitz had organized all that in Cleveland, and had the money to do so. He became a professional manager, most recently of the Baltimore Symphony. Our Second Viennese School cycle was a great success in Cleveland also. And they published a marvelous program booklet! We did the second Schoenberg quartet with Bethany Beardslee: it was fantastic.[23]

RS By the way, the second Schoenberg quartet was the last one you learned, not counting the early quartet from 1897.[24]

WL That was because we needed a soprano who could sing it in a way that matched our conception of the piece, and with whom we could thoroughly work our way through it. We could only do that with a local singer – who else would take the time out to do it? So we prepared our first performance with Helen Laird, a teacher at the College-Conservatory and an excellent singer who became Dean of the music school at Temple University in Philadelphia. Later on, from 1969 to 1975, we worked with Bethany Beardslee, and from 1975 to 1980 with Benita Valente.[25] But what

[21] In *Simon Boccanegra*, December 13, 1969.

[22] Performance Wednesday, August 7, 1968; the cast included Cornell MacNeil, Roberta Peters, Jan Peerce, and Ezio Flagello.

[23] Bethany Beardslee (1927–) was well known for her performances of contemporary music and her collaborations with contemporary composers including Stravinsky, Babbitt, Boulez, and Perle. She sang the vocal music of the Second Viennese School with leading orchestras and sang the second Schoenberg quartet with several quartets, including the Pro Arte Quartet with Kolisch, as well with the LaSalle Quartet.

[24] The LaSalle Quartet played the second quartet by Schoenberg for the first time on May 23, 1967.

[25] Benita Valente (1934–) had a distinguished operatic career at the Metropolitan Opera and elsewhere; she also sang oratorio, Lieder, and chamber music, including the second Schoenberg quartet, which she recorded with the Juilliard Quartet.

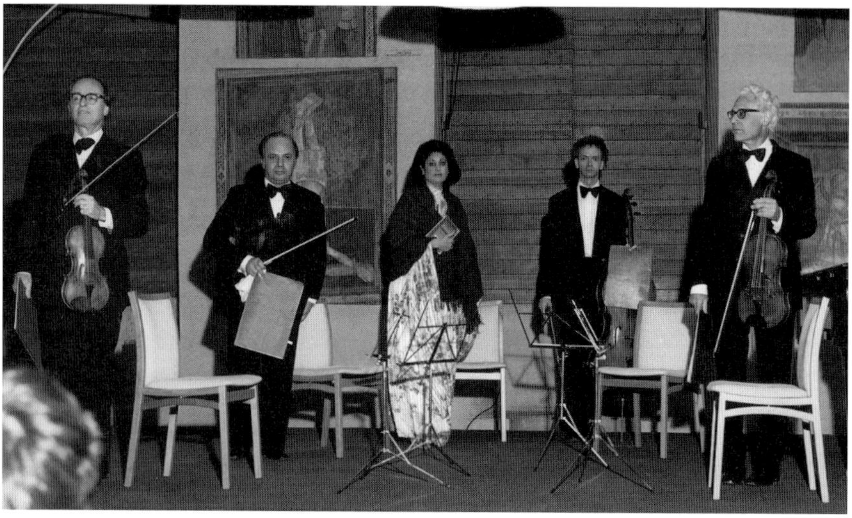

35 The LaSalle Quartet with Benita Valente, Perugia, March, 1980

were we to do about the recording date with Deutsche Grammophon in the summer of 1969? Neither Helen Laird nor Bethany Beardslee could make this date. But our manager in England told us he knew a wonderful young singer who we absolutely had to hear, she was from Wales and she was my kind of singer: she could learn, and she'd already sung the second Schoenberg quartet – he sent me a tape. The quartet's playing was simply dreadful, but she actually sang very beautifully. Not entirely the way I would have it, but we could give it a try. It was Margaret Price.[26]

We met in Vienna just before we played the Second Viennese School cycle in 1969 and rehearsed in the hall at the Museum of Modern Art. The hall was dark, we were seated on the stage, and we worked on the third movement of the second Schoenberg quartet. Margaret Price had a wonderful voice but there was still a lot of room for improvement. After two hours we said we thought that was enough, we would rehearse this movement again tomorrow, and then also the fourth movement. I thought to myself, my god, this could take a long time, but she can really sing. The question was whether she could learn it the way we want it. The next day she came to the rehearsal and we began the third movement again. We played it through from beginning to end, and there was nothing more to do, everything was perfect! Overnight she'd made all our corrections so completely her own that the whole movement was completely convincing. We were utterly taken aback and asked her how

[26] Margaret Price (1941–2011), leading soprano, was noted for her performances of Mozart and Verdi as well as for her Isolde in the Carlos Kleiber recording of *Tristan und Isolde*.

she'd done it. She said she had an accompanist who helped her, he was sitting in the back of the hall.

We hadn't seen him, as the hall was dark. It was James Lockhart, the director of the Welsh Opera Company, Margaret was in a relationship with him at the time. He was an outstanding conductor and rehearsal pianist, he knew what it was to really work hard. He'd written down every word we said the day before and had worked with her that afternoon and evening, and now it was all set. She was used to working that way. We then worked on the fourth movement, and it went the same way: in two days the whole piece was ready. After the Vienna cycle we did the second Schoenberg quartet with her once more in Graz and then recorded it for Deutsche Grammophon in Munich: that was no problem at all. Margaret Price is the best singer we ever worked with. At that time she was a complete unknown, but afterwards she had a great career.

On the way back to the Four Seasons hotel from the recording session Lockhart asked me whether by any chance I knew a young conductor who could conduct *Aida* at the Welsh Opera. I told him I could indeed recommend someone: James Levine, he was still very young, but he could conduct *Aida* even better than a lot of other conductors. That was Jimmy's debut in Europe: *Aida* at the Welsh Opera Company. He could conduct that opera standing on his head.

RS The first of the Schoenberg quartets you studied was the third.

WL Yes, we began to learn it while we were still at Juilliard, at Eugene Lehner's prompting, and also the Juilliard Quartet's.

RS Am I right that of the five quartets by Schoenberg the third is your favorite?

WL Yes, indeed it is, it's full-fledged Schoenberg, there's nothing romantic remaining as there is in the first and second quartets, it's the twelve-tone Schoenberg. And I find it to be the strongest of the five, even stronger than the fourth, which is also a twelve-tone piece. But Schoenberg had composed the third quartet when his twelve tone technique was still brand new, and like everything that's really new, it's 'on fire': extreme, uncompromising, fabulous.

RS When you were talking about the concerto for string quartet by Louis Spohr you mentioned that the Schoenberg concerto for string quartet[27]

[27] Concerto in B♭ for string quartet and orchestra (1933), a free adaptation of Handel's Concerto Grosso, Opus 6, Nr. 7. The concerto is dedicated to the Kolisch Quartet, who premiered it in 1934.

was so extraordinarily difficult that there was no question of preparing it at that time. But you did play it later on, nevertheless.

WL We performed it once with James Levine and the Cincinnati Symphony and then once more with the Chicago Symphony, also conducted by him. It was an extremely difficult work to learn, starting with the fact that there was no piano reduction of the piece. How can you prepare a work for soloists and orchestra without ever having heard the orchestra part prior to the first rehearsal? So to begin with I commissioned a young music student from the Cleveland Institute of Music who Jimmy put me in touch with to make a piano reduction. But what he did was so complicated that nobody could play it. The same thing happened to Schoenberg with the piano reductions that Alban Berg made for him: they were also too complicated. Students take pride in leaving nothing out. By the way you have the same problem with the piano reduction of the Brahms violin concerto. The usual piano reductions are pretty thin, they only keep what's really indispensable in the orchestration, and so Artur Schnabel undertook to make a piano reduction in which you really could hear everything. And he did, it's a fabulous piano reduction, but so complicated no one can play it! So anyway I had to start all over again from scratch and make a piano reduction of the Schoenberg quartet concerto myself. That's a good piano reduction, somebody should publish it!

EL Not only did you make the piano reduction, you also bought a set of orchestra parts.

WL Yes, we still have them. The Cincinnati Symphony didn't have the parts for this concerto. So I bought them and used them to assemble a full score. In the meantime Schirmer has published a printed score, but there wasn't any then.

RS It doesn't seem to be a piece that could be heard very often.

WL No, it's just too difficult and even ungrateful, the orchestra is too overpowering. You either have to reduce the orchestral forces substantially or else augment the quartet, otherwise you can't hear the denser parts. For instance, there are fingered octaves in the left hand, I don't know what Schoenberg had in mind when he asked for that, it's just like his violin concerto, he's assuming he'll have a violinist with six fingers. There's a recording from 1937 with the Kolisch Quartet and the Los Angeles Philharmonic under Otto Klemperer, but unfortunately the technical quality is very poor. We really asked around about recordings of the piece and got whatever there was to be had. Since then some good recordings have been made. Recently we heard a recording made in San Francisco, fantastically well-played by a young quartet, the Pacifica Quartet. It's the same thing time and again: as time goes on the players get better and after you've played a lot of even more difficult music such a piece gets easier. And as regards technique, today's quartets are the absolute pinnacle of perfection.

17 *Commissions and Premieres*

ROBERT SPRUYTENBURG: From the very outset, contemporary music was and remained the heart of the LaSalle Quartet's repertory, starting with the quartets by Bartók, Berg, and Webern that you worked on while you were still at Juilliard in the 1940s, when these pieces still qualified as 'new music.' But it was your experience at Darmstadt, starting in 1954, where you got to know the young composers of your own generation, that provided the real impetus to your career as an advocate for the music of the present. Thanks to the support of the Sunday Group in Cincinnati, these and other acquaintanceships with contemporary composers led to your commissioning sixteen string quartets over the years from 1956 to 1983, fourteen of which you premiered, and you also premiered five other works that had not been commissioned by the LaSalle Quartet.

From the Darmstadt composers alone you commissioned nine quartets, from Franco Evangelisti and Gottfried Michael Koenig in 1959, from Henri Pousseur in 1961, from Giuseppe Englert in 1962 and again in 1966, from György Ligeti in 1968, Mauricio Kagel in 1965, and Luigi Nono in 1980, all of which except for Kagel's quartet and Englert's second quartet you premiered as well.

And you commissioned and premiered works from outside the Darmstadt milieu too, another eight quartets in all: from Hans Erich Apostel in 1956, from Wolf Rosenberg in 1957 and again in 1962, and from Herbert Brün in 1957 and 1961, Earle Brown in 1965, Gerhard Samuel in 1978, and Michael Gielen in 1983.

You also premiered Penderecki's quartet in 1962 and Lutosławski's in 1964, neither of which were commissioned by the LaSalle Quartet, as well as a quartet by Robert Mann of the Juilliard Quartet, early in your career, in 1953, and then much later on the quartets by William DeFotis in 1979 and by László Kalmár in 1982.

Among this impressive series of new works the quartets by Lutosławski and Nono, as well as Ligeti's second quartet, the one you commissioned, have by now become established classics of the string quartet repertory.

WALTER LEVIN: That's right, these quartets are surely the most successful pieces in our repertory from the second half of the 20th century.

Witold Lutosławski

RS Of all the works you premiered, the Lutosławski quartet seems to me to be the one closest to your heart, and with 98 performances it's the one you played most often.[1]

WL That's because it really is a performer's delight, and a showpiece as well: it sounds terrific and it's a pleasure to play it every time. It always appeals to the audience and it's engaging too: a right and proper piece of good music! Also it's not difficult to maintain in repertory once it's been learned, so there's no problem with taking it on tour. Of course, there are things you have to practice: cadenzas and individual solos, but Lutosławski's quartet isn't really difficult in the way that the *Allegro Misterioso* in Alban Berg's *Lyric Suite* is, or like the second Ligeti quartet, where there are these insanely fast passages with constant string changes that are very difficult to execute technically at the required velocity. By comparison, the Lutosławski quartet is very playable and always comes off sounding just exquisitely good.

RS Lutosławski wasn't one of your Darmstadt acquaintances. Where did you first get to know him?

WL In Warsaw. In February 1964 the LaSalle Quartet was returning from a Mediterranean and Eastern European tour, and the last concert we played was an evening at Warsaw's Philharmonic Hall. Afterwards there was a reception at the American Cultural Attaché's – a memorable occasion. Many prominent Polish musicians were present, and as usual at such events we circulated among them, talking with first one and then another. After a while Lutosławski turned up too. He rushed right over to us and told us how good it was to see us and how happy he was that we would be premiering his new string quartet! This was news to us, and we were simply dumbfounded, which must have been obvious from the expressions on our faces. He was shocked to learn that we knew nothing whatsoever about it, neither about his new string quartet nor that we would be giving the premiere.

It turned out that the Swedish Radio had commissioned works from two composers for the tenth anniversary of its 'new music' series: Ligeti was writing a requiem and Lutosławski was writing a string quartet. And

[1] Renowned Polish composer Witold Lutosławski (1913–1994) studied mathematics at the University of Warsaw 1931–1933 before deciding to become a musician: a pianist and a composer, eventually becoming a conductor as well, noted in particular for his performances of his own works. Initially interested in transformations of folk music, in the 1950s he moved to a highly individual adaptation of twelve-tone technique, and then, influenced by Cage as well as by Calder's 'mobile' sculptures, to what he called 'limited aleatorics,' through which he allows his interpreters great freedom while ensuring that their results remain within predetermined bounds, much as the elements of Calder's mobiles move freely but only within the limits given by their, in this case mechanical, construction.

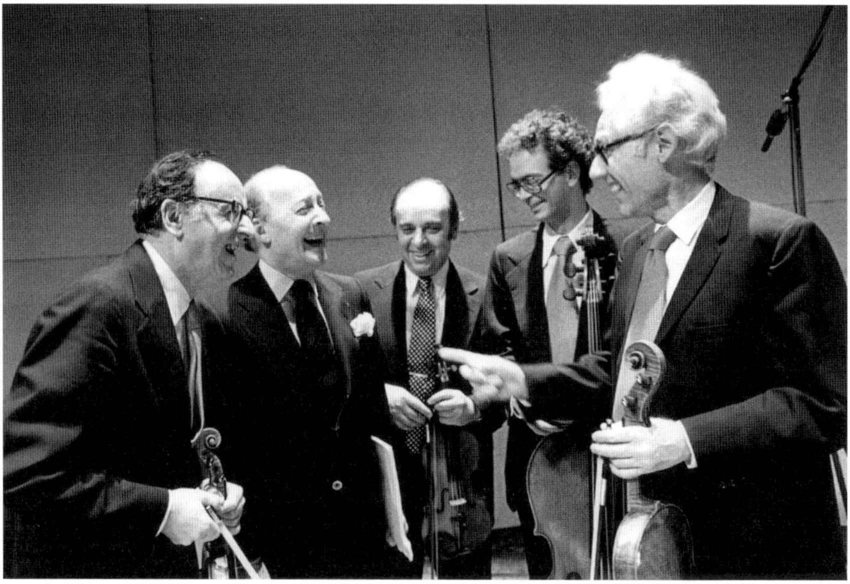

36 The LaSalle Quartet with Witold Lutosławski before the lecture-recital in Cincinnati, March, 1977

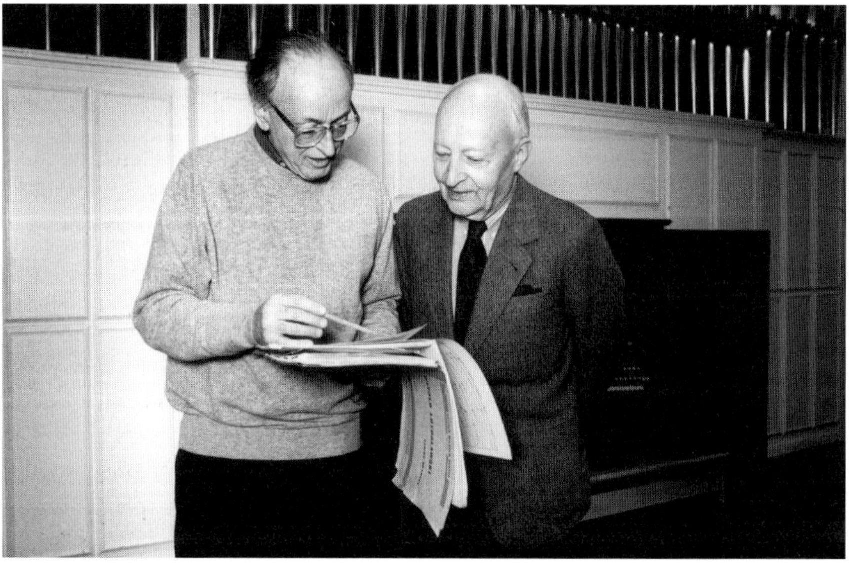

37 Walter Levin and Witold Lutosławski after the lecture-recital in Basel, February, 1990

since the people at the Swedish Radio knew the LaSalle Quartet was willing to play new music, they'd asked our Swedish manager, Margarete Haegefeld, if we could give the premiere of Lutosławski's quartet. She agreed at once and they settled on a date during our next tour of Europe, which was already planned and would take us to Stockholm in March,

1965. Only she forgot to tell us about these arrangements too. Naturally the situation was very embarrassing for Lutosławski, but he was quick to reassure us that it was not a difficult piece at all and not even very long. Nevertheless, our prior experience with composers as well as performers had been that they could badly underestimate the time required both to write a new work on the one hand and to prepare it for a premiere on the other. So a premiere a year hence seemed very close, especially since the quartet itself was not even finished yet.

We actually didn't begin to get the music until sometime in November, 1964. To our horror it arrived in a big package with nothing in it but the four individual parts, and not even for the whole quartet at that, but just for the first section of it.

RS And it was always the LaSalle Quartet's practice to learn and to play complex and above all new pieces from the score.

WL Of course! Every member of the quartet should know what the other three are playing and how the four parts fit together into a whole. So we wrote to Lutosławski asking him to please send us a score. But as it turned out there was a good reason why there was no score: in this piece Lutosławski used a technique that he called 'controlled aleatorics.' What he meant by that was that there are sections in which the individual player can shape his part independently, within predetermined limits, without regard to the other three. So to a certain extent it's left to chance how the parts will fit together in these *ad libitum* sections. Lutosławski sent us a long letter in English explaining why this meant that it was impossible to meet our urgent request for a score for the piece. It's a very interesting document, which I would like to read to you:

> You wrote that you 'must have a score so that each one knows what the other one is doing and at what points events coincide.' The point is that one of the basic techniques used in my piece is that, in many sections of the form, each particular player is supposed not to know what the others are doing, or, at least, to perform his part as if he were to hear nothing except that which he is playing himself. In such sections he must not bother about whether he is behind or ahead of the others. This problem simply does not exist because of measures which have been taken to prevent all undesirable consequences of such freedom. If each performer strictly follows the instructions written in the parts, nothing could happen that has not been foreseen by the composer. All possible lengthening or shortening of the duration of the sections as played by each particular performer cannot affect

the final result in any decisive way. The lack of a score is partly compensated by a whole system of signals written in the parts, fragments of the piece scored traditionally, frequent use of cues, etc. In a given part I have written the part of another instrument when the first instrument is to accompany the second one....

... You may ask me why I attach such great importance to the non-existence of a score of my piece. The answer is quite simple: if I did write a normal score, superimposing the parts mechanically, it would be false, misleading, and it would represent a different work. This would suggest e.g. that the notes placed on the same vertical line should always [be] played at the same moment, which is contrary to my intention. Further, it would prevent each performer from being free enough in his rubatos, ritenutos, accelerandos, pauses and above all in his own tempos. That would deprive the piece of its 'mobile'[2] character which is one of its most important features.....

... To satisfy your wish, however, I did write a sort of score, which departs considerably from the norm. You will see in it that there are very few moments in the whole piece in which the different parts coincide precisely. I have marked these places with broken vertical lines. Short fragments scored traditionally are to be played normally. Throughout the rest of the score each performer plays quite independently of the others. He must only observe certain general indications such as the approximate tempo, the approximate pauses (in brackets), the approximate rhythmical values, etc. I put each section on a separate page in order that you might see clearly what happens in each separate mobile. As you see, each part of a given section is to be read as in the parts

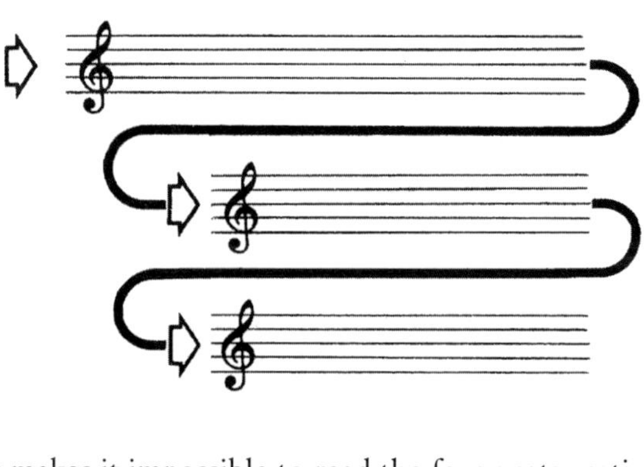

This makes it impossible to read the four parts vertically, except when the notes are placed on the same broken vertical line. I

[2] Lutosławski gave the following explanation of the 'mobile' character of his string quartet: 'When I used the term "mobile" I had in mind the variable lengths of the

have done this purposely in order to avoid the false assumption that other notes might be understood as coinciding…

RS What was Lutosławski's basic idea for his string quartet?

WL He wanted to bring to the domain of ensemble music what he called 'the immensely rich possibilities of soloistic music-making.' In order to do that he worked out the concept of collective playing *ad libitum*, which means that every individual can play freely without being tied to precisely notated rhythmical relationships. Nevertheless, it was to be a completely composed piece, which is to say that the musical materials of the piece are not improvised by the players. A risky undertaking but a brilliant concept, which he used in many works, starting with *Jeux vénitiens* in 1961 and *Trois poèms d'Henri Michaux* in 1963, and then later on, in 1967, in his Second Symphony. In the string quartet the collective *ad libitum* playing principally affects the common pulse, which is what a conductor ordinarily beats and is something the existence of which you take for granted in quartet playing. But here this common pulse is missing, and as a result of the fact that each of us is playing his part independently of the others, there arise aleatorically very complex rhythmic structures and new relationships every time the piece is played, which gives the piece a rhythmic texture of undreamt of flexibility that simply could not be notated in a conventional score. And even if you were to try to notate it, it would be almost impossible to realize it precisely in performance.

One of the chief developments of 20th century music is that it often reaches a degree of rhythmical complexity that approaches the limits of what human beings can execute in performance. I am thinking, for example, of the *Misterioso* movement of Alban Berg's *Lyric Suite* or the second string quartet by Ligeti, where the most complicated rhythms are precisely written out and you have to adhere to them when you play the piece. This puts an overwhelming burden on the freedom of each individual player, and often it takes a very long time before you've made such a piece so much your own that you're free enough to play it like a Mozart

individual sections in the different parts, which results from the ad libitum ensemble playing. Now since in this work there are very long sections, lasting many minutes, great differences arise from one performance to another. Therefore I made use of a term that describes the mobility of the work's layers, which is determined by the way in which it is performed. Nevertheless, it is to be emphasized in this regard that this variability in the length of the sections was not my objective in using this technique; rather what I was concerned with here was simply a loosening of the temporal relationships, with a specific facture that one could describe metaphorically as "flowing," in the sense in which one speaks of a "flowing" weave, of "flowing" silk. As paradoxical as it may sound, composition with this method may be compared with making a sculpture out of imperfectly solid, almost fluid materials.' – Quoted in Tadeusz Kaczyński, *Gespräche mit Witold Lutosławski* (Leipzig, 1976) pp. 25–26.

or Beethoven quartet. This problem disappears with Lutosławski. His constrained aleatorics allows him to achieve an unlimited richness of rhythm without putting any kind of restrictions on the players, who each play their part however they like. And as a result the quartet has a great liveliness to it and comes out sounding new every time it's played, at least as regards its details. Besides which, as is always the case with Lutosławski, it's a very expressive music.

RS What did the 'sort of score' look like that Lutosławski finally did put together for you? A conventional score surely wouldn't be appropriate for his concept of collective playing *ad libitum*.

WL No, it wouldn't. In the first place, the piece consists of a number of different sections, each of which is notated on its own page. The four parts are indeed notated vertically one above the other in the usual sequence, that is, first violin, second violin, viola, cello, but each part is enclosed in its own frame or box, and is to be understood as being played independently of the others. As a result it is impossible to read the four parts vertically. Whenever different parts are meant to coincide, as happens from time to time, the notes to be played simultaneously are joined vertically by a dotted line. In each section, every player is to repeat his part until a pre-defined signal event occurs: at the end of one section, for instance, it says in the three upper voices: 'repeat until the cello enters, then go on to the next section.' Or elsewhere it says in the first violin part: 'Stop immediately when the second violin plays two octaves.' These signals make it possible to transition from one section to the next without a break, so that the whole piece is heard as a single continuous movement and not as a sequence of discrete sections. But the listener doesn't notice any of this: once the players have gotten to know the piece, the transitions from one section to the next are seamless, inaudible.

RS In his letter to you Lutosławski also mentions that each of the players is to be free in the execution of *rubato*, *ritartando*, *accelerando*, pauses, and, above all, tempo. This asynchronicity is also an innovation. What did he have in mind?

WL Indeed, there had never been anything like it before. The lack of a common pulse or meter among the four players makes possible a further rhythmic freedom, through which a rhythmic texture of unimaginable flexibility arises. But you can see that you can't learn such a piece without a score, for how else are you to know what's in the other parts and whether you're to play – and are playing – independently or together? And since each player is playing something completely different, I would also like to know whether they're actually playing what's written in their parts and are following the instructions in it. The 'sort of score' that Lutosławski ultimately sent us is more than sufficient for this purpose. Incidentally, the form this score took was his wife Danuta's idea: she cut up the individual parts and glued them onto large sheets of paper for him.

RS Was she also a musician?

WL No, but she always helped him a lot.

RS A problem that is often spoken of in connection with the controlled aleatorics in Lutosławski's work is how he can control the harmony when for long stretches the simultaneities depend on the choices the players make independently of one another.

WL That's a technical problem that Lutosławski solved with the help of the mathematical concept of combinatorics – he had studied mathematics at the University of Warsaw before deciding in favor of a career as a musician and a composer. The basic idea is this: if in slowly moving harmonies a particular chord lasts long enough the sequence in which the notes of the chord appear ceases to matter, you hear a sound-field that consists of those pitches. The Alberti bass accompaniment of the classical period rests on the same principle: if a chord is repeatedly arpeggiated it makes no difference to the harmony which note of the arpeggiation comes first: what you hear harmonically is the chord as a whole, as a sound-field, independent of the sequence of notes.

Lutosławski applies this old and well-known principle of complementary harmony in a new way, so that, for instance, in one section of the string quartet he defines an eleven-note chord that is divided among the upper three instruments: the first violin and the viola each repeat four of the eleven tones and the second violin the other three, each in a changing sequence and rhythmically varied. So a fluctuating but static sound-field arises, in which the harmony is completely stable despite the internal movement, namely the self-same arpeggiated eleven-tone chord. In composing sections that are to be played freely the composer has to be able to foresee the worst harmony that could arise as a result of playing a given number of tones *ad libitum*, and then decide whether this least favorable simultaneity of tones is acceptable according to his criteria, or not. If this worst case is acceptable, the implication is that all the other possible combinations can only be better and will therefore also meet his harmonic criteria.

The stationary sound-fields in Lutosławski's *ad libitum* parts presuppose relatively slowly changing harmonies and would therefore tend to make these pieces sound static. In order to compensate for this, in the works in which he uses his technique of controlled aleatorics, as in his string quartet, Lutosławski alternates between *ad libitum* sections and sections that are conventionally notated in order that the harmonies in them can move more quickly. Here you have to play precisely together as an ensemble.

RS What are the conventionally notated sections like?

WL They are also rhythmically complex, but written out. Take for instance the place where the first violin plays in 9/8 time, and its tempo is set at dotted quarter note = 120. At the same time, the second violin plays in 2/2 time with quarter note = 160. The viola plays in 3/4 time with quarter note = 120, and the cello plays in 5/8 time with eighth note = 200. All of this is to be played very precisely together, though each of us is playing in a different tempo and a different meter. But if you work it out, you discover that in one and the same bar the first violin plays nine notes, the second violin plays eight, the viola six, and the cello five, but they are all to be together on the downbeats, as is shown in the score by a dotted vertical line. The conventionally notated parts of the piece sound no different from the *ad libitum* parts, and the notational differences aren't audible to the listener.

RS It must have been a real effort for you to learn the Lutosławski quartet, since everyone is accustomed to the norm of always playing together.

WL Absolutely! To begin with, until we really knew the piece well, we were tripped up by our deep-seated inhibitions against playing our parts independently of one another, and we caught ourselves again and again unintentionally paying attention to what the others were doing in order to play exactly together with them. For instance, there are places where each of us is playing his part and after a definite but unpredictable interval is supposed to stop: he stops but the others are to keep on playing, and then another one stops, and so on, and it's not until everyone has stopped that we all go on to the next section. But in rehearsals it often happened that we would all stop at exactly the same instant, which is absolutely incorrect! We really had to work hard at learning to play independently. This independence has by and large been driven out of anyone educated in western classical music.

RS When you teach the piece today, do the young quartets have this problem also?

WL Exactly the same: they're all very anxious about playing together, even when they're not supposed to.

RS But for all its compositional innovations, as regards tone production Lutosławski's quartet is clearly less advanced than some pieces by other composers from the same period.

WL That's right, there are hardly any unusual sounds present. There's a lot of *pizzicato*, and in some sections you play with mutes, but there's scarcely any *sul ponticello*, and no *col legno* at all. In a few places Lutosławski uses quarter-tone intervals as an means of intensifying expression. He also makes generous use of *glissandi*. But no new sounds have been invented, as has long been the norm in avant-garde music. So while the quartet is rather cautious as regards innovative sounds, expressively it is nevertheless incredibly intense.

RS After you had finally gotten Lutosławski's 'sort of score' and had studied the quartet, did you also have the opportunity to work through it with him prior to the premiere?

WL No, we just corresponded with him about certain questions, we didn't work with him. But our having pressed him repeatedly for a score had made him uneasy, and thereafter he was always afraid that we'd completely misunderstood the piece. He wrote to say that he would like to hear us play the quartet prior to the premiere, and so we played it for him one morning in the bar of the Hotel Vacuna in Helsinki, while we were on tour a few days before going on to Stockholm. Of course we were just as anxious about how he would react to it as well. I proposed that we first of all play it through from start to finish just exactly the way we had prepared it, and that he wait to give us his comments afterwards. He and his wife Danuta sat there and listened to our performance. And when we were finished there was dead silence for minutes on end, or so it seemed to us. We were completely demoralized, we thought we'd completely mistaken his intentions and hadn't understood the piece at all. Finally he told us not to change a thing, to leave everything just as it was! Later on, in articles and interviews, he often said that this preview had been a superlative and unforgettable experience, as it had been his usual experience that nothing ever worked in rehearsals, at least not to begin with.[3]

[3] 'At rehearsals what I usually experience is a total chaos that suggests only the vague outline of my piece. Often they don't even play the notes I've written. Then gradually, at first slowly, the major contours begin to emerge, and after a couple of performances the work finally sounds the way I had imagined it. For this reason, rehearsals can often be depressing for a composer: he thinks it's all his fault, and he's afraid that his piece will never turn out the way he wanted. Because I'm familiar with this sort of misery,

The premiere in Stockholm a few days later was altogether a sensational success, which began with a marvelously unexpected incident: at the beginning of the piece there is an instruction in the first violin part to 'repeat the phrase between the repeat marks until you see the audience has become completely quiet.' It's often the case when you've just gone on stage, sat down, and are about to begin a piece, that you end up having to wait a bit until the audience settles down. Lutosławski composed the audience's settling down into the piece itself. At the premiere the audience had settled down completely by the time I'd played this opening phrase twice, but just as I was about to go on and begin the first movement proper, a door slammed and somebody stomped into the auditorium and crassly forced his way into the second row so everybody had to stand up to let him pass. There was a big uproar, and so I went on playing the opening phrase over and again – it went on forever! Lutosławski thought it was just terrific! Ordinarily I would never have the nerve to delay the beginning for so long. My professional colleagues who were present in the auditorium, Györgi Ligeti among them, claimed afterwards that I had engaged this man as an extra for the performance. That was absolutely not the case – I would like to emphasize that.

György Ligeti

RS Whereas Lutosławski's quartet, which you premiered, was commissioned by the Swedish Radio, the impetus for Ligeti's[4] second quartet came from the LaSalle Quartet, to whom it is dedicated in memory of Alfred J. Friedlander. But it says in the score that the quartet was composed on commission from J. K. S. and the SWF radio network in Baden-Baden. Who was J.K.S.?

it was for me an almost overwhelming surprise when the LaSalle Quartet performed my string quartet for me for the first time. That was in Helsinki, a few days before the premiere, when scarcely anything about the interpretation could still be changed… I sat there listening almost without moving, nearly paralyzed by the effect of this experience. I would never have believed that my quartet could be presented with such artistic perfection, so full of feeling. I could only say: leave it just as it is! Leave it just so! Don't change a thing!' - In Kaczyński, *Gespräche*, pp. 211–212.

4 Romanian-born Hungarian composer György Ligeti (1923–2006) studied and subsequently taught at the Franz Liszt Academy in Budapest where his teachers included the composer Zoltán Kodály. Fleeing to the West following the Hungarian revolution in 1956, he went first to Vienna and then to Cologne, where he met and worked for three years with Karlheinz Stockhausen and Gottfried Michael Koenig at the WDR electronic music studio, eventually falling out with them as too dogmatic and factional. Ligeti taught at the Hamburg Academy of Music and Theater 1973–1989. He achieved international renown for his 1961 orchestral work *Atmosphères*; other well-known works include *Aventures* (1962) and *Nouvelles Aventures* (1962–1965), *Requiem* (1963–1965), *Lontano* (1967), *Lux Aeterna* (1966), and the opera *Le Grand Macabre* (1975–1977).

WL Jane K. Steinfirst was the wife of Alfred Friedlander, our friend in Cincinnati who was a cousin of Gerald Warburg and who helped us finance our Amati instruments. To take her mind off the tragedy of Alfred's death in 1965 she went with us on our next European tour, in the fall of 1966. She went everywhere with us, she was with us here in Basel and then also with us in Vienna. And in Vienna Ann Santen's sister gave a huge party at the Bristol Hotel, she rented the whole ballroom for it. Ligeti was there too – we'd known one another ever since he first came to Darmstadt after immigrating from Hungary in 1956. We'd been trying to negotiate a quartet commission for him for the past ten years or so. We talked about it again at this party in Vienna, and this time he only wondered who would pay for such a thing, it would cost a lot of money. To which Jane promptly replied that she would pay for it. And the SWF also chipped in: we usually arranged things so that they got the broadcast rights for our premieres.

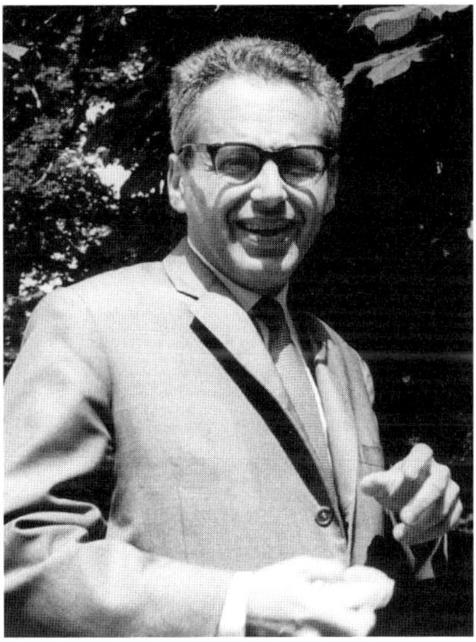

38 György Ligeti, Darmstadt, late 1950s

RS Ligeti, like Lutosławski, is an incredibly original composer, but in a completely different direction. How would you characterize his second quartet?

WL In many respects it's a much more classical quartet than you might suppose at first glance. The piece has five movements, which puts it in a 200 year old tradition in the string quartet genre: early on Haydn wrote some five movement string quartets, though most of his quartets after that have four movements, but then Beethoven's Opus 132 has five movements, and his Opus 131 of course has seven. For Ligeti nevertheless the most significant antecedents are the fourth and fifth quartets by Bartók, both of which have five movements. Ligeti's second quartet plays with tradition throughout. Behind the new elements in the foreground elements of older styles appear as if through a scrim: hidden allusions, formal reminiscences – often distorted as if in a dream, at other times extremely compressed in time, or stretched out to the point of paralysis, of stasis. There are no literal quotations, instead the music quotes the manner, the gestures of traditional music, its basic repertory of gestures and rhythms, but abstracted from how they appear in traditional music. So what usually orients the listener is lacking: there are no themes, no motifs, no workings out of thematic-motivic relationships, no developments – the quartet even avoids any recognizable meter. In this way Ligeti establishes a multi-layered referential background of tradition as the subtle matrix for a completely new music.

Ligeti was highly ambivalent about tradition but also quite articulate about the nature of his ambivalence – let me read you what he said about that in an interview around the time we gave the premiere in Baden-Baden: 'To negate tradition … I make something new, but somehow to let tradition appear indirectly nonetheless by way of allusions: for me that's utterly essential. I don't know how you would explain that psychologically. Maybe I somehow have a need to secretly hang on to the umbilical cord when I so radically cut myself loose from tradition, like an astronaut who is still connected to the satellite by a cable even though he's free to move around in space.'

RS But still, it's surely the sense of hearing something absolutely new that makes the biggest impression when you listen to the quartet.

WL True enough but, in spite of that impression, much of what seems new in the quartet is simply an exaggeration of what already existed: the parameters of traditional music are driven to extremes. For instance in the first movement the first violin may have six notes to a beat while the second violin has seven, or vice-versa, and at the same time the viola also has six but the cello has five, so the quartet as a whole is playing five against six against seven. These relationships change from beat to beat and from bar to bar, giving rise to an immensely complex counterpoint that is, moreover, notated completely and precisely. But it's so fast and so complicated that the ear can't keep up with it. It's a music at the limits of comprehensibility. But so is the *Misterioso* in Berg's *Lyric Suite*, it's a textbook canon – you can explicate every note in the score as such, but you can't hear it: the music is so fast, and sounds so strange as a result of being played *sul ponticello* and *con sordino* that you can no longer hear it as a canon. So Ligeti's quartet is also in the tradition of Berg's *Lyric Suite*, but the result is a completely new kind of music.

RS What is also characteristic of Ligeti is his ability to produce previously unheard sonorities from traditional instruments.

WL Yes, that's quite typical of Ligeti. For instance, if you listen to a recording of his orchestra piece *Atmosphères*, you haven't a clue how the sonorities are achieved: it sounds like electronic music. But it's being played by a completely traditional big symphony orchestra using nothing but old and well-known instrumental techniques. Nevertheless, the sonorities resulting from how they're combined are quite literally unheard of. Ligeti has a unique ability to use traditional instruments to realize the new sonorities he imagines, and to do so with extraordinary precision. If nothing else, this mastery of instrumental sonorities would make him one of the most important composers of our time.

RS How is Ligeti's approach to creating new sonorities by means of traditional techniques realized in the quartet?

WL A good example of it is the second movement, which otherwise has the air about it of a traditional slow movement. The four instruments enter repeatedly, one after another, each on the same note, a G sharp, in unison, except for the cello's first two entrances, two octaves below the others, which include a double stop with a C sharp also, after which, on its third entrance, the cello joins the others in a perfect unison. The sonority at each entrance is very precisely defined: the entrances are to be imperceptible, *con sordino, senza vibrato, sul tasto, pianissimo.* The only thing that changes is the timbre of each instrument, going from *sul tasto* on the first entrance, then *flautando* on the second – but for the cello *col legno tratto* – and then in the ordinary way and then *sul ponticello*, at the bridge. Vibrato takes over from these timbres in the fourth bar, followed immediately by *molto vibrato.* Also the strings on which the G sharp is played are changing: another subtle change in timbre, since the same pitch has a different color on different strings. The intervals between the repeated entrances become shorter, so that the color changes follow one another more rapidly, which gives rise to a color accelerando, an accelerating motion within a single pitch, the unison G sharp.

The opening of this movement is reminiscent of the opening of the slow movement of Bartók's fourth quartet with its canon-like layers of a stationary sound, first without, then with, vibrato. At the beginning of the Bartók a stationary chord is built up that subsequently serves as the harmonic foundation for a big cello solo. In the Ligeti there is no such cello solo, the band of sound is itself the point and the substance of the whole movement. Texture and timbre alone articulate its progress. That's new: a music that renounces practically all the traditional means of expression. But the idea that the function of a melody, a sequence of different pitches, could be realized by a sequence of different colors, that even a single pitch could suggest a quasi-melodic motion via changing colors, was already described by Schoenberg in 1911 in his *Harmonielehre*, where he introduces this concept of a 'color melody' and extends it even further, saying that by layering different tone colors a color harmony could be produced, and by varying the density of the tone color changes, a color rhythm also, so that you could use the same rules to compose with tone colors as had previously been done with pitches.

Schoenberg tried out this idea as early as 1909, in the third of his *Five Pieces for Orchestra*, Opus 16. He originally even called the piece 'Colors.' But this idea was only explored systematically after 1950, with the development of electronic music, which allows the internal structure of each and every sound, its frequency spectrum, which produces its color, to be varied at will. Ligeti's experience at WDR's electronic music studio in Cologne was surely important in making him aware of the technical possibilities of composing with tone colors. But he'd already had the idea for such a music much earlier, prior to his emigration from Hungary. Ligeti says in an interview that the idea of a music that required neither melodies nor chords nor rhythms came to him suddenly, already in 1950, like a nocturnal vision, a hallucination, so to speak seen optically as well as heard: a tremulous surface, a static music that scintillates iridescently, a music in which all the colors shimmer.

Ligeti only succeeded in realizing this idea years later, after his emigration to the West and his acquaintance with the western avant-garde generation of Stockhausen, Boulez, and Nono, and his electronic music studies in Cologne. The results of this development were the orchestra works *Apparitions* (1958–1959) and *Atmosphères* (1961), the work the sensational success of which at its world premiere catapulted him into the front rank of the western avant-garde. The second movement of the string quartet as well as parts of the other movements are translations of this static conception of form into the transparent universe of chamber music.

RS So variations in tone color play a central role in Ligeti's music and in his second string quartet in particular. But how did he notate them in the score?

WL That's actually a problem. While there is, for example, a rudimentary sign in classical notation for gradually changing a pitch, in that one connects the starting note and the ending note of a *glissando* with a straight line, there is no notational symbol at all for gradual changes in tone color. We are fundamentally still using a notation for instrumental and vocal music that originated over 700 years ago for a music with a fundamentally different character. Attempts at a thorough-going reform have repeatedly been unsuccessful, so that in the second half of the 20th century composers have repeatedly had to develop their own notation for each new piece, with the result that its performers have to learn a new musical notation in order to be able to play it. This has made it very difficult to learn new pieces and prevented many people from playing them, in particular pieces that are notated purely graphically: images that one has to interpret.

Achieving precision with a musical notation that was invented for something completely different has become ever more difficult over the years. In his second string quartet Ligeti had to rely on an elaborate verbal description of the sequence of changes that vary the tone color here. But Schoenberg and Berg also had already had to struggle with such problems. Take a look for example at a score by Alban Berg: look at the lengths he went to trying to explain verbally what he meant by his notation, so that people would understand it. These explanations make what he wanted perfectly clear, but they also make it extremely tedious for the performer, who has to translate them into the terms of his instrument, what he is supposed to do, technically, practically, in order to realize Berg's intentions.

RS Were Ligeti's verbal instructions in the score to begin with, or did he add them as a result of what happened in your rehearsals?

WL No, they were already there. He always notates very precisely his conception of how something should sound and doesn't leave anything to chance. Ligeti never employed chance methods in his music, as was the fashion among some composers after John Cage arrived at Darmstadt in 1958.

RS Ligeti's music is further characterized by the two extremes of stasis and a hectic frenzy.

WL These two extremes of movement previously appeared separately in Ligeti's music, shimmering stasis for example in his orchestral work *Atmosphères*, and, in radical contrast to that, violent ruptures, as in the two pieces *Aventures* and *Nouvelles Aventures*. These two extremes of motion are brought together in the second string quartet, so that paralytic stasis and violent outburst not only confront one another abruptly but also invade one another in various ways. This underlying strategy regarding motion joins the five movements into a characteristic transformation, like a series of variations. In the first movement in particular the extreme contrasts collide with one another directly: hectic activity and paralytic stasis, whispering *pianissimo* and explosive *fortissimo*.

RS Perhaps we could talk a little bit about the third and fourth movements, both of which also represent typical characteristics of Ligeti's music.

WL The third movement is a kind of scherzo-intermezzo, with the indication '*come un meccanismo di precisione*,' 'like a precision mechanism.' A rather delicate mechanism though, a watchmaker's nightmare. Its precision leaves something to be desired, apparently the machinery has sand in the gears, it gets noisier and noisier and loses its strict metrical footing. Towards the end something breaks with a loud bang, and after a brief pause the ticking peters out into nothing. Machine-like ticking has always fascinated Ligeti: he even wrote a piece for 100 metronomes.[5] Here in his second quartet he makes of it a *pizzicato* movement, which also connects with a tradition: there are already *pizzicato* scherzo movements in the Debussy and Ravel quartets. Nevertheless, Ligeti's model here is surely the *pizzicato* movement from the fourth Bartók quartet. The *pizziccato* third movement in the Ligeti quartet is certainly the wittiest and most entertaining in the piece, not least thanks to the virtuosic multiplicity of its *pizzicato* effects. Along with the normal plucking there is *pizzicato* at the bridge and the so-called 'Bartók *pizzicato*,' which snaps back percussively against the fingerboard, as well as *pizzicato* on the fingerboard. And knocking with the fingertips instead of plucking. And the rattling *pizzicato* that you get by holding one of the left hand fingers so that the nail is against the string and pulling sideways on the string so that it snaps back against your fingernail. In the long run that wears out a lot of fingernails.

Incidentally the movement is also an oblique parody of ensemble playing, a late offshoot of Mozart's *Musical Joke*, the so-called 'village musicians sextet,' though in the Ligeti what you see are four musicians who honestly try to play together as exactly as possible. That's not so easy, actually it's very difficult in this piece, and sometimes it falls apart. They start out together very bravely, but right away a slight accelerando by the first violin messes everything up, the others don't follow, and it all becomes just hopelessly confused, but then they're together again, surprisingly – but not for long. 'See you at the fermata,' as it says in *The Well-Tempered String Quartet*,[6] the Bible of all amateur quartets.

It's all precisely notated by Ligeti: the confusion is intentionally composed, it's in nowise arbitrary on the part of the performers or due to their lack of ability. At the beginning of the piece everyone starts together with four notes to the beat, but already in the fourth measure the first violin makes a little accelerando: it begins to play five notes to the beat, the others are still playing four, but they notice what's happened, and the second violin is the first to go along with it, he also wants to play five to the beat. But by then the first violin has already reached six, the others are still at four – so typical: the lower-pitched instruments always tend to lag behind. Now the first violin reaches seven notes per beat, the second violin has reached six, and in the meantime the viola has made it to five while the cello is still at four. In the sixth measure it's nine in the first

5 *Poème Symphonique* (1962).

6 *The Well-Tempered String Quartet: A book of Counsel and Entertainment for all Lovers of Music in the Home* (New York, 1938). 'The Joy of String Quartets' might be a more apt contemporary title for this good-humored work, first published in Germany in 1936.

violin, eight in the second violin, seven in the viola, and six in the cello, and you can imagine what a chaos that is. But now they are to get back together, slowly, in that the three others catch up: the first violin stops at twelve, and by the ninth measure they are once again exactly together.

It's evocative of meaningless precision, of mindlessly running to keep up: this too has its tradition. It's a regularity that gradually gets confused and turns into chaos: a clear pulse that begins to curdle in the acceleration and ends up coagulating into an expanse of iridescent stasis. Textural transformations like that already appeared in the first movement, and slow transformations of tone color, as well as a sliding around in microtones in the second movement. Now, in the *pizzicato* third movement we've got gradual accelerations as well as creeping changes of pitch and tone color, all at the same time. The pitches are changed by sliding the left hand slowly up or down while the *pizzicato* motion accelerates from about ten beats per second at the beginning up to sixteen. But sixteen attacks per second is the limit of our ear's ability to perceive discrete attacks individually. Beyond that a blurring arises, in that the individual events merge into one another. At the same time, sixteen attacks per second is also the limit of what can be repeated manually, even using two fingers. Over and over again Ligeti plays with the physiological limits of perception and execution in this way, in which actions switch into a new quality.

RS The fourth movement is once again a kind of scherzo. What distinguishes its character from the preceding movement?

WL It's a bitter and angry scherzo marked '*presto furioso*, *brutale*, *tumultuoso*.' There are only two levels of dynamics: triple *fortissimo* and triple *pianissimo*, no transitions, no tone color poetry. In this sense the fourth movement is related to the first. By the way, there's an interesting story about the manic-eruptive character of the fourth movement. At the first, private, performance of the piece in 1968 in Cincinnati, a neurologist friend of ours remarked that the sequence of spastic twitchings and sudden paralysis in this movement bore an astounding similarity to the course of an epileptic fit with its characteristic losses of consciousness of 5–30 seconds' duration, which correspond exactly to the paralytic halts in the quartet. Analogous medical diagnoses of a piece of music aren't all that uncommon: surely the most astounding of all was the question we were asked by a doctor after he heard the *presto-delirando* movement from Berg's *Lyric Suite*: he wanted to know if the composer had suffered from asthma, the movement was the acoustic protocol of an asthma attack. Berg was in fact asthmatic. Ligeti on the other hand was in good health, as far as I know.

In an interview for SWF Ligeti himself made a completely different analogy to this movement: 'Here everything that has gone before is compressed. In astronomy there are dwarf stars: the same mass as our sun is compressed into a millionth of its volume and has an unbelievable density, but is, nevertheless, the same mass.' Whereas in the score the instructions for the players are quite prosaic: 'This movement (with the exception of some *pianissimo* places) is to be played with exaggerated haste, as if crazed, always with the utmost force, the bow pressed hard against the strings (scratching noise). It will have been played correctly if at the end a lot of hairs have come loose from the bow.'

RS What was it like for you to learn Ligeti's second string quartet?

WL It is certainly among the most difficult of all the pieces we ever played, I can assure you of that. The first movement is so difficult that we often despaired of whether it was possible to play it at all. The notes simply come so fast and are so hard, and nothing is repeated. Learning it all was sometimes really discouraging, even depressing, and it took rather a long time before we were able to play it musically. We even had to postpone the first performance for a year, because we couldn't learn the piece quickly enough. But once you've learned it, it's a very grateful piece that's a pleasure to play. But it's not a piece that you can easily keep in your active repertory, since you have to keep working on it, over and over again. Even today it's a very difficult piece for a quartet to learn. Composers are always confronted by the question of how far they can take difficult techniques. Otherwise it can happen that the interpreters just say to themselves that nobody can hear such-and-such anyway, so we'll just do whatever we like. A quartet came to me once and tried to play the first movement, but they couldn't play it at all. They'd surely told themselves I wouldn't be able to hear that anyway.

RS But they'd come to exactly the right address!

WL Indeed. But it was all the more astonishing when the Vogler Quartet, which we didn't know at all at that time, played the Ligeti quartet flawlessly at the Evian String Quartet Competition in 1986.[7] They had prepared it with Eberhard Feltz at the Hanns Eisler Academy of Music in what was then East Berlin, and thoroughly too – it was really wonderful! And they won the first prize to boot!

RS Did you work with Ligeti to prepare his second string quartet?

WL Only at the very end. When we got the music, we corresponded with him for further details, after which he always made small changes in

[7] The LaSalle Quartet sat *in corpore* on the jury of the Concours d'Evian.

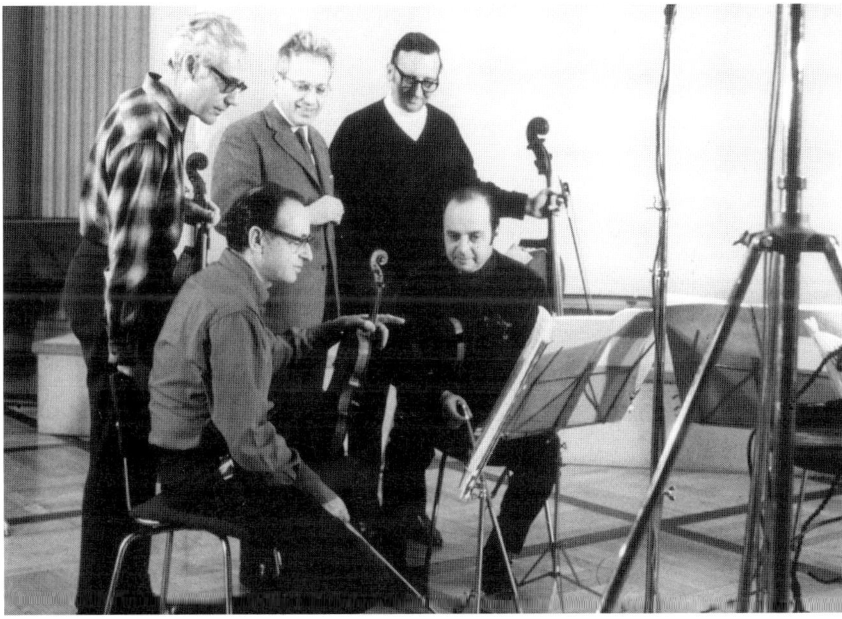

39 The LaSalle Quartet with György Ligeti at Deutsche Grammophon, Munich, 1969

the score to represent his ideas more clearly and precisely. After we had learned the piece, we played it for him. But then he made life very difficult for us. It was absolutely fascinating how he could hear so extraordinarily precisely, how he knew exactly what he wanted, and simply never settled for less. He was extremely critical but at the same time very charming. He would say, for instance, 'The way you play that is absolutely amazing, but it has nothing whatsoever to do with my conception of it!' Then we'd start all over again. But he could also be quite unpleasant. He was present when we recorded the quartet for WDR in Cologne prior to recording it for Deutsche Grammophon and he thoroughly hassled us once more for good measure.

RS What were his objections?

WL It was never precise enough for him.

RS Not precise enough in all parameters?

WL Well, his conception of the piece was completely different from ours, and in his mind's ear he heard what he conceived with great precision. What constitutes being precise enough depends on how something is conceived, not on what can be achieved technically. When is something *ponticello* enough and when is it *pianissimo* enough, what are the relationships between tone color and dynamics – he was very sensitive to that. He not only had very precise ideas of what he wanted but his ideas were much more extreme than the ones we had arrived at. He was also present when we recorded the quartet for Deutsche Grammophon, the same as when we recorded Luigi Nono's quartet with Nono himself present. Those are really authentic recordings.

RS You played the piece a total of 54 times, and played it every season from 1969 to 1974. So during that time it was a real repertory piece. Then you didn't take it up again for nearly ten years, not until 1983, and you only played it four times after that. Do you remember what prompted you to take it up again after such a long time?

WL It was because that year in Vienna they wanted to have a cycle with three important works that were either dedicated to us or that we had premiered: Ligeti's second string quartet, the Lutosławski quartet, and the quartet by Nono. We played a series of three concerts, with one of these quartets on each of them.

EVI LEVIN: That was on my 60th birthday. Our two sons, Thomas and David, came to Vienna as a surprise, and Luigi Nono and Nuria were staying in the same hotel as we were.

WL In the Hotel Schubert on the Schubert-Ring, and then we were at Hatto Beyerle's for a party.

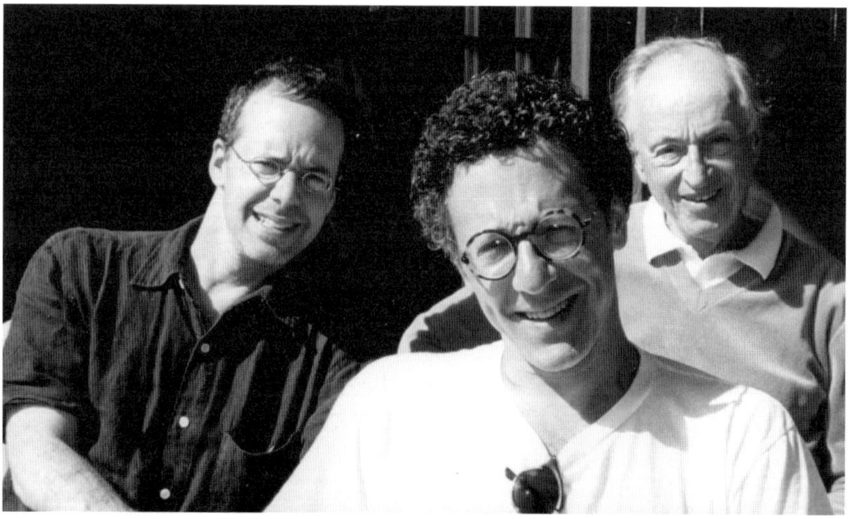

40 David, Thomas, and Walter Levin in Flims, September 14, 1999

Luigi Nono

RS You began asking Luigi Nono[8] to write a string quartet in the mid-1950s, at Darmstadt, about the same time you started asking Ligeti to write one.

WL That's right. And he promised us he would think about it. Which he did: he thought about it for the next 25 years. The quartet was finally written between July, 1979, and January, 1980, as a commission from the city of Bonn for the 30th Beethoven Festival. We premiered it on June 2, 1980, in Bad Godesberg, in Bonn.

RS Does anyone know why Nono needed such a long period of gestation?

WL Nono's approach to composition changed rather a lot in the decades between when we first met him and when he began work on the string quartet. His earlier music, up through his 1960 opera *Intoleranza*, had an immediate contemporary relevance, characterized by his political awareness as an active and combative member of the Italian Communist Party. Then, starting in 1960, Nono worked in the electronic studio in Milan, and during this time he integrated new materials into his music: documentary sounds, distorted electronically, often in combination with live instrumental sounds, that alluded to specific situations in society: to the situation of metal workers in his 1964 *Fabbrica illuminata*, the trial of the Auschwitz executioners in his 1966 *Ricorda cosa ti hanno fatto in Auschwitz*, the student revolts in his 1968–1969 *Musica-manifesto no. 1*. Such a stance took courage, since it repeatedly led to scandals, in the case of the premiere of *Intoleranza* in Venice in 1961 to a real rampage organized by fascists, complete with stink bombs.

So most of Nono's works from the 1960s are quasi-musical manifestos that pointedly document his solidarity with working people and with the victims of war, torture, and oppression. In the 1970s this posture changed. His piece for piano and tape … *sofferte onde serene* …,

[8] Italian composer Luigi Nono (1924–1990) studied music with composer Gian Francesco Malipiero at the Venice Conservatory but took a law degree from the University of Padua. Encouraged by composer and conductor Bruno Maderna, Nono's first acknowledged work, *Variazioni canoniche sulla serie dell'op. 41 di A. Schoenberg*, was presented by Hermann Scherchen at Darmstadt in 1950, and established Nono as both an avant-garde composer and a political radical. He was subsequently recognized as one of the leading figures in the 'Darmstadt School,' along with Pierre Boulez and Karlheinz Stockhausen, for serial works like *Il canto sospeso* (1955–1956) and the opera *Intoleranza* (1960). Following a number of works oriented toward political activism – Nono was an engaged member of the Italian Communist Party – the string quartet *Fragmente – Stille, An Diotima* (1979–1980) marked an inward turning in his work that was and remains controversial and is by no means fully explicated.

is the start of a development towards quieter, sweeter textures with a gentle surface, almost like chamber music, a music that is subjective and expressive, and often introverted. There has been a lot of argument as to whether this signals a shift in Nono's prior beliefs, even a betrayal of them, which is something that Nono has vehemently denied. Disciples are always outraged when their prophets appear to contradict some supposed doctrine of theirs, for instance when Schoenberg began writing tonal pieces again, towards the end of his life, or when, after Schoenberg's death, Stravinsky himself, the antithesis of twelve-tone orthodoxy, wrote twelve-tone pieces.

In any event it appears to be the case that Nono's development in the 1970s opened the way for him to compose a string quartet, a genre in which the great classical-romantic tradition is always implicated, and which Nono had always avoided. In many important respects, however, he does decline to follow this tradition in his string quartet.

RS Nevertheless, in the complexity of its many levels of meaning and its use of quotations and allusions, Nono's quartet is a serious contribution to the genre of the string quartet as traditionally conceived.

WL But it's a complexity that works not with obvious allusions but rather with hidden ones that the listener cannot possibly catch. You could liken it to Alban Berg, who also uses quotations, but he too demands that you pay very close attention in order to catch them. And you have to know what's being quoted. What good is it to listen to Berg's *Lyric Suite* without knowing Zemlinsky's *Lyric Symphony*? And no one knew the *Lyric Symphony* at the time when Berg's piece became famous, since at that time the *Lyric Symphony* was hardly ever played, and a few years later performances of it were forbidden altogether by the Nazis. Nevertheless, once you know what it's about, you hear the *Lyric Suite* differently.

RS I can imagine that on account of its intellectual demands the Nono quartet was a kind of homage to the LaSalle Quartet.

WL No, actually I don't think so, not at all. The composers we approached with commissions worked at their own level. They didn't need us in order to be motivated to work at that level. It may be, however, that they didn't hesitate to write demanding works for us in part because they knew that we would take performing them very seriously. They certainly knew how we went about playing difficult music from the past. Our attitude towards both new and old music was known to them, so it was worth their while to compose something quite difficult both technically and intellectually, and in most cases that's what they did.

RS The quartet bears the multiply ambiguous three-part title *Fragmente – Stille, An Diotima*. How would you describe the essential characteristics of Nono's string quartet? Is the title descriptive, and if so, in what way?

WL Something of Nono's 25 years of quiet deliberation and maturation has entered into the work itself: it also takes its own good time. It's a long piece: something like 40 minutes, with many pauses, but to be played without a break. It consists of a sequence of relatively short sections with very different textures: the 'fragments' of the title, dream-like, meditative images, sometimes pierced, lightning-like, by shards of other music. In between, framing the fragments or framed by them, are silences, long pauses, and long-held fermatas, the '*Stille*' of the title. High notes predominate, a bright, iridescent sonority. The lowest registers of the cello and the viola are infrequent. So there's no classically-balanced, rich string quartet sonority, as there still is with Bartók and Schoenberg, and there's scarcely any opportunity for vibrato, for the notorious 'beautiful tone.' Contra the classical ideal of polyphony the piece is predominantly homophonic, chordal; at the beginning it's almost univocal, with only the sparsest harmonies.

The most important interval, both harmonically and melodically, is the tri-tone, disdained from the Middle Ages on as the essence of dissonance. There are no extended melodies, and therefore there's no melodic imitation or polyphonic development. The thematic element is for the most part limited to three and four note motivic cells and short rhythmic patterns. A peculiarly unique compound sonority results from the simultaneous use of different string color effects: *sul tasto, sul ponticello, dietro ponticello, col legno battuta, col legno tratto, flautando, flageoletti*. What is characteristic of this compound sonority is the high proportion of noise produced by these effects. Motion is improvisatory, hesitant, and halting. There is no definite meter, so that only rarely is there any sense of a regular pulse. Even where a meter could arise it's undermined by many fermatas and pauses of highly various durations.

RS Apparently these pauses are such a fundamental feature of the piece that they have contributed to the title.

WL Exactly, and Nono had something extreme in mind with these fermatas and pauses, much more extreme than we had imagined. He wanted them to be very long and highly differentiated, and for these fermatas and *Luftpausen* he invented a whole set of new signs, which are defined at the front of the score. We had a lot of trouble with these signs when we were rehearsing for the premiere: how long is 'very long'? And how short is a 'long *Luftpause*'? Nono found the pauses we were making between the 'islands' of sound insufficiently differentiated and almost always too short: it seemed to him that we were always making it sound like Webern's *Bagatelles*: it sounded too metrical to him. But notating his conception in the manuscript had been very difficult for him, though not as difficult as for György Kurtág, who simply gave up on notating his intentions in the score at all: you can't tell from a Kurtág score how the piece is supposed to go. And when you talk with him about it, he changes his mind from one time to the next.

RS Did Nono also change his mind while you were learning the piece?

WL No, he knew exactly what he wanted, he just hadn't specified it precisely in the score. I persuaded him to define the length of the pauses at least somewhat more precisely by adding upper and lower bounds, for instance 7–11 seconds for a mid-length fermata: that still leaves enough room for the individual player's sense of what's right. But for a long time he resisted defining the pauses even to this extent, he was anxious to leave that up to the individual players, and he always hoped that we would get far enough along with the piece to sense the necessity of these particular lengths.[9]

But even as schooled as we were on the new music that we already knew, this proved to be too much for us. We were used to learning pieces in which the composer indicated, at least approximately, what he had in mind, and we were never able to play the piece entirely to Nono's satisfaction until he gave us these more specific durations for the pauses. As a result, the piece kept getting longer and longer: our premiere in June, 1980, took 30 minutes, our recording for Deutsche Grammophon three plus years later, in December, 1983, took 38 minutes, and this additional length was a consequence of nothing else but our holding the fermatas, chords, and pauses longer – eight minutes! That amounts to more than 25% of the piece as we first played it!

RS Do you have the impression that Nono was able to know exactly how long he felt a pause should be between two given fragments and between another pair ten minutes further on in the piece?

WL Certainly, I have complete faith in his ability to do that. Just as with

[9] In his preface to the score Nono attempts to communicate a feeling for these fermatas by means of a poetical text: 'The *fermati* are always to be felt as being of different kinds, leaving the imagination open to dream-like spaces, sudden ecstasies, inexpressible thoughts, deep silent breaths and the stillness of timeless singing.'

Ligeti: these people know exactly what they want, but they do have to notate it so that their intention can be understood by interpreters also.

RS Can you imagine that nowadays other ensembles would be able to hold the pauses and fermatas correctly just using their own subjectivity or intuition in Nono's sense, without having his time limit indications?

WL Of course I can imagine that, but now these durations are written in the score! So they've never had the problem. But there are interpreters nowadays whom one can rely upon with such indeterminacies, because they have so much more experience with this kind of music and perhaps also because they are particularly sensitive and gifted. The Arditti Quartet, for instance, can do that. But at the time it was completely new to us. We weren't all that avant-garde, not at all.

RS You were pioneers.

WL Yes, but we weren't quite so gifted in this direction and so we were able to arrive at how to play the piece only laboriously by way of written indications. Maybe others could feel their way into it, we couldn't!

RS We've spoken at length now about the pauses that so fundamentally articulate the Nono quartet. But these pauses frame the 'sound-islands,' that is, the 'fragments' mentioned in the title of the piece.

WL Yes, the piece is a sequence of contrasting fragments, of 'islands' that often last only a few seconds: intuitive, dream-like associations that emerge from the silence and die away again into the pauses.

RS Could you describe how these sound islands are constructed?

WL There are many characters that pervade the piece through many variations, and these characters are the basic elements out of which the piece is composed. The piece begins with a one bar recitativ by the first violin, an almost ascetic line, with sparse harmonies. The most important interval, as I've said, is the tri-tone, an interval of three whole tones. Here at the beginning it's the interval between A and E♭ – 'Es' in German – certainly no accident for the son-in-law of Arnold Schoenberg. The notes of this violin recitativ are colored by being doubled in the other instruments, all of them with a large component of noise. While the first violin begins *flautando*, then *sul ponticello*, the second violin begins *col legno battuto sul ponticello*, then *normale*, then again *col legno battuto sul ponticello*, followed by *col legno tratto*. The viola plays *sul ponticello*, then *col legno battuto*, and then *col legno tratto sul ponticello*, and the cello first plays *col legno battuto*, then *dietro ponticello*. After this first bar comes the first fermata: 'first violin and cello as long as possible,' further defined as 9–13 seconds. Holding a chord for that long, in a fermata, when you're sitting on the stage, seems like forever. You get the feeling that any moment the public will walk out on you if something doesn't happen very soon.

A second texture is based on quintuplets, fleeting groups of five notes played tremolo. Tone color alternates between *sul tasto* and *sul ponticello*. There is a third texture, a '*gettato*': high harmonics, alternating between *sul tasto* and played *sul ponticello* in a drum roll with a 'thrown' bow, all four instruments, but each in its own rhythm. Here the traditional half-tone steps of the chromatic scale are distorted by quarter-tones, which play an important role in the piece as a source of color. A further element is a short, signal-like fanfare: the sharpest rhythmical figure in the piece, and one that is repeated many times. The four instruments all play double-stop tri-tones. Then, exactly in the middle of the piece, as its painfully restrained essence, the central lyrical phrase, concentrated in just five bars: '*mit innigster Empfindung*' it says, '*pianissimo, sotto voce*.' These instructions quote another very personal quartet: they appear in the famous *Heiliger Dankgesang* movement of Beethoven's Opus 132.

This is particularly revelatory as regards Nono's ambivalent feelings about expression: the harmony here is eight-voice homophony, all four instruments play double stops. But it's a distorted harmony: quarter-tones oppose the pure assonances of the overtones. Intonation, already iffy because of the many register changes, and therefore of the left hand position, in this widely spaced harmony, is further put in mortal peril by the double stops and, on top of that, the quarter-tone distortions, the constant *pianissimo, sotto voce, legato*. And despite all that, '*mit innigster Empfindung*,' 'with the utmost feeling.' Vibrato is absolutely out of the question, on purely technical grounds. And yet it is the only place in the whole piece where all four instruments play with normal tone production. Nono invoked this allusion again and again in conversation and in letters: '*mit innigster Empfindung*.' Further on in the piece this phrase is recalled six times, fragmentarily, drawn out, and every time with the words '*mit innigster Empfindung*.' It is the most often repeated texture in the piece.

At the opposite extreme to such introverted and reflective lyricism is a rhythmically lively, imaginatively rich invention on the hexachord C E F♯ G A B♭. Each instrument plays only one or two of these pitches, but constantly changes register, color, articulation, and entrance rhythm. This gives rise to a wittily moving and transparent texture based on a single, static hexachord. So those are the basic elements of the piece.

RS You just mentioned the quotation from Beethoven's Opus 132. It would appear that quotation in general is a salient feature of Nono's quartet.

WL Yes, there's a lot of quotation in this piece, but always hidden, quasi-subcutaneous, underground. The listener doesn't notice it. The quotation of '*mit innigster Empfindung*' is only for the players to take note of, not the listener. Then at the end of the piece Nono hides a Renaissance chanson by the Flemish composer Johannes Ockeghem: '*Malor me bat*,' 'I've been struck by misfortune.' It's a lover's lament, indicated in Nono's score by quotation marks, and in parentheses it says 'freely adapted.' Freely adapted! In fact so freely and so thoroughly integrated with the piece as to be unrecognizable. The melody is exclusively in the viola, and this is the only place in the quartet in which there is a lengthy melody for a single instrument. But if you don't know about the quotation in advance, it's impossible to recognize it. Recognition is only possible when you already know what's going on, which is that it's note for note the same as in the Ockeghem, but totally distorted rhythmically, pulled apart, and surrounded by other pitches. Incidentally it was this solo that redeemed the piece for our violist.

RS How is Nono's quartet composed, technically speaking? Is it twelve-tone music?

WL No, it isn't based on a twelve-tone row, as one might expect of Schoenberg's son-in-law, but it is, nevertheless, atonal. But the genetic pitch material from which the piece is constructed, its structural backbone, is also hidden. The piece is based on the so-called '*scala enigmatica*,' an invention of the Bolognese composer Adolfo Crescentini: a remarkable, eccentric mix of elements of the major, minor, whole-tone, and chromatic scales, that was published in 1888 in the *Gazzetta Musicale di Milano* with a challenge to harmonize it. Many composers did just that in fact, among them Giuseppe Verdi in the first of his *Quattro Pezzi Sacri*, an *Ave Maria* for four part *a cappella* choir. But if you don't know that, then it's also very hard to hear it in Verdi also.

For Nono the elements of the *scala enigmatica* are the raw materials of the quartet, they structure its harmonies and simultaneities. The scale contains two tri-tones, which surely, along with the hidden homage to Verdi, contributed to Nono's choice of the *scala enigmatica* as his pitch source for the quartet. The tri-tone is actually a fundamental element of the piece. In a conversation I had with him Nono also felt a connection

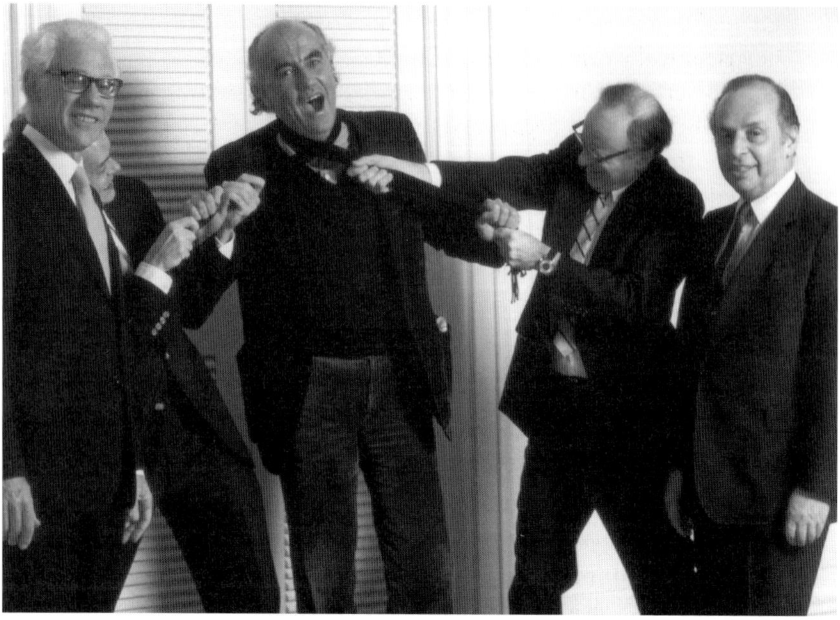

41 The LaSalle Quartet with Luigi Nono, Hamburg, December, 1983

between this scale and the Lydian mode of the *Heiliger Dankgesang*, the 'sacred song of thanksgiving' movement of Beethoven's quartet Opus 132, from which he borrowed the *sotto voce 'mit innigster Empfindung,'* 'with the utmost feeling.'

RS So far we've talked about the first two parts of the title, *'Fragmente'* and *'Stille,'* which have to do with the character and elements of structure of the quartet. But *'An Diotima'* seems to be something completely different: a kind of dedication.

WL That's another hidden layer of the piece, one that refers to Friedrich Hölderlin. Diotima, the priestess character in Plato's *Symposium*, who teaches Socrates the essence of love, is the name given by Hölderlin to the female figure in his novel *Hyperion*, but also his poetic name for the woman with whom he had a passionate and tragic love affair: Suzette Gontard, wife of the Frankfurt banker Friedrich Gontard, in whose household Hölderlin was employed as a tutor. So the name Diotima is fraught with all kinds of meaning and therefore invites speculation.

There are 53 places in the score where Nono has written fragments of quotations from Hölderlin's poems and letters to Suzette Gontard. Since the premiere there has been a great deal of speculation and even controversy about the meaning of these quotations, but despite intensive research and analysis their meaning remains undisclosed. But the

Hölderlin quotations in the score are meant only for the players, in nowise are they intended as naturalistic, programmatic indications of how to perform the piece. So for the listener they don't exist.

There had been secret texts and messages hidden in scores previously: '*Muss es sein*' in Beethoven's Opus 135, and in 1857 Franz Liszt copied verses from Schiller's poem *Die Ideale* into the score of his symphonic poem of the same name. There are innumerable anagrams of people's names in Alban Berg's music, also the quote from Zemlinsky's *Lyric Symphony* in the *Lyric Suite* and even, in its last movement, but suppressed by him for publication, a poem by Baudelaire.

RS So no one knows what Nono meant by these quotations, what their hidden, even secret, message is?

WL No. They do appear in any case to testify to a need to communicate something that goes beyond what is possible to do with instrumental music alone, ultimately a need for the human voice.[10] Schoenberg was the first to risk that in the string quartet literature, in his second quartet: two movements with soprano on poems by Stefan George. Nono denied himself that possibility: the texts remain unheard. But in the score he meticulously documented where they come from, which suggests that Nono's understanding of them derived from their original contexts. It was so important to him that the players know these contexts that he sent us a copy of the bilingual German-Italian Adelphi edition of Hölderlin's Diotima texts that he had worked from. In it the places that he quotes are all underlined by him.

RS In a letter to Hans-Jürgen Nagel, the director of the Bonn Beethoven Festival, Nono wrote that 'The fragments of Hölderlin should resonate in each of the members of the LaSalle Quartet, independently of the music.' Did they resonate with you?

WL That's a very difficult question: what did he mean by 'resonate'? The Hölderlin text fragments and apparently also their whole history were very important to Nono. But in order to understand the poems, you have to know the whole story about Hölderlin and Suzette Gontard. And maybe that's what he meant. There's also a hidden back story to

[10] In his preface to the score Nono writes that 'the fragments of poems by Hölderlin are ... diverse moments, thoughts, silences, songs from another universe, from other heavens, meant to rediscover in another way the possibility of not having to say goodbye [this in turn is a quotation from a letter from Hölderlin to Suzette Gontard]. The performers may sing them however they may understand them, sing them as if they were sounds that strive to attain to the sweetest tones of their innermost lives.'

these quotations, but I'm reluctant to get into Nono's private life, just as I'm reluctant to get into Berg's affair with Hanna Fuchs as it enters into his *Lyric Suite*.

RS So you didn't concern yourself much with Hölderlin in connection with Nono's quartet?

WL On the contrary, I worked through the bilingual edition that he sent us. But I'm not such a lover of lyric poetry or an expert on it that the Hölderlin poems could have had much of an impact on me, especially as regards the quartet. It was and remains difficult for me to establish the connection between this piece and the text fragments. But that's my problem, not his.

RS When did you begin to work with Nono on the quartet?

WL It was in Vaduz, when we were there on tour at the beginning of September, 1979. At that time he still hadn't written any music, just a few possibilities on staff paper, which we were supposed to try out. There wasn't anything like a whole piece or even any parts of one, but he wanted to work with us, experimenting with sounds and combinations of sounds. And when something corresponded to what he had in mind, he wrote it down. Over and over again he wanted to hear what it sounded like when we produced strange sounds with the instruments or distorted intonations or dissonances.

To begin with these were more in the nature of experiments with individual sounds in various combinations. Sometime after this meeting in 1979 he began to send sections of the quartet to us in Cincinnati, and then we met once more in Perugia in March of 1980, during our tour when we played all the Schoenberg quartets. Nono was there with Nuria, his wife, to hear her father's quartets,[11] but he was so depressed that he wasn't able to come to the concerts. Nevertheless we were able to play parts of the piece for him in Perugia, so that he could compare how he imagined it sounding, his notation, and the acoustic result of our playing.

Of course it's incredibly exciting to be involved in the genesis of a new piece by a composer of the stature, the quality, and the intelligence of a Nono and to experiment with him regarding what he has in mind, a creative process that is usually inaccessible to anyone else. I've always envied the members of the Schuppanzigh Quartet, who worked with Beethoven, and we often wished we could have eavesdropped on these working sessions or had a recording of them. That's how we worked with Nono on his quartet, even after we'd premiered it in Bad Godesberg

[11] Nono's wife Nuria is Schoenberg's daughter.

and performed it in Badenweiler. We then made a video recording of the quartet in Baden-Baden, together with Nono and Peter Wapnewski:[12] the broadcast was called 'Keynotes.' We worked with him over and over again on all these occasions.

People often think that a composer is finished with a composition once it's been premiered. But at the premiere or even in the first rehearsals the composer may come to perceive important things differently. We know for example from a letter of Leopold Mozart to his daughter Nannerl that Wolfgang rehearsed the quartets dedicated to his friend Haydn in his apartment.[13] Supposedly Haydn was playing in the quartet, and there must have been discussions about these new pieces in which Mozart requires a wide range of dynamic nuances. We can imagine Haydn responding by asking how the players were supposed to know that, since they weren't notated in the parts: if that's what you want, then write it down! But by then the manuscripts were already at the printer. So the improvements were made directly on the plates without ever being copied into the manuscript, as a result of which we can, today, reconstruct what probably happened at the rehearsals in Mozart's apartment.

RS You once said that after one of these concerts you found Nono's comments on the performance waiting for you at your hotel.

WL That was after the concert in Badenweiler.

RS He didn't want to talk to you about his comments?

WL No, he wanted them written down. He'd thought them over after the concert and then written down what occurred to him all over big sheets of paper, so that we could read them while rehearsing.

RS Completely unstructured and spontaneous. It surely wasn't easy for you to make something coherent out of these unstructured notes.

WL No, it wasn't easy, but we made the effort.

[12] German literary scholar and medievalist Peter Wapnewski (1922–2012), author of books on medieval German poetry, also wrote extensively on Wagner and on the poetry and literature of the 19th and 20th centuries. He was the founding rector of the Wissenschaftskolleg (Institute for Advanced Study) in Berlin (1982–1986), where Levin was later on in residence during the academic year 1991–1992.

[13] On January 22, 1785, Leopold Mozart wrote to his daughter: 'I just now got 10 lines from your brother, in which he writes ... that this past Saturday [January 15] he heard his good friend Haydn and other good friends play the 6 quartets that he sold to Artaria for 100 ducats.' Unfortunately, the '10 lines' have been lost, and it is questionable as to whether all six quartets were really played on that day. The last one, K. 465, was only just finished on January 14, 1785.

RS What were his most important objections?

WL Again and again it was the pauses and the fermatas, they weren't long enough and differentiated enough for him. And then he was concerned about our intonation in connection with the quarter tones.

RS Did he have a precise idea about how they should sound?

WL Certainly, and in Vaduz we worked a lot on these quarter tones and high registers so that the intonation would not be 'clean,' that is, there weren't to be any 'pure' intervals, they were all to be intentionally imperfect, edgy, irritating. We had difficulty with that, because these deviations in intonation were also still new to us, even though Ligeti had asked for something similar in his second quartet. And for neither composer are they really precisely quarter tones, something that Ligeti at least acknowledged in his instructions in the score, which Nono did not. How big were these departures from pure intonation to be?

And paired with big changes in register, and therefore in the left hand position, and in the extreme registers, having to play not quite pure double stops in the highest register of the violins, where the notes lie very close together anyway, that's very difficult. You can't use vibrato, if you do, the vibrato overrides the quarter tones. It was all technically very demanding and we had to work hard at it, since we had always worked to achieve the opposite, to maintain the purity of our intonation when making big changes in register, in the left hand position.

RS Was he satisfied with your interpretation in the end?

WL We made the recording with Deutsche Grammophon in December, 1983, and Nono was present at the sessions. He was satisfied with the recording to some extent, otherwise he wouldn't have approved its release.

RS I don't believe you've taught Nono's quartet very often. What are the most common problems with teaching it? Are the pauses and fermatas the stumbling block once again?

WL Yes, but there are also problems with the rhythms, with ensemble, and with playing the right notes. There are some places that are rhythmically difficult, everything is written out, this is not an aleatoric piece. There are a great many difficulties in the piece, at every level, including technique, for instance *ricochets*, *col legno*, *gettato*, but then also sound color and dynamics.

RS After the premiere you played the piece regularly, with very few pauses, between June, 1980, and January, 1986, 33 times in all.

WL Really? I wouldn't have thought that possible, I would have said a dozen times. But people were interested in it because of the controversy as to whether it was a reactionary piece by Nono. This controversy called attention to the piece and people asked us to play it, we even played it twice at La Scala! But it was quite a while before other quartets performed it. The Diotima Quartet in Paris learned it in the late 1990s, and also the Pellegrini Quartet, and then the Arditti Quartet. There's even a film about the Nono quartet with them. It gradually became an epochal piece, as a result of which younger quartets also took an interest in it, since you can become famous for being able to play such a difficult piece. Just like Ligeti's second quartet, which has also become a repertory piece by now.

RS Did your interpretation of the piece continue to change in the course of these six years?

WL No, hardly at all, no more than our interpretation of the Beethoven quartets, which also didn't noticeably change. Of course every piece changes: as you become more familiar with it you can devote yourself to different aspects of it. It probably sounded better after a while. We were able to realize it without too much trouble, or without having to concentrate so much on the details of execution, for instance, on ensemble, so we could concentrate instead on how we were performing it.

Franco Evangelisti

RS You once said that the commissioned works didn't always match your expectations.

WL Yes, that's right. But we very quickly gave up on having such expectations. We could rely on the composers we commissioned only insofar as we knew them personally and knew some of their pieces, the ones we had heard. But that wasn't enough by a long shot to form an idea of what somebody would come up with if he were to write a string quartet: it could be a bolt from the blue! I prefer quartets that already exist, but in order to get new quartets, you first of all have to order them.

RS But quartets were sometimes written for you unbidden: for instance the Greek composer Anestis Logothetis[14] wrote a piece for the LaSalle Quartet in 1964 with the title *Osculationen*. Evidently that was a purely graphical score?

WL Yes, it was, and we didn't play it either. We weren't such imaginative interpreters as to be able to do justice to music that isn't written out. We plainly and simply didn't have the gift for that. There are people who find such graphical scores enormously challenging, but we didn't, quite the contrary. The furthest we went in this direction was Franco Evangelisti's *Aleatorio*.[15] It's a commissioned work that we asked him for after we met him in Darmstadt.

What Evangelisti tried to do in *Aleatorio* was to create a work in which the players are to a certain extent drawn into the composition process. It's a short piece in three parts, for which there is a stock of instructions in which Evangelisti suggests some basic material but by and large leaves open what's to be done with it.[16] There are the most

[14] Anestis Logothetis (1921–1994) studied mechanical engineering in Vienna at the Technical Institute and composition at the Academy of Music. After further studies in Rome and Darmstadt he worked in the electronic music studio in Cologne. Until 1959 he composed twelve-tone pieces, notated conventionally. Later he favored graphical methods for more fluid forms. These works allow for great freedom in the choice of instruments as well as all the other parameters of music and often are fascinating visual works of art.

[15] Franco Evangelisti (1926–1980) studied in Rome and Freiburg and worked in the electronic music studios in Rome, Cologne, Warsaw, and Gravesano. He later taught composition at the Casella Conservatory and at the National Academy of Santa Cecilia in Rome. He lectured widely abroad and wrote many articles. A major theoretical treatise remained unfinished at his death. He organized a number of festivals of new music, in particular in Italy, and founded the Gruppo d'Improvvisazione di Nuovo Consonanza (the New Consonances Improvisation Group) in 1964. *Aleatorio* was composed in 1959 and premiered by the LaSalle Quartet under the auspices of the Darmstadt Summer Courses for New Music on July 14, 1962, in Kranichstein. Also on the program were Herbert Brün's third string quartet, Henri Pousser's *Ode pour Quatuor*, and the premiere of Penderecki's 1960 string quartet.

[16] In the introduction to *Aleatorio*, which can be regarded as the 'rules of the game' for the piece, Evangelisti writes: '*Aleatorio* is a synthesis of the sounds that are possible with stringed instruments. It consists of three parts, α, β, and γ; α and γ each are four bars long, β is eight. Each of these parts is characterized by typical ways of playing the stringed instruments. α uses the traditional tone colors (bowed) and so it has the most traditional character. β offers the widest range of possibilities for changing and combining dynamics, tempi, expression, and tone color. γ, the third part, principally uses noises: *col legno*, *sul ponticello*, knocking on the body of the instrument, Bartók pizzicato, etc. In performance *Aleatorio* may be repeated, on the condition that the character of the parts has been fundamentally changed, so that a constant change in tempo, tone color, and intensity results. For the performance of *Aleatorio* it is important that the players agree as to the character of each part, the sequence in which the parts are to be played, and the tempi. These decisions are to

various signs: *cambio metronomo*, that is, 'change tempo,' or *cambio intensità*, 'change intensity,' and a sign indicating that you can make a pause. All these suggestions can be followed or not, but you can only follow them where they're given. The order of the three parts can also be exchanged, but in no case can the order of the bars within a part be permuted. The result of these performance instructions is that something completely different comes out when two different ensembles take the same material and assemble a piece from it.

RS But did Evangelisti have an idea about how the piece should sound?

WL Only a very general idea, which he often expressed negatively: he knew exactly what it shouldn't sound like. We once tried to make something of his instructions that would sound as much as possible like '*Hänschen klein*' – it's the same tune as the song 'Lightly Row' in English, I believe. We did this precisely because it was the sort of possibility that he wanted to preclude. When we played it for him, he nearly fell off his chair, for it proved to him that his instructions weren't nearly thorough enough to make such a thing impossible.

RS Was he mostly concerned with sounds, timbres, sonorities?

WL With timbral and rhythmic aspects of the piece and with avoiding what Webern also sought to avoid in the *Bagatelles*, Opus 9: any kind of repetition, always different sounds, not only among the different instruments but also among the different distorted sounds within each instrument. Webern attempted something similar in his unpublished *Bagatelle* with voice,[17] nothing but noises and a *Sprechstimme* with single syllables, really very strange. And that's the direction that music subsequently took. Composers no longer wanted anything that sounded beautiful or romantic or was even only reminiscent of what had been acceptable in the music of the period they had just overcome. These composers really did intend to finally make 'degenerate music.'

RS How is *Aleatorio* notated?

be made jointly prior to the performance: they are not to be left to the judgment of the individual players. Many versions are possible, but nevertheless no more than two are to be played on any given concert, and none is to last longer than at most five minutes. They may be separated by a pause. The composer recommends that the players write out in score each of the versions they have worked out.'

17 The LaSalle Quartet played Webern's *Bagatelle* for string quartet and soprano with Bethany Beardslee at the Ravinia Festival on July 12, 1972.

WL Evangelisti writes notes, but with many instructions as to what is to be done with them. He wants the players to make up their parts out of the instructions and the predefined bars, newly reassembled every time. You can, for instance, play them in a different sequence, you can use every imaginable kind of tone production and rhythm, even tempo. But if at some point he indicates a change of tempo, it's up to you to decide what new tempo to take. So he gives you as raw material notes that you can arrange differently from bar to bar and thereby can vary beyond recognition. For instance, you might take as a basic idea that it should be rhythmically very simple and sound like a Viennese waltz. Or just the opposite: that you do something really outrageous: no conventional sounds, nothing but noises. So you have to construct a new piece every time, cobbling the materials together according to the instructions and then seeing what comes of that when the four parts are put together. Totally different sonorities can result from that.

RS Did you yourself do this for all four parts?

WL No, we worked on it together. Each of us made proposals not only for his own part but also for the others and for the overall idea. It was so to speak a matter of composing as a quartet. We spent many hours finding out what we could make of it, and rehearsing the results. Then each of us worked out his own part, and finally we came up with two versions that we kept. Evangelisti was always inventing new systems to guide the players in assembling a piece. And *Aleatorio* is an instance of this.

RS Was he in agreement with your versions?

WL He didn't have any choice. We often played the two very contrasting versions one after the other. And he found that very beautiful. A radio broadcast recording of our two versions was included in the CD set of Evangelisti's complete works.

RS Evangelisti's concept of aleatorics, of chance, is very different from what you find in Lutosławski, Cage, and Earle Brown.

WL Evangelisti was concerned with the relationship between a clearly defined system of thought with rules, referential systems, and structures on the one hand, and the immediacy of improvisation on the other.

RS What did composers like Evangelisti and Earle Brown have in mind in stepping back as authors in favor of so to speak giving precedence to the interpreters?

WL But they did that only up to a certain point. They wanted to draw the players back into the process of shaping a piece, as was the case in the baroque. At that time there was much less of a distinction between composer and performer than there was after the 18th century, when the composer wrote the piece. In the 18th century composer and performer were still often one and the same person: Mozart played his own piano concertos and violin concertos. But the two roles became separated with the advent of the virtuoso literature. Already Beethoven no longer performed his quartets with colleagues who were themselves composers, as had still been the case with Mozart, but rather needed professional quartets to play them.

A few years later on in the 19th century composition got to be so complicated that the two branches of the profession separated. Okay, Schumann still played his own piano pieces, and Brahms also, and Louis Spohr performed his own quartets, which in any case weren't exactly top notch. But after the Schuppanzigh Quartet, which was the first really professional quartet in Europe, professional quartets didn't play quartets that they themselves had composed. Brahms didn't play his own quartets, he left that to his friend Joachim, with whom he also corresponded about the performance of his works. This separation of the professions also had negative consequences in that the interpreters no longer knew exactly what the composer had in mind, and sometimes weren't remotely interested in taking the trouble to find out. Evangelisti and others wanted to restore to some extent the influence of the interpreters.

RS But not as a conscious return to pre-classical music?

WL Not a conscious return to the style, rather a conscious return to the practice of involving the interpreters more, instead of just writing instructions for them. It was a reaction against the overly detailed instructions in the music of the Second Viennese School. In Berg's *Lyric Suite* there are so many instructions regarding dynamics, emphases, and phrasing in every bar that you often can't see the music for all the words and lengthy instructions.

RS Or Bartók, who prescribes the length of a piece down to the second.

WL Exactly, that's another example. But composers had put not only interpreters in a strait jacket of instructions but also themselves, as in the 1950s, the high tide of serial music, when composers were pursuing the ideal of an autonomous work of art. They wanted to replace the subjective decisions that they otherwise had to make at every step in the compositional process with ever more complex systems of rules that were to regulate the decisions and justify them. In that the music so to speak composed itself by means of an external mechanism, they hoped to escape the curse of subjectivity. Of course that meant there was scarcely any freedom left over for the composer's own decisions: he held fast to his self-imposed rules, and that very quickly got to be overly restrictive.

And then when John Cage came to Darmstadt for the first time in 1958 these composers made the horrifying discovery that compositions resulting from such fixed systems of rules very much resembled those that were absolutely arbitrary creations of chance. So it seemed necessary to break out of these self-imposed restrictions again. Evangelisti's *Aleatorio* as well as the quartets by Earle Brown and Lutosławski are the result of this new awareness.

Mauricio Kagel

RS Mauricio Kagel[18] was another acquaintance from Darmstadt from whom you wanted a quartet. I listened to the recording of the Cincinnati performance: the audience was laughing out loud. What was happening on-stage?

WL It's a piece of instrumental theater, as is so often the case with Kagel, and for the most part very critical and sarcastic, satirical and witty. On top of which it's a parody of the LaSalle Quartet, tailor-made to fit each of the quartet's four members. It begins with our somewhat phlegmatic but generally good-natured cellist, Jack Kirstein, coming on stage by himself with his instrument. He walks over to his chair, stands leaning on the back of it for a moment, then walks slowly around the other chairs and leans on the back of the first violin's chair, glances at something in the wings, sits down cautiously, and looks at the first violin's music. It's a very clear indication that he would like to lead the quartet himself once, but then he thinks to himself that maybe that wouldn't be such a good idea after all.

That's a wonderful way to start a quartet. And the audience begins to giggle. So the cellist walks back to his seat, sits down, and threads a

[18] Mauricio Kagel (1931–2008), born in Buenos Aires of Russian Jewish parentage, where he studied music, history of literature, and philosophy. Kagel lived most of his adult life in Cologne, though he taught at the State University of New York at Buffalo 1964–1965. A film maker as well as a composer, he was best known for his music-theater pieces, and for his extensive use of the music of previous composers, e.g., Beethoven, Mahler, in his own compositions.

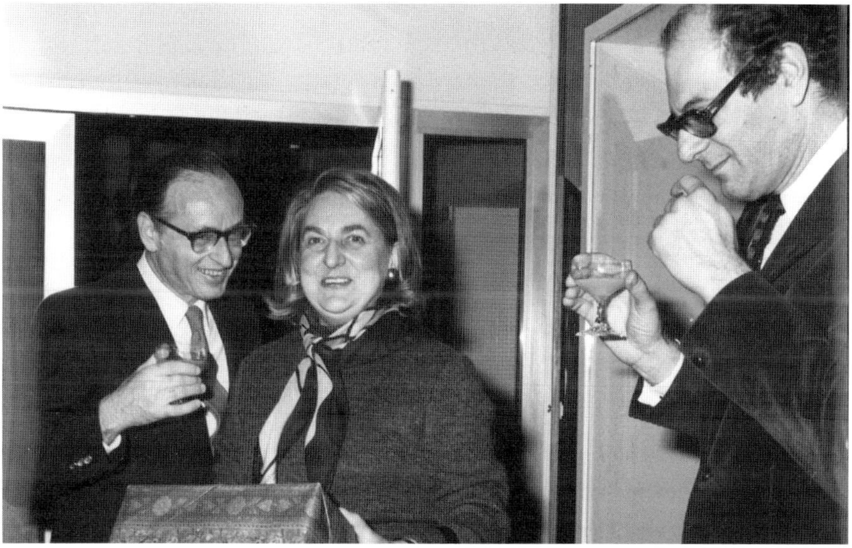

42 Walter Levin, Dorothee Koehler (Deutsche Grammophon), and Mauricio Kagel, Hamburg, February, 1974

knitting needle between the strings of his cello, peers at his music, and plucks at the knitting needle with an absolutely idiotic expression on his face. Really crazy! In the course of the piece Henry Meyer plays a wonderful *cantilena*, but I take out a towel and cover his hands and fingers and violin with it, because I don't want to listen to the *cantilena*, but he goes right on playing it anyway. Then I myself put on some elegant kid gloves and begin playing with them on. Nothing but such scurrilous inventions. The audience was rolling on the floor with laughter, because you wouldn't expect any such thing from the LaSalle Quartet, which was after all a rather buttoned-down, earnest group, that played serious music. And all of sudden we were doing theater!

RS Were the stage directions and blocking written in the score?

WL Yes, completely, and very precisely. Which is why it's so difficult to perform this piece in different places. For instance, Henry and I have to start playing backstage, that is, without the audience being able to see us, and then the way we make our entrance on stage is very precisely described, step by step. So everything has to be staged and then thoroughly rehearsed: very difficult.

RS So you didn't play it very often?

WL No, it was too difficult.

RS What did the score look like, since it was a piece of instrumental theater?

WL There are of course many verbal instructions, but also ordinary music, which you also have to play. But the stage directions are in the score: 'Puts a kid glove on the left hand' or 'Takes a hand towel and throws it over the violin of the second violinist.' And you have to use different bows, that's also explained at the front of the score.

RS You once said that you needed a whole tool chest in order to play the piece. Were all the tools in it defined?

WL Yes, and we had to have them custom made. For example, a toothed rod that would make a noise when you drew it across the strings. But it couldn't be so sharply toothed that it would cut the strings, that wasn't what was intended. So we had a whole chest of tools for producing the required noises, and there was a catalog of such tools that the player had to bring with him. In new works like this there's usually a prefatory list of instructions, requirements, and remarks, often quite a lengthy one, and in which there's a lot about notation, since the composer has to invent new signs for the new effects, and you have to learn what they are and what they mean. But there are such lists already with Schoenberg also: at the head of the score he defined what he meant by *Hauptstimme* or how he conceived of dynamic nuances, that is, everything that seemed important to him in rendering the piece in performance. Such lists of instructions and requirements grew longer and longer as music developed, and you have to pay close attention to them. Sometimes it's so difficult that you have to learn two whole pages of instructions when you begin to learn a new piece. And you have to really digest them thoroughly, so that you're not having to constantly refer back to them in order to play the piece.

RS Was the Kagel quartet especially difficult for you to learn, or was it for all that a players' piece?

WL It was something completely new to us, because it's a theater piece, and, for example, we had to learn to play while walking.

RS Kagel composed the quartet 1965–1967, but you didn't play it the first time until 1974.

WL That was because he'd given the premiere to another quartet. You just can't do that with a commissioned work for which you've been paid! We were very offended by that and afterwards let some time pass before we played it ourselves. And then he was very anxious that we record his quartet for Deutsche Grammophon. But after we'd played it a few times, I told Rainer Brock, our producer at Deutsche Grammophon, that an audio recording of the piece made no sense, that without the visual component no one could understand the piece, and that from a purely acoustical standpoint the piece isn't convincing. What's decisive, as is often the case with Kagel, is the combination of sight and sound, which is also very witty. You would have to make a video recording of it, but at that time there weren't any videos and video disks as yet, which would, of course, have been ideal for it. Kagel didn't want to hear about that and was so offended that for many years afterward he didn't speak to us at all. But later on our relationship improved somewhat.

RS So you didn't rehearse the quartet with him.

WL No, we gave our first performance in Cincinnati without him, and then only played the first part. He hadn't yet sent us the second part, which we only got much later: it's much less theatrical and as a quartet is much more traditional than the first part. He was in the audience when we subsequently played it in Hamburg and in Frankfurt. I do believe he was satisfied with our performance.

Gottfried Michael Koenig

RS Another acquaintance from Darmstadt who you asked to write a quartet was Gottfried Michael Koenig.[19] The piece he wrote for you in 1959 is the very first commissioned work you premiered.[20] Koenig was one of the most prominent theoreticians of serial music. How was his quartet composed?

WL It's constructed as a strict serial piece, that is, pitches, durations, and tone color are all conceived as functions of time: in this sense Koenig serialized all the parameters of music. But the compositional process is aleatoric, that is, the values of the serialized parameters have been selected by chance, indeed by means of a computer program. So he

[19] Gottfried Michael Koenig (1926–) studied music in Braunschweig, Detmold, and Cologne, where he subsequently worked with composers Mauricio Kagel, Franco Evangelisti, György Ligeti, Herbert Brün, and Karlheinz Stockhausen in the WDR electronic music studio. A pioneer not only in electronic music but also in computer-assisted composition, Koenig was from early on an important essayist and theoretician of the Darmstadt avant-garde and a contributor to its 'house' organ, the famous periodical *Die Reihe*. He has taught at the University of Utrecht since 1964 and was director of the electronic music studio there until 1986.

[20] The LaSalle Quartet premiered the work on April 5, 1960, in Cincinnati.

doesn't leave these choices up to the interpreters: the piece is fully composed and notated completely traditionally.

RS How a piece is made is one thing, how it works is another. What do you think of the piece now?

WL When I listen to it now, I find it a particularly attractive, many-sided, and very successfully composed piece.

RS But what was your opinion of it at the time you premiered it?

WL At that time I very rarely allowed myself to judge new pieces. To begin with you're so caught up in learning such a piece and performing it that you hardly ever have enough distance to judge it so to speak as an outsider would. You only hear what you haven't succeeded in bringing off. For example, it was a long time before I could listen to the third and fourth Schoenberg quartets as an outsider. It was like that with the second Carter quartet also, until years later I heard it again and asked myself how I could ever have had a problem with it: today I think it's a terrific piece!

RS But you didn't play Koenig's quartet very often, altogether only four times.

WL Unfortunately, concert organizers were only rarely interested in it. We played it in Munich and in Cologne and then also recorded it in Cologne. Our recording is included in the CD set of Koenig's chamber music.

RS Do you know the second quartet that Koenig composed in 1987?

WL No, but I would be very interested in hearing it, and also in knowing whether there is a recording of it available.[21]

RS Did you have much contact with Koenig at the time?

WL Certainly, he also came to our concerts. I once had an argument with him too: he asked why we wasted so much time playing Mozart and other such old-fashioned music. Was it just so we could appear at the

[21] The quartet was premiered by the Arditti Quartet on June 24, 1988, in Pontinia, Italy; there is no recording available (as of August 2013). For a review of both quartets see Konrad Boehmer, '*Doppelter Ausbruch: über die Streichquartette 1959 und 1987 von Gottfried Michael Koenig*' in Schott's *Neue Zeitschrift für Musik* for March-April, 2006, pp. 29–31.

chamber music society concerts where there are nothing but old people in attendance? Were we museum curators? He told us to just play new music, we were wonderful at it. What he wanted was a quartet like what the Arditti is today. I thought his position was rather doctrinaire.

Henri Pousseur

RS Yet another commission from the Darmstadt circle was Henri Pousseur's quartet *Ode pour Quatuor*.[22] Reading the reviews in the newspapers, the piece must have encountered a lot of resistance at the time.[23]

WL It was certainly the most problematic commission for a quartet we ever made. At first we got only a part of it, consisting of periods repeatedly interrupted by pauses. The first part was quite long, but Pousseur wrote to tell us that there would be yet another, second part. When it arrived, it turned out to be not much different from the first part. In any case the impression that this piece, which does after all last twenty minutes, makes on the audience is simply one of paralysis. It's also the only piece that caused an audience uproar when we performed it in Paris at Boulez' Domaine Musical.

RS One of the critics came up with the pun '*Die Öde von Pousseur*,' Pousseur's 'Wasteland.'

WL That's a good one! But not unjustified, after a while the work is exhausting: you already know what's happening next, and then it happens again, replete with pauses. But it's the only piece that we ever had such a flop with. Even so, we didn't simply drop it, but all the same we no longer felt much like playing it again.

RS Apparently Pousseur was a gifted speaker.

WL Indeed, and he was also fluent in German and English. He was a very intelligent man and also a very good teacher: he was always able to get jobs as a lecturer, also in Buffalo, in upstate New York, at

[22] Belgian composer Henri Pousseur (1929–2009) was associated with the 'Darmstadt School' in the 1950s, in particular with Pierre Boulez, Karlheinz Stockhausen, and Luciano Berio. His music employs seemingly opposing tendencies such as serialism and aleatorics and embraces and mediates disparate historical styles, often within the same piece, as in his best known work, the opera *Votre Faust*.

[23] The LaSalle Quartet premiered Pousseur's *Ode pour Quatuor* on July 14, 1962, at Kranichstein (Darmstadt).

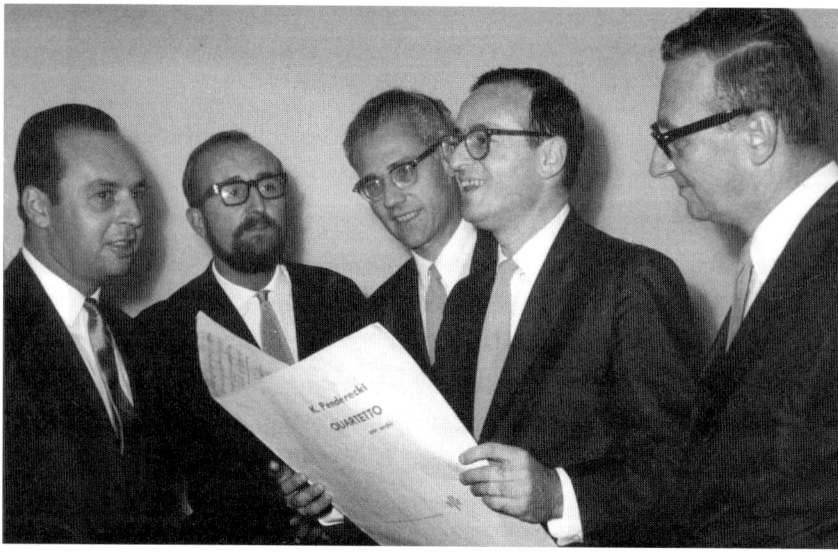

43 The LaSalle Quartet with Krzysztof Penderecki, Warsaw, 1962

the university, which was a real center for new music in those days. He once gave a lecture there on Webern, at the end of which we played the *Five Pieces* Opus 5, the *Bagatelles* Opus 9, and the quartet Opus 28.

Krzysztof Penderecki

RS You didn't meet Krzysztof Penderecki[24] in Darmstadt but rather in Vienna. What was the occasion?

WL In June, 1961, I went to Vienna to hear a performance of Schoenberg's *Die Jakobsleiter*, the orchestration of which had been completed by Winfried Zillig.[25] While I was there I met Jozef Patkowski,[26] the director of the experimental music studio in Warsaw whom I'd met through Herbert Brün. Patkowski was there with a young composer: Krzysztof Penderecki. Patkowski told me Penderecki had just written a string quartet

[24] Krzysztof Penderecki (1933–) studied at the Kraków Academy of Music and later taught there as well. His 1960 *8'37"* for 52 stringed instruments employed numerous extended instrumental techniques; the work secured him an international reputation after it was retitled *Threnody to the Victims of Hiroshima*.

[25] On June 16, with the Cologne Radio Symphony Orchestra under Rafael Kubelik.

[26] Jozef Patkowski (1929–2005) studied music, musicology, and physics before founding the Polish Radio's Experimental Studio in 1957; he was its director until 1985.

that no one wanted to play,[27] and asked me if I would have a look at it. The following day we went out together for coffee and I looked at the quartet, which Penderecki had brought with him.

RS Why didn't anyone want to play it?

WL Because his quartet avoids almost everything that at the time was held to be the proper sound of a string quartet. He used a continuum from noise to precisely established pitches. Whole sections consist of practically nothing but very high notes that are not precisely defined, and overall there is in this piece a certain element of freedom not only with regard to pitches but also to rhythm. There's scarcely a single normal string tone, rather almost exclusively distorted sounds and noises. At the time that Penderecki composed the quartet, these characteristics were so shocking for most string players that it wasn't performed for quite some time. Also, as he explained to us, in his piece you have to thump and hit the bodies of the instruments, which led to loud protests from the musicians, who objected that they couldn't be expected to go thumping and beating on their precious Stradivarius instruments. We didn't have that problem, because we didn't have any Stradivarius instruments, besides which doing that sort of thing didn't bother us. So we told him we would be very interested in playing his quartet.[28]

RS What was Penderecki's main idea in composing his quartet?

WL As a reaction to the traditional 'beautiful sound' he wanted to use only noise. So there are many struck, percussive sounds, and various techniques of producing them, for which he had to invent a new notation, since prior to his quartet there had been no such sounds on stringed instruments. As soon as sounds appear in a new piece that hadn't existed before, every composer has to invent a new notation for them, and then the interpreters have to deal with that.

RS But there are still musical staffs and notes and traditional dynamic markings in Penderecki's quartet?

WL Certainly, it's otherwise still relatively 'normally' notated, as there are also 'normal' sounds present.

27 The quartet was composed in 1960.

28 The quartet was premiered by the LaSalle Quartet at Darmstadt on July 14, 1962, in Kranichstein. Also on the program were Herbert Brün's third string quartet, Henri Pousseur's *Ode pour Quatuor*, and the premiere of Evangelisti's 1959 *Aleatorio*.

RS Were Penderecki's instructions regarding his notation sufficient, or did he have to expand on them after you had rehearsed the piece?

WL No, they were clear enough for us. After all, there were two pages of instructions at the head of the score.

RS But every new notation creates a problem of passing the meaning along to future generations, since if there's a gap in the generations the performance tradition is lost.

WL That's why there are these instructions at the head of the score, we didn't have any more than that to go on either.

RS But you could ask Penderecki what he meant.

WL Yes, of course, but we learned the piece first without him and only played it for him shortly before the premiere. But you're right, scores must be self-explanatory, otherwise they can't convey the composer's ideas and intentions.

RS Evidently you really enjoyed playing Penderecki's quartet, as there was an almost uninterrupted series of 41 performances over a ten-year interval.

WL It's an entertaining piece, sonically and rhythmically interesting, on top of which it's short: it only lasts about seven minutes. And once you've learned it, it's not difficult, so it's well-suited to be an active repertory piece.

RS Later, in 1968, Penderecki wrote another string quartet.

WL But we never played that one. Penderecki soon took a turn to being a commercial composer, in my opinion. It was quite obvious that he'd found a formula for himself. But in Warsaw at that time he was a bright young man and fun to be around, and we got along very well with him.

Giuseppe Englert

RS You surely read that Giuseppe Englert[29] died recently?

[29] Giuseppe G. Englert (1927–2007) studied organ and composition at the Zurich Conservatory. At Darmstadt since 1955, he taught composition, improvisation, and electro-acoustic and musical computer sciences at the Université de Paris VIII (Vincennes) 1970–1992. Englert's concert tours in Europe, Israel, and America often featured live electronics as well as more conventionally composed works.

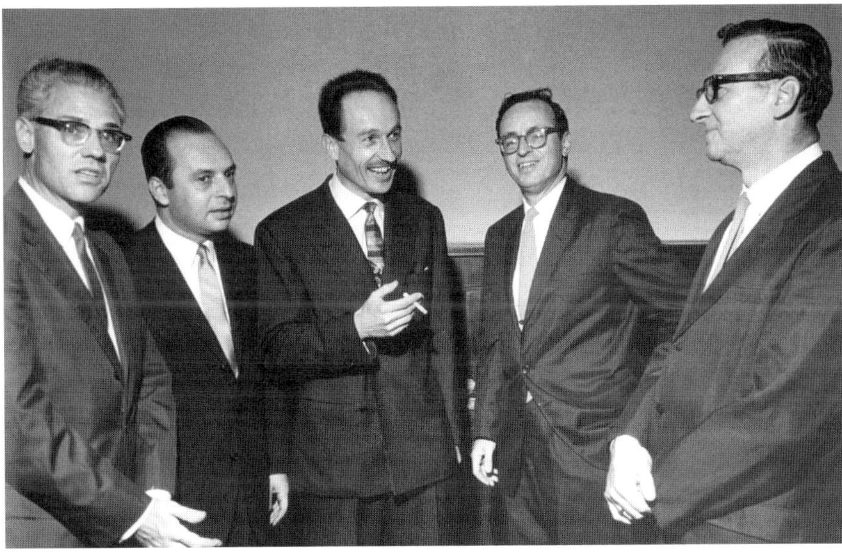

44 The LaSalle Quartet with Giuseppe Englert, Warsaw, 1962

WL Yes. He was a good friend. He wrote two quartets for us, the first one in 1962–1963, *Les Avoines folles*,[30] the second in 1965–1966, *La Joute des Lierres*.[31]

RS Where did you first get to know Englert?

WL He was another composer whom we met at Darmstadt, early on, in the mid-1950s. He was there for the first time in 1955.

RS After composing the two quartets he changed direction and turned to computer music. In this sense the quartets are so to speak early works.

WL Yes, but they're very good pieces. And he was already making some use of the computer in composing them.

[30] The title *Les Avoines folles* (*Wild Oats*) is taken from the poem *'Colloque Sentimental'* by Paul Verlaine (1844–1896). The work was premiered by the LaSalle Quartet on October 13, 1964, in Cincinnati.

[31] *La Joute des Lierres* was inspired by Ghelderode's novel *Le Jardin Malade*, in which 'the ivy, wisteria, pristine vineyards fight a battle of octopuses, smothering shrubs and hustling walls.' According to Englert the quartet is a triple fugue; the 'joust' perhaps alludes to the fugue's intertwining and conflicting themes. Ghelderode was the *nom de plume* of the Belgian writer Adémar Adolphe-Louis Martens (1898–1962) whose works are considered theater of the absurd. His best known work is *La Balade du grand Macabre*, on which Ligeti based his opera *Le Grand Macabre*. *La Joute des Lierres* was premiered by the LaSalle Quartet on May 11, 1971, in Cincinnati.

RS Even then?

WL Yes, at that time he used a computer to work out his tone-rows. He was strongly oriented to mathematics, he found mathematical methods very attractive, and there are strict and therefore programmable mathematical concepts for the kinds of combinations and permutations of tone-rows that characterize twelve-tone composition. You very quickly get in over your head if you try to work out all the permutations and combinations by hand, all the possibilities that are implicit in a given tone-row. So he developed a systematic approach that derived a wide range of possibilities from the basic materials but didn't force him to spend years calculating everything. He had the computer make the calculations, but the fundamental structures were his own. So the result was a combination of composing in the classical sense on the one hand, in which the composer invents the materials of the piece himself, and on the other hand a working out of the permutations of these materials with the help of a computer.

RS Evidently he was most interested in the unforeseen results of this procedure: that is, as he himself said, he was interested in getting to results that surprised him, even though he knew how they were produced. These surprises made him happy, which is why the headline of his obituary was so appropriate: 'The joy of something never heard before.'[32]

WL Indeed, much like what Evangelisti was after later on. But I don't believe Englert went as far as Evangelisti, and certainly not in his quartets, he didn't allow the interpreters the freedom to decide what they would play. Also, Englert didn't write any aleatoric music, that is, music that doesn't specify exactly what is to happen but the course of which is to be decided by the performers with the help of certain instructions. Evangelisti did that in *Aleatorio*, which in this respect is a ground-breaking piece. But that's not the case with Englert. The two quartets are also notated conventionally. He used his unexpected results in order to be surprised by what could be composed with his materials, and then wrote them out.

RS In his quartets Englert refers to texts by Verlaine and by the Belgian poet Ghelderode. Did you ever ask what significance these references had for him?

WL No, we never talked about that. Evidently they were a kind of impetus for him in writing the quartets, and something about them inspired him, but I don't know what it was.

[32] *Neue Zürcher Zeitung*, March 31, 2007.

RS You premiered Englert's first quartet in 1964, a year after he finished composing it, but you didn't play his second quartet until 1971, five years after its composition.

WL That was because Englert did the same thing as Kagel: he let the Società Cameristica in Rome play his second quartet before we did. After which we postponed our performance. The work was written for us and dedicated to us and then given to someone else to premiere, without even telling us about it. That wasn't right.

RS Diplomats might call that an 'unfriendly act.'

WL Exactly. It was completely uncalled for, we liked him a lot, he was a close friend. And he knew it wasn't right, what he was doing.

Pierre Boulez and Karlheinz Stockhausen

RS Pierre Boulez[33] and Karlheinz Stockhausen[34] are two of the most prominent representatives of Darmstadt, but you didn't commission a quartet from either of them.

WL No, we didn't. Boulez had already written a quartet, the *Livre pour Quatuor*, in 1948, but he didn't want us to play it and wouldn't give us the music.[35]

RS Why not?

[33] Pierre Boulez (1925–) achieved early notoriety for his slogan 'Schoenberg is dead' but went on to become one of the most important composers, conductors, and musical institution builders of the later 20th and early 21st centuries, beginning with his leading role in the formation of what Luigi Nono dubbed 'the Darmstadt school' of serialism in the 1950s, as exemplified by his 1953–1955 *Le marteau sans maitre*.

[34] The music of Karlheinz Stockhausen (1928–2007), perhaps Darmstadt's most prominent theoretician, ranges from his early work in the electronic music studio in Cologne through the serialism of his famous Klavierstücke to the later mixed media operas, from one of which, *Mittwoch aus Licht* he drew his rather infamous 'Helicopter Quartet' for string quartet and four helicopters, one for each member of the ensemble. It was premiered at the Holland Festival 1996 by the Arditti Quartet in helicopters of the Royal Netherlands Air force.

[35] The *Livre pour Quatuor* has never been performed in its entirety. It was given partial premieres by the Marschner Quartet in 1955 (parts I and II), by the Parrenin Quartet in 1961 (parts V and VI) and 1962 (part III). The Arditti Quartet gave an 'almost complete' performance in 1985 (parts I–III and V–VI). In 1968 Boulez transcribed part I for string orchestra as *Livre pour cordes;* Boulez conducted the premiere in 1989. A 1999 live recording with the Chicago Symphony Orchestra conducted by Boulez was released in volume 19 of the orchestra's 'From the Archives' series.

WL He didn't like the piece. He felt that he would have to rework it once again. And he did, he rewrote it for chamber orchestra. It was only after he had thoroughly reworked it to match his new conception that he allowed quartets to play it as such.

RS And later on he didn't want to write another quartet?

WL No, the string quartet was too conventional for him. It wasn't clear to him how he could deal with this form, which is so burdened with tradition, without being untrue either to himself or to the tradition, which really does presuppose a certain format. An interesting problem, but one that I believe ultimately didn't interest him.

Composers at that time were interested in new sounds and unconventional instruments like percussion, in percussive sounds generally, and prepared piano. But they had not yet gotten as far as prepared quartet. Lachenmann is doing that now, but back then it would have been going too far, though Karlheinz Stockhausen actually was already interested in it. We spoke with him often about a string quartet commission, and in principle he was interested in writing a piece for us. But he kept asking us whether we would be willing to use different gongs as well as our regular instruments. He wanted to distort the sonority of the quartet through the use of other instruments, in this case gongs, really big gongs, that would have to be custom built for us in order to produce the sounds he had in mind. I remember a conversation that I had with him somewhere in America in which I asked how we were supposed to take big gongs with us on tour when they sometimes wouldn't even let us take our violins and cello on board the plane with us. But that didn't interest him.

RS As Beethoven once said, what do I care about your miserable fiddle when the spirit moves me?

WL Exactly. What do I care about your tours. I have a specific idea as to how the piece I want to write should sound, and for that I need gongs. But he never followed through on this idea, but rather, much later, wrote a helicopter quartet, for which other noises are present instead of gongs. But ultimately Stockhausen's ideas weren't in line with our general direction as a quartet.

RS But you did invite both Boulez and Stockhausen to Cincinnati?

WL Certainly, because the people in our Sunday Group, for whom we always previewed the new quartets, wanted to know what the avant-garde music of the Darmstadt composers was like and how it differed from the works we'd already introduced them to. So we invited Boulez and Stockhausen to give lectures about their new music and to play recorded examples of it. That was in the late 1950s and early 1960s, when they weren't yet so famous.

Stockhausen was also eager to visit the University of Cincinnati neurology department, because his mother, who had been diagnosed as depressed, had been killed by the Nazis in 1941 in the course of their euthanasia campaign against the mentally ill and the terminally ill. Maurice Levine, James Levine's uncle, was not only a great supporter of the LaSalle Quartet but also the director of the neurology department and Stockhausen wanted to learn something about euthanasia. Maurice Levine didn't only educate his psychiatry students as specialists but wanted to give their knowledge a broad horizon, to which end he invited people from other disciplines to lecture his students in a Friday afternoon seminar that he called the 'Perhaps Seminar.' Stockhausen was invited to lecture at this seminar, as I was once also – I gave a talk on how I went about choosing a new work to play:[36] a nice little lecture on my 'Ten Commandments,' the criteria in accord with which I made my choices. 'Because I like it' is not one of the criteria!

Herbert Brün

RS We come to the composers who were close friends of yours: Herbert Brün,[37] Wolf Rosenberg, and Michael Gielen. Brün wrote three string quartets, and you played all of them. Were they all commissioned by you?

WL Not the first quartet, which he'd written in 1952, that is, before we were able, with the help of the Sunday Group, to make commissions. But the other two were commissioned by us, and we also premiered them.[38]

RS What were Brün's compositions like then? After he wrote the two quartets for you he turned to electronic music and music composed with the help of computers. Were his quartets still based on the ideas of the Schoenberg school?

36 The text of this lecture is given in Appendix VI.

37 For more about Herbert Brün see pp. 41–42.

38 The LaSalle Quartet played Herbert Brün's first quartet for the first time on June 21, 1954, during the ISCM Festival in Tel Aviv. The LaSalle Quartet premiered Herbert Brün's second quartet (composed 1957) on April 1, 1958, in Cincinnati, and his third quartet (composed 1961/62) on March 20, 1962, also in Cincinnati.

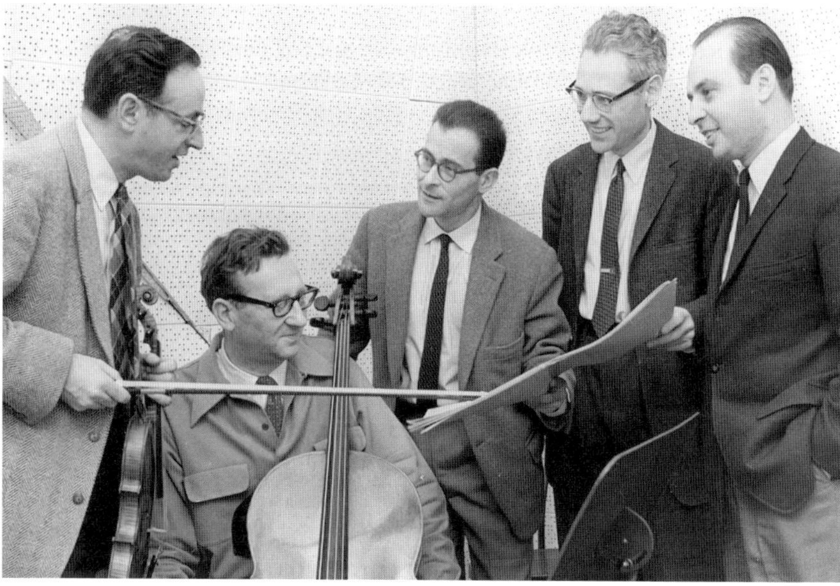

45 The LaSalle Quartet with Herbert Brün, Cincinnati, 1962

WL Yes, insofar as Herbert had studied with Stefan Wolpe, very much of the Schoenberg school,[39] but then Herbert had always also very much gone his own way, and there is a component of his compositions that is very different from most Schoenberg students: Herbert was a gifted jazz musician. In Palestine he had made his living as a pianist playing jazz with a string bass player and a drummer in the evenings in cafes, bars, and hotels. Even as a young man he had a genius for improvising at the piano, he was practically born with this ability.

This component of rhythm, of jazz, that comes from a completely different direction, always enters into his music and makes it sound completely different from pure twelve-tone music. Pierre Boulez recognized that immediately when we played Herbert's third quartet at his Domaine Musical in Paris,[40] and he didn't like it. He called it entertainment music. But I like Herbert's quartets a lot, and we played them a number of times. They're not to everyone's taste. They're first rate, but there's sometimes

[39] Levin rather exaggerates the Schoenberg school's influence on Wolpe. Though as a student Wolpe was taken with Schoenberg's atonal music, and later studied briefly with Webern in Vienna (1933–1934), the range of influences on this exceptionally polymathic composer included Busoni, the Weimar Bauhaus, Kurt Schwitters, and Hanns Eisler; Morton Feldman recalls Wolpe exhorting him to 'write for the man in the street,' scarcely a characteristic position of the Schoenberg school.

[40] The concert with Brün's third quartet at the Domaine Musical took place on February 13, 1963. On this occasion the *Ode pour Quatuor* by Henri Pousseur was also played, see p. 279.

a stubborn streak in the way he pursues a compositional idea, which I'm not always certain was so successful. There are some places in his pieces where there is a repetitiveness, and a style of music, that I don't like at all, but on the whole I like the pieces very much.

RS Was there a development from the first to the third quartet?

WL Yes, of course. He became much more an ascetic stylistically, he developed his own sense of twelve-tone music. But in and of itself twelve-tone or atonal music is no determinant of style: you can't compare Webern's Opus 28 with Berg's *Lyric Suite*, they're worlds apart. It would be like saying that someone wrote tonal music. What can that possibly mean? What's important is what can be done with this system. Even Schoenberg didn't strictly follow his twelve-tone system, and when people pointed that out to him he got very angry.

RS What was Brün like personally? You once read us a few letters from Wolf Rosenberg, who must have been an incredible wit. Was Brün that also?

WL He was much more strict. He wrote very precisely, also wittily, but in a very sharp albeit familiar style. He was also like one of the family, since my parents were close friends of his parents and the whole Brün family. Herbert knew me since the day I was born. We had made music together since I was six or seven years old.

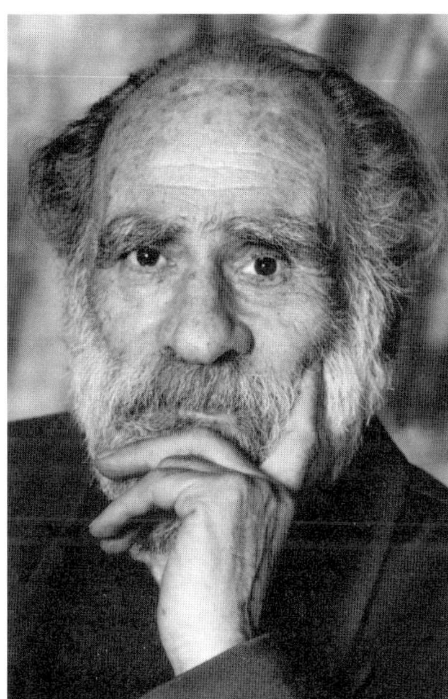

46 Wolf Rosenberg, 1993

Wolf Rosenberg

RS I've not been able to find out much about your life-long friend Wolf Rosenberg.

WL I'm not surprised. He's not someone anyone knows much about, either as a person or as a composer. In honor of Rosenberg's 70th birthday Paul Fiebig at SWF interviewed some of his closest friends and acquaintances, including myself, and eventually published them: that's where you'll find the most comprehensive appreciation of Rosenberg as a person, a human being, and a composer.[41] His wife, Pamela, became the Intendant of the Berlin Philharmonic.[42]

RS He was older than you, wasn't he?

WL Yes, Rosenberg was born in Dresden in 1915, so he was nine years older than me.[43] His parents were dead, he grew up in Dahlem with his grandfather, and also went to the Gymnasium there. From early on he was an opera fanatic, he went to the Staatsoper, and he knew the operas inside and out. But I only got to know him later, in Palestine, through Herbert Brün. Both of them were studying with Wolpe at the conservatory in Jerusalem. At that time I was 14 and he was 23, which at that age is a huge difference. When I went to New York after the war to go to Juilliard, Rosenberg went to Cyprus to play cocktail piano in a bar. He always made his living as cocktail pianist, also in Jerusalem. He was already a fanatical record collector: he had a huge collection of old 78 shellac recordings. My knowledge of opera and of Mahler comes from him. My first encounter with Mahler's *Lied von der Erde*, for instance, I owe to Rosenberg, the 1936 recording with the Vienna Philharmonic under Bruno Walter. Rosenberg was also a great expert on the art of singing and wrote a very interesting book on it: *Die Krise der Gesangskunst*,[44] *The Crisis in the Art of Singing*. He also made many broadcasts for SWF and other German radio stations.

RS Rosenberg's life and yours seem to have had much in common.

WL Yes, unbeknownst to us to begin, though we lived only five minutes away from one another, in Dahlem of all things, and we both went to the Staatsoper. Then we both emigrated to Palestine, which is where we met. There are such coincidences in life. How could it be that in Paris in December, 1945, I was at the same concert as Henry Meyer, almost three years before I first met him?

41 A transcription of the broadcast of January 20, 1985, by SWF in Baden-Baden, 'Wolf Rosenberg on his 70th Birthday' (with contributions by Wolf Rosenberg, Wolfgang Hildesheimer, William DeFotis, Hans G Helms, Uwe Schweikert, Herbert Brün, and Walter Levin, ed. Paul Fiebig) is to be found together with memorial contributions following Rosenberg's death by Nike Wagner, Gottfried Michael Koenig, Paul Fiebig, and Ulrich Dibelius, in *Fragmen* [sic], vol. 31, ed. by Helmuth Kreysing, Saarbrücken, 1999.

42 Pamela Rosenberg (born 1945) was the Intendantin of the Berlin Philharmonic 2006–2010.

43 Rosenberg was born in Dresden on January 17, 1915; he died in Frankfurt am Main, January 18, 1996.

44 Karlsruhe, 1968.

RS Was Rosenberg so to speak only incidentally a composer?

WL Yes, but then who is primarily a composer these days? He couldn't make a living at it. He didn't compose very much, but among what he did compose are three string quartets, of which we commissioned and premiered the second and the third. The first was destroyed in the fire at Stefan Wolpe's New York apartment[45] and was never performed. We recorded his third quartet for Deutsche Grammophon.

RS There's an interview in Cincinnati with Hans G Helms, in which he says about Rosenberg's quartets that 'they are the most exquisite result of the collaboration between composer and interpreter and that 'the interpreter's conception and the composer's conception are married to one another.'[46] That contradicts what I've otherwise heard you say, namely that you never undertook to influence the process of composition.

WL What Helms said isn't at all that far-fetched, as we have indeed worked with composers, and they in turn have prized the way we played and the way we dealt with their music. We've never denied the fact that we wanted pieces that satisfied a certain intellectual demand. Insofar as our way of playing had something to do with our choice of composers and our sympathies with them, there was, perhaps indirectly if not directly, a connection between them. And that is probably what Helms is referring to. If you look at the list of composers and pieces we played, then you will see that overall there is a single, conceptually rigorous orientation, which has a whole lot to do with our interpretive style. The commissions and our approach to interpretation aren't independent of one another. We were conscious of how we played. We played the way we did because that's how we intended to play, not because that's what we felt like. We felt the way we intended to, and not vice-versa. Helms knew us very well, starting with Darmstadt. And he knew that there were things that we didn't play. Why didn't we play Shostakovich? Never. Not even early on in our career. Why are you laughing?

EVI LEVIN: I'm just looking at Rosenberg's letters to you. He greets you with

[45] The quartet was composed in 1945; for the fire in Wolpe's apartment, see pp. 96–97.

[46] *'Mit der Intensität der Verzweiflung'* ('With the Intensity of Despair'), WDR, September, 1980. Hans G Helms (1932–), wrote and directed many broadcasts for the West German radio and television networks on subjects ranging from contemporary music to city planning. His lectures 'Composing with Language' (1964) and 'Presuppositions for a New Musical Theater' (1966) are widely respected as Darmstadt classics; Helms was a close friend of Rosenberg, Hildesheimer, Brün, and Levin, and was acquainted with most of the leading figures of the 1950s and later musical avant-gardes.

'Dear Charles' and 'Dear Aloisius'! And signs one of them 'Tabula Rasenberg.' Such delightful whimsy!

WL Yes, Rosenberg was like that, and Herbert too. That's how I grew up.

Michael Gielen

RS The next of your long time friends is Michael Gielen.[47] How did you come to meet him?

WL We met him through his uncle, Eduard Steuermann, in Salzburg, in 1954. Gielen was an assistant in an opera performance there, I believe it was *Dantons Tod* by Gottfried von Einem. At that time Gielen was a rehearsal pianist at the Staatsoper in Vienna and also conducted there. Gielen was as a matter of course very interested in the Second Viennese School. On the occasion of Schoenberg's 75th birthday in 1949 he performed all of Schoenberg's solo pieces for piano in Buenos Aires. We shared the same musical interests and ideas and got along very well with one another. He came to our concerts in the cities where he was engaged as a conductor, for instance in Brussels and in Amsterdam. He was Music Director in Stockholm when we premiered the Lutosławski quartet.

We were together at Darmstadt now and then also. We were once invited to dine with the mayor on opening day, and I was seated next to Gielen. At this time the question of where Jimmy Levine should go to learn conducting had just come up. I told Gielen I had a really exceptionally gifted student who wanted to be a conductor. Where would Gielen send him? To Vienna, he said. I was taken aback: to Vienna? Yes, he said, send him to Karajan. Of all people! Gielen said if someone wants to conduct, he has to learn how to communicate his ideas to the orchestra, and in his opinion nobody did that better than Karajan. I might not like Karajan's ideas, but he was a master of the art of conducting, and I shouldn't underestimate that: Karajan could communicate his ideas to any orchestra in almost no time, just by the movements of his hands, which was something he, Gielen, couldn't

47 Michael Gielen (1927–), pianist, composer, and conductor, gave the South American premiere of Arnold Schoenberg's complete piano works in 1949. He was a conductor at the Vienna Staatsoper (1950–1960), the Royal Swedish Opera (1960–1965), and the Frankfurt Opera (1977–1987). Gielen was principal conductor of the Cincinnati Symphony Orchestra (1980–1986) and the SWF Orchestra in Baden-Baden (1986–1999). Gielen championed contemporary composers and conducted the premieres of works by Henze, Ligeti, Pousseur, Stockhausen, and Zimmermann, among others. He is also noted for his Beethoven, Bruckner and Mahler.

do, he had to explain what it was he wanted! And then he told me the following story.

Gielen was an assistant at the Staatsoper in Vienna and often had to prepare singers or even the orchestra for Karajan, who apparently had a very high regard for him, since once when Karajan had been engaged to conduct *Tristan und Isolde* at La Scala he asked Gielen if he could do him the favor of going to Milan and rehearsing the orchestra for him. Gielen's reaction was to say to Karajan that the way he would rehearse *Tristan* probably had little if anything to do with the way Karajan intended to conduct it. Karajan's response to this was to say that this was exactly why he wanted Gielen to prepare it for him, he wanted the orchestra to learn the whole work in exactly the same way that Gielen would prepare a symphony orchestra. Karajan didn't have time to do that, what he wanted Gielen to do was to rehearse the orchestra completely according to his own lights, his own idea of how it should be done.

So Gielen went to Milan and worked with the orchestra, he was allowed any number of rehearsals and worked with the orchestra the way he always does, after which they knew *Tristan* backwards and forwards. After which Karajan came to Milan to begin his own rehearsals. Gielen took a seat in the auditorium as Karajan began to conduct. The orchestra played just as Gielen had rehearsed them to, and, he told me, it was not to be believed: within a very few minutes the sound of the orchestra had changed into a Karajan-sound. And their whole manner of playing changed without Karajan having said even a single word. The orchestra had instantly become a Karajan orchestra and nothing was left of what Gielen had done. Gielen was mortified, and went to see Karajan at the break in order to apologize, but instead Karajan congratulated him, saying his work was fabulous, the orchestra played exactly the way he wanted them to! Karajan could really do that! But it's only possible if the orchestra knows the whole piece so thoroughly that they can concentrate on the conductor.

RS So Jimmy Levine was in good hands.

WL No, actually he never went to Vienna, we prevented his going there. The atmosphere in Vienna would have been destructive for him.

RS How did Gielen come to write his string quartet?

WL Gielen came to Cincinnati in 1980 as Music Director of the Cincinnati Symphony, on our initiative, and our relationship naturally became closer as a result. He did incredible things with the orchestra, it was a fantastic time, a golden age. The recordings! He performed so many works that are never played, for instance by Bernd Alois Zimmermann, and invited so many soloists that no one had ever heard of, he programmed the entire Second Viennese School and conducted a Beethoven cycle that you simply must hear! The first recording he made with the Cincinnati Symphony was of Beethoven's *Eroica* and it's still one of the best *Eroica* recordings there is.

And then radio station WGUC in Cincinnati, the university's radio station, wanted to commission a significant work to celebrate their 25th anniversary. WGUC's director, Ann Santen, asked me who they might commission, and I proposed Gielen, who was also a composer, and had written a string quartet when he was a young man.[48]

RS How would you describe Gielen's quartet?

WL It has five movements and formally it's conceived symmetrically: the two outer movements are short, the second and fourth movements are significantly longer, and the middle movement, the center of the piece contentwise, is the longest. In the second and fourth movements Gielen refers to poems by Baudelaire, great allegories of decay and decline: '*Une Charogne*', 'A Carrion,' and '*Le Cygne*,' 'The Swan.' The title of the quartet, '*Un Vieux Souvenir*,' 'An Old Memory,' comes from the last stanza of 'The Swan.' Originally he wanted a woman to speak the lines along with the music, but because that would mean trouble with meeting the deadline, as well as higher performance costs, which would mean that the piece would be performed less often, I was able to talk him out of it. The connection to Baudelaire's poems is now achieved by the musicians' speaking or shouting individual lines of the texts.

The first movement begins with two sound images, which are the basic elements of the piece: a *ricochet col legno* on muted strings of the cello represents the swan that can no longer fly and beats its wings helplessly in the dust of the street, then a *glissando* in diminished fifths in the viola, which stands for the slime in the rotting carrion. In addition, the two outer movements have a theatrical aspect: the first movement plays with the group dynamics of the four musicians, in particular with the competitive behavior of the two violinists. The second violinist dreamily plays a lovely melody from Zemlinsky's *Lyric Symphony*: an homage both to Zemlinsky and to Alban Berg, who also quoted a theme from the *Lyric Symphony* in his *Lyric Suite*. The quotation functions here much like the madeleine in Marcel Proust: it evokes the aura of memory. Whence the title of the piece. The first violinist, who definitely wants to be in charge, is annoyed and inter-

[48] Michael Gielen's *Variationen für Streichquartett* were written in 1949.

rupts the second. Gradually the two exchange their roles, until the first violinist has taken over the lovely melody and it's the second violinist who is annoyed. The violist and the cellist also exchange their materials in the course of the movement, a process represented formally by a canon in retrograde.

The second movement, with the title '*Une Charogne*,' is introduced by two eight-part fields of *glissandi*: the image of the rotting carrion. The movement has elements of *recitativ* and *arioso* as well as *scherzo*. The middle section of the movement is the 'strange music' that per Baudelaire's words arises from putrefaction.

The central third movement consists of a montage of variations of diverse ideas in a 'moment form,' that is, a sequence of disconnected fragments confronting one another like strangers. It's a series of 'jump shots,' to use the language of film makers. What these 'moments' or fragments have in common is their tense, compulsive character. The length of the 'moments' and the pauses between them by the way was determined by a so-called Fibonacci series.[49] Along with the spoken and shouted scraps of text the movement also has an acoustically violent noise aspect: stamping the feet.

The fourth movement, '*Le Cygne*,' is a further development of the variations of the third movement and a transformational reprise of the second movement. Only one new element is added: a melody in parallel chords, related to Gregorian chant, that Gielen calls '*Schwanengesang*,' 'Swan Song.' There are five variations on this song, each appearance both more hymn-like and more ecstatic than the one before, while all the other materials are subject to a process of disintegration. At the end the swan song falls to pieces also.

In the last movement the theme is alienation, the hopelessness of human relationships, which is also represented gesturally: the musicians turn away from one another. The idea that this movement attempts to express is to resist this hopelessness in full consciousness of it: the sound collapses under its overwhelming pressure.

Even today I find this quartet to be an extremely demanding and uncommonly strong piece, with its basic idea taken from these poems by Baudelaire. But we didn't have an easy time with it, it's not an easy piece, and not many quartets play it. We never took shortcuts in learning new pieces, we always allowed ourselves plenty of time to learn them.

49 Leonardo Fibonacci (~1170–~1250), Italian mathematician, promoted the use of Arabic numerals in preference to Roman numerals, citing their ease of use in arithmetic, in particular in bookkeeping. The series that bears his name was one of the examples he used: each number in it is the sum of the previous two, e.g., 0, 1, 1 (=0+1), 2 (=1+1), 3 (=1+2), 5 (=2+3), etc. The ratio of any two adjacent numbers in the series approximates the golden mean, e.g., 233:377 = 0.618.

RS What specifically were your problems in learning Gielen's quartet?

WL There were elements of the piece that had never been tried before, such as having us speak, declaim, shout, and stamp our feet while playing. There were also some difficult problems with rhythm and sonority, though we were used to dealing with things like that. What was extraordinarily difficult for us was the rhythmical foot stamping, which is prescribed very precisely in the score. So you have to learn to play and at the same time stamp your feet in a completely different rhythm: it's not easy to concentrate on performing two different motions, that's a difficult problem of coordination. Besides which, when you stamp your feet, the violin shakes, and the bow can easily skid on the strings. So you have to learn to hold your upper body still while playing the violin while at that same time stamping your feet. And when on top of that all four players are doing different things, precision and ensemble are in mortal peril.

RS Which means, by way of contrast with the Lutosławski quartet, that in Gielen's quartet, ensemble, playing together, is all important.

WL Indeed. In the Gielen quartet everything is precisely notated, and it's not his intention to allow the players any freedom in this regard. Singing and speaking texts in a foreign language while we were playing was also very difficult for us. On top of which he had a very precise idea of how he wanted the texts to be declaimed: they were intended more for actors than for musicians. He knew all about actors: his father, Josef Gielen, was a director. But we'd never had to do anything like that before!

RS Is it indicated in the score, how he wanted to have the texts declaimed?

WL No, it's not indicated in the score. There's only the text and the dynamic indication, the rhythm is also precisely notated.

RS How are future quartet generations who know neither you nor Gielen supposed to know what is meant?

WL Indeed, how would they know? In *Pierrot Lunaire* Schoenberg tried to define how the *Sprechstimme*[50] should sound, and what good did that do?

[50] *Sprechstimme* (spoken voice) is a vocal technique of speaking rhythmically with the syllables at different, and often sliding pitches, as notated by the composer. *Pierrot Lunaire* is perhaps the most ambitious attempt to notate the technique, but Schoenberg also used variants of it in his *Ode to Napoleon Bonaparte*, *A Survivor from Warsaw*, and *Moses und Aaron*. Kurt Weill also used the *Sprechstimme* for parts of *The Three Penny Opera*.

Pierre Boulez thinks that Schoenberg's instructions are no good and he has the *Sprechstimme* sing the notes, which is exactly what Schoenberg didn't want. But Boulez thinks it's more beautiful that way and that's how he recorded it. No composer is immune to such treatment, no matter what lengths he goes to avoid it.

Ultimately our conventional musical notation is never unambiguous. It's already centuries behind the times, and composers have constantly invented new things for which it doesn't provide any conventional signs. In Gielen's case you can hear recordings such as ours, which we made under his supervision, and which he approved, and if there are other recordings he approved as well, then you can make the comparisons yourself. So that gives some idea of what he intended. In other instances you would have to take care to realize as precisely as possible what's in the score and to seek out what the composer said about his own work as well as recordings made or approved by him. For instance, Gielen gave a number of lecture-recitals together with us in which we discussed the work with him and played examples from it, and in which he also addressed such questions of realization.

RS Did you work on the quartet with Gielen only after it was finished or did you work on it while he was writing it?

WL We got involved rather late. We had some questions for him when we were working on it while he was in Cincinnati. But we only played it for him relatively shortly prior to the premiere,[51] and made a few changes then. In addition to which he rewrote parts of it where his rhythmic notation had been unnecessarily complicated.

RS So you only found out rather late that his ideas about the declamation were different from yours?

WL Yes, and at the time of the recording he was still objecting to our dynamics, speech gestures, and French pronunciation.

RS So did those recording sessions for Deutsche Grammophon run less smoothly than usual?

WL Not really, as I find composers' comments valuable. I wish Beethoven could have been present at our recordings! I would have loved to have heard his comments and recorded his ideas about his quartets rather than ours! It's a shame that we don't know what composers from

[51] The premiere of Gielen's string quartet took place on October 15, 1985, in Cincinnati.

times prior to our own had to say about the playing of their interpreters. We do have recordings by the Rosé Quartet of some pieces of Brahms that they worked on with Brahms himself, and they also played the piano quintet with him. This would seem to be as close to so-called authentic performance practice as you could hope to get. However, the fact that performance practice changed so radically in the course of the following years argues that under some circumstances the traditional way of playing something is no longer necessarily authoritative.

The concept of music changes with every newly composed piece, and every new style also changes our view of the past. Now that we've learned Schoenberg and the whole twelve-tone school as well as a lot of what followed in tone colors, tempi, and contrapuntal transparency, we can play quite differently than anyone would have thought of doing 50 or 75 years ago, to say nothing of 100 years ago.

RS Perhaps Brahms simply had to be satisfied with what was possible at the time.

WL Certainly. Composers like Brahms were fortunate to have a quartet like the Rosés. But when you listen to how they play Beethoven, how it sounds: was that really the ideal that Beethoven had in mind? They were certainly closer to Beethoven and to the performance practices of his time, since some of the teachers in Brahms' time had played the pieces in Beethoven's time. But even so you're already two generations removed from Beethoven: Joseph Böhm played Beethoven's last quartets and had worked on Opus 127 with him. And Böhm was Joseph Joachim's teacher, and the teachers of my generation had all studied with Joachim in Berlin. My teacher Bergmann had also played for Joachim. And Joachim had carried on the tradition from Böhm in his complete performances of the Beethoven quartets. But whether such a tradition is valid for decades and centuries is a big question, because music develops in different directions and opens our ears to possibilities that no one had thought possible previously.

RS In addition, it's a small step from tradition to betrayal, as is easily seen in French and Italian: *tradition* and *trahison* in French as well as *tradizione* and *traditore* (traitor) are etymologically closely related. But the fundamental problem is that the notation for new sounds and new kinds of expression is simply insufficient.

WL Indeed, musical notation is and remains inadequate.

Friedhelm Döhl

RS You might consider Friedhelm Döhl[52] a distant member of the Darmstadt circle: he did write a dissertation on Webern.

WL Yes, and a very interesting one too. He's a fabulous musician.

RS Where did you meet him?

WL We got to know him in Berlin. Our au-pair girl in Cincinnati, who was a student of mine, Hete Nolte, told us about him. She was from Münster, had studied in Detmold, played the violin, and very much wanted to study violin with me. She came to the Hotel Ernst in Cologne to play for me. I told her that I only taught in Cincinnati, so she would have to come to Cincinnati to study. She could live with us if she was willing to be an au-pair for us, we had two small children. She thought that was a great idea, and so she came to live with us in Cincinnati and had violin lessons with me. While she was studying in Detmold she'd become friends with a composer by the name of Friedhelm Döhl, and she insisted I should meet him, he was a wonderful man, I would like him a lot. And the next time we were in Berlin to play a concert at the Akademie, a man came backstage to the Green Room after the concert and introduced himself as Friedhelm Döhl, saying he'd gotten a letter from his former girlfriend Hete telling me to say hello from her and that we should get to know one another. After the concert we went out to dinner, he and his wife Julia, and we hit it off right away.

Hete was right, he was the kind of person I like a lot. A real German intellectual musician, and he was interested in what we were doing. He told me he'd just taken a position as rector of the Academy of Music in Basel and that he very much wanted me to give a summer course in chamber music there. So our courses in Basel got started when Döhl became the rector there. It was a golden age for this school. What a rector! What all he undertook, what he publicized, how he raised money, he got the whole city going! A phenomenal rector for this music school. And we were happy to be there too: every summer we gave a two week string quartet course here, and quartets came here from all over the world to attend it.

[52] Friedhelm Döhl (1936–) studied composition, musicology, art history, and philosophy at Freiburg and Göttingen. After teaching in Düsseldorf and Berlin he was appointed rector of the Basel Academy of Music in 1974, moving in 1982 to Lübeck as professor of composition at the Academy of Music there, and becoming its director in 1991. He served as president of the German section of the ISCM 1980–1983.

RS But these short teaching sessions weren't really what you had in mind.

WL No, that's right, they weren't. But even so it was in Basel that we got a foot in the door for teaching in Europe. We'd previously not been able to do that. And then when Döhl went to Lübeck a few years later, it was high on his list of things to do to get me to go there too. That's how I started teaching the chamber music course at Lübeck. And now whenever I'm in Lübeck I get together with Döhl, who has retired by now, but he's still one of the brightest minds around and a very good composer. Among other things he wrote a string quartet that we performed.[53] We also played it at the Basel Academy of Music, and our recording of a performance of it in Cincinnati has been released commercially. Pieces like that by composer friends were always of interest to us: our choice of repertory always had a human component. We also played Herbert Brün and Rosenberg because they were friends.

RS The title of the work, *Sound of Sleat*, refers to a strait in Scotland, and although Döhl does not regard his work as program music,[54] in his notes for the premiere Döhl suggests that the piece was inspired by the Scottish landscape and talks about the two meanings of 'sound' as the word for both the geographical feature and for the acoustic phenomenon as well as the double meaning of 'Sleat' as a place name,[55] and as the name given to the monochrome atmosphere where sea and sky meet at the horizon.

WL That very well may be. But I never think much about the background of a composition: what's important to me is the composition itself.

RS How does the piece seem to you today?

WL It's a beautiful piece in the tradition of Webern, it even quotes his Opus 5.

[53] *Sound of Sleat*, 1971–1972, commissioned by WDR, was premiered in the United States by the LaSalle Quartet on April 20, 1982, in Cincinnati.

[54] Beyond its affinity to nature, Döhl understands his quartet as an autonomous 'sound landscape' or 'sound scene.' In his foreword to the score, Döhl writes that he is concerned 'not with the individual parts but with their sum, so to speak a surface in motion, in which the individual parts and moments flow into one another now to a greater now to a lesser extent.'

[55] The Sound of Sleat is a sea channel which separates the peninsula of Sleat on the island of Skye from the Scottish mainland.

Earle Brown

RS Earle Brown[56] was also a Darmstadt participant, starting in 1956, and also lectured there. Was that when you commissioned a string quartet from him?

WL Yes, and we premiered it in 1965 at the Festival for Contemporary Music in Donaueschingen.[57]

RS Where would you place Earle Brown's quartet stylistically?

WL As in Lutosławski's quartet and Evangelisti's *Aleatorio*, Earle Brown permits the players a certain measure of freedom in shaping the piece, but within limits that he precisely defines. But in contrast to Lutosławski's 'limited aleatorics,' Brown doesn't rely on chance but instead offers a framework he can control, a selection of possibilities, and he expects the players to improvise freely in shaping these possibilities together in performance. For example, he writes the pitches, how they are to be played, and their dynamics, but neither rhythm nor meter. Each player is to derive the duration of the notes from his personal reactions to the graphical notation. When they are close together on the time-axis of the score the notes are shorter, and longer when they are further apart from one another. Which means that each player is to play his part independently of the others. The places at which he asks the four instruments to play together are indicated by a vertical arrow above each part. Brown called this way of engaging the players in the creative process 'creative ambiguity.' But he doesn't go as far in this direction as Evangelisti in *Aleatorio*.

RS How is Brown's quartet conceived in terms of its sonorities?

WL He used the whole repertory of techniques: normally bowed notes as well as *pizzicato*, *sul ponticello*, *col legno battuto* and *col legno tratto*, and so on, and also all these techniques behind the bridge or even 'inarticulate,' as he calls it: the notes aren't to be made to sound fully, but by

[56] Earle Brown (1926–2002) studied at Schillinger House in Boston, a school oriented to Joseph Schillinger's mathematical theories of art and music. He was one of the first composers to produce an entirely graphically notated score, his famous *December* of 1952. Through John Cage he met pianist David Tudor, who performed his work at Darmstadt, where it came to the attention of Pierre Boulez and Bruno Maderna. Brown's 'open form' composition as well as his use of graphical notation has had an enormous influence ever since, particularly on the 'downtown' music scene in New York in the 1980s.

[57] On October 16.

means of slight slippage of the bow just to be hinted at. These places aren't notated as specific pitches in the score but rather with a kind of arabesque in the note-beams that indicates their relative pitch, duration, and rhythm. The actual pitches are left to the discretion of the individual player, while the technique used to produce them is precisely defined.

RS How would you describe the form of Brown's quartet?

WL As is the case with the quartets by Evangelisti, Penderecki, and Koenig, it's a relatively short piece, it lasts about ten minutes. It's a single movement, but it consists of many sections of a diverse character. The transitions from one section to the next are meant to be flexible too, that is, to be up to the discretion of the individual player. But then all four players are to finish their transitions within five or six seconds.

The last section, which is to last between one and two minutes, Brown characterizes as an 'open form' in which each player is allotted eight to ten 'events' – as he calls them – that he can play as often as he likes, in whatever sequence and whatever tempo he pleases. Brown himself said that Alexander Calder's mobiles were his inspiration for this open form. Dynamics, tone production, and rhythm are in part left to the discretion of the individual players, otherwise they are to follow the directions given. The material for these 'events' is derived from preceding sections of the piece, but not always from the same instrumental part. So this last section is a free-form coda which is to be assembled spontaneously by the players.

RS Did you work together with Brown when you were rehearsing the piece?

WL Of course. He lived in New York, so it wasn't hard to meet with him. He was also with us prior to the premiere in Donaueschingen, and when we recorded the piece for the SWF. Later we put together a second version and he was there when we performed it.[58] He was very enthusiastic about it. I still find it a very good piece, even today.

RS And with 32 performances between 1965 and 1976, and another one after an interval of ten years, in 1986, it's one of the commissioned works that you played most often.

[58] Earle Brown was Composer in Residence at the College-Conservatory of Music in Cincinnati in the winter semester 1985–1986. A lecture-recital on his string quartet with him and the LaSalle Quartet took place on February 10, 1986.

Robert Mann

RS Apparently Robert Mann, the first violinist of the Juilliard Quartet, was also a composer,[59] since there's a string quartet by him, *Five Pieces for String Quartet.*

WL Absolutely. We premiered it on the occasion of our farewell concert in Colorado Springs,[60] as his Juilliard Quartet colleagues declined to play it: that led to an almost insurmountable rift between them. We then played it in Cincinnati also and at the Juilliard School, where they recorded our performance.

RS At the Sacher Foundation there's a devastating newspaper critique of the piece after the concert in Cincinnati: a total demolition. We listened to the recording of the performance at Juilliard and couldn't begin to figure out what could have unleashed such an adverse critique. We found it very entertaining and diverting, also humorous, there's even a quote from Beethoven's quartet Opus 59, No. 2. It's very energetic, for large stretches even forceful. A really good piece!

WL Yes, at a distance the piece just gets better and better. At the time I found it somewhat coarse and superficial, not really my thing. But the confrontation with so many different kinds of pieces in the course of the decades would lead anyone to revise their previous judgments again and again.

RS Did Mann compose later on as well?

WL Yes, his wife was a story-teller. He composed music for fairy tales for children's concerts and for Rudyard Kipling's 'Just So Stories.'

Gerhard Samuel

RS Another friend of many years was Gerhard Samuel.[61]

[59] Mann composed more than 30 works for speaker and various instrumental combinations, which he performed with his wife, the actress Lucy Rowan. He also wrote an 'Orchestral Fantasy' that was performed by Dimitri Mitropoulos, as well as a duo for violin and piano, a duo for cello and piano, and a concerto for orchestra.

[60] The farewell concert in Colorado Springs took place on March 11, 1953. Also on the program were Haydn's quartet Opus 77, Nr. 2, and the Ravel quartet.

[61] Gerhard Samuel (1924–2008) studied at the Eastman School of Music and then at Yale, where he was a student of Paul Hindemith. Following two summers working

WL We brought Gerhard to Cincinnati as a professor of music and the conductor of the Philharmonia Orchestra, the student orchestra of the College-Conservatory. He was a phenomenal conductor and orchestral educator. There were performances with the Philharmonia Orchestra that could stand comparison with any professional orchestra. And what didn't they study! Beethoven's and Mahler's Ninth Symphonies, among other things. Christian Tetzlaff was the concertmaster for those, that's the kind of orchestra it was, they could really play! Gerhard also dug up all sorts of interesting things, for example the symphony by Hans Rott, Mahler's school friend, from which Mahler derived some of the ideas for his first symphony. The recording they made of this piece is extraordinary.[62] He could get an orchestra to play really brilliantly. He was a born conductor, from his baton technique on up, a wonderful, first rate musician, but somehow he never made the breakthrough to an international career.

RS You commissioned a quartet from Gerhard Samuel in 1978. How did that come about?

WL We'd heard some of his music and were surprised by its lyrical character, its expressivity and sensitivity, as these were rather unusual for music written in the decades following the Second World War. After all these years in which composers experimented so intensively in their search for a new language and new means of expression, I found this return to certain romantic and emotional aspects of music astonishing and interesting. On the other hand, this kind of nostalgia can also resurrect some highly questionable aspects of both composition and interpretation. But up to a point such a reversal is justified. Gerhard always wrote pieces with a lyrical and romantic character and did so in his own completely unique way.

RS Would you on that account call his quartet a traditional rather than an experimental piece?

WL In any case he employed many compositional techniques that reveal the piece to be an heir of the 18th through the 20th centuries. But it is a

with Serge Koussevitzky at Tanglewood, he became Dimitri Mitropoulos' assistant in the Minneapolis Symphony. In 1959 he was appointed Music Director of the Oakland (CA) Symphony, where he established an international reputation for his innovative programming. Samuel was Associate Conductor of the Los Angeles Philharmonic 1970–1973; he was the conductor of the College-Conservatory's student orchestra 1976–1997.

62 Samuel's recording of the Rott symphony with the student orchestra was released commercially by Hyperion.

twelve-tone piece, since after his studies with Hindemith he occupied himself intensively with twelve-tone music and had an extraordinary admiration for the music of Schoenberg and Berg. The quartet is in a single movement of about fifteen minutes' duration and is based completely on a number of twelve-tone rows that he derived from a basic row by means of various combinations and permutations. Individual rows are associated with particular instruments or with certain sections or transitions. And since all the rows are related to one another, you can hear the commonalities among them. It's a complex and intellectually demanding piece.

RS Does the quartet also use predominantly traditional sonorities?

WL Yes, there are scarcely any distorted sounds like *sul ponticello* or *col legno battute*, and also no percussive sounds like thumping the instruments. That wasn't what interested him. What was important to him were a clear formal structure and carefully organized materials, but above all else a fluency of expression, so that the music communicates to the listener. That has to do with instrumental gestures that are closely related to the vocal gestures of the human voice. The only sound element that particularly characterizes this quartet is given by the long passages of *glissandi*, about which Gerhard said that the last piece he rehearsed with the Philharmonia Orchestra before starting work on the quartet had been Strauss' *Don Quixote*, the last note of which, portraying Don Quixote's death, is a very long *glissando*. He was obsessed by this *glissando* for a very long time and it found its way into the quartet. But of course it doesn't represent a novel technique of tone production.

RS Did Gerhard Samuel also integrate elements of chance and improvisation, as was often the case in the 1960s and 1970s?

WL No, the piece is completely written out, there are no elements of chance, and the players aren't asked to improvise or to contribute to the compositional process. There are a few rubato-like places that are rhythmically free and not metrically determined: they give the feeling of a cadenza for the four instruments together. But that isn't new either. It's a traditionally composed piece throughout, one that doesn't necessitate any new approaches to performance. But then that wasn't Gerhard's intention: it was the content of the piece that interested him. Knowing the pieces of his that we'd already heard, that was what we expected and hoped for.

RS A few years later, in 1981, Gerhard Samuel wrote a second quartet. Did you play that one too?

WL No, we never played it. It was premiered by the Sequoia Quartet, in which Robert Martin[63] is the cellist.

William DeFotis

RS You also played a quartet by William DeFotis[64] a few times. Who was William DeFotis?

WL Bill DeFotis was a student of Herbert Brün at the University of Illinois in Champaign-Urbana; he subsequently studied with Rosenberg in Munich. He was twenty-four years old when he wrote the quartet for us, he was an exceptionally gifted musician.

RS How was the quartet composed?

WL It's very short: around five minutes long, and a derivative piece: he quotes Webern among others. It's certainly not a very important work, but he was a great admirer of the LaSalle Quartet and he wrote it for us. So all due respect for the work of a young composition student! I think it's also important to give young composition students the opportunity to hear their work. The Arditti Quartet does that to a great extent. We didn't do enough of it. If a music school has a good composition department then it's incumbent upon them to get the student quartets to play the works of their fellow students in order to give them the opportunity to hear their works. I actually wanted to introduce that idea in Basel. The performances don't have to be prepared to the level required for public performance. Bill DeFotis died not long ago, unfortunately. He was stricken with multiple sclerosis when he was still quite young, only twenty-seven years old. It was terrible, as the years went by he was more and more crippled, and finally in a wheelchair. But he continued to write music.

[63] Robert Martin had been the cellist in the children's trio with Linda Sharon and James Levine in Cincinnati in the 1950s; see pp. 165–166.

[64] William DeFotis (1953–2003) studied composition with Herbert Brün at the University of Illinois and with Wolf Rosenberg in Munich; he subsequently studied conducting with James Dixon in Iowa. He taught and conducted the student orchestra at Baylor University in Waco, Texas, 1983–1984, and then at William and Mary College in Williamsburg, Virginia, 1986–2003.

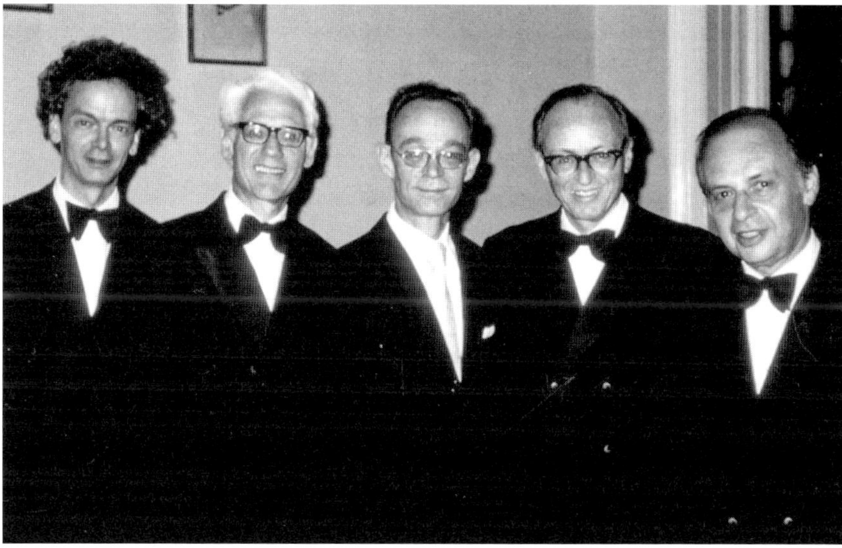

47 The LaSalle Quartet with László Kalmár, Budapest, 1982

RS Evidently he was, like Gerhard Samuel, a gifted conductor. Owing to the crippling effect of his multiple sclerosis, in the end he was able to conduct solely by means of his facial expressions.[65]

László Kalmár

RS László Kalmár[66] remains an unknown composer even today. What prompted you to perform his string quartet *Morfeo*?

WL We gave a concert in Budapest, after which Bálint Varga came to see us, he was at that time the director of the promotions department of the state publisher Editio Musica and represented them in their international business. Bálint Varga recommended that we learn the quartet *Morfeo* by László Kalmár. We gave the official premiere of the piece in

65 'So attuned was he to his music and so at one was he with his orchestra that, when he lost motor control and could no longer hold the baton, he conducted a Haydn symphony with facial movements. His orchestra of students responded as though they, their conductor and Haydn were indistinguishable. As far as DeFotis was concerned, nothing, including multiple sclerosis, could stop the music.' *The Virginia Gazette*, Williamsburg, February 8, 2003.

66 László Kalmár (1931–1995) composed his string quartet *Morfeo* in 1977. The work lasts about four and a half minutes and consists of eight short movements in the style of Webern's *Bagatelles* Opus 9.

the great hall of the Liszt Academy.[67] That was evidently a great occasion for Kalmár, as he was not very well known and was quite a modest man. When we went with Bálint Varga to visit his publisher we also met György Kurtág[68] there.

RS Do you know any other compositions by László Kalmár?

WL No, I don't know anything about his other pieces, I also don't know anything about his career or his personal circumstances.[69]

Hans Erich Apostel

RS After you managed to get Fred Smith, the director of the College of Music in Cincinnati, to accept your programming Bartók's fifth quartet on the LaSalle's first concert as Quartet in Residence, you evidently took seriously your stated intention to perform a contemporary or otherwise unknown work in every one of your concerts. And the program for your second concert[70] already included the first quartet, Opus 7, by Hans Erich Apostel,[71] who was at that time almost completely unknown.

WL Indeed. Apostel was among the composers whose works were branded 'degenerate' by the Nazis, as a result of which they disappeared from the concert programs in Germany and Austria. Unfortunately that's still the case today.

[67] On May 30, 1982; the LaSalle Quartet had previously played *Morfeo* in Cincinnati, on April 29, 1980.

[68] György Kurtág (1926–), Hungarian composer and close friend of György Ligeti. His second string quartet, *Officium Breve in Memoriam Andeae Szervánsky* (1988–1989), appeared too late for the LaSalle Quartet, which had disbanded in 1987. They did not play Kurtág's first quartet, written in 1959.

[69] Kalmár studied composition with Ferenc Farkas, who was also Ligeti's and Kurtág's teacher. He went to work for Editio Musica in 1957, where he remained for the rest of his life, eventually serving as Editor in Chief and Artistic Director. For many years he wrote only chamber and choral music, in a refined style reminiscent of Webern, at one point writing a score, *Lectiones*, meant to be read but not performed. In 1982 he unexpectedly produced a large-scale, almost late-romantic work for orchestra, *Horae* (the Horae are the classical Greek goddesses of the seasons). Further works in the same style followed. (Personal communication from Bálint Varga.)

[70] On January 12, 1954.

[71] Pianist, composer, and conductor Hans Erich Apostel (1901–1972) studied composition with Arnold Schoenberg and Alban Berg and was close to Expressionist painters Emil Nolde and Oskar Kokoschka. Proscribed by the Nazis as 'degenerate,' he resumed his work with contemporary music after the war, serving as president of the Austrian branch of the Gesellschaft für Neue Musik 1947–1950. As an editor at Universal Edition, he was responsible for the new editions of Berg's operas *Wozzeck* and *Lulu*.

RS How did you come across Apostel's quartet Opus 7?

WL It was another discovery at Frank's, the sheet music store in New York where I later also discovered Zemlinsky's third string quartet. In 1952 I chanced upon a pocket score of Apostel's quartet Opus 7 there and realized immediately that it was an unconventional and rewarding work. It wasn't difficult to persuade my colleagues that we had to play the piece. I knew of Apostel as a student of Schoenberg's and Berg's. The piece was composed in 1935, the year of Berg's death, and Apostel had wanted to dedicate it to his teacher, who he very much admired, on the occasion of Berg's 50th birthday. When Berg died that year, the piece, which had been planned as a five movement work, wasn't finished yet, and Apostel decided to let the quartet end with the slow fourth movement.

RS How did you make the piece palatable to the audience?

WL In the same way as with Bartók's fifth quartet: we gave a lecture-recital the Sunday before the concert, this time in the Taft Museum, where there was more room than in our studio at the College of Music. We analyzed the piece, played examples from it, and then performed it. As it happened, Virgil Thomson, the critic for the *New York Herald Tribune* was present at this lecture-recital. He knew us, since he'd recommended us to Carol Truax as the group she should engage as Quartet in Residence at Colorado Springs. He wrote a review of our lecture-recital for his paper.[72]

RS You once said that Apostel was the only composer from the Second Viennese School who you got to know personally. How did you come to meet him?

WL We wrote to him about a number of questions that had arisen while we were rehearsing his quartet Opus 7. That resulted in a long-running exchange of letters, and when we were on tour in Europe for the first time in 1954 we played the quartet for him in Vienna. He got to be a real friend of ours. When we played his second quartet in Graz and Linz a few years later, he came with us. He was so pleased, excited, and above all grateful that his music was finally being played. Evidently we played it well, as it was very well received by the audience. That's always the problem with new music, and with difficult music in general, namely

[72] In his review, Thomson, who was hearing Apostel's music for the first time, stated that he would not be surprised if Apostel's string quartet would eventually come to enjoy a real popularity, as he thought there were not all that many chromatic-atonal pieces that were so deeply felt and so marvelously well-composed.

that it's really unbearable when it's badly played. You can't blame the audiences for that. Schoenberg's and Berg's quartets suffered from that for a long time, and Beethoven's quartets still suffer from it.

RS Was it then in Vienna, on your first European tour, that you commissioned his second quartet?

WL Exactly. We found Apostel's first quartet, his Opus 7, to be a very beautiful piece and wanted to support him financially via a commission for another quartet, as at that time he was having to eke out a living by giving piano and composition lessons and working as an editor at Universal Edition, who also published his works. When I was at Darmstadt next I was able to speak with Otto Tomek, who is now the director of the new music department at WDR, but who at that time was with Universal Edition and had come to Darmstadt as their representative. He thought the commission idea was excellent, and I asked what he thought such a commission would cost. He wondered if $200 would be possible.[73] Not much of an honorarium per se, but that was a lot of money in Austria in the mid-1950s. Apostel then composed his second quartet, Opus 26, in 1956, and we premiered it the following year in Cincinnati.

RS How would you describe the style of Apostel's first quartet? Is it a twelve-tone piece?

WL No, it's not a strict twelve-tone piece, it's written in a free atonality, like Berg's Opus 3. Apostel takes as a model the classical form: the first movement is an *Allegro* in sonata form, the second movement is composed on the principle of 'continuous variation' that was already beloved of Brahms and Schoenberg. The material that Apostel develops in this movement is based on the *Wozzeck* theme from Berg's opera. The third movement is a scurrilous scherzo with a sweeping rhythmical vitality: it certainly has the most striking profile of all the movements in the piece. It's based on motives that are derived from the names Alban Berg, A, B♭, and Hans Erich Apostel, H, that is, B natural, E, and A. The quartet ends with a *Largo* with the character of an extended song of lamentation that refers thematically to the previous movements, above all to the variations movement.

Apostel's music is distinguished by the prominence of its rhythmic components and by its irregular meters. The form of his works is always very clear. They are extremely dense emotionally and their materials are highly concentrated. He's a highly individual composer. The quar-

[73] $200 in 1956 nominally equates to about $1,700 today (2013), but the actual value in the Austria of those years far exceeded what this figure would suggest.

tet has an emotional quality that sets it apart from almost everything else that was written at that time. In my opinion Apostel is a very great composer, whose orchestral works, songs, and other chamber music are wholly deserving of a place in the repertory of 20th century music. But that recognition has still not been granted them.

RS Between the composition of the first and the second quartets there is an interval of 21 years. Over such a long period one could expect, if not a change of style, then at least a stylistic development. Do the two quartets differ in this respect?

WL No, fundamentally they do not. The second quartet is even more concentrated in that it is a single movement in cyclical form. It's a difficult piece, also difficult to play, but in my opinion far more accessible than for instance the third Schnabel quartet. But as to whether there is a stylistic development, I can't really say, as I hardly know any of Apostel's other music. How could I? No one plays it! But as regards the second quartet: I can tell right away that it's by Apostel.

RS All in all you played Apostel's first quartet some twenty times, whereby it's striking that after the first performance in Cincinnati in 1954 you didn't take it up again until the early 1970s, and even then played it only three times. You played it most often starting in the 1980s. Whereas you only played the second quartet five times altogether, the last four all in 1958, the year after the premiere. Was the second quartet a disappointment?

WL No, it wasn't a disappointment. The problem was that nobody wanted to hear Apostel. It was a lot of work to convince concert organizers to accept his work on our programs. The first quartet is also the weightier of the two pieces and easier to argue for. And it's simply the case that we feel more drawn to some pieces and like them better, while others were a lot of trouble for us. Nevertheless I think Apostel's second quartet is a wonderful piece. It's certainly still playable today, there's no doubt about that. I worked on it recently with the Doric Quartet, who had a big success playing it in England.

RS Later, in 1962, Apostel also wrote his *6 Epigramme* Opus 33 for string quartet.

WL Yes, but we didn't have an opportunity to play them. It's a serial piece in the style of Webern, just seven minutes, and follows a tempo progression from *grave* to *vivace*.

Igor Stravinsky

RS When we were talking about Zemlinsky you mentioned that Stravinsky also came to visit Cincinnati. What was the occasion for that visit?

WL In 1964 there was an exhibition of paintings by Stravinsky's wife Vera in a Cincinnati art gallery whose owner we knew and who always came to our concerts. We were invited to the vernissage. It was only at the last minute that we learned that Stravinsky would be coming too, and we seized the opportunity to meet him. We immediately got into a conversation and he asked us what we would be playing in the concert we were about to give, which he hoped to come to. When we said we would be playing Zemlinsky's third quartet, he was enthralled, since he didn't know that Zemlinsky had also been a composer. He knew him only as a conductor, for whom he had only the most ecstatic praise, having heard him conduct *The Marriage of Figaro* in Prague. But the next day Stravinsky wasn't feeling well and couldn't come to our concert, which was really too bad.

RS Did you also take advantage of this opportunity to ask him if he would be willing to compose a new string quartet for you?[74]

WL Of course! His response was simply to say, why not? We should talk to Robert Craft! Craft[75] was his assistant and advisor in musical matters, whom we knew quite well, since he was a student at Juilliard when we were, a highly intelligent and gifted man. He handled all of Stravinsky's negotiations and told us that a string quartet would be hopeless, it would cost at least $5,000[76] and he, that is, Stravinsky, would make no concessions. He couldn't say how long it would turn out to be, it might be two minutes, it might be twelve. But at the time $5,000 seemed like an impossible sum for us, we didn't want to ask for that much from the friends who supported our commissions: they were used to giving $200 or at most $250.[77] There's no question that this

[74] Stravinsky's previous works for string quartet include his *Three Pieces* (1914), *Concertino* (1920), and *Double Canon* (1959).

[75] Robert Craft (1923–), recorded virtually all of Stravinsky's symphonic works and made pioneering recordings conducting the works of Schoenberg, Berg, and Webern. His *Conversations with Igor Stravinsky* (Garden City, NY, 1959) and subsequent books on Stravinsky are classic if somewhat controversial accounts of the composer's life and work.

[76] About $38,000 in today's (2013) dollars.

[77] About $1,500–$1,800 in today's (2013) dollars.

was a bad decision. We should have paid it ourselves. But hindsight is always better than foresight.[78]

RS So that's why there was no new quartet by Stravinsky?

WL That's why, unfortunately.

Observations on the Commissions

RS Looking back at the music of the classical and romantic periods, there was the sonata form with exposition, development, and recapitulation, there was thematic development, there were relationships among voices, and starting with Brahms there were no longer subsidiary voices, everything is thematic. For the composers who used a completely new compositional technique, for instance Evangelisti or Brown, or Ligeti and maybe Lutosławski too, none of that matters anymore, and nevertheless their music is 'good' music. So what does the intellectual claim of this kind of new music consist of?

WL It differs greatly from composer to composer. In the extreme cases it has to do with producing sounds with the classical instrumentarium that are not normally associated with those instruments: for instance thumping or striking the bodies of the instruments to make a percussion ensemble out of a string quartet. The result sounds completely different from any other instrument.

RS But is it then still a string quartet or is it music for four stringed instruments?

WL It's music for four stringed instruments. But string quartet is a very flexible concept. No matter what sorts of sounds you produce with the instruments of a string quartet: two violins, a viola, and a cello, you can say it's a string quartet.

RS Okay, but you do expect a certain intellectual demand, as the Shostakovich quartets aren't in the classical sense unambiguously string quartets either, but music for four stringed instruments, that you didn't want to play. Wherein lies the difference?

[78] The quartet had also just finished paying for the Amati instruments (see pp. 141–143), which, though acquired at an enormous discount from the seller, Gerald Warburg, had nevertheless represented a very substantial outlay for an ensemble working in what was by no means a lucrative corner of the music business.

WL I think that the claim can be found on both sides of the so-called classical string quartet. By means of harmony, repetition, ostinato you can produce a kind of reactionary and vacuous music that is so simple and so banal that it's of no interest to me. If it's genuinely simple music, I have no problem with it, it's just that it doesn't interest me. I'm not interested in Shostakovich because for me his music doesn't convey any new information. So that kind of music belongs to what we know already.

But there is also a kind of music that isn't what we already know, that leaves all that behind or simply discards what's already known, and doesn't have a single ordinary note in it. That's the music that interests me. I'm not in a position to judge whether it's good music or bad, and that's not a question that interests me either. What attracted me to the Penderecki quartet was that it's a piece that works exclusively with modulations of sound, that the piece begins with nothing but percussive noises, to which more and more notes are then added, that is, normally played notes, and that the sonority then gets completely distorted again, and the piece becomes ever more complex rhythmically. So it's a form that arises from the combination of an ongoing transformation of its overall sonority and a continuous increase in its rhythmic complexity: that's something I find interesting. On top of which it was a challenge: nobody else wanted to play a piece like that. We knew of nothing else like it and in our opinion it was something that should be given a hearing.

Whether you like something or not ... I find the whole idea of only playing music you like questionable. Music always only began to interest me when I didn't like it, when I didn't understand it, because it was so complex or so different that I couldn't make heads or tails of it. That was what attracted me to Schoenberg when I first heard his quartets on the roof of Peter Gradenwitz's house in Tel Aviv. That's supposed to be a string quartet? The same question, over and over again. As if there ever was such a thing as an eternal and unchanging category. If there were such a thing, Beethoven would never have written a single note! If you just keep composing what already exists, then it's impossible for music to renew itself. Cage for instance is a musician who set everyone's teeth on edge: anything so vacuous and boring can't possibly be music! It was 'minimalist music' at a time when the concept didn't even exist yet. It's that sort of thing that attracted me. And I never knew in advance whether I would like something or not. Once we'd learned a piece and played it, if it turned out not to be something we liked, we could just let it go, as we did with the second Elliott Carter quartet. Why did we do that? Don't ask me, nowadays I think it's a really good piece!

RS If you consider the period in which the great quartets you premiered were written, for instance the quartets by Lutosławski, Ligeti, Nono,

Kagel, and Gielen, it's astonishing how diametrically opposite to one another they are in their construction. And Evangelisti and Koenig again represent completely different directions.

WL Absolutely, the differences in their approaches to composing are enormous.

RS Was it to be expected that the pieces I just mentioned would turn out to be so different from one another at the time you commissioned them?

WL Indeed, certainly you could expect that, since we intentionally sought out composers who, based on the works of theirs that we'd already heard, had the most sharply defined individual character. They were anything but unknown to us.

RS But in Ligeti's case it took ten years for him to write his quartet, and Nono took 25 years. Nono at least surely changed over this period of time.

WL That's why Nono's quartet was such a big surprise for us when we first got it. But we'd already known him for a long time as a person and a composer. Well, okay then, composers change from work to work and sometimes from month to month, but the earnestness and the general character of their approach to composing doesn't change. A Ligeti doesn't all of a sudden become a waltz king, he doesn't turn into a composer of entertainment music aimed at a very superficial success. He had a very clear idea of where his music was going. The works for orchestra that he wrote after his emigration to Western Europe: incredible! And you could tell that this was someone who had really thought about his music. We didn't know his first quartet, because he had kept it more or less a secret and didn't want it played. But we thought Ligeti was someone you could get a quartet from. And then it turned into something quite special, this second quartet by Ligeti.

Our commissions weren't always as satisfying for us as were the works you just mentioned. Here and there were some works we didn't particularly care for and that we left by the wayside. But by and large we were quite certain that the composers whose works for orchestra and chamber music for mixed ensembles we heard at Darmstadt, for instance, were composers who weren't at all concerned about popular taste but rather who were out to realize their own ideals and devil take the hindmost, and whose music in any case had a very strongly individual character with a definite spice to it. And that was just what we wanted.

RS When you consider the fact once more that the quartets by Lutosławski, Kagel, and Ligeti were composed within a span of only five years, and those by Nono and Gielen within another five year span, and all of them together within a span of only twenty years, the extreme differences in approach to composition represented by these works becomes all the more remarkable. I don't know if there had ever before been such great extremes in so short a time in the history of music. For instance, I don't believe that the contemporaries of Haydn and Mozart felt that their quartets were different to such an extreme degree. Perhaps the quartets of Beethoven and Schubert, but even in this case their composition technique represents the same approach. How would you explain the extreme differences in compositional approach among the 'new music' composers?

WL It has to do with the fact that at the beginning of the 20th century we completely lost any sense of there being a valid style that could promise any kind of stylistic unity. Every composer was completely on his own in the search for a new language and for new means of expression. There were only certain aspects that they all still had in common, atonality for instance, and the increasing importance of tone color: in all these pieces tone color and its constant variation and extension on the traditional instruments of the string quartet plays an increasingly important role. In the Penderecki quartet, for instance, you have to strike the instruments in order produce percussive sounds, in other pieces there's scarcely any use of normal tone production, all the notes are distorted, for instance by playing on or behind the bridge or bowing or striking the strings with the wood of the bow.

The formal criteria that had previously been taken for granted as an integral part of composition have also changed radically: the established forms like the sonata, like the strophic or song form, the variations form, the rondo form, by means of which you could always identify the formal aspects of a piece, even with a new and different content, play hardly any role any more. In the later 20th century pieces form has almost nothing to do with the forms of the classical and romantic works. For instance, when you look at the quartets by Lutosławski, Kagel, Nono, and Gielen, they're works that redefine all the criteria that prevailed when they were written, so much so that it's not possible to establish any kind of similarities among them. Ligeti's second quartet, however, is still a five movement piece that is oriented towards recognizable forms.

So for many years there haven't been any binding criteria for musical composition. The fact that in recent years now there is a counter-tendency to reverse this again, and we've seen the appearance of neo-conservative, neo-classical, and neo-romantic works, in which the 20th

century's extremes are repudiated for the sake of making music comprehensible to the listener again – that's another story. But at the time in which we were particularly interested in the new music and participated in it with our enthusiasm and our ability to play it, music had gotten itself into an extreme of multiplicity and diversity: there was almost nothing in common between any two works, and we had to learn each new work from the ground up, like the alphabet, so it was often very difficult to take up these works and make them our own.

RS Is the kind of composition that the quartets by Brown, Evangelisti, and Lutosławski represent, in which the players have to contribute to the compositional process, still analyzable in the usual sense?

WL A new form of analysis is required. Everything is analyzable, of course, you can see how a piece is 'made,' how it's put together: every piece is 'made' in this sense. Composers also write to tell you how it's made. Even when you're asked, as an interpreter, to contribute to the compositional process, that doesn't mean that they haven't 'composed' something, in the original sense of the word. You also have to analyze what you're contributing as a player to the composition of pieces like Evangelisti's *Aleatorio* or in the quartet by Earle Brown. That means that sometimes you have to analyze not just the note heads but also the instructions for the piece that a composer has written.

RS So then it's still true, what Schoenberg said: 'What's important is not how it's made but rather what it is.'[79]

WL Yes, and how it sounds! Of course Schoenberg was defensive about analyzing twelve-tone music. What mattered was what resulted from it. You can also write bad twelve-tone music, academic twelve-tone music, music that uses all twelve tones and follows all the rules and is still utterly banal. No system, not even the twelve-tone 'system,' can prevent stupidity. Once he'd invented it, Schoenberg scarcely ever kept strictly to his own system. It was too boring for him!

[79] 'I can not warn often enough against overestimating these analyses, since they really only lead to something that I've always fought against: to a knowledge of how it is *made*, whereas I have always aimed to help understand what it *is*' (Schoenberg's emphases). From a letter to Rudolf Kolisch dated July 27, 1932, in Arnold Schoenberg: *Ausgewählte Briefe*, Erwin Stein, ed. (Mainz, 1958), p. 179.

18 Other 20th Century Composers

ROBERT SPRUYTENBURG: You played a number of other 20th century composers, both European and American, in addition to those you commissioned and premiered.

WALTER LEVIN: Yes, and many of them were by relatively unknown composers or by composers whose reputation was as something else, as in the case of the pianist Artur Schnabel and writer Theodor W. Adorno.

Artur Schnabel

RS Schnabel's third quartet was one of the more important and exceptional pieces you revived. How did you come across it?

WL That's another one of these fantastic chains of coincidences. To begin with, I'd heard about Schnabel even when I was a child, and not only because he was such a prominent pianist and musician. The whole time my mother was in Berlin she studied with Georg Grünberg, who was a cousin of Schnabel's and a fabulous pianist who unfortunately suffered from stage fright and couldn't give concerts. Schnabel said that Grünberg was a far more gifted pianist than he himself was. Schnabel was also living in Berlin at that time, he picked out the Bechstein concert grand that my mother then bought. I knew his 1932 recording of the Beethoven first piano concerto with the London Symphony Orchestra under Malcolm Sargent, and in the 1930s he also made the first complete recording of the Beethoven sonatas. And then in Palestine my teacher Bergmann had asked me if I knew Carl Flesch's *Art of Violin Playing*, which he said I had to get for myself. I looked for it but couldn't find it in the second hand music shops. So I wrote to Herbert Brün's uncle Paul who had stayed in Berlin and asked him if he could send me a copy. In 1939, just before the war broke out, he sent me the *Art of Violin Playing.*

The second volume of the *Art of Violin Playing* has an appendix with twelve examples of different musical styles, with the music and a bar by bar analysis on facing pages: phenomenal! That's how I happen to know the a minor concerto by Spohr, Opus 47, *In the Form of a Vocal Scene.* And the next to the last example was the third movement of Schnabel's sonata for solo violin, 'In the Form of a Suite.' Flesch was well known as Schnabel's partner on the violin, with whom he played sonata recitals in Berlin, and together they published an edition of the Mozart and

Brahms violin sonatas with the fingerings and interpretation markings in the piano parts by Schnabel and the bowings and fingerings in the violin parts by Flesch. The Schnabel solo sonata is a huge piece, 45 minutes long, and notated without bar lines.[1] So that was how I learned that Schnabel was a composer of avant-garde music. It was my first encounter with Schnabel's music. I was fifteen at the time and I've never forgotten it. I couldn't believe my eyes! Schnabel wrote music like that but played only classical repertory?

RS That's absolutely astounding. Wasn't he concerned about getting his music heard?

WL In any event he scarcely did anything to promote his compositions and took no active role in their performance. Someone who had known him well once told me that Schnabel found himself in a dilemma about this: for a whole generation of music lovers he was famous as a pianist of Viennese Classicism, that is, as the great interpreter of the piano music of Mozart, Beethoven, and Schubert. And apparently he was afraid of confusing his public with the fact of his also being an avant-garde composer who wrote music in a highly original atonal idiom. He knew Schoenberg personally and all the other Viennese composers of his day: he had grown up in Vienna. He didn't want to upset people with the idea that their idol wrote a kind of music that they had a lot of reservations about or were even hostile to.

And it's still that way today: hardly anyone plays Schnabel's music. When the Academy of Art in Berlin took over Schnabel's estate in 2001 they put on a series of concerts in which at least almost all his chamber music was performed. I recommended the Minguet Quartet, the Vogler Quartet, the Pellegrini Quartet, and the Petersen Quartet as performers for his string quartets. Christian Tetzlaff and Stefan Litwin were to play the sonata for violin and piano[2] and Tetzlaff was to play the solo violin sonata. They had already studied both these works with me in Cincinnati. There's a fabulous recording of their performances. In America Schnabel also wrote three big symphonies, but you never hear them either.[3]

1 Composed in 1919.

2 Composed in 1935.

3 Schnabel's first symphony, written in 1938, was premiered in 1946 by Dimitri Mitropoulos and the Minneapolis Symphony. His second symphony, written 1941–1943 was not performed until Jürg Wyttenbach conducted it with the Deutsches Symphonie Orchester Berlin in 2001. The third symphony, from 1948–1949, has yet to receive a public performance, but, together with the first and second symphonies, has been recorded by the American violinist and conductor Paul Zukovsky. Schnabel's compositions also included a piano concerto, a *Rhapsody* for orchestra, choral works and songs,

RS Did you also know Schnabel's five string quartets?

WL Yes, the first quartet had already been published by Universal Edition in 1927. The second, third, and fourth were composed while Schnabel was still in Berlin, the fifth in America, in Colorado of all places.[4] I got the Schnabel Memorial Committee, who were arranging for the publication of his works, to make copies of the handwritten scores for me, and after I'd had a look at them I thought that the third was the most advanced. I was eager for us to learn it, to the great consternation of my colleagues: a long, very difficult piece, more than 35 minutes long and useless as an audience pleaser. I don't know whether anyone had ever played it again after the premiere by the Kolisch Quartet in Berlin in 1929.

RS At that time did you know it had been premiered by the Kolisch Quartet?

WL No, I only found out about that at the Kolisch memorial celebration at the Schoenberg Institute in Los Angeles in 1980.[5] There were lectures, and we played the third Schoenberg quartet. In a review of our concert a critic noted that it was interesting to see that we too played the Schoenberg quartet from the score. The Kolisch Quartet's performing copies of the scores were on exhibition, and they had glued them together exactly the way as we had: they looked exactly the same! And there were their parts, also glued together from the score, for the third Schnabel quartet, which we were working on just then.

RS What did you find so fascinating about Schnabel's third quartet?

WL I find it an astonishing piece because it's so different from everything else that we know and also from every model that he may have had in mind, it's completely original in form and diction. These characteristics alone show him to be a composer of genius. He does write in an outspokenly

a number of pieces for solo piano, and various works for chamber ensembles, including five string quartets, a string trio, and a piano quintet.

4 Schnabel's first quartet dates from 1918, his second from 1921, the third from 1922, the fourth from 1930, and the fifth from 1940. The first quartet was premiered by the Premyslav Quartet in Frankfurt in 1919; after the Second World War it was taken up by the Juilliard Quartet. The second quartet was premiered in 1924; the circumstances of its premiere, as well as those of the fourth quartet, are unknown. The third quartet was premiered by the Kolisch Quartet in Berlin in 1929; the fifth by the Galimir Quartet in New York in 1941. See Werner Grünzweig's program book for the concert series presented in connection with the exhibition 'Artur Schnabel – Musiker/Musician' (Berlin, 2001).

5 Established at the University of Southern California in 1970, where Schoenberg had taught 1935–1944, the Arnold Schoenberg Institute's archive was transferred to the newly founded Arnold Schoenberg Center in Vienna in 1998.

atonal harmonic idiom, but it's quite clear that he is working in the classical tradition: he develops his themes, he uses the techniques of variation as well as a very much extended sonata form. Although the work is in a single through-composed movement, you can still distinguish three movements within it, a model that we already know from Schoenberg's first quartet and Zemlinsky's second. All of these elements allude to the classical tradition, but the way in which the piece is composed is absolutely original. I don't know any other piece that sounds even remotely like Schnabel's third quartet. Sometimes it's reminiscent of Reger, Bartók, Schoenberg, or Berg, but only incidentally and then for just a moment, fleetingly. When a composer succeeds in composing something that's completely and uniquely itself, I'm fascinated, it's an extraordinary achievement!

RS Do you find the fourth and fifth quartets less interesting than the third?

WL Yes, because they're harmonically less complex. Reading them, I find them somewhat more primitive, almost artless, I might say. But I would have to actually hear them. I often change my mind considerably when I hear a piece that I've previously only read. But who's playing Schnabel quartets these days?[6]

Mátyás Seiber

RS Another composer who you particularly esteem is Mátyás Seiber.[7]

WL Absolutely, and I don't understand why his works are so seldom performed. He was a Hungarian, a thoroughbred of a musician who had an interesting career: after studying composition with Zoltán Kodály in Budapest he got a job as a cellist in a dance orchestra on an ocean liner, went to South and North America, and had the opportunity to hear jazz in New York. In 1928 he began teaching at the Hoch Conservatory in Frankfurt, where he established the world's first curriculum for the scientific study of jazz, and he also directed at theaters in Frankfurt. So his music has components similar to Herbert Brün's:

[6] Schnabels's third quartet was recorded by the LaSalle Quartet for Deutsche Grammophon; the first quartet has been recorded by the Whitman Quartet and by the Pellegrini Quartet, the fourth quartet by a free-lance quartet in New York; and the fifth quartet by the Pellegrini Quartet.

[7] Hungarian composer Mátyás Seiber (1905–1960) left Germany in 1933 and settled in England in 1935. He taught composition at Morley College in London from 1942 until his death in an automobile accident while on a lecture tour of South Africa. Seiber was instrumental in finding a position for Ligeti after the failed Hungarian revolution in 1956; Ligeti later dedicated his 1961 *Atmosphères* to Seiber's memory.

both of them are composers with jazz in their blood: in his second string quartet Seiber writes a blues movement. There's an exceptionally prominent rhythmic component in Seiber, and he loves to use dance forms. But his compositions were also influenced by Bartók and Schoenberg. His music is extraordinarily attractive, and I think the second and third quartets are really very good. I don't know the first one, I don't even know if it still exists or whether it's been lost.[8]

RS But you didn't play Seiber's quartets very often, actually you played his second quartet only four times, and his third quartet, the *Quartetto Lirico*, just once.

WL But we recorded it, in London I believe. It's a beautiful piece! It's dedicated to the Amadeus Quartet, and they also premiered it. But they didn't much like it, it was too modern for them. It was also supposed to be performed in 1954 at the ISCM festival in Israel, where we were to play Roger Sessions' second quartet and Leon Kirchner's first. When we arrived, Seiber was very unhappy, because the Israeli quartet that was supposed to play his *Quartetto Lirico* had apparently only played it through one time, over the weekend. It was so bad that he said he couldn't allow them to perform it. Whereupon he asked us if we would play it.

RS At sight?

WL Indeed. But we had to say no. For that he would have needed an ensemble like the Arditti Quartet, they wouldn't have hesitated to play it at sight, and they would have played it very well.

RS So you got to know Seiber at the ISCM festival in Israel in 1954. Did you meet him again later on?

WL We corresponded with him, but we never ran into him again. He was a wonderful, very refined gentleman, a type similar to Lutosławski, serious-minded and highly cultivated.

Theodor W. Adorno

RS Is it fair to say that Adorno[9] was one of the central figures at Darmstadt?

[8] Seiber's first quartet was composed in 1924; his second in 1935, and his third, the *Quartetto Lirico*, in 1948–1951.

[9] Theodor W. Adorno (1903–1969), German philosopher, musicologist, and sociologist was,

WL No, you couldn't really say that. He belonged to the older generation. He did give some important lectures at Darmstadt, but he was a sort of 'opposition figure.' There was a real row between Adorno and Heinz-Klaus Metzger over Adorno's radio broadcast 'Modern Music is Growing Old.'[10] Adorno was someone who on the one hand enjoyed enormous prestige but on the other hand provoked conflicts, in particular with the younger generation at Darmstadt. He was also suspicious to them as a representative of the people who had emigrated to America.

RS And who 'had it good.'

WL Yes, it was assumed that the emigres had all had a good time of it in America. The younger generation hadn't much of a clue about what difficult fate emigration had been for a great many people. The fact that there were some who were able to succeed even under these dreadful circumstances, like Lion Feuchtwanger and Thomas Mann in Los Angeles, was rather the exception than the rule. For a man like Schoenberg emigration was a very hard fate. These are things that the younger generation simply can't begin to imagine. You can read about them, and you can try to understand them, but it's not the same as having lived through it.

Adorno was in England and New York before he settled in Los Angeles, where he was in contact with Thomas Mann about *Doktor Faustus*, and *Doktor Faustus* was a thorn in many people's sides. All such things provoke conflict and contradiction even among highly intelligent people. Just as with Toscanini, these were people who had taken their moral opposition to Hitler seriously and now were reproached with having taken a high moral stand while having no idea how difficult it was back home. Adorno was also subject to all these contradictions, as was

together with Max Horkheimer, a founder of the Frankfurt-based Institute for Social Research, which attracted a circle of scholars and writers including Walter Benjamin, Herbert Marcuse, Leo Lowenthal, and Erich Fromm, later known as the originators of 'critical theory,' first systematically articulated in Adorno and Horkheimer's *Dialectic of Enlightenment* (1944). A prolific writer, Adorno's *Philosophy of New Music* (1949), *Minima Moralia* (1951), *Dissonanzen* (1956), *Mahler* (1960), and *Quasi una Fantasia* (1964) were touchstones of the intellectual self-understanding of the 'Darmstadt School' avant-garde, a position furthered, though not without controversy, by his role as musical advisor to Thomas Mann in the writing of Mann's novel *Doktor Faustus*. Adorno emigrated to England in 1934, and in 1937 joined Horkheimer in New York, where the Institute for Social Research had relocated under the auspices of Columbia University. In 1941 he relocated to the Los Angeles area for the duration of the war, returning to Europe in 1949.

10 Adorno's '*Das Altern der neuen Musik*' was broadcast by the South German Radio (SDR) in April, 1954; Metzger's response, '*Das Altern der Philosophie der neuen Musik*' ('The Philosophy of New Music is Growing Old') appeared in 1957. The ensuing controversy continued for many years.

the older generation in general, as was Hermann Scherchen. On the one hand they were admired and their great achievements during the Weimar Republic were well known, on the other hand it was difficult to come to grips with the post-war situation. What position should one take now with respect to the German past? It's still a difficult problem for most Germans and for the younger generation too: it's possible that Germany is beginning to find itself only just now, nearly 70 years after the Nazis seized power.

Another factor was the dependence of the West on America, and more generally the relationship with America, which also played a role at Darmstadt. Many of the people who came to Darmstadt, for instance Stefan Wolpe, represented the Weimar Republic generation, they came from the circles around Schoenberg, first in Vienna and then in Berlin, and had emigrated to America. That made people uneasy, suspicious, since the issue of 'restitution' was so pervasive. Schoenberg himself never came to Darmstadt, although he would have been more than welcome there: unfortunately he died too soon.

RS You met Adorno on that memorable occasion when you had to take over Kolisch's course on the quartets of the Second Viennese School.[11] Did you have any subsequent contact with him?

WL No, I did my best to avoid it. He couldn't abide anyone walking in the footsteps of his god, Kolisch. But we did both participate in the Webern memorial concert in Darmstadt[12] in which Kolisch and Eduard Steuermann played Webern's violin pieces, Carla Henius sang his songs – with Adorno at the piano! – and we played his string quartets. That was a very beautiful concert. A great many famous people participated, while we were the junior partners. But all the same they listened to us, even Adorno listened to us, and Kolisch had listened very closely, since he asked us afterwards whether we realized that the pauses we made between each of the *Bagatelles* were longer than the *Bagatelles* themselves. We actually hadn't realized that, and it was something we took care of right away!

RS How did you come to play Adorno's *Two Pieces for String Quartet*?

WL I found out about them when Heinz-Klaus Metzger and Rainer Riehn began publishing Adorno's compositions in 1980, they were published by edition text + kritik, another imprint of the publisher of their journal

[11] See p. 121.

[12] See p. 227.

Musik-Konzepte.[13] Rolf Tiedemann, the executor of Adorno's estate, had withheld Adorno's music for quite a long time. Adorno himself had no particular interest in promoting his compositions, and had done nothing about getting them published. It took a while before Metzger succeeded in getting Tiedemann to agree to allow them to be published. The *Two Pieces for String Quartet* were also played again in 1988, though not by us of course, at the big Adorno symposium in Frankfurt, along with Adorno's orchestral and choral pieces. Sigfried Schibli, who wrote a dissertation on Adorno, wrote a little book about it. It was a lovely festival, I heard a lot of Adorno's music there for the first time.[14]

RS Who played the *Two Pieces for String Quartet* there?

WL The Buchberger Quartet. There's a recording of this whole event.

RS You played Adorno's *Two Pieces for String Quartet* in 1986.[15] That was the last piece you learned before the end of your career. I listened to it: it's a good, typical, piece of Schoenberg-school writing.

WL Indeed, absolutely. Berg also wrote a nice letter to Schoenberg about it, describing it as belonging to this school and none other, and recommending Adorno to Schoenberg.[16] But Schoenberg didn't like Adorno. As a student of Berg's in Vienna Adorno had become thoroughly familiar with the methods and practices of the Schoenberg circle. But he kept himself off to one side and was skeptical of the new orthodoxy. In his lifetime Adorno was opposed to all a priori systems, composition systems included. In any case he never kept to the laws of the Schoenberg method – nor did Schoenberg, by the way – and Schoenberg was allergic

[13] *Kompositionen Band 1: Lieder für Singstimme und Klavier* and *Kompositionen Band 2: Kammermusik, Chöre, Orchestrales* (both Munich, 1980); *Klavierstücke* (2001); *Kompositionen Band 3: Kompositionen aus dem Nachlass* (2007).

[14] The concert took place on September 17, 1988, at the Frankfurt Alte Oper as part of a series commemorating the 50th anniversary of the Nazi's *Kristallnacht* pogrom of November 9–10, 1938. See Schibli, *Der Komponist Theodor W. Adorno* (Frankfurt, 1988). A portion of the papers presented at the conference were later published by Metzger and Riehn in *Theodor W. Adorno: Der Komponist*, volume 63/64 of *Musik-Konzepte* (1989).

[15] The LaSalle Quartet's sole performance of Adorno's *Two Pieces for String Quartet* was on October 28, 1986, in Cincinnati.

[16] 'The performance of [Adorno's] insanely difficult quartet was a coup for the Kolisch Quartet, who learned it in eight days and played it perfectly. I find [Adorno's] work *very good* and believe that you will also find it satisfactory once you get to know it. – In any case, in its seriousness, its compression, and above all the unblemished clarity of its every aspect, it is appropriate to regard it as belonging to the Schoenberg school (and nowhere else!).' Quoted by Walter Levin in his essay '*Adornos Zwei Stücke für Streichquartett op. 2*,' *Musik-Konzepte* 63/64 (1989), pp. 74–99.

to criticism from his own rank and file. He probably took Adorno's reservations about the twelve-tone method as a betrayal.

RS Could you perhaps give a short description of the *Two Pieces for String Quartet*?

WL Both pieces are highly ambiguous mixed forms that elude traditional analysis and in keeping with the new methods of analysis these forms have to be derived from the structures themselves. The two pieces were composed separately, one in 1925 in Vienna, the other in 1926 in Frankfurt, and only afterwards brought together as Opus 2, and then in reverse chronological order: the 1926 piece first, the 1925 piece second. The first piece can be conceived of either as a sonata or a rondo. The development of the musical ideas, of the thematic substance, is accomplished in the sense of Schoenberg's 'continuous variation' by constant alteration and development of the material. Literal repetition would contradict the way this music is to be understood as 'suffering fate,' a favorite concept of Schoenberg's and Berg's. In this movement what is remarkable is the elective affinity of this Berg student with Schoenberg: stretches of the music sound like Schoenberg's fourth quartet, which is dated 1936. The second piece is a theme with twelve variations. In that he connects the variations having related characters and tempi into larger units, Adorno shapes the movement into a through-composed three part song form. What is striking is the similarity of this movement in its overall disposition and in many of its details to the third movement of Schoenberg's second quartet, the '*Litanei*' movement.

Ernst Toch and Ernst Krenek

RS You supported Apostel and took up the cause for Zemlinsky, who had been forgotten. But the most forgotten composer of the 20th century was, according to his own statements, Ernst Toch.[17] Weren't you interested in his work? He did write thirteen string quartets.[18]

[17] Ernst Toch (1887–1964) came to the attention of the Viennese public as a seventeen year old when the world famous Rosé Quartet premiered his sixth quartet in 1905. After being awarded Frankfurt's Mozart Prize for composition in 1909, he studied piano and composition at Frankfurt's Hoch Conservatory. In 1933 he emigrated to London and in 1935 to America, where he obtained an appointment as professor of composition and music theory at the University of Southern California in Santa Monica in 1936, where he wrote the scores for sixteen films produced by Paramount. Toch wrote seven symphonies, the third of which was awarded a Pulitzer Prize in 1957.

[18] Toch's first five quartets were written 1902–1903; the sixth in 1904–1905; further quartets were written in Europe in 1908, 1910, 1919, 1921, and 1924. Two more were written in America, in 1946 and in 1953–1954.

WL Well, in post-war Austria Apostel was practically starving. Toch was in America, in Hollywood, and he at least didn't have it at all bad there. Of course he was an emigre, but he was a professor of composition and music theory at the University of Southern California at Santa Monica and also had an income from movie scores for Paramount Studios in Hollywood. There were very good composers and musicians working for the movie companies. The members of the Hollywood Quartet for instance all played in the Warner Brothers and 20th Century Fox's studio orchestras. At this time Hollywood really was an incredible 'Weimar of the West.'

I knew a few pieces by Ernst Toch, but in one way or another they didn't particularly appeal to me. Ultimately there has to be an impetus to do anything: it might well have been that I would discover a Toch quartet sometime and then become an enthusiastic Toch promoter. But that didn't happen. It was the same with some composers in Schoenberg's wider circle in Berlin who didn't belong to his inner circle and for whom I had very little interest. Roberto Gerhard, for instance, is a discovery that I've just recently made, through the sister of Catherina Lendle, a student of mine, who wrote an essay on Gerhard and convinced Catherina to play Gerhard's first quartet.[19] I hadn't known about him before then.

And there are a few more composers who we should have performed. But we quite consciously set limits to what we would do, since we weren't able to learn pieces quickly in the way some quartets are able to today. We learned slowly, and therefore our repertory was necessarily limited, and only gradually broadened in the course of time. You can't possibly play the whole quartet repertory anyway. For instance we never played a string quartet by Krenek,[20] who was by no means a bad composer, quite the contrary in fact. I've had a look at some of his quartets again and again, but they aren't to my taste. Hans Landesmann, at the time the general secretary of the Wiener Konzerthaus, asked me whether the LaSalle Quartet might not play some quartets on the occasion of Krenek's 80th birthday. And Krenek himself wrote to us from Los Angeles asking if we wouldn't once play a quartet of his. But it never happened.

[19] Roberto Gerhard i Ottenwaelder (1896–1970), Catalan composer, studied piano with Enrique Granados and composition with Schoenberg; he was Schoenberg's only Spanish student. He emigrated to England in 1939 and spent the remainder of his life in Cambridge. He wrote two quartets, the first in 1950–1955, the second in 1961–1962.

[20] Ernst Krenek (1900–1991) studied with Franz Schreker in Berlin; he was briefly married to Mahler's daughter Anna in 1924. Krenek wrote eight quartets, the first two in 1921, then again in 1923, 1923–1924, 1930, 1936, 1943–1944, and, after a long interval, again in 1980. The fifth quartet, from 1930, was premiered by the Kolisch Quartet. Krenek's 1926 'jazz' opera, *Jonni spielt auf*, secured his reputation as a 'degenerate' composer despite not being Jewish; he came to America in 1938, where he had a somewhat peripatetic academic career while continuing to compose prolifically.

RS Did you know, by the way, that the Buchberger Quartet, who once studied chamber music with you in Cincinnati, has recorded some quartets by Ernst Toch?

WL You see! Herr Toch did eventually get his due, so to speak second hand! Hubert Buchberger is a very fine individual and professor of music at the Frankfurt Academy of Music.[21]

Elliott Carter

RS One of the works in the repertory of the LaSalle Quartet that you played remarkably infrequently was the second string quartet by Elliott Carter.[22]

WL We played it in the same year after it was premiered by the Juilliard Quartet, at Brandeis University, with Carter present, then once on tour in America, and then once in Cincinnati, and then never again. At that time it just wasn't our thing. Still, there's a recording of the concert in Cincinnati which I think is very good. It now gives me a lot of pleasure when I listen to it and I can't begin to imagine why we didn't like the piece at the time. It's very strange, I can't explain it, but one's taste can change a lot over the years in one direction as well as the other.

RS After learning so much more music in the course of your career your ears were open all of a sudden.

WL Yes, you hear things completely differently. And besides which if you listen to it from the standpoint not of a participant but simply as a piece of music, without recalling how difficult it was to learn, then you hear it completely differently yet again.

RS Was Carter's second quartet so off-putting that you paid no attention to his later quartets?

WL You can't be casually concerned with Carter, you have to really work

[21] The Buchberger Quartet studied with the LaSalle Quartet in Cincinnati in the spring of 1986.

[22] Elliott Carter (1908–2012), celebrated and prolific American composer, studied with Gustav Holst and Walter Piston at Harvard and then with Nadia Boulanger in Paris, 1932–1935. He wrote five quartets (1951, 1959, 1971, 1986, and 1995). The LaSalle Quartet first performed his second quartet on June 16, 1960, at Marshall College in Bedford, Connecticut. Two further performances were given, the first at Brandeis University in Waltham, Massachusetts, on July 13, 1960, the second in Cincinnati on May 16, 1961.

very hard to get at his pieces. But we didn't find the prospect of working that hard particularly appealing once we'd rehearsed the second quartet very intensively and hadn't liked it. And so we left the others alone. By the way, there's a wonderful score edition of all five Carter quartets,[23] and the young Pacifica Quartet has released a complete recording of them, and both the Juilliard and the Arditti Quartets have recorded the first four quartets as well.

Wallingford Riegger and Roger Sessions

RS You played Wallingford Riegger's second quartet a few times, the first time in Cincinnati, evidently on the occasion of his 70th birthday.[24] Did you also know Riegger personally?

WL Yes, I met Riegger in 1946 at the Yaddo music festival, near Albany in upstate New York, not far from Galamian's Meadowmount. I was concertmaster there during my first summer studying with Galamian and we played Riegger's orchestra piece *Dichotomy*, one of his first twelve-tone pieces. Riegger was a very intelligent, pleasant, and educated individual. There were the most interesting people at Yaddo then: along with Riegger, Dika Newlin[25] was also there, the student of Schoenberg's. She had just finished writing her doctoral dissertation on Bruckner, Mahler, and Schoenberg, in which she analyzes the affinities of these three composers as heirs to the romantic tradition.[26] An incredible study, I read it right away. She had assembled so much information: colossal! She was someone who really knew what she was doing. But my aversion to Bruckner remained unaffected by that.

RS So Riegger was a twelve-tone composer?

WL Yes, totally, he was one of the first American composers to write atonal

23 *Elliott Carter: The String Quartets* (New York & London, 1998).

24 Wallingford Riegger (1885–1961), American composer and cellist, was in the first class to graduate from the Institute of Musical Art, which later became the Juilliard School of Music, after which he studied at the Academy of Music in Berlin and made the beginnings of a career as a conductor in Germany. His music was influenced by Schoenberg's twelve-tone music as well as by the works of his friends Henry Cowell and Charles Ives. He wrote three string quartets, in 1938–1939, 1948, and 1957.

25 Dika Newlin (1923–2006), American composer and musicologist, began studying with Schoenberg in Los Angeles at the age of 16. She later translated a number of Schoenberg's essays into English, which were published under the title *Style and Idea* (New York, 1951) as well as *Schoenberg Remembered: Diaries and Recollections 1938–1976* (New York, 1980).

26 *Bruckner, Mahler, Schoenberg* (New York, 1947).

and twelve-tone music, he belonged to the American avant-garde. He was also one of the very few American composers who was taken seriously in New Music circles in Europe at that time. The powerful effect of his music often depends on a vehement, even aggressive sense of rhythm. We played his second quartet on our South American tour in 1968, along with Earle Brown's quartet, since we'd been asked to play American string quartets.[27]

RS Was Riegger present when you played his second quartet in Cincinnati in 1955?

WL No, unfortunately, we never met him again.

EVI LEVIN: I took a few lessons in music theory from him in New York, on Herbert Brün's recommendation.

WL Riegger was a good composer who was also interested in the Second Viennese School. Roger Sessions was another exceptional personality: we played his second quartet at the ISCM Festival in Israel in 1954.[28]

RS Sessions must have been a colossal genius. For instance, he'd learned French, German, Italian, and Russian and corresponded with Serge Koussevitzky in Russian!

John Cage

RS When did you get to know John Cage[29] personally?

WL I don't remember anymore whether we met Cage at Darmstadt[30] or whether we met him before then in California, through our fellow student from Juilliard, Robert Craft.

[27] The LaSalle Quartet performed Riegger's second quartet seven times altogether; five of those performances were on their 1968 South American tour.

[28] Session's second quartet was composed 1950–1951; it was premiered by the Pro Arte Quartet in Madison, Wisconsin, when Kolisch was the quartet's first violin.

[29] John Cage (1912–1992), perhaps the most influential of all 20th century American composers, studied with Henry Cowell and Arnold Schoenberg, may fairly be said to have originated the use of chance or 'aleatoric' elements in music, beginning most notably with the third movement of his *Concerto for Prepared Piano and Chamber Orchestra* of 1950–1951.

[30] Cage came to Darmstadt for the first time in 1958; at that time the 'Darmstadt school' serialists found his aleatoric approach to composition, so far removed from any kind of strict rule governance, deeply disturbing.

RS In the Sacher Foundation collection there is a marvelously unstructured, so to speak an aleatoric lecture by Cage that he gave in Cincinnati in February, 1967. How did Cage come to be in Cincinnati?

WL As you know, Cage was not only a composer but also a painter: Alice Weston once put on an exhibition at the Contemporary Arts Center in Cincinnati in which among other things Cage's plexiglass paintings were shown. Cage had given a lecture in Cincinnati, to which we were also invited. Afterwards we told him we were about to begin working on his string quartet[31] and would very much like to work on it with him. Other people at the university were trying to get him an appointment of some kind and we suggested that he come as a guest of the College-Conservatory of Music. He agreed immediately and then spent a semester teaching composition at the College-Conservatory and giving lectures there.

RS Were those always unstructured lectures?

WL Yes, they were, and so was Cage.

EL I also heard him once at the Women's Club in Cincinnati. As he was about to start his lecture, one of the ladies went up onto the stage to close the window, and he told her 'No, don't close the window! The noises outside are part of my lecture!'

WL He was an incredibly mischievous imp and had such a sense of humor! And he was always able to laugh at himself, and whole-heartedly too.

RS His laughter in the Cincinnati lecture is inimitable! He tells the story about how he was about to throw a receipt into a trash basket in the parking lot of a supermarket but the wind blew it away and he didn't make any effort to catch it and so he was one of those people who simply don't pick up after themselves. Whereupon he falls into an incredibly contagious outburst of laughter.

WL Typical Cage! He had a manner of speaking and making fun of himself that immediately put you in sympathy with him. His laughter was in

[31] The *String Quartet in Four Parts*, composed in Paris and New York, 1949–1950, is dedicated to the composer Lou Harrison; it was premiered at Black Mountain College in 1950. It was the second of five quartets by Cage; the first, from 1936, has been lost, and Cage did not return to the genre until his 1983 *Thirty Pieces for String Quartet*, which was followed by his *Music of Four* in 1987–1988 and *Four* in 1989. The LaSalle Quartet first played the *String Quartet in Four Parts* on February 14, 1967, in Cincinnati; they played it eight more times between 1970 and 1973, and recorded it for Deutsche Grammophon in 1972.

fact contagious. He had a colossally charismatic presence and had the gift of being able to present complex subjects in such a way that even lay people could understand them. He was a wonderful, a sympathetic, individual.

RS Were you in frequent contact with Cage during the semester he was in Cincinnati?

WL Of course! He often came to our house, and his friends too. That was a wonderful time, and those visits really were the high points of the year. And of course we rehearsed his *Quartet in Four Parts* with him.

RS What was it like to work with Cage?

WL He had a very good ear and was very critical. When he didn't agree with something, he said so, in a very nice way, but without letting it go. Still, Cage was never unpleasant, he was a friendly person. It was completely different, working with Ligeti: he could often be quite unpleasant. Whereas Cage also laughed at himself when he had some criticism to make, and that took away the sharpness of it.

RS Cage's *String Quartet in Four Parts* was composed 1949–1950, that is, prior to his 'chance' music. Was tone color what the quartet was predominantly about?

WL The impression you get listening to it is old-fashioned, it sounds like medieval music. But it's harmonically very innovative.

RS But it sounds positively archaic. In the *New Grove Dictionary* it says that 'The string quartet translates the sonic imagery of the prepared piano to the medium of the string quartet.'

WL But that's only partly true – in one way it's a kind of 'prepared string quartet,' although the prepared string quartet was really only first introduced much later on, by Helmut Lachenmann. In the Cage quartet each player is assigned certain notes, which are always to be played on the string indicated, usually in a most uncomfortably high position. This gives rise to a sonority that is a complete departure from the usual string sound. The notes assigned to each player are recombined over and over again, so that a new sonority results every time. It was Cage's intention that the notes produced simultaneously by the individual players should meld into a single new sound. That presupposes playing without vibrato, which is why the piece gives the impression of 'medieval music.' But it also depends on the players' being in complete agreement about the exact length of each note. So it forces an incredible ensemble discipline on the players.

RS I would infer from this that the piece is conventionally notated.

WL Yes, completely conventional.

RS In his Cincinnati lecture Cage also quotes one of his composer colleagues who said after the premiere that the only thing interesting about the piece was how it sounds. Whereupon he once again burst out in his inimitable laughter.

WL Exactly! That's so typical of him.

RS In the lecture I just mentioned Cage also mentions that some members of the LaSalle Quartet hadn't looked forward to learning the piece, which occasioned yet another outburst of laughter from him.

WL My colleagues often had that reaction at first. They were sometimes reactionary and rejected anything that they didn't know, just like the music lovers. My colleagues didn't find it appealing to have to learn what they didn't know. They would rather have played what they did know. When Henry Meyer was new to the quartet and we were starting to study Bartók's third quartet he thought it was disgusting. Only as we came to work on the other Bartók quartets, one after the other, did he gradually become familiar with Bartók's style, and then it wasn't a problem for him anymore. But it was always this same reaction. Webern was also strange to them to begin with. I had to persuade them or explain to them what this music was about and why it was important to play such pieces. You can certainly play something you don't like occasionally. They had to learn that. They thought that quartet playing meant just playing what you liked.

RS You never commissioned Cage to write a quartet for you. Would it have been an aleatoric piece?

WL I don't think the direction Cage took corresponded to ours. We did play aleatoric pieces, for instance Evangelisti's *Aleatorio* and the Earle Brown quartet, in which as an interpreter you also have to participate in the compositional process. But even that went beyond what seemed to us to be our strength. None of us were composers, and I had learned not to attempt to do something for which you don't have the necessary talent. That's dilettantism, and I'm not inclined that way.

Leon Kirchner

RS Leon Kirchner[32] must have been quite an impressive personality.

WL Jimmy Levine commissioned Kirchner to compose a piece for the Boston Symphony Orchestra in 2006 when he was eighty-seven years old and still very active! That summer he, Elliott Carter, and Milton Babbitt performed the speaking roles in Stravinsky's *Soldier's Tale* under Jimmy's direction at Tanglewood. He was the youngest of the three composers![33] That must have been just sensational! I hope there'll be a recording of it.

RS Kirchner's first quartet was one of the American quartets that you played at the ISCM Festival in Israel in 1954.

WL Yes, as an American quartet we were invited to Israel by Peter Gradenwitz to play Kirchner's quartet as well as Roger Sessions' second quartet. Nobody in Israel could play them. On the return trip we recorded Kirchner's first quartet for the French radio. It's a good piece: after the premiere Szigeti called it the seventh Bartók quartet, though I wouldn't really call it that at all myself. By now there are four quartets by Kirchner. I just read a review in the New York Times about a complete performance of them by a quartet I don't know.[34] That made me want to listen to his first quartet once again: I haven't heard it for a long time.

RS Did you also get to know Kirchner personally?

WL Yes, but only much later, when he was invited by the Chicago Symphony to be Composer in Residence at the Ravinia Festival.

Gunther Schuller

RS You performed Gunther Schuller's first quartet quite a few times, eleven altogether.[35] Where did you meet him?

[32] Leon Kirchner (1919–2009), studied with Arnold Schoenberg, Roger Sessions, and Ernst Bloch. He wrote four string quartets (1949, 1958, 1966, and 2006). The third quartet includes a part for electronic tape; the piece won the Pulitzer Prize for music in 1966.

[33] Elliott Carter was born in 1908, Milton Babbitt in 1916.

[34] It was probably the Orion Quartet, whose performance of the four Kirchner quartets in New York was reviewed in *The Times* on March 9, 2007.

[35] Gunther Schuller (1925–) is noted for his pursuit of a 'fusion' of jazz and classical music. He wrote what was probably the first analytically rigorous study of jazz, *Early Jazz:*

WL He was at Darmstadt in 1956 also.

RS That's about the last thing I would have expected!

WL Indeed. At that opening night dinner with the mayor of Darmstadt, when I was talking with Otto Tomek, the director of the New Music department at WDR about Hans Erich Apostel, who the LaSalle Quartet wanted to support financially with a commission for a string quartet, someone at the table behind us turned around and said he'd just heard us talking about our intention to commission a string quartet and wouldn't we like to commission one from him too? It was Gunther Schuller, who had just written his first quartet, which was subsequently published by Universal Edition. He was at Darmstadt to conduct one of his pieces, that's how we met him. A few years later, in 1960, we learned his first quartet and invited him to Cincinnati for the performance, about which he was very enthusiastic. It was on this occasion that he heard recordings of the LaSalle Quartet at our house and recommended us to Columbia Records in New York.[36] Schuller had studied for a while in Cincinnati at the College of Music when it was still a Catholic school, where we also taught when we first came to Cincinnati. At seventeen he was the principal horn in the Cincinnati Symphony Orchestra, prior to his being engaged as co-principal by the Metropolitan Opera in New York two years later.

RS But you didn't respond to his request for a string quartet commission after you met him at Darmstadt.

WL No, I wanted first of all to learn the quartet he'd just written. It's a very beautiful piece, not easy, but good. Hasn't he written more quartets by now?

RS Yes, there are now four quartets, and in 1988 he wrote a concerto for string quartet and orchestra.

WL That's really interesting! I don't know any of these pieces. We rather lost track of Schuller when he went to Boston and became the director of the New England Conservatory. Jimmy Levine likes him a lot and enjoys playing his music.

Its Roots and Development (London and New York, 1968), which he followed with *The Swing Era: the Development of Jazz 1930–1945* (New York and Oxford, 1989); both are considered standard works of jazz research. His book *Horn Technique* (Oxford, 1962) remains a standard work. Schuller has written four string quartets (1957, 1966, 1986, and 2002) as well as a concerto for string quartet (1988). The LaSalle Quartet played his first quartet for the first time in Cincinnati on February 2, 1960.

[36] See pp. 148–149.

RS It's really too bad that you lost contact with Schuller, since when you read his *Compleat Conductor*[37] with its analyses of the pieces he takes as examples …

WL … it's completely in line with our approach, absolutely. And when I listen to the recordings[38] you recently brought with you, it's really incredible! They show once again that there are no good orchestras, only good conductors, conductors who know how to work with an orchestra, although the orchestra on these recordings is actually a hand-picked orchestra made up of some of the best musicians in New York. A good orchestra can even be a hindrance if the players have too high an opinion of themselves. There may be good individual players in them, but they only play well when they're led by a conductor who demands a high level of performance: then they can achieve fabulous things. The NBC Symphony, for instance, was made up of nothing but virtuosos, but as an orchestra it was impossible. It was only brilliant when it was conducted well, as it was by Toscanini. I think we should nominate Schuller to be the conductor of the Basel Symphony. Wouldn't that be a nice idea?

RS He's a year younger than you.

WL So he's still a young man! And for conductors that's a young age anyway. At 86 Pierre Monteux agreed to a 25-year contract with the London Symphony Orchestra, and the contract had a provision for extensions.[39]

37 Gunther Schuller, *The Compleat Conductor* (Oxford, 1997).

38 Beethoven, Symphony Nr. 5, and Brahms, Symphony Nr. 1, with a New York free-lance orchestra conducted by Gunther Schuller. The concertmaster is David Nadien, who had been a student of Galamian's together with Levin in the late 1940s.

39 The intent of such a contract is, of course, 'for life': Monteux would have been 111 by the time the 25-year term of the contract was up. But Monteux died three years after the contract was agreed to, at the age of 89.

19 *Questions of Interpretation*

ROBERT SPRUYTENBURG: If you've attended your chamber music courses for as many years as I have, what is always astonishing is how you are able to take a fresh look at every piece you work on with young ensembles, and that evidently your previous musical interpretation is never the last word for you.

WALTER LEVIN: That's right, it's always a 'work in progress.' There's no such thing in my opinion as 'the last word,' not for interpretation, not for how to play, not for how to practice. There was no 'last word' for us. And that also distinguished us from many other quartets.

RS Yes, I noticed that about you right from the very beginning, and that's what I admire so much, that you never stand still.

WL No, I don't. I would find it boring. I also find it impossible purely theoretically: there simply can't be any definitive interpretations. There's only the path you take, and in retrospect you always have to question whether the choices you make all the time are still valid. If they aren't, then you have to change them.

RS And sometimes this means going back to a position you held previously.

WL That certainly can happen.

Tempo Changes over the Years

RS There was a beautiful example of that once when you were working with the young Ullmann Quartet on Beethoven's Opus 127. Since there are no metronome marks for the last quartets, the question arises as to how fast the introductory *Maestoso* should be. You prompted the Ullmann Quartet to play it relatively quickly, and I took the liberty of looking at my watch: the *Maestoso* lasted fourteen seconds, exactly the same as your 1974 live concert recording from Cincinnati. I was completely taken aback, since in your 1976 recording for Deutsche Grammophon it lasts about twenty seconds: that's almost half again as long.

WL That's absolutely astounding!

RS What's astounding is that you've now gone back to that earlier tempo.

WL It also makes a difference sometimes, whether you're playing or listening.

RS But when you listen to the WGUC live recordings of the LaSalle Quartet from Cincinnati and other radio recordings, you soon realize that, despite the interpretive 'work in progress,' ultimately your interpretations have remained unbelievably constant over the years. But I remember that you once said in a chamber music class that when you take up a given piece again after not playing it for some time your first reaction is often that you just can't play it the way you did before! Whereupon I went looking for examples of pieces that you played differently in the course of time. It was very frustrating, because I found scarcely any, only a very few. One of them is the third movement of the Debussy quartet, the *Andantino*. In a radio broadcast with Roman Brotbeck ten or so years ago[1] you said that you were very unhappy with your 1971 recording for Deutsche Grammophon, as you now wouldn't play the third movement so slowly.

WL No, that's right.

RS But since you didn't play the Debussy quartet again after the spring of 1972,[2] it's not possible to show that by comparing the Deutsche Grammophon recording with later recordings of live performances. Debussy writes eighth note = 80, the LaSalle Quartet played eighth note = 60 on the Deutsche Grammophon recording as well as in earlier live recordings from Cincinnati, and in a class you gave here in Basel in 1993 you once proposed that the young Amar Quartet play eighth note = 72.

WL And is that what they did?

RS I can't tell, because I don't have a recording of the concert at the school. On the Amar Quartet's later commercial recording they play eighth note = 63.

1 Roman Brotbeck (1954–), Swiss musicologist, lectures at the Bern Academy of the Arts; he was Director of the Bern Biennales in 2008, 2010, 2012. The German-Swiss Radio broadcast comparing recordings was on November 26, 1991.

2 The live recordings are from 1956, 1960, and 1970. In both the 1956 live recording and the studio recording fifteen years later the *Andantino* takes exactly 7' 05". All in all the LaSalle Quartet played the piece twenty-one times.

WL If Debussy writes eighth note = 80, I would try it that way now, even if it goes against everything we're accustomed to. You can do something unusual once in a while! If we didn't do that, it might have been because I wasn't always able to get my own way, as a quartet does consist of four people and we did in fact earnestly discuss such questions. It's certain that we experimented with that tempo but then agreed instead on the tempo we recorded for Deutsche Grammophon. Have you ever looked into what tempo people usually take for this movement?

RS Yes, and the LaSalle Quartet plays what one might call the usual tempo.[3]

WL To be perfectly honest, I have to say that it didn't seem as important to me as it would be in Beethoven. And also we didn't play the Debussy quartet all that often. But there is a recording by the Capet Quartet: that's straight from the source, since they studied it with Debussy himself. I'd like to hear how quickly the Capet Quartet plays the slow movement of the Debussy quartet.[4] I have the recording somewhere, it was originally made for Columbia.

But tempo isn't the only criterion that is open to question. Our interpretations did differ over time, but mainly in details. We never made radical changes in our interpretation of a piece. It would take some very compelling reasons to do that, for instance, if we came by some information that we didn't have before. But that happened only very occasionally.

RS As for example with the *piano* in the first bar and the *forte* in the second bar at the beginning of the first movement of Mozart's F major quartet, K. 590, that have to be linked with a crescendo.

WL Yes, exactly. We didn't do that, because at that time we didn't know that such a dynamic indication implies a crescendo. Or ornamentation, grace notes on or before the beat. For instance, how long should the appoggiaturas, the grace notes, be at the beginning of the first movement of the D major quartet, K. 575? Like this? (Levin sings):

3 Based on a comparison of the tempi taken in recordings by 24 quartets at the beginning of the movement. The tempi vary from a low of eighth = 56 (Linday) to a high of eighth = 69 (Auryn, Casals, Keller); the average is 62.3. The LaSalle Quartet's eighth = 60 is notably shared with the Budapest, Cleveland, and Juilliard quartets.

4 The Capet Quartet's 1928 opening tempo is quite fluidly interwoven with its realization of Debussy's *'doucement expressif,'* but a basic pulse of eighth = 48 is soon established, with the result that theirs is the most drawn out of all recordings of this movement (10' 07" vs the LaSalle Quartet's 7' 05"). Whether the Capet's recorded tempo represents or is at least not inconsistent with Debussy's views when they last discussed the quartet with him is unknown and probably unknowable.

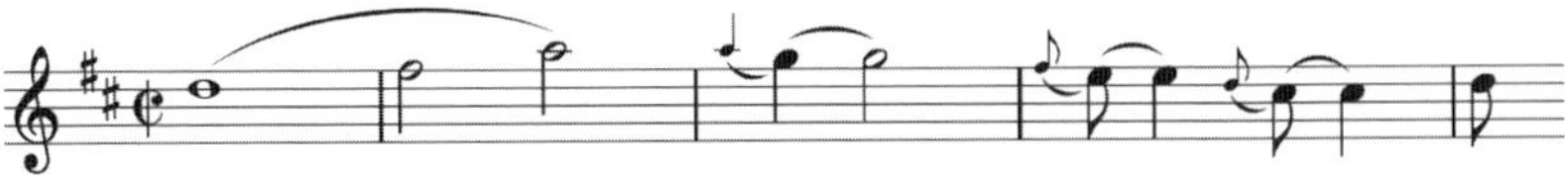

Or like this:

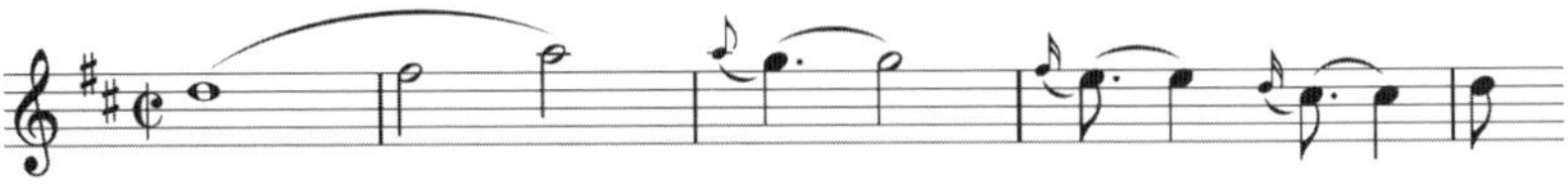

or this:

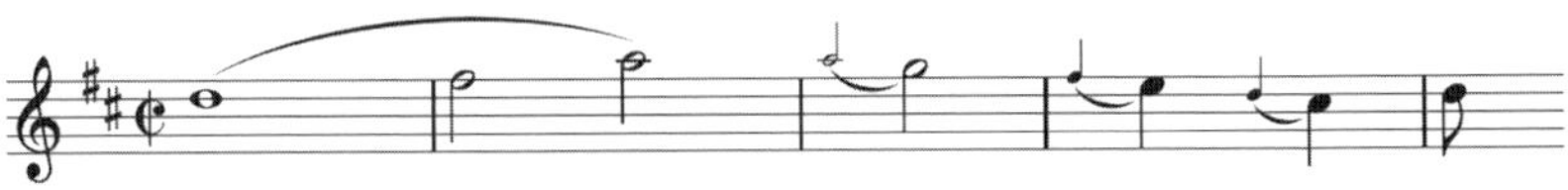

or this?[5]

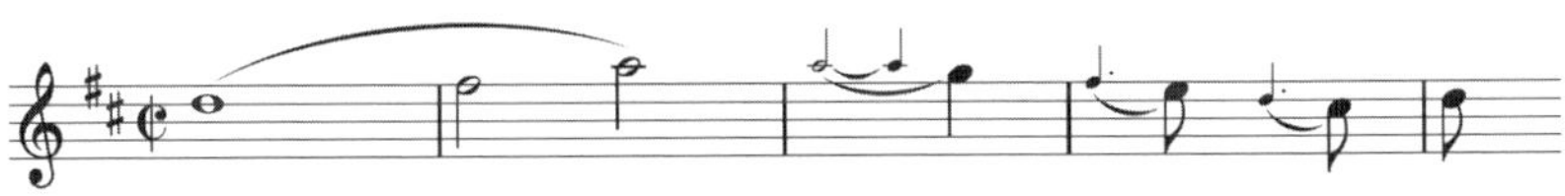

We experimented a lot with that, and it's possible that we also tried out the different possibilities in concert. Also the decision was left up to my colleagues, who usually tended towards something rather conventional. I was always the one who wanted to go against the grain: '*épater le bourgeois.*' Our tempi in Mozart also changed somewhat. And not only in the direction of quicker tempi, sometimes slower tempi too.

RS I listened to all your live recordings of K. 590. The one from 1950 is insanely fast, but after that they're all the same, almost to the second, in all movements.

WL Yes, that's how it was with us. For instance, we recorded the first Schoenberg quartet for Deutsche Grammophon and a year later were there again to record something else, and they asked us to bring the Schoenberg with us since they needed another take at one place. It was in the same studio and the set up was exactly the same as the year before, so that acoustically the retake would exactly match what they already had. And when we'd played the section they needed, Rainer Brock told

[5] The *Neue Mozart Ausgabe* (Kassel, 1955–1991) gives as a further variant.

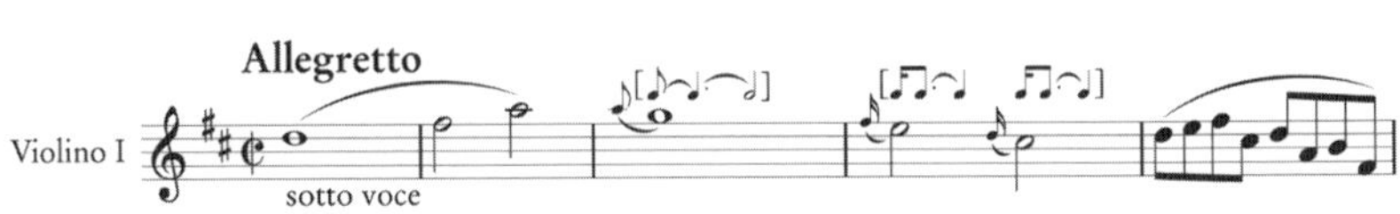

us that we'd taken nearly one whole second longer than the previous year, and this for a section that was about five minutes long. We could do that, we could in fact reproduce a tempo down to the second. We didn't need to check whether that was so or not, it was simply the case. Our sense of tempo was very highly developed. But when we wanted to change a tempo, we could do that too: it wasn't the case that in concert we would unintentionally revert to our prior tempo.

RS I find that all the more astonishing in that you never played a piece in a relentlessly fixed tempo but rather there was a give and take to your tempi, a rhetoric, and nevertheless it would end up being exactly the same length in all your performances. Really astounding!

WL Indeed. You have to develop a feeling for tempo, it doesn't just come to you. And then you can do a retake of something a year later with exactly the same *ductus* and sound and everything else in all respects except maybe one or the other fingering.

But to get back to your question about changes in interpretation: ever since I began to play Beethoven in earnest, my conception of his works has remained by and large the same. I was already familiar with Kolisch's study of tempo in Beethoven when I was at Juilliard, which he'd published in *The Musical Quarterly* in 1943.[6] I got a copy and studied it closely. And through the Juilliard Quartet we knew Eugene Lehner, the violist from the Kolisch Quartet. I could have talked about tempo questions with him all day long. And from the outset we paid close attention to Beethoven's metronome markings and tried them out in our rehearsals. Whether we actually played them in performance is another question. You have to carefully consider to what extent the metronome markings are to be taken as absolute

[6] Kolisch, 'Tempo and Character.' In 1817 Beethoven published two brochures supplying metronome marks for most of his major works up until then (but not including the concerti and the piano sonatas). These did include his symphonies 1–8, his string quartets up through Opus 95, and his very popular septet, Opus 20. Metronome marks for the 9th symphony are found in a letter of October 13, 1826, to his publisher, Schott; his metronome marks for the 'Hammerklavier,' Opus 106, are in a letter of April 16, 1819, to Ferdinand Ries. Metronome marks for Opus 112, *Meeresstille und glückliche Fahrt*, are found in the manuscript. Kolisch's pioneering work represents his attempt to define tempo categories based on his analysis of the musical character of Beethoven's themes and motives in relation to his metronome marks, in order to arrive at a coherent system for determining the tempi for those of Beethoven's works for which the composer did not supply metronome marks. Kolisch's work has remained controversial: see the essays in *Rudolf Kolisch, Tempo und Charakter in Beethovens Musik*, *Musik-Konzepte* 76/77, available in English in *The Musical Quarterly*, vol. 77, 1993. See also Arnold Schoenberg's '*Über Metronomisierung*' in *Beethoven, das Problem der Interpretation*, *Musik-Konzepte* 8 (1985), and, in the same issue, Peter Stadlen's '*Beethoven und das Metronom.*'

and to what extent they have to be qualified by other considerations. Kolisch himself reconsidered many aspects of the question when he published the expanded version of his study that he worked on with David Satz, he extended them and made them more precise, and once again completely revised the tempo categories he had worked out previously. All of which goes to show that questions of tempo are not an exact science but rather that this is a very complex subject involving many aspects that have to be taken into account and that you have to think through completely. But fundamentally I find Beethoven's metronome markings to be of decisive importance for the interpretation of his works, and most of the arguments that have been made against them are simply banal.[7]

RS Despite which you still have to fight for them today!

WL Indeed. And I'm the last person who wouldn't fight for them. I just got an email from a former student who is now a conductor in America in which he'd worked out for all the Beethoven symphonies just how long each movement has to be if you observe Beethoven's metronome marks exactly. He calculated the lengths both with and without the repeats. And if you compare his results with recordings by various conductors, it's astonishing. There are some movements in Toscanini's recordings that are to within a few seconds of their theoretical length. And no one plays a whole movement of Beethoven in a single, rigidly strict, tempo without any rhetorical nuances. But it is indeed astonishing how close some conductors come to the calculated theoretical lengths. I think it's a very interesting subject, which is why I prefer to concern myself with interpreters other than myself.

RS The only other example I've found of a change in concept besides the *Andantino* of the Debussy quartet is in fact in Beethoven: the Minuet of the A major quartet Opus 18, No. 5. In 1953 you played this movement at the tempo indicated by Beethoven: dotted half = 76, but in 1962 you slowed the tempo to dotted half = 60–63.

WL That really is a marked difference. I can't tell you how we arrived at that decision. But didn't we also play Opus 18, No. 5, in our Cincinnati debut concert, along with Schubert's *Quartettsatz* and the fifth Bartók quartet?

7 E.g., 'They are not by Beethoven,' 'they do not really convey his intentions,' 'Beethoven's tempi are unplayable,' 'our modern metronome differs considerably from Beethoven's,' 'they are "inartistic,"' 'his metronome didn't work properly.' See Kolisch, 'Tempo and Character.'

RS Yes, you did, and that's exactly the concert I'm talking about. It's an interesting example, because in Kolisch's tempo categories for the works for which Beethoven didn't give metronome marks the Minuet from Opus 18, No. 5, represents one of the points of reference for minuets of the waltz-type, which also includes the second movement of the a minor quartet Opus 132, the *Allegro ma non tanto*. Kolisch suggests a tempo of dotted half = 72 for this movement, while Beethoven's own indication in Opus 18, No. 5, is dotted half = 76. But you're of the opinion that Kolisch's proposed tempo for the *Allegro ma non tanto* in Opus 132 is too fast.

WL Yes, much too fast.

RS Exactly, and in 1962 you took the second movement of Opus 18, Nr. 5, slower than Beethoven's indicated tempo in the same proportion as you took the *Allegro ma non tanto* of Opus 132 slower than Kolisch's proposal.[8]

WL So that was a conscious decision. It can happen that you find what the composer has prescribed for something to be *'contre coeur*.' It was relatively rare for us to be in fundamental disagreement with one of Beethoven's tempo indications, enough so to have really changed it, and radically so. And in those cases we experimented with alternative tempi, and I can also imagine that the performances changed over the years, since once you begin to have doubts about a tempo you then come back to it again and again: is the change we've made really justified? But there are also some movements in which we deviated from Beethoven's tempo markings from the very beginning of our career.

RS As for example in the slow movement of Opus 74, the *Adagio ma non troppo*, which you play somewhat slower than Beethoven's metronome mark.

WL Yes, but all the same much faster than it's usually played.[9]

RS Another example concerns the tempo of the second movement of Opus 18, No. 1: for this *Adagio* Beethoven prescribed eighth note = 138, which

8 In the live performance recordings the LaSalle Quartet takes the second movement of Opus 132 at dotted half = 60, whereas their recording for Deutsche Grammophon is at dotted half = 54. Most quartets take a tempo of around dotted half = 58; only the Hagen Quartet's dotted half = 69 comes close to Kolisch's proposed dotted half = 72; the Emerson Quartet, by contrast, takes the movement at dotted half = 52.

9 Beethoven's metronome mark is eighth = 72; The LaSalle Quartet plays eighth = 60, but one often hears eighth = 50. In the faster moving parts (measures 87–102 and 115–136) the LaSalle Quartet does reach the tempo indicated by Beethoven.

is a very fleet tempo that nobody takes, not even the LaSalle Quartet. You played eighth note = 112–120.[10]

WL I'm certain we tried it at Beethoven's tempo. But we didn't play the piece very often.

RS Altogether only twice, and there's only one live recording from Cincinnati, a concert on February 11, 1958.

WL Too bad, since there's then no evidence as to whether we tried out other tempi. On the other hand, there are tempi in Beethoven that you can't keep up for the whole movement, namely those complex movements in which extremely different characters are contrasted. For example in the first movement of Opus 95 we only play Beethoven's tempo at the beginning and whenever this theme returns. But I can't play the lyrically contrasting theme that immediately follows in the same aggressive tempo as the beginning, and that's not what he intended either, in my opinion.

RS This movement prompts a comparison with certain pieces by Schumann, the ones with his contrasting characters of Eusebius and Florestan. In Opus 95 there are also two completely incongruent themes.

WL Indeed, exactly. And that's the case in many of Beethoven's pieces, for instance in the first movement of the *Eroica* you also have this kind of contrast between different sections. But complex movements like that are always held together by the constraint imposed by the principal tempo.

RS But there is the classical 'rule' that the first and second themes of a sonata first movement are to be played in about the same tempo, that is, that the difference should be undetectable.[11] In this context I've always been astounded by the first movement of Beethoven's Opus 18, No. 6. You play the first theme at a tempo of whole note = 72–76, which is, as by no one else, almost the tempo given by Beethoven, whole note = 80, whereas you play the second theme at whole note = 54, a radical difference. So the question is, what did you have in mind with this difference?

10 Only the Hagen Quartet takes a comparably fleet tempo, eighth = 126; all the other ensembles considered are significantly slower.

11 As examples Sandra Rosenblum in her *Performance Practices in Classic Piano Music* (Bloomington, 1988) cites Daniel Gottlob Türk's 1789 *Clavierschule* and Johann Nepomuk Hummel's 1828 *Ausführliche theoretisch-practische Anweisung zum Pianoforte Spiel;* see pp. 372 and 363.

WL I simply can't imagine this second theme in Opus 18, No. 6, in the tempo given by Beethoven: for me it makes no sense at all in this tempo. As we've already noted, there are other pieces by Beethoven that are like that for me, the first movement of Opus 95 being one of them.

RS That was my next question: do you regard the first movement of Opus 18, No. 6, as being in the same category as the first movement of Opus 95?

WL As similar, yes. The first theme in Opus 18, No. 6, is exceptionally propulsive: for its first appearance and then whenever it returns the extreme tempo that Beethoven indicates is justified. But then there are also other characters in this movement, and I find the characters in Beethoven to be dramatically much more differentiated than they ever are in Haydn and Mozart. This particularly distinguishes the late Beethoven, and some of his earlier pieces anticipate the late Beethoven: Opus 18, Nr. 6, and Opus 95 are to a certain extent already 'late' Beethoven pieces, for which the concept of a single tempo for a whole movement no longer holds. Okay, you might question whether the difference has to be as radical as we made it. But if you don't make the distinction, then I can't understand what people are thinking of.

RS I tried to make comparisons with other ensembles, but the attempt failed because not one single quartet plays the first theme at the tempo indicated by Beethoven. I compared the Emerson, Juilliard, Alban Berg, and Pražák quartets, and it's astonishing how even the quartets who studied with you, like the Berg Quartet and the Pražák Quartet don't come close to the whole note = 80 indicated by Beethoven but play whole note = 69. And then of course there's much less of a difference with the reduced tempo for the second theme.

WL None of them dare to do it! There are a lot of quartets that studied with us or, later, studied with me, that start out playing pieces like Opus 18, Nr. 6, boldly and, in my opinion, very well, and then a few years later it's all been smoothed over again.

RS Too bad!

WL I think it really is too bad when something that really does have character is suddenly made commonplace again. People are always afraid of their own courage! '*Epater le bourgeois*' was what I was always about, my whole life. There are a few quartets who still retain this character to a certain extent, even today, but not many.

Bartók's Tempo Indications

RS Another composer whose metronome marks are controversial is Bela Bartók. How did you deal with his peculiar metronome marks and his indications of the lengths of the movements? In some pieces he gives the length of individual sections down to the half second and gives metronome marks that don't exist on a conventional metronome. How did he himself determine the tempi when he gives metronome marks of, for instance, 130, 70, or 35, which don't exist on the metronome? And Kolisch reported that he'd noticed many times that Bartók could tell the slightest deviations from his indicated tempi.[12]

WL In this case I don't share Kolisch's opinion. Bartók himself didn't keep to his own metronome markings. There are recordings, for instance those that he made with Szigeti of his sonatas for violin and piano, for which he also gave metronome marks, and he just plays whatever he wants.

RS Okay, but he's also the composer.

WL That's just it! It makes a difference, whether you're the composer interpreting your own works or whether as the composer you're trying to convey to someone else as precisely as possible how you want something to be rendered. That he may only have been rigorous about just these tempi and no other, I could imagine, to some extent, and might even believe, but he was surely interested in other aspects of rendering music as well. Eugene Lehner, the violist of the Kolisch Quartet, told us about how Bartók had come to Vienna, they had played one of his quartets for him, and he had nothing to say about anything except the tempi, nothing else mattered to him. I simply don't believe that. Either they played it so well that he had nothing else to say about it, or what Lehner said just wasn't true. I do believe that Bartók had a very precise idea about tempo relationships and put a lot of emphasis on that. And that he had a very fine feeling for tempo is something I can also imagine. When he asks for tempi that aren't on the metronome, for instance 130, then that simply means that he wants something a bit slower than 132, the next higher mark on the metronome. But even so, when you listen to him playing, he not only doesn't observe his own tempo indications very closely but also plays classical works very romantically, meaning with big fluctuations in tempo. From this standpoint his metronome markings aren't to be taken as absolute. But as an interpreter you should at least take the trouble to approximate the indicated tempo as closely as possible.

[12] In Kolisch, 'Tempo and Character,' p. 131, note 10.

RS Of course we now have electronic, digital metronomes, so that you set any pulse you want. Did you experiment with Bartók's metronome marks or did you just give up on them?

WL Even then we had electronic metronomes with a continuous scale, by means of which you could set any arbitrary intermediate value, and we also had the Tempowatch,[13] with which you can check your tempo. We aimed to get it precisely. Whether we always succeeded in that, is another question.

RS The playing time given for the last, and extremely complex, movement of the fifth quartet, for instance, is so short that it's simply physically impossible to realize it.

WL But we took the trouble to try to learn it at Bartók's indicated tempi. But then when you know the piece thoroughly, you can deviate somewhat for the sake of articulating the musical structure, and you can do that in Beethoven too. But you're right: Bartók's tempo and duration indications in the last two quartets are something you have to consider as almost manic. But you can also hear how the Kolisch Quartet played the fifth quartet: there's a recording of it.[14]

Tempo in Berg's Opus 3

RS We spoke somewhat earlier about the LaSalle Quartet's ability to reproduce the same tempo in a given piece over the course of many years. Now I've come across a case which in this context seems very atypical: Berg's quartet Opus 3, which you played quite often and in almost every season from 1959 to 1986, 97 times all in all. The recordings from Cincinnati that I've listened to, namely the earliest, a couple in the middle, and the last one, reveal that over the years both movements of this piece got slower. Was that a conscious decision?

WL I wouldn't think so.

RS The differences are quite large. To put it in minutes and seconds, in

13 Invented by American oboist and composer Cecil Effinger in 1969 for conductor Robert Shaw, the Tempowatch is a device akin to a stop watch to assist in determining an actual tempo: the user starts the Tempowatch on a given beat and stops it after six more beats; the Tempowatch then displays the exact tempo in beats per minute.

14 Bartók prescribes a duration of 6' 21.5" for the last movement of his fifth quartet. The Kolisch Quartet took 6' 34". The LaSalle Quartet took 6'48" in 1953, 6' 56" in 1963, and 7' 6" in 1979; the Juilliard Quartet took 6' 49" in 1950 and 6' 50" in 1963.

1959 the first movement lasted 8' 14" and in 1986 9' 5", which is a 50 second difference. And the second movement went from 8' 48" to 9' 43", which is almost a minute longer.

WL That's something like ten percent.

RS And in the middle of these years the lengths of the two movements were also more or less in the middle, which is itself rather astonishing.[15]

WL I can't explain it. Unfortunately there are no metronome marks for these pieces.

RS No, but I tried listening to the piece with the metronome and with the Tempowatch, but it has so many tempo changes that it couldn't be done. That's why I gave the lengths in minutes and seconds, I wasn't able to give the differences in metronome marks.

WL Yes, that's right, because this piece is a written-out *rubato*, the tempo is always in flux. It's also precisely, even overly precisely indicated, but only in relative terms. I would say that our getting slower had to do with our striving for clarity and transparency, which in time got to be more and more important to me, and these qualities can sometimes be had only at the cost of a somewhat more measured tempo. But if the dramatic aspect of the piece is lost as result of that, it would be too bad. I hope that isn't the case.

RS No, absolutely not! In particular the earliest recording, from 1959, is still markedly, I might say youthfully, impetuous.

WL Right, at that time we still took a very vigorous approach to it. Berg's Opus 3 is a very complex piece, and apparently it increasingly seemed to me in the course of time that what happens in the piece isn't clear enough, that you actually can't follow it. In general that's one of the problems with the early works of the Second Viennese School, the first Schoenberg quartet is also so dense and is of such a complex polyphony that you simply can't follow it if it goes past the ear too quickly and there

15 After listening to all of the LaSalle Quartet's live recordings, it is apparent that between 1961 and 1979 the first movement varied only between 8' 28" and 8' 47" (the Deutsche Grammophon recording made in 1968 at 8' 55" is almost as long as the longest live performance, in 1986), whereas the second movement varies between 9' 4" and 9' 30". In contrast to Opus 3, the live recordings of the *Lyric Suite* manifest an almost eerie consistency, remaining overall within ±5% over the course of the 36 years 1951–1987, with the fourth movement remaining within ±2%.

isn't enough differentiation among principal and secondary voices and the various motivic elements aren't expressed clearly and transparently. But neither of these are pieces that have to be played in a single rigorous tempo, since they don't have the forward drive of a Beethoven quartet but rather are pieces that so to speak expand and contract and are very rhetorical and similar to speech, what I call 'composed *rubato*.'

You have to balance all that very precisely: there are people who play such pieces so slowly that every single note is spelled out. But then it becomes unclear in a different way, in that you can no longer grasp how the individual notes relate to the whole. So clarity, detail, and context are important, but so is a forward moving flow. To balance all that is very difficult in some pieces. That's why Berg's Opus 3 is known among quartet players as a 'bone of contention,' because there are so many different possible ways to render it. If you want to motivate a quartet to give up and disband as quickly as possible, just assign them Opus 3 to learn.

RS You didn't play Opus 3 off and on in phases, but practically continuously, almost in every season. I have to assume that you didn't rework it from the ground up every time.

WL No, we continued to work on it, again and again, but not from the ground up.

RS Since you usually wrote the tempi you had decided on into your scores, could later performances nevertheless be taken at different tempi?

WL Of course that could happen, since we were always questioning our previous decisions. How was it with our performances of the first Schoenberg quartet? Have you made the comparisons? I would be very interested to know the results, since the first quartet also doesn't have any metronome markings, and it's also an extremely complex piece.

RS That's exactly why I've just listened to all the available live recordings of the piece from Cincinnati. Surprisingly, it's only the second part that gets longer as the years go by, the others stay remarkably close to one another in length.[16]

WL And what about for instance Beethoven's Opus 127, and with the late Beethoven quartets in general? There are no metronome marks for any of these pieces.

16 Schoenberg's first quartet is a through-composed but nevertheless four movement work, the movements of which are to be played without pause.

RS Of the later quartets I've paid the most attention to Opus 127 in this respect. And in this case also the performance lengths of the live recordings from 1966 to 1980 are for the most part unbelievably close together. So Berg's Opus 3 really does seem to be an exception.

WL Yes, that does seem to be the case.

Studio vs. Live Performance Tempi

RS What's perhaps most striking about the LaSalle Quartet recordings is that the live recordings are for the most part faster than the studio recordings.

WL That's obvious.

RS Yes, but why?

WL It's because in a public concert you have an audience, and that gives you a very different kind of adrenalin rush than when you have to try to recreate the atmosphere of a live performance in a cold studio at 11 o'clock in the morning. It's hard to do, and although we were often successful at doing so, sometimes we weren't.

RS So did you play faster than you meant to in the concerts or slower in the recording studio? As we've already seen, you have a highly refined and exact sense of tempo: weren't you ever struck by this difference?

WL Of course you're more cautious when you're making a studio recording, because you want to avoid slip-ups. That alone can lead to a somewhat slower tempo. But how big a difference is there, did you measure that?

RS Yes, I've had a closer look at some pieces for which there are both live performance recordings as well as studio recordings for Deutsche Grammophon. Of course it only makes sense to look at pieces for which the composer has supplied no metronome marks. Brahms' quartet Opus 67 is a good example. Your basic tempo in the first movement is always dotted half = 104 in the live recordings, but in the studio recording it's 96–100, so that in the studio recording this movement at 9' 35" is about half a minute longer than it is in the fastest live recording. In the second movement your basic live tempo is quarter note = 120, in the studio recording 104, and at 7' 18" the movement lasts a good minute longer than the fastest live performance. And in the third movement, the live performance basic tempo of half = 126–132 is noticeably faster than the 120 of the studio recording.[17]

WL Those are in fact very clear differences.

RS Yes, but just for that reason I generally much prefer the recordings of your live performances, of Opus 67 also, on account of their energy and intensity and devil take the hindmost attitude. In Beethoven's Opus 127 too the studio recording for Deutsche Grammophon is clearly the slowest: in the first movement the difference, as we've already discussed, is mostly owing to the slower introductory *Maestoso*, but in the second movement the basic tempo in the studio recording is quarter note = 92 versus 104 in the live performances, so that in the studio recording the movement lasts something on the order of a minute and a half longer. And the last two movements are also half a minute or so longer in the studio recording. In the Scherzo the basic tempo in the studio recording is 60 whole bars per minute, in the live performances it's 62–63, and in the finale you play half note = 112–116 versus 120–126 in the live performances.

WL Yes, and those are also interesting differences. In the late Beethoven quartets our interpretation developed over a long period of time and our approach changed somewhat over the years. It takes quite a while before you really come to possess an intuitive knowledge of such pieces and have made them your own, and sometimes your criteria for rendering them change. For instance I now find the '*Alla Danza Tedesca*' of Opus 130 in our recording to be simply too slow.

RS In the Deutsche Grammophon recording you play whole bars, that is, dotted quarters at 56–58, but in the live performances 60–63. That's a noticeable difference. Kolisch proposed a tempo of dotted quarter = 72 for this movement, which is a tempo that only the Hagen Quartet takes. The Busch Quartet goes as far as dotted quarter = 76, and that is already well beyond what can be executed clearly, owing to the complex microdynamics and rhythms.

WL Yes, but I also find Kolisch's suggested tempo too fast. In my opinion the character of this piece is not a fast one. It's by no means an innocuous movement, but it is, as you say, in many respects extremely complex.

17 Other ensembles choose tempi that are significantly slower than the LaSalle Quartet's: for example, in the first movement the Quartetto Italiano plays dotted half note = 88, the Alban Berg Quartet dotted half note = 96; in the second movement the Quartetto Italiano plays quarter note = 92, while the Alban Berg's quarter note = 104–112 is in the range of the LaSalle Quartet's studio recording.

Besides which I want to hear the melody as such and not the moving figures in the accompaniment. To me all this speaks in favor of a moderate tempo. I had to argue about this with my colleagues also, and it's possible that as a result I over-emphasized my position when we recorded it and then played it too slowly. That can also happen.

RS There are ensembles, also soloists, who are outspoken supporters of the artistic merits of studio recording, for instance, Glenn Gould.

WL Yes, in the last eighteen years of his life he only played in the studio.

RS And other musicians really are better on stage: you have to record them live.

WL Sure, but at that time no one was doing that. For instance at the premiere of Ligeti's second quartet in Baden-Baden we also played Beethoven's Opus 130 with the *Grosse Fuge*, and this concert was broadcast and recorded by SWF.[18] A few days prior to that we'd also made a studio recording of the *Grosse Fuge* at SWF. But the live performance is fabulous by comparison, it has an incredible verve, which the studio recording doesn't have.

Repeats in Sonata-form First Movements

RS The repeats in sonata-form first movements are another theme. From the very outset of your career on through to 1960 you always faithfully took all the repeats in sonata-form first movements. And then there was a period between 1961 and say 1973–1975 when you didn't take the repeats, but then after that, and on through to the end of your career, you once again took all of them. Your concert of April 25, 1972 seems to be a kind of turning point, as that's when the Mozart d minor quartet, K. 421, turns up again for the first time with the repeat of the exposition in the first movement, but in the same concert you still played Brahms' Opus 67 without the first movement repeat: you didn't take that repeat again until 1976, when you brought the piece back into your active repertory. How did you come to the decisions, first to eliminate the repeats, and then to restore them?

WL I don't know any more. Apparently we were aware that it was a problem, and we probably believed, as did all interpreters, that you could take

[18] On December 14, 1969.

them or leave them, depending on the length of the program, so that if the program seemed to us to be too long or demanding we simply skipped the repeats, without thinking very much about whether or not what we were doing made sense. I only became aware of the issues with these repeats, and with the research and the thinking about them, over the past twenty years, that is, after the LaSalle Quartet had retired. I did know something about this before then, but in the last few years the issue has gotten a great deal of attention. Whether you take the repeats or not isn't really up to the interpreters but rather to the composers. In the classical period the rule was that if the composer didn't want a repeat taken he had to indicate that explicitly.[19] I only first began to seriously study the research and literature on this subject in Berlin twenty years ago, when we were at the Institute for Advanced Study there between October 1991 and June 1992. So in the last few years I've learned a lot that I should have learned sooner, in which case that knowledge could have been applied consistently by the LaSalle Quartet.

RS But you started out taking all the repeats.

WL We did that because purely as a matter of feeling I always found the balance better that way when the repeat in the exposition, at least, of sonata-first movements was taken. Should the development and recapitulation also be repeated? For most ears today it doesn't make sense from the point of view of dramatic structure to repeat the most dramatic part of the movement. But at least in their late works both Haydn and Mozart distinguish very carefully as to whether they do or don't want the exposition repeated, and the second part of the movement also.[20]

[19] For example: for the reprise of the Minuet after the Trio in his string quartets K. 387 and K. 575 Mozart writes '*Menuetto da capo senza repliche*,' i.e., with neither of the repeats. A complex and revealing instance is the second minuet in Mozart's String Trio ('Divertimento'), K. 563, which has the form Minuet – Trio 1 – Minuet – Trio 2 – Minuet. After the first trio Mozart writes '*Menuetto da capo, la replica piano*,' i.e., the repetition of the minuet is to be played softly. After the second trio Mozart writes '*Menuetto da capo senza replica*,' i.e., without repeats.

[20] Of Mozart's last six symphonies, Nrs. 35–41, number 38, K. 504, is the only one in which the repetition of the development and the reprise is prescribed in the first movement, whereas it is prescribed in the last movements of Nrs. 36–41. Repetition of the exposition in the first and fourth movements is prescribed in Nrs. 36–41, whereas in the first and fourth movements of the symphony Nr. 35, K. 385 ('Haffner'), there are no repeats. With the prescribed repeats symphonies Nr. 36 and Nr. 41 last about 40 minutes, Nr. 38 (three movements) about 37 minutes, and Nr. 40 about 35 minutes. At the tempi prescribed by Beethoven the *Eroica* symphony, Opus 55, long considered to be revolutionary in length, lasts about 44 minutes. In his string quartets up to and including Opus 76, Nr. 3 (1797), Haydn writes a repeat for both the exposition and for the development and reprise. That he meant this in earnest can be seen in Opus 76, Nr. 3, where at the end of the reprise he writes '*la*

Beethoven distinguishes this very precisely in his quartets Opus 59.[21] I always argued in favor of repeating the development and recapitulation in the first movement of his e minor quartet Opus 59, Nr. 2, just as he indicated, but we never actually did it. It's completely obvious that Beethoven was serious about the repeat, since he even wrote transitional bars that you otherwise would never hear!

RS Too bad, since with both repeats taken the first movement would be about as long as the second.

WL Exactly. And those proportions are completely different: it's a mistake not to take the repeat of the development and recapitulation in this piece. To give a very crass answer to your question: the fact that we didn't take the repeats was due to our ignorance!

RS It was also a matter of the *Zeitgeist*, since in the 1960s most interpreters didn't take the repeats. We have some recordings with the Amadeus Quartet, including Mozart's quartet K. 590. One of them is from around 1955, in which they repeat the exposition in the first movement, but they don't do that in the later recording of theirs that we have. The repeats simply weren't taken in symphonies either in the 1960s. If you listen for instance to the complete Beethoven symphonies with Karajan from the 1960s, he skips all the repeats.

WL So the times do seem to play a role as well. I don't know what criteria Karajan had, but for the Amadeus Quartet it was certainly a matter of feeling and not a matter of information, which wouldn't have mattered to them at all. But why they took that repeat once and then not again, I can't say. It's very odd, and today it disturbs me greatly when quartets simply skip the repeats.

RS But as far as I can tell based on live recordings, there are two pieces in which you never took the repeat of the exposition, not once in your whole career: the first example is the first movement of Mozart's quartet K. 499, and it's a short movement anyway.

seconda volta più presto,' i.e., a '*Verdi-stretta*' to end the movement. In his last movements, starting with Opus 74, Nr. 3, Haydn as a rule only asks for the repeat of the exposition (Opus 76, Nr. 6, is the last of his quartets in which the repeat of both parts of the movement is requested).

21 In the quartet Opus 59, Nr. 1, there are no repeats in the first movement; in the fourth movement only the exposition is repeated. In the first movement of Opus 59, Nr. 2, Beethoven prescribes the repeat of both parts of the sonata-form first movement, none at all in the Finale; in Opus 59, Nr. 3, in the first movement only the repeat of the exposition and again none at all in the Finale.

WL The first movement? I can't imagine our doing that. I guarantee you we often played it with the repeat. We played it in 1954 on our European debut tour, it was the first piece on the program, along with the third Bartók quartet and Beethoven's quartet Opus 59, Nr. 3, and I absolutely guarantee you we took the repeat then.

RS It's too bad that we can't find out for sure, as the first live recording that I was able to find is from 1964 and from then on in all the live recordings from Cincinnati and SWF on through to the last performance in 1981 there isn't a single one with the repeat.[22] The other example concerns the first movement of Beethoven's quartet Opus 130: as far as I've been able to determine, you never took the repeat of the exposition here either. Could that have been because of the length of the whole quartet when you play the *Grosse Fuge* as the finale?[23]

WL That's certainly one consideration. Nevertheless, I'm not entirely convinced that you really have to take this repeat. The late Beethoven quartets have a style all their own. Today I would take the repeat in any case, because my criteria are different today.

Expressive Interpretation of the Second Viennese School

RS You once said that the way you played Webern was a thorn in the side of the devotees of serialism, because you didn't play his pieces so to speak 'four square' but rather very romantically and expressively. Where did this approach to them come from?

WL It was a thorn in the side above all for the young composers in Sweden. We caused quite an uproar when we played Schoenberg's third quartet on a concert of avant-garde music. These people were highly engaged by the new music, they'd even been taught by Ligeti. So they came '*en force*' to our concert, and we played Schoenberg's third quartet very romantically, that is, with expression, which is to say, with *portamenti* and *rubati*. We always played it as a late-romantic work. In general we felt that Schoenberg was a composer who worked with themes, accompaniments, and expressive melodies, even in his twelve-tone works, and that's how we played them. These people in Stockholm were furious!

22 The recordings from November 13, 1952, in Colorado Springs, and from March 9, 1954, in Cincinnati, are among the few that are missing in the archive of the LaSalle Quartet.

23 If the exposition is repeated in the first movement and the *Grosse Fuge* is played as the finale Beethoven's quartet Opus 130 lasts about 50 minutes.

How could we play Schoenberg like that, it was a complete falsification. So I asked them how they would play it: drily and repulsively with a miserably thin tone? Where does it say that in the score?

We got into a big row about that, and I told them to their face that they were on the wrong track. It's not right, not at all, it's nowhere written that you have to play the works of the Second Viennese School that way! The Kolisch Quartet also didn't play them like that, and Schoenberg was in complete agreement with their being played expressively. He viewed himself as a classical-romantic composer in the line of Brahms, whose work he had simply continued and carried further. Okay, harmonically, and the way in which it's constructed, it's twelve-tone music and atonal. But what's that supposed to mean? This is exactly what Boulez reproached Schoenberg for: he wrote atonally, but otherwise composed just the way Brahms had, which he, Boulez, found inconsistent, even trivial. He thought that if you wrote atonal harmony then you simply had to bring the other parameters of music into accord with that, which ultimately meant that they had to be serialized.

RS There's also the edition of the *Piano Variations*, Opus 27, by Webern that Peter Stadlen published.

WL Yes, it's still in print at Universal Edition. Stadlen was a great opponent of the serial approach to interpreting Webern or analyzing him, he claimed that Webern was an expressive composer, an extremely expressive composer. And the *Variations*, which are today regarded as the high point of twelve-tone composition, in which all that remains are single, distributed notes, that is, where everything is done strictly 'by the book,' weren't at all to be played that way: Webern thought it was a very romantic piece, to be played with *rubato*, and that's how he instructed Stadlen to play the piece. So Stadlen wrote Webern's instructions into the score and published them. Stadlen also played the premiere of these piano variations. Stadlen was in general a very romantically inclined individual. For instance he published a big study of tempi in Beethoven,[24] in which he argued strongly against Beethoven's metronome markings and made comparisons based on recordings by various conductors: all that is very tendentious and in part also mistaken. But he was someone who had been a very strong advocate of new music, as evidenced, for example, by his playing these variations by Webern.

RS But this way of playing Webern, and the works of the Second Viennese School generally, romantically and with expression, apparently didn't catch on.

[24] *'Beethoven und das Metronom,'* in *Musik-Konzepte* 8 (1985); see also p. 341 n.6.

WL It has by now, I would say. The Juilliard Quartet also didn't play Webern as 'serially' as the Darmstadt school would have had it. At Darmstadt all the parameters of music, including its interpretation, were to be serialized and correspondingly rigorous. But Hermann Scherchen conducted at Darmstadt and he was an extraordinarily expressive exponent of the Second Viennese School: you can hear it in his recordings, I myself first heard Schoenberg's *Pelleas und Melisande* in Palestine under Hermann Scherchen, a highly romantic piece.[25] So at Darmstadt not only was serialization the order of the day, but the younger generation also strongly rejected any kind of expressive interpretation. You have to understand that as a reaction to what had preceded this rediscovery of the Second Viennese School in Europe, which was possible only after the Second World War. These young people wanted nothing more to do with any music, musicians, or way of making music that had been acceptable to the Nazis, because it represented something that they wanted nothing more to do with, also politically. I can understand that very well. '*Schoenberg est mort!*' as Boulez wrote. But those are all tendentious attitudes, very much bound up with their time. By now Boulez has also changed a lot.

RS The second part of that slogan is of course 'Long live Schoenberg!'

WL Exactly. Yesterday there was a wonderful two hour broadcast on Radio Berlin Brandenburg, RBB, honoring the 50th anniversary of Toscanini's death and the 140th year since his birth,[26] in which all of what we've been talking about also came up for discussion, and the fact is that the kind of interpretation that Toscanini represented is still a thorn in people's sides even today. The myths that are being written about it all over Europe, particularly in Germany, where to this day nobody has a clue what he was about! They never listen to his recordings! And if you do listen to them, then it turns out that all these assertions of theirs are just plain wrong, and that he succeeded in achieving a level of interpretation that penetrated every aspect of rendering music and brought it into the most delicate balance, while in Europe you could perceive only tasteless exaggeration in everything. If someone in Europe says that somebody conducts metronomically, what that means is just that they don't make the wildest leaps in *rubato*. It was a great broadcast, you should have heard all that was said about the style that was accepted as a matter of course during the Hitler time in Germany and Austria and got a big reputation. The

[25] For the young Walter Levin's encounter with Hermann Scherchen on the beach in Tel Aviv in 1939, see pp. 44–46.

[26] The broadcast was on May 17, 2007. Toscanini was born on March 25, 1867, and died on January 16, 1957.

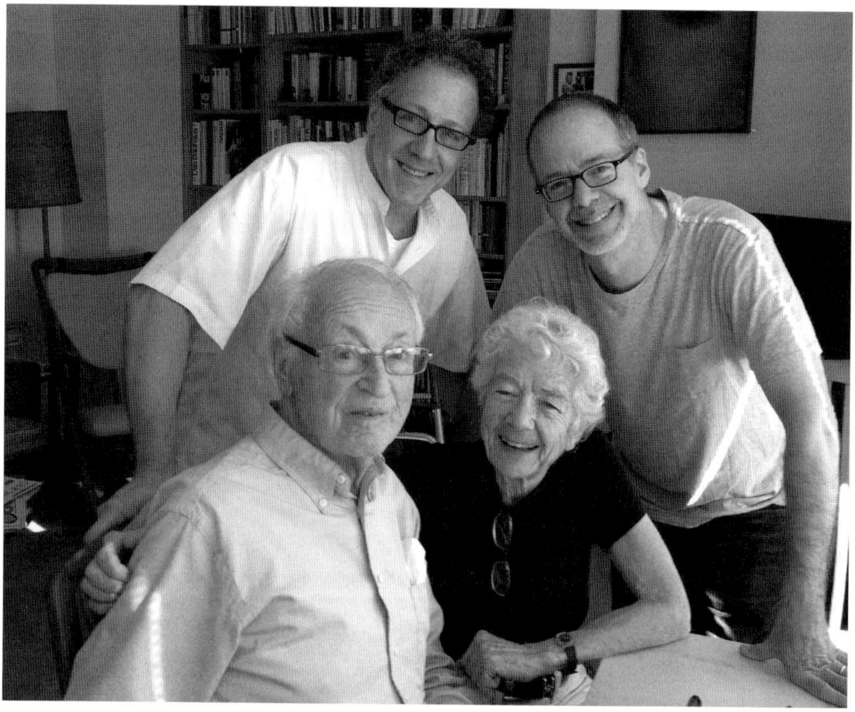

48 Levin family, seated: Walter and Evi Levin; standing: David and Thomas Levin, Chicago, August 28, 2012

one chiefly responsible for that, who also cooperated with the Nazis and performed for them, was Wilhelm Furtwängler. Listen to his recordings! It's not to be believed, how music can be played that way.

RS Toscanini's recordings aren't in the least metronomic!

WL No, not at all! On the contrary! Sometimes they're even almost too free for me, rhythmically. It's scarcely to be believed, the way he conducted Beethoven's *Coriolan* overture. You had to have heard the rehearsals for that![27] I was at one of these rehearsals and then was at the concert, when Myra Hess[28] played Beethoven's third piano concerto following the *Coriolan* overture. You have to have heard how he worked with the NBC Symphony to achieve these *rubati*! In Beethoven! Where issues of inter-

[27] The rehearsal on November 23, 1946 was recorded; the concert (also recorded) was on November 24, 1946.

[28] Myra Hess (1890–1965), English pianist, known for her Mozart, Beethoven, and Schumann, and also famous for the 1,700 lunchtime concerts she organized in London during the Second World War in defiance of the German bombing.

pretation are concerned there's a lot of gossip and very little knowledge of the facts. This has a lot to do with politics and with a kind of politics that young people didn't want to have anything to do with back then. And so they didn't want to have anything to do with the least hint of the kind of *rubato* and romanticizing musical interpretation that we used, and that's quite understandable.

The Conscience of the String Quartet

Afterword by Werner Grünzweig

In the estate of Herbert Brün, the American composer of German-Jewish origin who had been a close friend of Walter Levin's since their childhood together in Berlin, there is an undated note on the subject 'string quartet':

> *How to become a string quartet.*
> *How to be a string quartet.*
> *How to remain a string quartet.*
>
> *How to choose a repertoire and then the yearly new work.*
> *What does it mean: to look for a new composition for string quartet.*
> *The score: experiences, requirements, notations, competence, etc.*
>
> *String quartet: the conscience of the composer.*
> *Interpretatio.*
> *Musical ideas which require a string quartet.*[1]

The purpose for which this note was intended is unknown to us. The thoughts were probably meant to be topics for discussion with students at the University of Illinois, where Brün had taught since 1963. Originally the concept 'string quartet' was no more than an instrumental ensemble specification, but one that in the course of music history was ennobled by the works of Haydn, Mozart, and Beethoven, and since then has been understood as a genre, along with the symphony or the sonata. (Brün did note that there are musical ideas that demand a string quartet for their realization.) When Brün characterized this genre as 'the conscience of the composer,' he surely meant to refer to the place where a composer has to come to grips with the 'core' of his work, to the basic framework of composing, which holds for him the whole of musical content from the largest form down to the nuances of color.

But as a result of his own close acquaintance with Walter Levin, Brün himself would surely have meant the LaSalle Quartet, which premiered two of his own quartets and which many composers regarded as the ideal expression of this ensemble form, because they dealt with every kind of music without compromise and was as much opposed to the clichés under which older music is buried as it was successful in dismantling the prejudice against New Music. So it would be no wonder if Brün were to ascribe the function of a conscience to this ensemble, on account of its authority vis-a-vis both the older and the

[1] In the Herbert Brün Archive of the Akademie der Künste, Berlin.

newer (and newest) music. And if the LaSalle Quartet represented something like the 'conscience of the composer,' then its primarius, Walter Levin, was most certainly the conscience of this quartet. From the beginning of his professional career Levin had been wholly committed to this genre. He had given himself over to it absolutely, because in it he could realize everything he could imagine musically. The genre comprises an incomparably rich repertory from the 18th and 19th centuries, and beyond that the composers in the first decades of the 20th century demonstrated its potential for New Music as well. (For the musicians of the Wiener Schule around Arnold Schoenberg and many of their contemporaries the quartet even became a laboratory for compositional experiments *par excellence*.) In an era in which chamber music fell out of fashion, because it was no longer commonly played at home and the claim of the orchestral repertory to be the quintessence of ensemble music, Levin's guiding thought was to firmly re-anchor this form of music making in concert life. Its musical qualities, which he valued so much, he wanted to preserve for a new generation of composers and to develop them further: the concentration that follows from the restriction to four voices, the close and virtuosic ensemble playing of quasi-soloistic musicians, the immense possibilities of revealing new musical terrain.

The question that Brün posed at the outset, of how one becomes, is and then remains a string quartet, is a theme that equally occupied Levin again and again. To sensitize young quartets to these problematics seemed to him to be an urgent necessity, because some of the most important quartet ensembles of the 20th century had come to grief on the difficult working conditions and their internal conflicts, like the Viennese Kolisch Quartet, which was otherwise a model for the LaSalle Quartet in respect of the way it went about working on music.[2] Since a quartet develops the consensus that ensures the highest artistic quality only after many years of working together, ways must be found to keep four musicians together for a long time, not only so that they can get along well with one another but also so that they develop artistically. Here Levin recognized one of the most important tasks confronting a primarius: establishing a strict working discipline, so as not to endanger the *niveau* once it had been achieved.

The most important decisions that a quartet ensemble has to agree on include, as Brün noted, the choice of repertory and above all its expansion through new works. For the LaSalle Quartet that was always linked to the question of how to find out about new quartets or from whom to commission them. In the light of today's assembly line interpretations it seems astonishing that the LaSalle Quartet voluntarily imposed narrow limits on its taking up new works – Brün writes about the 'annual new work.' Levin was convinced that it was precisely a new and therefore unknown work that had to be played

2 See Claudia Maurer Zenck, '"*Ein Sauberruf!*" *Der Alltag des Kolisch Quartetts auf Reisen in der Zwischenkriegszeit*,' in *Annäherungen: Festschrift für Jürg Stenzl zum 65. Geburtstag* (Saarbrücken, 2007), pp. 187–221.

at the highest level of perfection – and indeed in order not to endanger the quality he once postponed an important premiere a whole year. Quantity was never a criterion here. Rather the musicians committed themselves for the long term to an intense engagement with carefully selected new works – or with composers whom they particularly valued to whom they therefore gave commissions. Not a few of the works that arose in that way and were premiered at the highest *niveau* subsequently entered the regular string quartet repertory. Such a way of working would be exemplary even today, when in the midst of an immensely rich production many works don't survive their premiere, simply because their poorly rehearsed performance conveys no sense of their actual value. (The number of works that have been lost to musical life through bad premieres is surely about equal to the number that have arisen as the result of commissions and stipendia.)

What astonishes over and over again in Robert Spruytenburg's conversations with Walter Levin is the extent to which all the events of Levin's life appear to serve one single purpose, one single goal. In retrospect everything seems to have an obvious sense, because it was aimed at his later life work, the quartet. If you like, you can already see in his appearance as a percussionist in the premiere of Herbert Brün's *Kindersymphonie* in Berlin in 1933 the foundation for the later rhythmically sharp style for which the LaSalle Quartet was famous. And however dark and unpredictable Levin's fate may have been at moments in his life, his forced emigration to Palestine nevertheless resulted in his having teachers that he wouldn't have had in Berlin. And on the other hand, his wish to escape from the confines of the country to which his family had been exiled opened up for him all the possibilities that America, culturally striving and bursting with economic vitality, had to offer in the middle of the 20th century. In New York he very deliberately put his musical education on a broad basis, but never for its own sake, rather in order to make him into the best possible quartet player.

The impression that Levin's life was cast from a single mold naturally arises from the way he presents it. When Levin tells stories, his life is condensed to a unity in which the most disparate and accidental things fit into a meaningful whole, so that one ultimately has the feeling that things could have turned out only that way and no other. In his two extended series of interviews – the one with Robert Spruytenburg and the other with Deutschlandradio Kultur[3] – his life's story serves as the thread that leads the reader or the listener through

[3] *Walter Levin und das LaSalle-Quartett. Eine musikalische Biographie in 26 Folgen. Wolfgang Hagen und Werner Grünzweig im Gespräch mit Walter Levin*, Deutschlandradio Kultur, 2009.

the recent (music) history of Europe, Palestine, the United States, and many more countries besides, in which a 'European' musical life is cultivated. In so doing he doesn't overrate his own life: what is more important to him is what the reader (or listener) can learn for himself from this life – about music, about modern history, about life in general. On top of which there is his pleasure in elegant formulations, in beautiful and often ambiguous anecdotes that are presented with a humor that reaches self-irony.

Altogether the strongest impression is that Levin actually embodies something like a conscience, a moral authority, even when he, instead of making absolutes of his experience, aims at inciting independent and critical thinking. For himself, he was implacably committed to the search for truth – for moral, artistic, and historical truth. The evidence for that he collected painstakingly for years: he can resort to an astonishing personal archive, for example the recordings of his own appearances going back to the late 1940s, in addition to which there are rare recordings of other musicians, music, family and professional documents, letters, personal notes, newspaper clippings, and photographs – everything that goes into a content-rich artist archive. The nearly 39 hours of interviews with Walter Levin that were broadcast on Deutschlandradio Kultur in 2009 were not hard to fill; what was difficult was to decide what to leave out. The incredible intensity of his memories, that make a compelling unity of the chance events of his life, was unique even for those who have interviewed many artists about their lives. Some of them that were too specialized and detailed for the radio broadcasts can now be obtained from the present book, which will serve musicians and those interested in music in the future as a compendium of many aspects of the music and the musical thought of the second half of the 20th century.

Fundamentally it was always Walter Levin's intention to give the music that was important to him its due, as it was always in danger of being lost in the workings of the music industry. For him it was a matter of his moral integrity, and it was this that made Levin fight and struggle for just this music his whole life long. He wanted to achieve something that at first seemed scarcely feasible, something like the self-evident integration of completely new works into 'normal' concert programs. He was never interested in the status quo, as little interested in it, by the way, as he was interested in restricting his field of activities to that of a performing musician. Levin the musician is only to be understood as uniting the teacher, the organizer, the instigator, the patron, the historian: in short, the mediator in one and the same person. Or in a different formulation: since for Walter Levin music always represented a communicative task, so his accounts of his life, his activities as a teacher, and his organizational strategies are not to be separated from his concept of music. The 'Levin project' was an indissoluble unity.

Teaching, which Levin pursued his whole life, was particularly natural for him. Teaching is where the teacher works out the concepts of his intuitive artistic understanding theoretically, not only for his students, but also for himself. When Schoenberg said that his *Harmonielehre*, a philosophy of music disguised as a theory book, was something he had learned from his students, what he meant was precisely this transition from intuitive understanding to explicit knowledge. For an intellectually voracious artist like Levin teaching was therefore an ideal field of activity, because it forced him to find the rational foundations for his intuitive grasp of music. Completely in line with Schoenberg's understanding he tried, together with his students, to solve musical problems instead of dictating from on high what was right and what was wrong. Every return to an important work brought new aspects to light even for the teacher, and so the teacher could not present himself, as Schoenberg put it, as infallible but rather as tireless, always seeking and sometimes finding.

For Levin the education of musicians was by no means enough, however: he also wanted to educate the audience. His life-long credo was that without informed listeners all the efforts of composers and musicians were in vain. The lecture-recitals that the LaSalle Quartet probably invented, and that Levin continued to give with great success after the quartet disbanded, won countless friends for the serious engagement with music. He demonstrated that the conventional form of the concert is not simply to be overcome by loosening up its stiff ambience. Rather what seemed to him to be destructive about the conventional concert business was a situation in which the audience for the most part didn't know the music being presented and moreover couldn't (or didn't want to) know it, whereas Levin's strategy was to achieve an active understanding of the music, a real approach to it, by means of explanations, sequences of examples, and repeated performances. As a result there is a social element in the life work and achievement of the musician Walter Levin – but not in the usual political sense, rather in the sense that he found the artistic potential that is hidden in many people, opened it up, and encouraged it. If you will, Levin taught more than music: he taught musicality, because he extended the idea of what music can be. In that he restored authenticity to older music through his thorough study of the sources, he made it attractive to contemporary listeners by sensitizing musicians and audiences to the creative impulse from which a completely new work arises. In this way art was understood to be a part of life and one that always repaid being concerned about.

Appendices

I Complete Repertory Alphabetically by Composer

The numbers of performances listed in this and the following appendices are based on the collection of LaSalle Quartet concert programs in the archive of the Paul Sacher Foundation in Basel. A comparison with the tour itineraries, however, shows that the programs for a number of the concerts are missing, mostly for the 1954 tour of Israel and the 1956 tour of Asia, as well as a few tours of the United States. The performance numbers listed here include only those documented in archive; the actual numbers of performances of some individual works are therefore somewhat higher, though the number of missing programs is small enough to ensure that the differences are, from a practical point of view, *de minimis*.

Composer	Work	Performances
T. W. Adorno	*Two Pieces for String Quartet*, Opus 2	1
H. E. Apostel	Opus 7	20
	Opus 26	5
B. Bartók	*Mikrokosmos*	15
	Quartet Nr. 1	8
	Quartet Nr. 2	10
	Quartet Nr. 3	78
	Quartet Nr. 4	36
	Quartet Nr. 5	19
	Quartet Nr. 6	56
L. v. Beethoven	Opus 14, Nr. 1	39
	Opus 18, Nr. 1	2
	Opus 18, Nr. 2	15
	Opus 18, Nr. 3	29
	Opus 18, Nr. 4	23
	Opus 18, Nr. 5	6
	Opus 18, Nr. 6	8
	Opus 59, Nr. 1	16
	Opus 59, Nr. 2	32
	Opus 59, Nr. 3	22
	Opus 74	9
	Opus 95	117
	Opus 127	36
	Opus 130	42

Composer	Work	Perform-ances
Beethoven, cont'd.	Opus 131	58
	Opus 132	74
	Opus 133, *Grosse Fuge*	148
	Opus 135	12
A. Berg	Opus 3	97
	Lyric Suite	100
	7 *Frühe Lieder*	1
L. Boccherini	Opus 41, Nr. 2	1
J. Brahms	Sextet, Opus 18	10
	Opus 51, Nr. 1	23
	Opus 51, Nr. 2	42
	Opus 67	98
E. Brown	*String Quartet*	33
A. Bruckner	Quartet in c minor	6
H. Brün	Quartet Nr. 1	4
	Quartet Nr. 2	6
	Quartet Nr. 3	10
J. Cage	*String Quartet in Four Parts*	9
E. Carter	Quartet Nr. 2	3
C. Debussy	String Quartet, Opus 10	21
W. DeFotis	String Quartet	3
F. Döhl	*Sound of Sleat*	2
G. Donizetti	Quartet Nr. 5	10
M. Dumler	Opus 47	1
A. Dvořák	Opus 96, 'American'	3
G. Englert	Quartet Nr. 1, *Les Avoines Folles*	6
	Quartet Nr. 2, *La Joute des Lierres*	4
F. Evangelisti	*Aleatorio*	34
M. Gielen	*Un Vieux Souvenir*	11
J. Haydn	Opus 9, Nr. 4	51
	Opus 20, Nr. 2	42
	Opus 20, Nr. 3	30
	Opus 20, Nr. 4	42
	Opus 33, Nr. 2	8
	Opus 33, Nr. 3	9

Composer	Work	Performances
Haydn, cont'd.	Opus 33, Nr. 5	26
	Opus 42	1
	Opus 50, Nr. 1	6
	Opus 50, Nr. 2	40
	Opus 50, Nr. 6	11
	Opus 55, Nr. 1	28
	Opus 64, Nr. 1	25
	Opus 64, Nr. 5	22
	Opus 64, Nr. 6	11
	Opus 71, Nr. 2	80
	Opus 71, Nr. 3	1
	Opus 74, Nr. 1	30
	Opus 76, Nr. 6	18
	Opus 77, Nr. 1	3
	Opus 77, Nr. 2	20
P. Hindemith	Quartet Nr. 3, Opus 22	15
M. Howe	String Quartet	1
B. Johnston	*9 Variations*	2
M. Kagel	Quartet Nr. 1	5
L. Kalmár	*Morfeo*	4
L. Kirchner	Quartet Nr. 1	15
G. M. Koenig	Quartet Nr. 1	4
G. Ligeti	Quartet Nr. 2	58
W. Lutosławski	String Quartet	98
R. Mann	*Five Pieces for String Quartet*	7
T. Mayuzumi	*Prelude for String Quartet*	18
F. Mendelssohn	Opus 12	22
	Opus 13	32
W. A. Mozart	K. 155	3
	K. 387	17
	K. 421	105
	K. 428	50
	K. 458	39
	K. 464	95
	K. 465	3

Composer	Work	Perform-ances
Mozart, cont'd.	K. 499	61
	K. 575	29
	K. 589	12
	K. 590	48
	K. 405, *Preludes and Fugues*	44
	K. 546, *Adagio and Fugue*	38
	K. 617, *Adagio and Rondo*	2
L. Nono	*Fragmente – Stille, An Diotima*	33
K. Penderecki	Quartet Nr. 1	41
W. Piston	Quartet Nr. 1	29
H. Pousseur	*Ode pour Quatuor*	9
H. Purcell	*Fantasies*	124
M. Ravel	String Quartet	199
M. Reger	Opus 121	10
W. Riegger	Quartet Nr. 2, Opus 43	7
W. Rosenberg	Quartet Nr. 2	1
	Quartet Nr. 3	12
G. Samuel	Quartet Nr. 1	10
A. Schnabel	Quartet Nr. 3	8
A. Schoenberg	Quartet D major (1897)	16
	Quartet Nr. 1, Opus 7	61
	Quartet Nr. 2, Opus 10	25
	Quartet Nr. 3, Opus 30	59
	Quartet Nr. 4, Opus 37	57
	Opus 4, *Verklärte Nacht*	11
	Opus 41, *Ode to Napoleon*	5
	String Trio, Opus 45	25
	Concerto for String Quartet	1
	Lieder Opus 2	2
F. Schubert	Opus 125, Nr. 1, D. 87	33
	Opus 125, Nr. 2, D. 353	3
	Quartet D. 173	4
	Quartettsatz in c minor, D. 703	57
	Quartet in a minor, D. 804	57
	Quartet in d minor, D. 810	21

Composer	Work	Performances
Schubert, cont'd.	Quartet in G major, D. 887	15
	String Quintet, D. 956	12
G. Schuller	Quartet Nr. 1	11
R. Schumann	Opus 41, Nr. 2	20
	Opus 41, Nr. 3	7
	Piano Quintet, Opus 44	14
M. Seiber	Quartet Nr. 2	4
	Quartet Nr. 3, '*Quartetto Lirico*'	1
B. Smetana	Quartet Nr. 1, *From my Life*	33
L. Spohr	*Concerto for String Quartet*	2
I. Stravinsky	*Concertino*	26
	Three Pieces for String Quartet	70
G. Turchi	*Concerto breve*	1
G. Verdi	Quartet in e minor	31
A. Vivaldi	*Sonata a quattro*	8
A. Webern	Quartet, 1905	73
	Rondo, 1906	47
	Piano Quintet, 1907	9
	Five Pieces, Opus 5	96
	Six Bagatelles, Opus 9	243
	Opus 28	125
	String Trio, Opus 20	14
	Bagatelle with Soprano	2
H. Wolf	Quartet in d minor	15
	Italian Serenade	6
A. Zemlinsky	Quartet Nr. 1, Opus 4	9
	Quartet Nr. 2, Opus 15	13
	Quartet Nr. 3, Opus 19	25
	Quartet Nr. 4, Opus 25	68
	TOTAL	**4725**

II Composers Ranked by Performance Frequency

Rank	Composer	Performances
1	L. v. Beethoven	688
2	A. Webern	609
3	W. A. Mozart	546
4	J. Haydn	504
5	A. Schoenberg	262
6	B. Bartók	222
7	F. Schubert	202
8	M. Ravel	199
9	A. Berg	198
10	J. Brahms	173
11	H. Purcell	124
12	A. Zemlinsky	115
13	W. Lutosławski	98
14	I. Stravinsky	96
15	G. Ligeti	58
16	F. Mendelssohn	54
17	K. Penderecki	41
17	R. Schumann	41
18	F. Evangelisti	34
19	E. Brown	33
19	L. Nono	33
19	B. Smetana	33
20	G. Verdi	31
21	W. Piston	29
22	H. E. Apostel	25
23	C. Debussy	21
23	H. Wolf	21
24	H. Brün	20
25	T. Mayuzumi	18
26	P. Hindemith	15
26	L. Kirchner	15
27	W. Rosenberg	13

Rank	Composer	Performances
28	M. Gielen	11
28	G. Schuller	11
29	G. Donizetti	10
29	G. Englert	10
29	M. Reger	10
29	G. Samuel	10
30	J. Cage	9
30	H. Pousseur	9
31	A. Schnabel	8
31	A. Vivaldi	8
32	R. Mann	7
32	W. Riegger	7
33	A. Bruckner	6
34	M. Kagel	5
34	M. Seiber	5
35	L. Kalmár	4
35	G. M. Koenig	4
36	E. Carter	3
36	W. DeFotis	3
36	A. Dvořák	3
37	F. Döhl	2
37	B. Johnston	2
37	L. Spohr	2
38	T. W. Adorno	1
38	L. Boccherini	1
38	M. Dumler	1
38	M. Howe	1
38	G. Turchi	1
	TOTAL	**4725**

III Works Ranked by Performance Frequency

Rank	Composer	Work	Performances
1	A. Webern	*Six Bagatelles* Opus 9	243
2	M. Ravel	String Quartet	199
3	L. v. Beethoven	Opus 133, *Grosse Fuge*	148
4	A. Webern	Opus 28	125
5	H. Purcell	*Fantasies*	124
6	L. v. Beethoven	Opus 95	117
7	W. A. Mozart	K. 421	105
8	A. Berg	*Lyric Suite*	100
9	J. Brahms	Opus 67	98
9	W. Lutosławski	String Quartet	98
10	A. Berg	Opus 3	97
11	A. Webern	*Five Pieces*, Opus 5	96
12	W. A. Mozart	K. 464	95
13	J. Haydn	Opus 71, Nr. 2	80
15	B. Bartók	Quartet Nr. 3	78
14	L. v. Beethoven	Opus 132	74
15	A. Webern	Quartet, 1905	73
16	I. Stravinsky	*Three Pieces for String Quartet*	70
17	A. Zemlinsky	Quartet Nr. 4	68
18	W. A. Mozart	K. 499	61
18	A. Schoenberg	Quartet Nr. 1	61
19	A. Schoenberg	Quartet Nr. 3	59
20	L. v. Beethoven	Opus 131	58
20	G. Ligeti	Quartet Nr. 2	58
21	A. Schoenberg	Quartet Nr. 4	57
21	F. Schubert	Quartet in a minor	57
21	F. Schubert	*Quartettsatz* in c minor	57
22	B. Bartók	Quartet Nr. 6	56
23	J. Haydn	Opus 9, Nr. 4	51
24	W. A. Mozart	K. 428	50
25	W. A. Mozart	K. 590	48
26	A. Webern	Rondo, 1906	47

Rank	Composer	Work	Performances
27	W. A. Mozart	K. 405, *Preludes and Fugues*	44
28	L. v. Beethoven	Opus 130	42
28	J. Brahms	Opus 51, Nr. 2	42
28	J. Haydn	Opus 20, Nr. 2	42
28	J. Haydn	Opus 20, Nr. 4	42
29	K. Penderecki	Quartet Nr. 1	41
30	J. Haydn	Opus 50, Nr. 2	40
31	L. v. Beethoven	Opus 14, Nr. 1	39
31	W. A. Mozart	K. 458	39
32	W. A. Mozart	K. 546, *Adagio and Fugue*	38
33	B. Bartók	Quartet Nr. 4	36
33	L. v. Beethoven	Opus 127	36
34	F. Evangelisti	*Aleatorio*	34
35	E. Brown	*String Quartet*	33
35	L. Nono	*Fragmente – Stille, An Diotima*	33
35	F. Schubert	Opus 125, Nr. 1	33
35	B. Smetana	Quartet Nr. 1, *From my Life*	33
36	L. v. Beethoven	Opus 59, Nr. 2	32
36	F. Mendelssohn	Opus 13	32
37	G. Verdi	Quartet in e minor	31
38	J. Haydn	Opus 20, Nr. 3	30
38	J. Haydn	Opus 74, Nr. 1	30
39	L. v. Beethoven	Opus 18, Nr. 3	29
39	W. A. Mozart	K. 575	29
39	W. Piston	Quartet Nr. 1	29
40	J. Haydn	Opus 55, Nr. 1	28
41	J. Haydn	Opus 33, Nr. 5	26
41	I. Stravinsky	*Concertino*	26
42	J. Haydn	Opus 64, Nr. 1	25
42	A. Schoenberg	Quartet Nr. 2	25
42	A. Schoenberg	String Trio, Opus 45	25
42	A. Zemlinsky	Quartet Nr. 3	25
43	L. v. Beethoven	Opus 18, Nr. 4	23
43	J. Brahms	Opus 51, Nr. 1	23
44	L. v. Beethoven	Opus 59, Nr. 3	22

Rank	Composer	Work	Perform-ances
44	J. Haydn	Opus 64, Nr. 5	22
44	F. Mendelssohn	Opus 12	22
45	C. Debussy	String Quartet, Opus 10	21
45	F. Schubert	Quartet in d minor	21
46	H. E. Apostel	Opus 7	20
46	J. Haydn	Opus 77, Nr. 2	20
46	R. Schumann	Opus 41, Nr. 2	20
47	B. Bartók	Quartet Nr. 5	19
48	J. Haydn	Opus 76, Nr. 6	18
48	T. Mayuzumi	*Prelude for String Quartet*	18
49	W. A. Mozart	K. 387	17
50	L. v. Beethoven	Opus 59, Nr. 1	16
50	A. Schoenberg	Quartet in D major (1897)	16
51	B. Bartók	*Mikrokosmos*	15
51	L. v. Beethoven	Opus 18, Nr. 2	15
51	P. Hindemith	Quartet Nr. 3	15
51	L. Kirchner	Quartet Nr. 1	15
51	F. Schubert	Quartet in G major	15
51	H. Wolf	Quartet in d minor	15
52	R. Schumann	Piano Quintet, Opus 44	14
52	A. Webern	String Trio, Opus 20	14
53	A. Zemlinsky	Quartet Nr. 2	13
54	L. v. Beethoven	Opus 135	12
54	W. A. Mozart	K. 589	12
54	W. Rosenberg	Quartet Nr. 3	12
54	F. Schubert	String Quintet, D. 956	12
55	M. Gielen	*Un Vieux Souvenir*	11
55	J. Haydn	Opus 50, Nr. 6	11
55	J. Haydn	Opus 64, Nr. 6	11
55	A. Schoenberg	Opus 4, *Verklärte Nacht*	11
55	G. Schuller	Quartet Nr. 1	11
56	B. Bartók	Quartet Nr. 2	10
56	J. Brahms	Sextet, Opus 18	10
56	H. Brün	Quartet Nr. 3	10
56	G. Donizetti	Quartet Nr. 5	10

Rank	Composer	Work	Perform-ances
56	M. Reger	Opus 121	10
56	G. Samuel	Quartet Nr. 1	10
57	L. v. Beethoven	Opus 74	9
57	J. Cage	*String Quartet in Four Parts*	9
57	J. Haydn	Opus 33, Nr. 3	9
57	H. Pousseur	*Ode pour Quatuor*	9
57	A. Webern	Piano Quintet, 1907	9
57	A. Zemlinsky	Quartet Nr. 1	9
58	B. Bartók	Quartet Nr. 1	8
58	L. v. Beethoven	Opus 18, Nr. 6	8
58	J. Haydn	Opus 33, Nr. 2	8
58	A. Schnabel	Quartet Nr. 3	8
58	A. Vivaldi	*Sonata a quattro*	8
59	R. Mann	*Five Pieces for String Quartet*	7
59	W. Riegger	Quartet Nr. 2, Opus 43	7
59	R. Schumann	Opus 41, Nr. 3	7
60	L. v. Beethoven	Opus 18, Nr. 5	6
60	A. Bruckner	Quartet in c minor	6
60	H. Brün	Quartet Nr. 2	6
60	G. Englert	Quartet Nr. 1, *Les Avoines Folles*	6
60	J. Haydn	Opus 50, Nr. 1	6
60	H. Wolf	*Italian Serenade*	6
61	H. E. Apostel	Opus 26	5
61	M. Kagel	Quartet Nr. 1	5
61	A. Schoenberg	Opus 41, *Ode to Napoleon*	5
62	H. Brün	Quartet Nr. 1	4
62	G. Englert	Quartet Nr. 2, *La Joute des Lierres*	4
62	L. Kalmár	*Morfeo*	4
62	G. M. Koenig	Quartet Nr. 1	4
62	F. Schubert	Quartet D. 173	4
62	M. Seiber	Quartet Nr. 2	4
63	E. Carter	Quartet Nr. 2	3
63	W. DeFotis	String Quartet	3
63	A. Dvořák	Opus 96, 'American'	3
63	J. Haydn	Opus 77, Nr. 1	3

Rank	Composer	Work	Performances
63	W. A. Mozart	K. 155	3
63	W. A. Mozart	K. 465	3
63	F. Schubert	Opus 125, Nr. 2	3
64	L. v. Beethoven	Opus 18, Nr. 1	2
64	F. Döhl	*Sound of Sleat*	2
64	B. Johnston	*9 Variations*	2
64	W. A. Mozart	K. 617, *Adagio and Rondo*	2
64	A. Schoenberg	Lieder Opus 2	2
64	L. Spohr	*Concerto for String Quartet*	2
64	A. Webern	*Bagatelle* with Soprano	2
65	T. W. Adorno	*Two Pieces for String Quartet*, Opus 2	1
65	A. Berg	*7 Frühe Lieder*	1
65	L. Boccherini	Opus 41, Nr. 2	1
65	M. Dumler	Opus 47	1
65	J. Haydn	Opus 42	1
65	J. Haydn	Opus 71, Nr. 3	1
65	M. Howe	String Quartet	1
65	W. Rosenberg	Quartet Nr. 2	1
65	A. Schoenberg	*Concerto for String Quartet*	1
65	M. Seiber	Quartet Nr. 3	1
65	G. Turchi	*Concerto breve*	1
		TOTAL	**4725**

IV Commissions and Premieres

Works marked with '(*)' are commissions.

Commissions and Premieres Alphabetically by Composer

Nr.	Composer	Work	Composed	Premiered
1	H. E. Apostel	Quartet, Opus 26 (*)	1956	Cincinnati 4/23/1957
2	E. Brown	*String Quartet* (*)	1965	Donau-eschingen 10/16/1965
3	H. Brün	Quartet Nr. 2 (*)	1957	Cincinnati 4/1/1958
4		Quartet Nr. 3 (*)	1961–1962	Kranichstein (Darmstadt) 7/14/1962
5	W. DeFotis	String Quartet	1977	Cincinnati 10/2/1979
6	G. Englert	Quartet Nr. 1, *Les Avoines Folles* (*)	1962–1963	Cincinnati 10/13/1964
7		Quartet Nr. 2, *La Joute des Lierres* (*)	1966	Cincinnati 5/11/1971
8	F. Evangelisti	*Aleatorio* (*)	1959	Kranichstein (Darmstadt) 7/14/1962
9	M. Gielen	*Un Vieux Souvenir* (*)	1983	Cincinnati 10/15/1985
10	M. Kagel	Quartet Nr. 1 (*)	1965–1967	Cincinnati 1/15/1974
11	L. Kalmár	*Morfeo*	1977	Budapest 5/30/1982
12	G. M. Koenig	Quartet Nr. 1 (*)	1959	Munich 2/28/1961
13	G. Ligeti	Quartet Nr. 2 (*)	1968	Baden-Baden 12/14/1969
14	W. Lutosławski	String Quartet	1964	Stockholm 3/12/1965
15	R. Mann	*Five Pieces for String Quartet*	1951	Colorado Springs 3/11/1953

Nr.	Composer	Work	Composed	Premiered
16	L. Nono	*Fragmente – Stille, An Diotima*	1980	Bad Godesberg (Bonn) 6/2/1980
17	K. Penderecki	Quartet Nr. 1	1960	Kranichstein (Darmstadt) 7/14/1962
18	H. Pousseur	*Ode pour Quatuor* (*)	1961	Kranichstein (Darmstadt) 7/14/1962
19	W. Rosenberg	Quartet Nr. 2 (*)	1957	Cincinnati 12/17/1957
20		Quartet Nr. 3 (*)	1962	Cologne 2/8/1963
21	G. Samuel	Quartet Nr. 1 (*)	1978	Cincinnati 10/31/1978

Commissions and Premieres in Chronological Order

Nr.	Composer	Work	Composed	Premiered
1	R. Mann	*Five Pieces for String Quartet*	1951	Colorado Springs 3/11/1953
2	H. E. Apostel	Quartet, Opus 26 (*)	1956	Cincinnati 4/23/1957
3	H. Brün	Quartet Nr. 2 (*)	1957	Cincinnati 4/1/1958
4	W. Rosenberg	Quartet Nr. 2 (*)	1957	Cincinnati 12/17/1957
5	F. Evangelisti	*Aleatorio* (*)	1959	Kranichstein (Darmstadt) 7/14/1962
6	G. M. Koenig	Quartet Nr. 1 (*)	1959	Munich 2/28/1961
7	K. Penderecki	Quartet Nr. 1	1960	Kranichstein (Darmstadt) 7/14/1962
8	H. Pousseur	*Ode pour Quatuor* (*)	1961	Kranichstein (Darmstadt) 7/14/1962

Nr.	Composer	Work	Com-posed	Premiered
9	H. Brün	Quartet Nr. 3 (*)	1961–1962	Kranichstein (Darmstadt) 7/14/1962
10	W. Rosenberg	Quartet Nr. 3 (*)	1962	Cologne 2/8/1963
11	G. Englert	Quartet Nr. 1, *Les Avoines Folles* (*)	1962–1963	Cincinnati 10/13/1964
12	W. Lutosławski	String Quartet	1964	Stockholm 3/12/1965
13	E. Brown	*String Quartet* (*)	1965	Donau-eschingen 10/16/1965
14	G. Englert	Quartet Nr. 2, *La Joute des Lierres* (*)	1966	Cincinnati 5/11/1971
15	M. Kagel	Quartet Nr. 1 (*)	1965–1967	Cincinnati 1/15/1974
16	G. Ligeti	Quartet Nr. 2 (*)	1968	Baden-Baden 12/14/1969
17	W. DeFotis	String Quartet	1977	Cincinnati 10/2/1979
18	L. Kalmár	*Morfeo*	1977	Budapest 5/30/1982
19	G. Samuel	Quartet Nr. 1 (*)	1978	Cincinnati 10/31/1978
20	L. Nono	*Fragmente – Stille, An Diotima*	1980	Bad Godesberg (Bonn) 6/2/1980
21	M. Gielen	*Un Vieux Souvenir* (*)	1983	Cincinnati 10/15/1985

V Discography

Recordings made for Deutsche Grammophon

	Work	Recorded	Released
1	Lutosławski, Penderecki, Mayuzumi	Dec. 1967	1968
2	H. Wolf, Quartet in d minor	Dec. 1967	1968
3	Schoenberg Opus 7, Berg Opus 3, Webern Opus 9, Webern String Quartet, 1905	Mar. 1968	1971
4	Berg *Lyric Suite*, Webern Opus 28	Dec. 1968	1971
5	Webern Opus 5	Mar. 1969	1971
6	W. Rosenberg Quartet Nr. 3, E. Brown String Quartet	Mar. 1969	1970
7	Mendelssohn Opus 12, Opus 13	Mar. 1969	1970 (only in Japan)
8	Schoenberg Opus 10, Opus 37	Jul. 1969	1971
9	Ligeti String Quartet Nr. 2	Dec. 1969	1970
10	Schoenberg Opus 30 + String Quartet in D major (1897)	Mar. 1970	1971
11	Debussy, Ravel	Jun. 1971	1972
12	Cage String Quartet in Four Parts	Dec. 1972	1976
13	Beethoven Opus 130 + Opus 133 (*Grosse Fuge*)	Dec. 1972	1973
14	Beethoven Opus 132	Dec. 1975	1976
15	Beethoven Opus 127	Jun. 1976	1977
16	Beethoven Opus 135 + Alternative finale to Opus 130	Dec. 1976	1977
17	Beethoven Opus 131	Mar. 1977	1977
18	Zemlinsky Quartet Nr. 2, Opus 15	Jun. 1977	1978
19	Schubert String Quintet D. 956	Dec. 1977	1979
20	Brahms Opus 67	May 1978	1981
21	Brahms Opus 51, Nr. 1	Dec. 1978	1981
22	Brahms Opus 51, Nr. 2	Dec. 1979	1981
23	Schumann Piano Quintet, Opus 44	Oct. 1980	1981

	Work	Recorded	Released
24	Zemlinsky Quartets, Nr. 1, Opus 4 + Nr. 3, Opus 19	Dec. 1980	1982
25	Zemlinsky, Nr. 4, Opus 25 + Apostel, Nr. 1, Opus 7	Dec. 1981	1982
26	Schoenberg Sextet *Verklärte Nacht*, Opus 4	Nov. 1982	1984
27	Schoenberg String Trio, Opus 45	Dec. 1982	1984
28	Nono *Fragmente – Stille, An Diotima*	Dec. 1983	1986
29	Webern String Trio, Opus 20 + Satz for String Trio, Opus posth.	Dec. 1983	1986
30	Schoenberg *Ode to Napoleon*, Opus 41 + Webern Rondo for String Quartet (1906) + Webern Piano Quintet (1907)	Aug. 1985	1986
31	Schnabel Quartet Nr. 3	Dec. 1985	1987
32	Mozart *Preludes and Fugues*, K. 405	Dec. 1985	1988
33	Gielen *Un Vieux Souvenir*	Feb. 1987	1987
34	Beethoven Opus 14, Nr. 1	Feb. 1987	1988

Recordings released by other firms

Live concert from Salzburg (August 20, 1976): Schubert *Quartettsatz*, Lutosławski, Ravel, Beethoven Opus 130 alternative finale as encore (released by Orfeo)

Gottfried Michael Koenig, String Quartet Nr. 1 (released by EditionRZ)

Franco Evangelisti, *Aleatorio* (released by EditionRZ)

Friedhelm Döhl, *Sound of Sleat* (released by Dreyer Gaido)

Giuseppe Englert, *Les Avoines Folles* and *La Joute des Lierres* (released by Gramont)

VI Choosing a New Piece[1]

We all have to make choices –

I am a string quartet player – and we have to choose from a large number of new works written every year the two or three that we have time to learn each season. As a matter of fact, we rarely get a chance to choose at all. Pressures of managers, concert societies, radio and recording companies, festivals and anniversaries – all tend to preempt personal choice. To ward off such pressures is thus an indispensable prerequisite if there is to be any choice at all.

The question is: how do we go about making such a choice? What are the criteria, what is taken into consideration? At first glance, this may seem to be a purely aesthetic problem. If that were the case, I'm afraid the four of us would never be able to agree on a single piece, what with the aesthetics of new music being a particularly foggy business. In the final stage of selection, aesthetics do play a role, but other factors have narrowed down the field to manageable proportions before then. Those factors have to do with the strange situation that exists in music today. Never before has such an astronomical distance separated the fully developed language of new music and the repertory of our official musical life, and thereby furthered the petrification of the 'eternal masterpieces.' Symphony orchestras, soloists, opera companies, all those concerned with box office, public demand, the press, will tend to reject works offensive to any of these. Works are often eliminated only with regard to these considerations.

The results can be seen in most public concert programming all over the world – a fatal tendency to cling to the safe and approved. Since (by its very nature) the bulk of music written during the past 50–60 years is neither safe nor approved, this attitude eliminates effectively most of the significant music written in our century. That was not always so. A semblance of tranquility had characterized relations between patrons, composers, performers, and the public during much of the 19th century. Socially accepted and financially supported, the composer reciprocated and tried to please, often to the detriment of the composition. This afflicts works of even the best composers, even Beethoven and Schubert. The uneasy truce was shattered beyond repair by World War I. The cataclysm gave the last impetus to a parting of the ways long since in preparation. The late Beethoven quartets, *Tristan*, *Parsifal*, and the Mahler symphonies had already revoked the alliance and had received in turn a sampling of the wrath in store for the nonconformist.

[1] Brief lecture presented by Walter Levin at the Perhaps Seminar's 'brown bag' lunch on May 2, 1968. The Perhaps Seminar was instituted by Dr. Maurice Levine (uncle of conductor James Levine) for students at the Psychiatry Department of the University of Cincinnati and medical residents and interns at the University's teaching hospital.

Freed by the chaos of war from the restraints of old associations and commitment, the music of the 1920s broke with practically every hallowed tradition. Wishing to follow its own laws, it mutinied against those of the establishment and the establishment retaliated with excommunication. The relevant new music was forced into strict segregation – still in force today. Specialist groups, societies (ISCM) for new music (for that matter also for new art – Museum of Modern Art, Contemporary Arts Center here [in Cincinnati]).

Actually, its enemies recognize the explosive nature of this music better than do its apologists. It is radical and always provocative, its gesture is often aggressive, its specific tone threatening. While it is impossible to pin down its content, its power of suggestion is attested by the fear it generates in totalitarian systems and in our own cultural industry. Fear of the new, uncategorized highly individualistic – its critical aesthetic self-reflection seems to have social relevance. When we are free to choose, we choose here.

10 Commandments

1 If it's beautiful – avoid it.

2 If the critics condemn it, it may be worth looking at.

3 If the critics praise it – leave it alone.

4 If it uses a new notation, try to transcribe it into conventional notation; if you succeed, forget it.

5 If it's naive – let it go.

6 If it's very naive, look at it very carefully, you're probably missing the point.

7 If it looks complex, look carefully and make sure it isn't just difficult.

8 If it strikes a familiar chord or a sympathetic tone, recommend it to a music lover.

9 If it fulfills your every wish, leave it alone; a good piece requires you to invent the wish to which it is the fulfillment.

10 If it sounds like a string quartet, it is not necessarily bad, but it probably is.

Selected Bibliography

Adorno, Theodor W., *'Das Altern der neuen Musik'* (1954), in *Dissonanzen: Musik in der verwalteten Welt* (Göttingen, 1991), pp. 136–157; 'The Aging of the New Music' in *Essays on Music, (*Berkeley, 2002), pp. 181–202

—— *Quasi una Fantasia: Essays on Modern Music* (London, 2012)

Akademie der Künste, *Geschlossene Vorstellung: Der Jüdische Kulturbund in Deutschland 1933–1941* (Berlin, 1992)

Aulich, Bruno, *Das stillvergnügte Streichquartett*, 1936; *The Well-Tempered String Quartet: A Book of Counsel and Entertainment for all Lovers of Music in the Home* (New York, 1938)

Boehmer, Konrad, *'Doppelter Ausbruch: über die Streichquartette 1959 und 1987 von Gottfried Michael Koenig'* in *Neue Zeitschrift für Musik*, (March–April, 2006), pp. 29–31

Bücken, Ernst, ed., *Handbuch der Musikwissenschaft* (Wildpark-Potsdam, 1928–1934)

Capet, Lucien, *La Technique Supérieure de l'Archet* (Paris, 1916); *Superior Bowing Technique* (New York, 2004)

Craft, Robert, *Conversations with Igor Stravinsky* (Garden City, 1959)

Czerny, Carl, *Über den richtigen Vortrag der sämtlichen Beethoven'schen Klavierwerke* (Vienna, 1963); *On the proper performance of all Beethoven's works for the piano* (Bryn Mawr, 1970)

Flesch, Carl, *Skalensystem* (Berlin, 1926); *Scale System* (New York, 1926)

—— *Die Kunst des Violinspiels* (Berlin, 1928–1929); *The Art of Violin Playing* (New York, 2007/2008)

Floros, Constantin, *'Das esoterische Programm der Lyrischen Suite von Alban Berg. Eine semantische Analyse,'* in *Hamburger Jahrbuch für Musikwissenschaft, Band 1* (1975), pp. 101–145

Glock, William, *'Schnabel und Berlin'* in *Artur Schnabel – Musiker/Musician* (Berlin, 2001)

Grünzweig, Werner, Program book for the concert series presented in connection with the exhibition *Artur Schnabel – Musiker/Musician* (Berlin, 2001)

—— *Walter Levin und das LaSalle-Quartett. Eine musikalische Biographie in 26 Folgen. Wolfgang Hagen und Werner Grünzweig im Gespräch mit Walter Levin*, Deutschlandradio Kultur (2009)

Hirshberg, Jehoash, *Music in the Jewish Community of Palestine 1880–1948* (Oxford, 1995)

Hummel, Johann Nepomuk, *Ausführliche theoretisch-practische Anweisung zum Pianoforte Spiel* (Vienna, 1828); *A Complete Theoretical & Practical Course of Instructions on the Art of Playing the Pianoforte* (London, 1829)

Keller, Hans, *The Great Haydn Quartets: Their Interpretation* (London, 1986)

Kolisch, Rudolf, '*Religion der Streicher*,' in *Rudolf Kolisch, Zur Theorie der Aufführung, Musik-Konzepte* 29/30 (Munich, 1983).

—— 'Tempo and Character in Beethoven's Music,' in *Musical Quarterly*, vol. 29, Nr. 2 (April, 1943), pp. 169–187 (part 1); vol. 29 Nr. 3 (July 1943), pp. 291–312 (part 2). Expanded German version in *Musik-Konzepte* 76/77 (Munich, 1992). An English translation of the expanded version was published in the *Musical Quarterly*, vol. 77 (1993), with an introduction by Thomas Y. Levin.

Leibowitz, René, *Schönberg et son école: l'étape contemporaine du langage musical* (Paris, 1947); *Schoenberg and His School: The Contemporary Stage in the Language of Music* (New York, 1949)

Levin, Walter, '*Zwei Stücke für Streichquartett op. 2*,' *Musik-Konzepte* 63/64 (Munich, 1989), pp. 74–99

—— 'Immigrant Musicians and the American Chamber Music Scene 1930–1950,' in Reinhold Brinkmann and Christoph Wolff, eds., *Driven into Paradise: The Musical Migration from Nazi Germany to the United States* (Berkeley, 1999)

Maurer Zenck, Claudia, '"*Ein Sauberruf!*" *Der Alltag des Kolisch Quartetts auf Reisen in der Zwischenkriegszeit*,' in *Annäherungen: Festschrift für Jürg Stenzl zum 65. Geburtstag* (Saarbrücken, 2007), pp. 187–221

Metzger, Heinz-Klaus, '*Das Altern der Philosophie der neuen Musik*,' *Die Reihe*, vol. 4 (1958), pp. 64–80; 'Just Who is Growing Old?' *Die Reihe*, vol. 4 (1960), pp. 63–80

Metzger, Heinz-Klaus and Rainer Riehn, eds. *Theodor W. Adorno: Der Komponist, Musik-Konzepte* 63/64, (Munich, 1989)

Moldenhauer, Hans, *Anton von Webern: A Chronicle of his Life and Work* (New York, 1978)

Mozart, Leopold, *Versuch einer gründlichen Violinschule* (Wiesbaden, 1991);

A Treatise on the Fundamental Principles of Violin Playing (Oxford, 1985)

Newlin, Dika, *Bruckner, Mahler, Schoenberg* (New York, 1947).

—— *Schoenberg Remembered: Diaries and Recollections 1938–1976* (New York, 1980)

Perle, George, '*The Secret Program of the Lyric Suite*' in *International Alban Berg Society Newsletter* 5 (June 1977)

Porter, Andrew, 'A Great Composer,' in *The New Yorker* (January 14, 1980), p. 84

Reich, Willi, *Alban Berg*, (Zurich, 1959); *Alban Berg* (New York, 1965)

Rosenblum, Sandra, *Performance Practices in Classical Piano Music* (Bloomington, 1988)

Rudolf, Max, *The Grammar of Conducting. A Comprehensive Guide to Baton Technique and Interpretation* (New York, 1995)

——*A Musical Life, Writings and Letters* (New York, 2001)

Scherchen, Hermann, *Lehrbuch des Dirigierens*, (Mainz, 1929); *Handbook of Conducting* (Oxford, 1989)

Schibli, Sigfried, *Der Komponist Theodor W. Adorno* (Frankfurt, 1988)

Schoenberg, Arnold, *Style and Idea* (New York, 1951)

—— *Ausgewählte Briefe*, Erwin Stein, ed. (Mainz, 1958), p. 179

—— '*Über Metronomisierung*,' in *Beethoven, das Problem der Interpretation*, *Musik-Konzepte* 8 (Munich, 1985)

Schuller, Gunther, *Horn Technique* (Oxford, 1962)

—— *Early Jazz: Its Roots and Development* (London and New York, 1968)

—— *The Swing Era: the Development of Jazz 1930–1945* (New York and Oxford, 1989)

—— *The Compleat Conductor* (Oxford, 1997)

Stadlen, Peter, '*Beethoven und das Metronom.*' in *Beethoven, das Problem der Interpretation*, *Musik-Konzepte* 8 (Munich, 1985)

Thomas, Theodore, *A Musical Autobiography* (New York, 1964)

Time Magazine, 'Music: Argument for Strings,' in *Time* (August 3, 1953)

Türk, Daniel Gottlob, *Clavierschule* (Leipzig and Halle, 1789); *School of Clavier Playing* (Lincoln, 1982)

von der Lühe, Barbara, *Musik war unsere Rettung* (Tübingen, 1998)

Weissweiller, Eva, *Ausgemerzt! Das Lexikon der Juden in der Musik und seine mörderschen Folgen* (Cologne, 1999)

Zemlinsky, Alexander, *Briefwechsel mit Schönberg, Webern, Berg und Schreker* (Mainz, 1995)

Zimmerlin, Alfred, *'Das Glück des nie Gehörten,' Neue Zürcher Zeitung* (March 31, 2007)

Index